Studies in the Dead Sea Scrolls and Related Literature

Peter W. Flint, Martin G. Abegg Jr., and Florentino García Martínez, General Editors

The Dead Sea Scrolls have been the object of intense interest in recent years, not least because of the release of previously unpublished texts from Qumran Cave 4 since the fall of 1991. With the wealth of new documents that have come to light, the field of Qumran studies has undergone a renaissance. Scholars have begun to question the established conclusions of the last generation; some widely held beliefs have withstood scrutiny, but others have required revision or even dismissal. New proposals and competing hypotheses, many of them of an uncritical and sensational nature, vie for attention. Idiosyncratic and misleading views of the Scrolls still abound, especially in the popular press, while the results of solid scholarship have yet to make their full impact. At the same time, the scholarly task of establishing reliable critical editions of the texts is nearing completion. The opportunity is ripe, therefore, for directing renewed attention to the task of analysis and interpretation.

Studies in the Dead Sea Scrolls and Related Literature is a series designed to address this need. In particular, the series aims to make the latest and best Dead Sea Scrolls scholarship accessible to scholars, students, and the thinking public. The volumes that are projected — both monographs and collected essays — will seek to clarify how the Scrolls revise and help shape our understanding of the formation of the Bible and the historical development of Judaism and Christianity. Various offerings in the series will explore the reciprocally illuminating relationships of several disciplines related to the Scrolls, including the canon and text of the Hebrew Bible, the richly varied forms of Second Temple Judaism, and the New Testament. While the Dead Sea Scrolls constitute the main focus, several of these studies will also include perspectives on the Old and New Testaments and other ancient writings — hence the title of the series. It is hoped that these volumes will contribute to a deeper appreciation of the world of early Judaism and Christianity and of their continuing legacy today.

Peter W. Flint
Martin G. Abegg Jr.
Florentino García Martínez

A Guide to the Dead Sea Scrolls and Related Literature

Revised and Expanded Edition

JOSEPH A. FITZMYER, S.J.

William B. Eerdmans Publishing Company
Grand Rapids, Michigan / Cambridge, U.K.

Published 2008 by
Wm. B. Eerdmans Publishing Co.
2140 Oak Industrial Drive N.E., Grand Rapids, Michigan 49505 /
P.O. Box 163, Cambridge CB3 9PU U.K.

Printed in the United States of America

13 12 11 10 09 08 7 6 5 4 3 2 1

Library of Congress Cataloging-in-Publication Data

Fitzmyer, Joseph A.
A guide to the Dead Sea scrolls and related literature /
Joseph A. Fitzmyer. — Rev. & exp. ed.
p. cm. — (Studies in the Dead Sea scrolls and related literature)
Includes bibliographical references.
ISBN 978-0-8028-6241-9 (pbk.: alk. paper)
1. Dead Sea scrolls — Bibliography. I. Title.

Z6371.D4F585 2008
[BM487]
016.2961'55 — dc22

2008004768

www.eerdmans.com

Contents

Preface

The student who undertakes the study of the Dead Sea Scrolls soon realizes the vastness of this modern area of studies related to the Bible. The bearing of the discovery of these texts on the technical study of the Bible is far from having been exploited. As of this writing, we are still waiting for at least two volumes in the official publication of the texts by the Clarendon Press of Oxford. So there is still much to be studied about the Scrolls and their bearing on the Hebrew, Aramaic, and Greek texts of the Bible, on Palestinian Jewish history and archaeology of the Roman period, and on the interpretation of both the Old and the New Testament. In many graduate or divinity schools with programs devoted to biblical studies or to the study of Northwest Semitic languages, seminars are often conducted in the reading and interpretation of the Dead Sea Scrolls. The student in such seminars is confronted immediately with the problem of finding out where the texts to be studied actually have been published or where to go to find secondary literature on them.

The term, "Dead Sea Scrolls," is employed today in two senses, one broad and the other narrow. In the broad sense, it denotes texts, not retrieved from the Dead Sea itself, but discovered in many caves of various areas (mentioned below) along the northwest shore of that Sea between 1947 and 1963, and even some texts from the Genizah of Old Cairo in Egypt, which are related to them. These "scrolls" are sometimes complete, but most of them are fragmentary texts or documents dating roughly from the fourth century B.C. to the eighth century A.D. In the narrow sense, the term denotes the texts found in 11 caves in the area of the Wadi Qumran, and so it equals "Qumran Scrolls," which fall into three categories: biblical texts, sectarian texts, and Jewish literary texts of the Second-Temple period.

In an effort to sort out all this material, to explain the various sigla that are used for texts from all these sites, to indicate where each text can be found in its *editio princeps,* and to guide the student to important secondary bibliography on many aspects of Scroll study, this book has been composed. It is the successor to *The Dead Sea Scrolls: Major Publications and Tools for Study* (Sources for Biblical Study 8; Missoula, MT: Society of Biblical Literature and Scholars Press), which first was published in 1975, reissued in 1977 with an Addendum, and later expanded in a revised edition of 1990 (Resources for Biblical Study 20; Atlanta, GA: Scholars Press). Since the vast majority of the fragmentary texts finally have been published in the decade since 1990, especially in the Clarendon Press series, Discoveries in the Judaean Desert (DJD), it has been almost impossible to revise the book in the same format. Consequently, a decision was made to retain the purpose and general outline of the earlier publication, but to present the texts from the Qumran caves and other sites in a more orderly mode, using mainly the numbers that have been assigned to most of them as the principal guide. For instance, the texts from the 11 Qumran caves are listed now not only by caves in their proper order, but primarily by the numbers used in the DJD series for the texts of a given cave, and no longer by the sigla in more or less alphabetical order, as was done in earlier forms of this book.

An effort has also been made, however, to list also those conventional sigla along with the numbers, when they exist (e.g., 4Q3 as 4QGen^{c}), and also to use numbers that have been assigned sometimes to texts that had been published outside of that series or before the DJD numbering system was devised (e.g., 1QapGen is now 1Q20). Likewise, when it is known that a text at one time bore a siglum different from that now in current usage, the short Latin word "olim" ("formerly") recalls the earlier abbreviation.

The complete listing of texts from Qumran, Naḥal Ḥever, Naḥal Ṣe'elim, Wadi Murabbaʿat, Ketef Jericho, Wadi Sdeir, Naḥal Mishmar, Masada, Cairo Genizah, Wadi Nar, Wadi Ghweir, Wadi Daliyeh, Khirbet Mird, and those of unknown provenience forms the first and major part of this book. An effort has been made to supply not only the volume number and plate(s) for a given text, but also the page numbers and often a brief mention of the contents of the text. That major part of the book is followed by important topics in the study of the texts that have been listed in it: bibliographies, translations, outlines of some of the lengthy writings; and finally important bibliography on a variety of selected topics in the study of the Scrolls.

In the latter part of the book, I have been guided mainly by own insights, knowledge, and notes amassed in the last decade and a half (written into an interleaved copy of the 1990 publication), but also by helpful, critical reviews of that revision and of earlier forms of the book. I have limited entries in the select bibliographies to those that are more important, but I am all too aware that I may have missed or neglected some that others may judge to be equally or more important. Yet the selected entries invariably will guide the reader to many other secondary titles.

In all, my purpose has been to provide the reader, and especially the beginning student of the Dead Sea Scrolls, with a list where one can find quickly the place in which a given text of the Scrolls has been published in its *editio princeps*. Anyone who uses the DJD series realizes immediately the need of such a guide as this to discover in which volume a certain text is to be found. A labyrinth or maze has been created in that series by the disorder in which the numbered texts appear in most of its thirty-some volumes.

A word should be said about the decision to include outlines of some of the lengthy texts. The outlines may be to a certain extent subjective; and others may prefer different ways of outlining the texts. Since most of the material in this book has grown out of an introductory course given to graduate students in biblical studies in recent decades, I have learned the value of supplying students with outlines of the longer texts to be read as an aide to their understanding of them. The outlines are included for their propaedeutic value, but they are not uniform, because they are dictated by the nature of the texts outlined. No attempt, for instance, has been made to outline the Psalms Scroll from Cave 11, because it would be a bare list of biblical and apocryphal psalms with prose insertions, such as is found under 11Q5 (11QPs[a]); that list already supplies all the needed information.

Full information (author/editor, complete title, place of publication, publisher, date) usually is given at the first occurrence; after that, a brief title is used. The reader should be aware that the sigla listed here are not always followed by all writers. Sometimes one encounters the older system (see p. 6), which should be abandoned; sometimes a writer uses in a foreign language the forms that are conventional in that language (e.g., 11QtgHiob will not be found below). At times, no siglum has been assigned to a text (e.g., the "Provisional List of Documents from the Judean Desert" of *EDSS*, 1013-49, in the column under "official sigla," gives a wordy description or title instead of a siglum [e.g., "4Q525 Wisdom Text with Beatitudes"; the siglum given below is rather "4QBeat," which I have found used by others]). Because a siglum is supposed to be an abbreviated title, one will find below an attempt to use such abbreviations, and even to create them when they do not exist. Sometimes an official siglum has been assigned in French (e.g., by Milik or Baillet), and I have retained it, when current English usage also does.

Finally, I have to express my thanks to many scholars who have helped me in this endeavor: to Eugene Ulrich for help in sorting out 4QPsalms texts;

to Daniel J. Harrington, S.J. for help with Wisdom Literature texts; to Emanuel Tov for help in sorting out various 4Q texts; to Eileen Schuller for needed correction of the list of 1QHodayot; and especially to the series editor, Peter W. Flint and his assistants, Kyung Baek and Chelica Hiltunen, for many recent additions to the bibliographies in the book and for information about electronic resources and data on the Scrolls. I am indebted also to J. Leon Hooper, S.J., director of the Woodstock Theological Center Library (housed at Georgetown University), and to his staff, for the help provided in obtaining many of the books mentioned in this work.

Joseph A. Fitzmyer, S.J.
Professor Emeritus, Biblical Studies
Catholic University of America

General Abbreviations

AASOR	Annual of the American Schools of Oriental Research
AB	Anchor Bible
ABD	D. N. Freedman (ed.), *The Anchor Bible Dictionary* (6 vols.; New York: Doubleday, 1992)
ABRL	Anchor Bible Reference Library
Abr-N	*Abr-Nahrain*
Abr-NSup	Abr-Nahrain Supplements
ADAJ	*Annual of the Department of Antiquities of Jordan*
AGJU	Arbeiten zur Geschichte des antiken Judentums und des Urchristentums
AION	*Annali dell'Istituto Orientale di Napoli*
AJBA	*Australian Journal of Biblical Archaeology*
ALD	Aramaic Levi Document
ALQ	F. M. Cross, *The Ancient Library of Qumran* (3d ed.; Minneapolis, MN: Fortress, 1995)
ALUOS	*Annual of Leeds University Oriental Society*
AncSoc	*Ancient Society* (Katholieke Universiteit Leuven)
ANES	*Ancient Near Eastern Studies*
ANRW	*Aufstieg und Niedergang der römischen Welt: II. Prinzipat* (ed. H. Temporini and W. Haase; Berlin/New York: de Gruyter, 1972-)
Ant.	Flavius Josephus, *Antiquities of the Jews*
AOAT	Alter Orient und Altes Testament
ASTI	*Annual of the Swedish Theological Institute*
ATTM	K. Beyer, *Die aramäischen Texte vom Toten Meer . . .* (Göttingen: Vandenhoeck & Ruprecht, 1984)
ATTME	K. Beyer, *ATTM . . . : Ergänzungsband* (Göttingen: Vandenhoeck & Ruprecht, 1994)

General Abbreviations

ATR	*Anglican Theological Review*
BA	*Biblical Archaeologist*
BAC	Biblioteca de autores cristianos
BARev	*Biblical Archaeology Review*
BASOR	*Bulletin of the American Schools of Oriental Research*
BASORSup	BASOR Supplements
BBB	Bonner biblische Beiträge
BBR	*Bulletin for Biblical Research*
BE	J. T. Milik, *The Books of Enoch: Aramaic Fragments of Qumrân Cave 4* (Oxford: Clarendon, 1976)
BeO	*Bibbia e Oriente*
BETL	Bibliotheca ephemeridum theologicarum lovaniensium
BHT	Beiträge zur historischen Theologie
Bib	*Biblica*
BibOr	Biblica et orientalia
BIES	*Bulletin of the Israel Exploration Society* (later renamed *Yediʿot*)
BIOSCS	*Bulletin of the International Organization for Septuagint and Cognate Studies*
BJRL	*Bulletin of the John Rylands (University) Library (of Manchester)*
BJS	Brown Judaic Studies
BL	*Bibel und Liturgie*
BN	*Biblische Notizen*
BSac	*Bibliotheca sacra*
BTB	*Biblical Theology Bulletin*
BWANT	Beiträge zur Wissenschaft vom Alten und Neuen Testament
BZ	*Biblische Zeitschrift*
BZAW	Beihefte zur *ZAW*
BZNW	Beihefte zur *ZNW*
CBQ	*Catholic Biblical Quarterly*
CBQMS	Catholic Biblical Quarterly Monograph Series
CJT	*Canadian Journal of Theology*
CPA	Corpus of Christian Palestinian Aramaic
CRAIBL	*Comptes rendus de l'Académie des Inscriptions et Belles-Lettres*
CRINT	Compendium rerum iudaicarum ad Novum Testamentum
DBSup	*Dictionnaire de la Bible, Supplément*
DJD	Discoveries in the Judaean Desert (of Jordan)
DSD	*Dead Sea Discoveries*
DSPS	J. A. Sanders, *The Dead Sea Psalms Scroll* (Ithaca, NY: Cornell University Press, 1967)
DSSCO	J. A. Fitzmyer, *The Dead Sea Scrolls and Christian Origins* (SDSSRL; Grand Rapids, MI: Eerdmans, 2000)
DSSE	G. Vermes, *The Dead Sea Scrolls in English* (3d ed.; London: Penguin; New York: Viking Penguin, 1987)

DSSHU	E. L. Sukenik, *The Dead Sea Scrolls of the Hebrew University* (Jerusalem: Hebrew University and Magnes Press, 1955)
DSSR	W. D. Parry and E. Tov (eds.), *The Dead Sea Scrolls Reader* (6 vols.; Leiden: Brill, 2004-5)
DSSSE	F. García Martínez and E. J. C. Tigchelaar (eds.), *The Dead Sea Scrolls Study Edition* (2 vols.; Leiden: Brill, 1997-98; in paperback, Leiden: Brill; Grand Rapids, MI: Eerdmans, 2000)
DTT	*Dansk Teologisk Tidsskrift*
EBB	*Elenchus bibliographicus biblicus*
EBib	Études bibliques
EDSS	L. H. Schiffman and J. C. VanderKam, *Encyclopedia of the Dead Sea Scrolls* (2 vols.; Oxford/New York: Oxford University Press, 2000)
ErIsr	Eretz Israel
ESBNT	J. A. Fitzmyer, *Essays on the Semitic Background of the New Testament* (London: Chapman, 1971; in paperback, Missoula, MT: Scholars Press, 1974; see *SBNT*)
EstBíb	*Estudios bíblicos*
ETR	*Études théologiques et religieuses*
EvQ	*Evangelical Quarterly*
EvT	*Evangelische Theologie*
ExpTim	*Expository Times*
FilNeot	*Filología neotestamentaria*
FO	*Folia orientalia*
FRLANT	Forschungen zur Religion und Literatur des Alten und Neuen Testaments
HAR	*Hebrew Annual Review*
HeyJ	*Heythrop Journal*
HSM	Harvard Semitic Monographs
HSS	Harvard Semitic Studies
HTR	*Harvard Theological Review*
HTS	Harvard Theological Studies
HUCA	*Hebrew Union College Annual*
IAA	Israel Antiquities Authority
ICASALS	International Center for Arid and Semi-Arid Land Studies
IEJ	*Israel Exploration Journal*
ILN	*Illustrated London News*
JANES	*Journal of the Ancient Near Eastern Society*
JAOS	*Journal of the American Oriental Society*
JBL	*Journal of Biblical Literature*
JBQ	*Jewish Bible Quarterly*
JBS	Jerusalem Biblical Studies
JBT	*Jahrbuch für biblische Theologie*
JDS	Judean Desert Studies

JEOL	*Jaarbericht ex oriente lux*
JETS	*Journal of the Evangelical Theological Society*
JHC	*Journal of Higher Criticism*
JJS	*Journal of Jewish Studies*
JNES	*Journal of Near Eastern Studies*
JNSL	*Journal of Northwest Semitic Languages*
JQR	*Jewish Quarterly Review*
JR	*Journal of Religion*
JRA	*Journal of Roman Archaeology*
JSHRZ	Jüdische Schriften aus hellenistisch-römischer Zeit
JSJ	*Journal for the Study of Judaism*
JSJSup	JSJ Supplements
JSOT	*Journal for the Study of the Old Testament*
JSOTSup	JSOT Supplements
JSP	*Journal for the Study of Pseudepigrapha*
JSPSup	JSP Supplements
JSS	*Journal of Semitic Studies*
JTC	*Journal for Theology and Church*
JTS	*Journal of Theological Studies*
KlT	Kleine Texte
MHUC	Monographs of the Hebrew Union College
MPAT	J. A. Fitzmyer and D. J. Harrington, *A Manual of Palestinian Aramaic Texts* (BibOr 34; Rome: Biblical Institute, 1978)
NAB	*The New American Bible*
NCAL	*Newsletter of the Comprehensive Aramaic Lexicon*
NDBA	D. N. Freedman and J. C. Greenfield (eds.), *New Directions in Biblical Archaeology* (Garden City, NY: Doubleday, 1969)
NEA	*Near Eastern Archaeology*
NovT	*Novum Testamentum*
NovTSup	NovT Supplements
NRT	*La nouvelle revue théologique*
NTA	*New Testament Abstracts*
NTAbh	Neutestamentliche Abhandlungen
NTOA	Novum Testamentum et Orbis Antiquus
NTS	*New Testament Studies*
OTA	*Old Testament Abstracts*
OtSt	*Oudtestamentische Studiën*
PalSb	*Palestinski Sbornik*
PAM	Palestine Archaeological Museum
PEFQS	*Palestine Exploration Fund Quarterly Statement*
PEQ	*Palestine Exploration Quarterly*
PTSDSSP	Princeton Theological Seminary Dead Sea Scrolls Project
QC	*Qumran Chronicle*

QL	Qumran Literature
RB	*Revue biblique*
RechBib	Recherches bibliques
REJ	*Revue des études juives*
RevExp	*Review and Expositor*
RevistBíb	*Revista bíblica*
RevQ	*Revue de Qumran*
RHPR	*Revue d'histoire et de philosophie religieuses*
RHR	*Revue de l'histoire des religions*
RivB	*Rivista biblica*
RSR	*Recherches de science religieuse*
RSV	Revised Standard Version
RTL	*Revue théologique de Louvain*
SBFLA	Studii biblici franciscani liber annuus
SBL	Society of Biblical Literature
SBLDS	SBL Dissertation Series
SBLEJL	SBL Early Judaism and Its Literature
SBLMS	SBL Monograph Series
SBLRBS	SBL Resources for Biblical Study
SBLSBS	SBL Sources for Biblical Study
SBLSCS	SBL Septuagint and Cognate Studies
SBLSP	*SBL Seminar Papers*
SBLSS	SBL Symposium Series
SBNT	J. A. Fitzmyer, *The Semitic Background of the New Testament: Combined Edition of Essays on the Semitic Background of the New Testament and A Wandering Aramean: Collected Aramaic Essays* (Grand Rapids, MI: Eerdmans; Livonia, MI: Dove Booksellers, 1997)
SBT	Studies in Biblical Theology
SDSSRL	Studies in the Dead Sea Scrolls and Related Literature
SE I, VI	*Studia evangelica I* (= TU 73 [1959]), *VI* (= TU 112 [1973])
Sem	*Semitica*
SHR	Shrine of the Book (Israel Museum)
SJLA	Studies in Judaism in Late Antiquity
SJOT	*Scandinavian Journal of the Old Testament*
SNTSMS	Studiorum Novi Testamenti Societas Monograph Series
SNTSU	*Studien zum Neuen Testament und seiner Umwelt*
SP	*Studia papyrologica*
SPB	Studia postbiblica
SR	*Studies in Religion/Sciences religieuses*
ST	*Studia theologica*
STDJ	Studies on the Texts of the Desert of Judah
SUNT	Studien zur Umwelt des Neuen Testaments

SWDS	*Scrolls from the Wilderness of the Dead Sea* (Smithsonian Institution Exhibit Catalogue; Cambridge, MA: American Schools of Oriental Research, 1965)
SymBU	Symbolae biblicae upsalienses
TAG	J. A. Fitzmyer, *To Advance the Gospel: New Testament Studies* (New York: Crossroad, 1981; 2d ed., Grand Rapids, MI: Eerdmans; Livonia, MI: Dove Booksellers, 1998)
TBT	*The Bible Today*
TDNT	G. Kittel and G. Friedrich (eds.), *Theological Dictionary of the New Testament* (10 vols.; Grand Rapids, MI: Eerdmans, 1964-76)
TDOT	G. J. Botterweck, H. Ringgren, and H.-J. Fabry (eds.), *Theological Dictionary of the Old Testament* (15 vols.; Grand Rapids, MI: Eerdmans, 1974-2006)
TGl	*Theologie und Glaube*
TLZ	*Theologische Literaturzeitung*
TRu	*Theologische Rundschau*
TS	*Theological Studies*
TSAJ	Texte und Studien zum antiken Judentum
TTZ	*Trierer theologische Zeitschrift*
TU	Texte und Untersuchungen
TynBul	*Tyndale Bulletin*
TZ	*Theologische Zeitschrift*
USQR	*Union Seminary Quarterly Review*
VDom	*Verbum Domini*
VT	*Vetus Testamentum*
VTSup	VT Supplements
WA	J. A. Fitzmyer, *A Wandering Aramean: Collected Aramaic Essays* (SBLMS 25; MT: Scholars Press, 1979; see *SBNT*)
WF	Wege der Forschung
WTJ	*Westminster Theological Journal*
WUNT	Wissenschaftliche Untersuchungen zum Neuen Testament
ZAH	*Zeitschrift für Althebraistik*
ZAW	*Zeitschrift für die alttestamentliche Wissenschaft*
ZDPV	*Zeitschrift des deutschen Palästina-Vereins*
ZKT	*Zeitschrift für katholische Theologie*
ZNW	*Zeitschrit für die neutestamentliche Wissenschaft*
ZPE	*Zeitschrift für Papyrologie und Epigraphik*
ZTK	*Zeitschrift für Theologie und Kirche*

I

The System of Abbreviations Used for the Dead Sea Scrolls

The system that was first used, when only Qumran Cave 1 was known, soon became outmoded, especially when other Qumran caves were discovered and it became necessary to distinguish various caves and multiple copies of the same document found in the same cave. As a result, a system was devised, which seems complicated but, once it is explained and studied, can be followed easily (see J. T. Milik, "Table des sigles," DJD 1. 46-48). Five elements can make up the siglum for a given text, but not all five are always used, since the first and the fifth are commonly omitted; but they become necessary at times. The five elements in the order in which they occur are: (1) the material on which the text is written; (2) the name of the site where the text was discovered, or its provenience; (3) the title of the work; (4) the copy of that work at the given site; (5) the language in which the text is written, since sometimes the same text is found in more than one language. Sometimes the order of (1) and (2) is transposed.

(1) Material

(skin)
pap (papyrus)
cu (copper)
ostr (ostracon)
lign (lignum, wood)
perg (pergamentum, parchment)

(2) Provenience

Q (Qumran: 1Q, 2Q, 3Q, etc.)
Maṣ (Maṣada)
Mur (Murabbaʿat)
Ḥev (Ḥever)
Sdeir (Wadi Sdeir)
Ṣe (Ṣeʾelim, Wadi Seiyal)
Mird (Khirbet Mird)
C (Cairo Genizah)

(3) Title of Work

Gen, Exod, Lev, Num, Deut, etc.
paleoLev (Leviticus copied in paleo-Hebrew script)
LXXNum (Numbers in the LXX version)
Samar (Samaritan version)
phyl (phylactery)
pHos (pešer [Commentary on Hosea])
tgJob (Targum of Job)
apGen (apocryphon, non-canonical literary work based on Genesis)
Sir (Sirach, Ecclesiasticus)
Tob (Tobit)
Jub *(Jubilees)*
En *(Enoch)*
TLevi *(Testament of Levi)*
TNaph *(Testament of Naphtali)*
Instead of a title, a (boldface or italic) number is often used; it denotes the numbered texts in the DJD volumes. Thus: 1Q**13** or 1Q*13* (= 1Qphyl). The boldface or italic number often is not used: 1Q13; this is what one will find below in this book.

(4) Copy of work

Superscript letters following title of the work

(5) Language

nothing or hebr (Hebrew)
ar, aram (Aramaic)

arab (Arabic)
cpa (Christian Palestinian Aramaic)
gr (Greek)
lat (Latin)
nab (Nabatean)

Normally, arabic numbers are used for caves, columns, and lines (sometimes separated by a colon, sometimes by a period, sometimes by a comma, depending on the custom of countries or periodicals). In some fragmentary texts, however, when there are several fragments that are not joined and have to be numbered separately within a work, the columns on them are then designated by lower-case roman numerals. Thus, 1Q27 1 ii 25 (which means text 27 from Qumran Cave 1 [in DJD 1], frg. 1, col. ii, line 25). In this case, a colon, period, or comma is not used. Similarly, 4QpIsa^{c} 4-7 ii 2-4 (which means the third copy [copy c] of a pesher on Isaiah from Qumran Cave 4 [cf. 4Q163 in DJD 5. 17-27], joined frgs. 4-7, col. ii, lines 2 to 4). In more recently published volumes of the series, upper case roman numerals are used for columns, which is a departure that conforms with Israeli convention from the original DJD system; it can be confusing at times.

Abbreviations Commonly Used in the DJD System

acc	account
ack	acknowledgement
admon	admonition, admonitory
ap, apocr	apocryphon
APHM	Arabic Papyri from Ḫirbet el-Mird
apoc	apocalypse
apostr	apostrophe
ar	Aramaic
arab	Arabic
BA	Babatha Archive
BarC or BarK	Bar Cochba or Bar Kokhba
beat	beatitude(s)
bened	benediction(s), blessing(s)
Ber	Bĕrākāh, Bĕrākôt (Blessing[s])
bil	bilingual
C	Cairo Genizah
cal	calendar(ic), calendrical
can	canonical

cer	ceremony
cit	citation, citing
col.	column
com	communal
comm	commentary
cont	contract
cpa	Christian Palestinian Aramaic
creat	creation
D	Damascus Document
DibHam	Dibrê Hammĕ'ôrôt (Words of the Luminaries)
did	didactic
div	divine
DM	Dibrê Môšeh (Sayings of Moses)
doc	document
En	Enoch
Enastr	Enoch astronomical texts
EnGiants	Enoch Giants texts
ep	epistle
eschat	eschatological
EschMidr	Eschatological Midrash(im)
Flor	Florilegium
frg(s).	fragment(s)
Ghweir	Wadi Ghweir
gr	Greek
H	Hôdāyôt (= Thanksgiving Psalms)
hebr	Hebrew
Ḥev	Ḥever (Wadi Khabra)
Hlk	Halakah
hym	hymn(ic)
ind	individual
Jub.	*Jubilees, Book of*
lat	Latin
lett	letter
lign	lignum (wood)
lit	liturgy, liturgical
LXX	Septuagint
M	Milḥāmāh (= War Scroll)
Mar	Marriage (or Mariage)
Mas	Maṣada
med	meditation
Melch	Melchizedek
mess	messianic (text)
mez	Mĕzûzāh

Mird	Khirbet el-Mird
misc	miscellany, miscellaneous
Mish	Naḥal Mishmar (Wadi Mahras)
MMT	Miqṣat Maʿăśê hat-Tôrāh (= Some Deeds of the Law)
mon	monastic
mss	manuscripts
MT	Masoretic Text
Mur	Wadi Murabbaʿat
myst	mystery, mysteries
nab	Nabatean
Nar	Wadi en-Nar
narr	narrative
NJ	New Jerusalem
ord	ordinances, ordonnances
ostr	ostracon
p	pēšer/pesher (= commentary); but sometimes wrongly used for pap
paleo	text is written in Paleo-Hebrew script
palimp	palimpsest
PAM	Palestine Archaeological Museum (now called Rockefeller)
pap	papyrus
par	parable
para	paraphrase
Pent	Pentateuch
perg	pergamentum (parchment)
phyl	phylactery
pol	polemical
pr	prayer(s)
PrNab	Prayer of Nabonidus
prom	promissory
proph	prophecy, prophetic
provid	providence
ps	pseudo-
Ps(s)	Psalm(s), Psalter
PsAp	Apocryphal Psalms
pur	purification
Q	(Wadi, Khirbet, or caves of) Qumran
quot	quotidien (daily)
rit	rite, ritual
Rock.	Rockefeller Museum (olim PAM)
RP	Reworked Pentateuch
S	Serek hay-yaḥad (Rule of the Community, or Manual of Discipline)
Sa	Appendix A of 1QS: Serek ha-ʿēdāh, Rule of the Congregation (1Q28a)

Samar	Samaritan
sap	sapiential
Sb	Appendix B of 1QS: Collection of Benedictions (1Q28b)
Sdeir	Wadi Sdeir
Sec	Second
Sef	Sepher (Book)
Sem	Semitic
ShirShabb	Serek širôt ʿôlat haš-šabbāt (= Order of the Songs of the Sabbath Sacrifice)
syr	Syriac
T	Testament
Tanh	Tanḥûmîm
Testim	Testimonia
tg	targum
unc	unclassified
unid	unidentified
vis	vision(s)
W	Work
WDSP	Wadi ed-Daliyeh Sale Papyrus (DJD 28)
Wiles	Wiles of the Wicked Woman
XII	Twelve Minor Prophets

Older System of Abbreviations (sometimes still encountered, but now to be avoided)

CDC	Cairo Damascus Covenant (now = CD)
DSD	Dead Sea Discipline (now = 1QS)
DSH	Dead Sea Habakkuk commentary (now = 1QpHab)
DSIa	Dead Sea Isaiah A (now = 1QIsa^{a})
DSIb	Dead Sea Isaiah B (now = 1QIsa^{b})
DSL	Dead Sea Lamech Apocalypse (now = 1QapGen)
DST	Dead Sea Thanksgiving Psalms (now = 1QH)
DSW	Dead Sea War scroll (now = 1QM)

II

The Dead Sea Scrolls: Major Publications

A. General Information

The texts of the Scrolls in their original languages are found in various publications, in printed and electronic forms, and in photographs and transcriptions. Some are more reliable and useful than others; and an attempt will be made to assess their value, with the aid of critical assessments given by other scholars who have made use of them.

The *editio princeps* of the vast majority of the texts can be found in the official series, Discoveries in the Judaean Desert, published by Clarendon Press of Oxford. To date, thirty-seven volumes of the series have appeared in the fifty years from 1955 to 2005: vols. 1-31, 33-36, 38-39. Two other volumes (32, 37) are awaited, and some further volumes are planned that will be re-editions of some texts, supply corrections to earlier volumes, and correlate scattered details. The contents of the different volumes in DJD will be listed below in their appropriate places, but the following is a list of the volumes presently available:

Discoveries in the Judaean Desert (of Jordan)

I	D. Barthélemy, O.P. and J. T. Milik, *Qumran Cave I* (DJD 1; Oxford: Clarendon, 1955; repr. 1964). Pp. xi + 165 + XXXVII pls.
II, IIa	P. Benoit, O.P., J. T. Milik, and R. de Vaux, *Les grottes de Murabbaʿât* (DJD 2 [in two parts]; Oxford: Clarendon, 1961). Pp. xv + 304 + CVII pls.
III, IIIa	M. Baillet, J. T. Milik, and R. de Vaux, *Les 'Petites Grottes' de*

	Qumrân: Exploration de la falaise, Les grottes 2Q, 3Q, 5Q, 6Q, 7Q à 10Q; Le rouleau de cuivre (DJD 3 [in two parts]; Oxford: Clarendon, 1962). Pp. xiii + 317 + LXXI pls.
IV	J. A. Sanders, *The Psalms Scroll of Qumrân Cave 11 (11QPs[a])* (DJD 4; Oxford: Clarendon, 1965). Pp. xi + 99 + XVII pls.
V	J. M. Allegro with A. A. Anderson, *Qumrân Cave 4: I (4Q158-4Q186)* (DJD 5; Oxford: Clarendon, 1968). Pp. xi + 111 + XXXI pls.
VI	R. de Vaux and J. T. Milik, *Qumrân Grotte 4: II, I. Archéologie, II. Tefillin, Mezuzot et Targums (4Q128-4Q157)* (DJD 6; Oxford: Clarendon, 1977). Pp. xi + 93 + XXVIII pls.
VII	M. Baillet, *Qumrân Grotte 4: III (4Q482-4Q520)* (DJD 7; Oxford: Clarendon, 1982). Pp. xiv + 339 + LXXX pls.
VIII	E. Tov with the Collaboration of R. A. Kraft, *The Greek Minor Prophets Scroll from Naḥal Ḥever (8ḤevXIIgr) (The Seiyal Collection I)* (DJD 8; Oxford: Clarendon, 1990; repr. with corrections 1995). Pp. xi + 171 + XX pls.
IX	P. W. Skehan, E. Ulrich, and J. E. Sanderson, *Qumran Cave 4: IV, PalaeoHebrew and Greek Biblical Manuscripts* (DJD 9; Oxford: Clarendon, 1992; repr. with corrections 1995). Pp. xiii + 250 + XLVII pls.
X	E. Qimron and J. Strugnell, *Qumran Cave 4: V, Miqṣat Maʿaśe ha-Torah* (DJD 10; Oxford: Clarendon, 1994). Pp. xiv + 235 + VIII pls.
XI	E. Eshel et al., in Consultation with J. VanderKam and M. Brady, *Qumran Cave 4: VI, Poetical and Liturgical Texts, Part 1* (DJD 11; Oxford: Clarendon, 1998). Pp. ix + 473 + XXXII pls.
XII	E. Ulrich, F. M. Cross et al., *Qumran Cave 4: VII, Genesis to Numbers* (DJD 12; Oxford: Clarendon, 1994; repr. 1999). Pp. xv + 272 + XLIX pls.
XIII	H. Attridge et al., in Consultation with J. VanderKam, *Qumran Cave 4: VIII, Parabiblical Texts, Part 1* (DJD 13; Oxford: Clarendon, 1994). Pp. x + 470 + XLIII pls.
XIV	E. Ulrich, F. M. Cross et al., *Qumran Cave 4: IX, Deuteronomy, Joshua, Judges, Kings* (DJD 14; Oxford: Clarendon, 1995; repr. 1999). Pp. xv + 188 + XXXVII pls.
XV	E. Ulrich, F. M. Cross et al., *Qumran Cave 4: X, The Prophets* (DJD 15; Oxford: Clarendon, 1997). Pp. xv + 325 + LXIV pls.
XVI	E. Ulrich, F. M. Cross et al., *Qumran Cave 4: XI, Psalms to Chronicles* (DJD 16; Oxford: Clarendon, 2000). Pp. xv + 302 + XXXVIII pls.

XVII	F. M. Cross, D. W. Parry et al., *Qumran Cave 4: XII, 1-2 Samuel* (DJD 17; Oxford: Clarendon, 2005). Pp. xix + 271 + XXVII pls.
XVIII	J. M. Baumgarten et al., *Qumran Cave 4: XIII, The Damascus Document (4Q266-273)* (DJD 18; Oxford: Clarendon, 1996). Pp. xix + 236 + XLII pls.
XIX	M. Broshi et al., in Consultation with J. VanderKam, *Qumran Cave 4: XIV, Parabiblical Texts, Part 2* (DJD 19; Oxford: Clarendon, 1995). Pp. xi + 267 + XXIX pls.
XX	T. Elgvin et al., in Consultation with J. A. Fitzmyer, *Qumran Cave 4: XV, Sapiential Texts, Part 1* (DJD 20; Oxford: Clarendon, 1997). Pp. x + 246 + XVIII pls.
XXI	S. Talmon, J. Ben-Dov, and U. Glessmer, *Qumran Cave 4: XVI, Calendrical Texts* (DJD 21; Oxford: Clarendon, 2001). Pp. xii + 263 + XIII pls.
XXII	G. Brooke et al., in Consultation with J. VanderKam, *Qumran Cave 4: XVII, Parabiblical Texts, Part 3* (DJD 22; Oxford: Clarendon, 1996). Pp. xi + 351 + XXIX pls.
XXIII	F. García Martínez, E. J. C. Tigchelaar, and A. S. van der Woude, *Qumran Cave 11: II, 11Q2-18, 11Q20-31* (DJD 23; Oxford: Clarendon, 1998). Pp. xv + 487 + LIV pls.
XXIV	M. J. Winn Leith, *Wadi Daliyeh I: The Wadi Daliyeh Seal Impressions* (DJD 24; Oxford: Clarendon, 1997). Pp. xxii + 249 + XXIV pls.
XXV	E. Puech, *Qumrân Grotte 4: XVIII, Textes hébreux (4Q521-4Q528, 4Q576-4Q579)* (DJD 25; Oxford: Clarendon, 1998). Pp. xviii + 229 + XV pls. + 2 figs.
XXVI	P. S. Alexander and G. Vermes, *Qumran Cave 4: XIX, Serekh Ha-Yaḥad and Two Related Texts* (DJD 26; Oxford: Clarendon, 1998). Pp. xvii + 253 + XXIV pls.
XXVII	H. M. Cotton and A. Yardeni, *Aramaic, Hebrew and Greek Documentary Texts from Naḥal Ḥever and Other Sites, with an Appendix Containing Alleged Qumran Texts (The Seiyâl Collection II)* (DJD 27; Oxford: Clarendon, 1997). Pp. xxvii + 381 + 33 figs. + LXI pls.
XXVIII	D. M. Gropp, *Wadi Daliyeh II: The Samaria Papyri from Wadi Daliyeh;* and M. Bernstein et al., in Consultation with J. VanderKam and M. Brady, *Qumran Cave 4: XXVIII, Miscellanea, Part 2* (DJD 28; Oxford: Clarendon, 2001). Pp. xv + 255 + LXIII pls.
XXIX	E. Chazon et al., in Consultation with J. VanderKam and M. Brady, *Qumran Cave 4: XX, Poetical and Liturgical Texts, Part 2* (DJD 29;

	Oxford: Clarendon, 1999). Pp. xiii + 478 + XXVIII pls. + five fold-out pls.
XXX	D. Dimant, *Qumran Cave 4: XXI, Parabiblical Texts, Part 4: Pseudo-Prophetic Texts* (DJD 30; Oxford: Clarendon, 2001). Pp. xiv + 278 + XII pls.
XXXI	E. Puech, *Qumrân Grotte 4: XXII, Textes araméens, première partie: 4Q529-549* (DJD 31; Oxford: Clarendon, 2001). Pp. xviii + 439 + XXII pls.
XXXII	P. W. Flint and E. Ulrich, *Qumran Cave 1: II, The Isaiah Scrolls* (DJD 32; Oxford: Clarendon, 2008). 2 vols. [in preparation].
XXXIII	D. M. Pike and A. C. Skinner, in Consultation with J. VanderKam and M. Brady, *Qumran Cave 4: XXIII, Unidentified Fragments* (DJD 33; Oxford: Clarendon, 2001). Pp. xiii + 380 + XLI pls.
XXXIV	J. Strugnell, D. J. Harrington, and T. Elgvin, in Consultation with J. A. Fitzmyer, *Qumran Cave 4: XXIV, Sapiential Texts, Part 2: 4QInstruction (Mûsār lĕMēvîn): 4Q415 ff., with a Re-edition of 1Q26* (DJD 34; Oxford: Clarendon, 1999). Pp. xvi + 584 + XXXI pls.
XXXV	J. Baumgarten et al., *Qumran Cave 4: XXV, Halakhic Texts* (DJD 35; Oxford: Clarendon, 1999). Pp. xi + 173 + XII pls.
XXXVI	S. J. Pfann, *Cryptic Texts;* and P. Alexander and Others, in Consultation with J. VanderKam and M. Brady, *Miscellanea, Part 1: Qumran Cave 4: XXVI* (DJD 36; Oxford: Clarendon, 2000). Pp. xvi + 739 + XLIX pls.
XXXVII	E. Puech, *Qumran Grotte 4: XXVII, Textes araméens, deuxième partie: 4Q550-575, 580-582* (DJD 37; Oxford: Clarendon, 2008). Pp. 578 + xxvi pls. [in preparation]
XXXVIII	J. Charlesworth et al., in Consultation with J. VanderKam and M. Brady, *Miscellaneous Texts from the Judaean Desert* (DJD 38; Oxford: Clarendon, 2000). Pp. xvii + 250 + 26 figs. + XXXVI pls.
XXXIX	E. Tov et al., *The Texts from the Judaean Desert: Indices and an Introduction to the* Discoveries in the Judaean Desert *Series* (DJD 39; Oxford: Clarendon, 2002). Pp. x + 452.
XL	Stegemann, E., E. Schuller, and C. Newsom, *Qumran Cave 1: III, 1QHodayot a, with Incorporation of 4QHodayot a-f and 1QHodayat b* (DJD 40; Oxford: Clarendon, 2008). Pp. 410 + XXVI pls.

The biggest difficulty that one has in using the volumes of this series is to find out in which volume a certain text is to be found: hence the need of a listing such as is being attempted here. When the texts of a specific cave are not too numerous, they are presented in one volume (e.g., the texts of Cave 1 in DJD 1; or most of the texts of Qumran Cave 11 [11Q2-18, 11Q20-31], which are grouped in DJD 23).). Since the fragmentary texts from Qumran Cave 4 number 582 (but with many subdivided as a, b, c, etc.) and are of many different genres (biblical, sectarian, and otherwise), they are found in many different volumes, and not in strict numerical order, although the biblical texts are kept separate from the non-biblical fragments. The disorder of the latter creates the greatest difficulty in finding out where a given text has been published in these volumes.

Moreover, since the first volume of DJD appeared only in 1955, the major scrolls of Qumran Cave 1, which were discovered in 1947, were published by American and Israeli scholars in publications that were not part of DJD. That too is the reason why most of the major texts of Qumran Cave 1 do not bear a number. The only exceptions are the Genesis Apocryphon (1QapGen), which is now known as 1Q20, and the War Scroll (1QM), which is now known as 1Q33, i.e., by the numbers that some fragments of these texts once bore, which were found by archaeologists in Cave 1 and published in DJD 1. 86-87, 135-36. These fragments are now treated with the main text, which was originally unnumbered, but now have the number of those fragments. The other unnumbered texts will be listed below in their appropriate places, along with some seventy other fragmentary texts of Cave 1, which do bear their own numbers.

For the official list of the documents from various places in the Judean Desert from which complete or fragmentary texts have come, together with numbers of their photographs and the museums where they are housed, see *The Texts from the Judaean Desert: Indices and an Introduction to the* Discoveries in the Judaean Desert *Series* (DJD 39; ed. E. Tov et al.; Oxford: Clarendon, 2002) 27-114. This list is an updated form of that published by Tov in *The SBL Handbook of Style* [ed. P. H. Alexander et al.; Peabody, MA: Hendrickson, 1999] 176-233) and as an article in *The Dead Sea Scrolls after Fifty Years: A Comprehensive Assessment* (2 vols.; ed. P. W. Flint and J. C. VanderKam; Leiden: Brill, 1998-99), 2. 669-717. See also S. A. Reed, *The Dead Sea Scrolls Catalogue: Documents, Photographs and Museum Inventory Numbers* (SBLRBS 32; rev. M. J. Lundberg and M. B. Phelps; Atlanta, GA: Scholars Press, 1994).

The text of the Scrolls can be found in microfiche form: E. Tov (ed.), *The Dead Sea Scrolls on Microfiche: A Comprehensive Facsimile Edition of the Texts from the Judean Desert* (Leiden: Brill and IDC Microform Publishers, 1992); with a *Companion Volume* (ed. E. Tov and S. J. Pfann) and an *Inventory List of Photographs* (by S. A. Reed and M. J. Lundberg) (Leiden: Brill, 1993). This form contains more than the Qumran texts, including texts from Masada, Ṣe'elim, Ḥever, and elsewhere, and it has many photographs from the Shrine of the Book that had not been previously made available. There are about a hundred positive microfiches, made from original negatives, which supply about 5200 photographs, as E. Tov reveals in his article, "The Unpublished Texts from the Judean Desert," *New Qumran Texts and Studies: Proceedings of the First Meeting of the International Organization for Qumran Studies, Paris 1992* (STDJ 15; ed. G. J. Brooke and F. García Martínez; Leiden: Brill, 1994) 81-88, esp. 83.

An electronic form of the texts is found in *The Dead Sea Scrolls Electronic Reference Library, Volume 1* (ed. T. H. Lim and P. S. Alexander; Oxford: Oxford University Press; Leiden: Brill, 1997); *Volume 2* (ed. N. B. Reynolds et al.; Leiden: Brill, 1999). This form was prepared by the Foundation for Ancient Research and Mormon Studies, Provo, UT; it presents digitized images of the most important (but not all) non-biblical texts, with bibliographical annotations (ed. E. Tov): *The Dead Sea Scrolls Electronic Library* (Volume 3: CD-Rom revised by E. Tov, N. B. Reynolds, and K. Heal; Leiden: Brill, 2006). See further section XIII below.

Individual photographs of texts, made from the original negatives of the 1950s, are available from the Israel Antiquities Authority, and the Ancient Biblical Manuscript Center in Claremont, CA. Such photographs of many of the texts can be viewed at the Hebrew Union College in Cincinnati, OH, the Oxford Centre for Postgraduate Studies, and the Huntington Library in San Marino, CA. The last-named institution is said to have the text of the Scrolls, made from its photographs, on two microfilm reels that are available (see *JJS* 43 [1992] 100), but Tov notes that, though the "microfilm contains valuable material," it "is not of good quality" ("The Unpublished Texts," 82). The Claremont Center also has color photographs made more recently with new photographic techniques.

A collection of photographs of fragments on 1787 plates can be found in R. H. Eisenman and J. M. Robinson (eds.), *A Facsimile Edition of the Dead Sea Scrolls Prepared with an Introduction and Index* (2 vols.; Washington, DC: Biblical Archaeological Society, 1991). The source of these photographs is not given, but they seem to be genuine, when they are compared with the fragments shown on plates in DJD. The photographs themselves have been somewhat reduced, but they are accompanied by PAM numbers. Tov says of this edition, "Some fifty per cent of the photographs . . . are of inferior quality and cannot be used well for scholarly purposes" ("The Unpublished Texts," 82). Now that most of the texts appear in DJD, this publication has lost much of its value, but it may still help, if used along with Reed's *Catalogue*, because it often has copies of older photographs of fragments that the editors did not use for the plates in DJD.

A transcription of many texts can be found in B. Z. Wacholder and

M. G. Abegg, Jr., *A Preliminary Edition of the Unpublished Dead Sea Scrolls: The Hebrew and Aramaic Texts from Cave Four* (4 vols.; Washington, DC: Biblical Archaeology Society, 1991, 1992, 1995, 1996). These transcribed texts were reconstructed from a concordance of unpublished non-biblical fragments based on editors' transcriptions produced in the late 1950s and early 1960s (see further the annotation on the "Preliminary Concordance" in section VI below). As a result, they were hopelessly out of date in the 1990s. The only value this publication has today is the record of a few significant readings and suggestions of Wacholder and Abegg.

Still of value are the early articles of E. Tov about documents that were still unpublished in the early 1990s because of the information that is contained in them about many texts: "The Unpublished Qumran Texts from Caves 4 and 11," *JJS* 43 (1992) 101-36; updated (with corrections) in *BA* 55 (1992) 94-104.

Valuable general information can be found further in various articles of DJD 39, which is mentioned above. They recount the history of the DJD series, give an additional annotated list of texts from the Judean Desert classified by content and genre, list the biblical texts, and then specific groups of texts (those written on papyrus, opisthographs, those written in paleo-Hebrew and cryptic scripts, and then Greek, Aramaic, and Nabatean texts). Articles also list overlaps and parallels in non-biblical texts from Qumran and Masada, catalogue scribal notations, and give a chronological index of all the texts from the Judean Desert.

Note also the preface of DJD 6, written by P. Benoit (pp. v-vi), which supplies information about the publication of that volume but also about the political events that affected the history of the publication of volumes in that series. Also important is the list that appears in DJD 7 (p. ix), where M. Baillet records the "Distribution des Manuscrits," i.e., the list of institutions that had contributed funds to aid the publication of the Scrolls and fragments and were to receive certain fragments, once they were published. Baillet lists only 13 texts, but the destination of many others should be recorded. Compare his list with that in DJD 1. xi.

B. Major Publications (according to Sites)

In the following list can be found all the places in which various Dead Sea Scrolls have been published. It provides information about the *editio princeps*, and sometimes also about preliminary or partial publications, when they have some details that may still be of value. References have been added in some cases to other articles or notes where different photos have been published or further information on a text has been supplied. The reader should realize that the long and tedious process of fitting fragments together and identifying them has at times required the reordering of material, even after it has once been published in a preliminary fashion, because it has subsequently been recognized that certain pieces should be associated differently. An effort has been made here to list the material according to the present state of knowledge about such questions. This means that the sigla on some occasions may differ from what has been given in a previous preliminary publication. The short Latin word *olim* ("formerly") is used to indicate the use of an earlier siglum, when and where this is known.

The texts are listed according to the numbered caves with their conventional sigla. The numbered Qumran caves designate only those in which written material has been discovered, not all the caves where artifacts or evidence of habitation have been found.

1. Qumran (Wadi Qumran, Khirbet Qumran, Caves of Qumran [see DBSup 9. 738-1014])

a. Cave 1

(i) Unnumbered Texts

1QIsa[a]

Burrows, M. (ed.), *The Dead Sea Scrolls of St. Mark's Monastery* (New Haven: American Schools of Oriental Reseach), 1 (1950) pls. I-LIV: contains all 66 chaps. of Isaiah with occasional lacunae, a few words missing at the bottom of some columns.

Cross, F. M. et al. (eds.), *Scrolls from Qumrân Cave I: The Great Isaiah Scroll, The Order of the Community, The* Pesher *to Habakkuk*. From photographs by John C. Trever (Jerusalem: Albright Institute of Archaeological Research and the Shrine of the Book, 1972) 13-123: Black-and-white and colored photographs of cols. I-LIV of 1QIsa[a]; the black-and-white photographs, however, are not as good as those of the first printing of 1950.

Parry, D. W. and E. Qimron, *The Great Isaiah Scroll (1QIsa[a]): A New Edition* (STDJ 32; Leiden: Brill, 1999): Transcriptions based on the scroll itself in the Shrine of the Book and checked against enhanced computer images of the J. C. Trever negatives, which had been scanned into digitized format. New photographs with selected bibliography of 1QIsa[a] (pp. xi-xxv).

Ulrich, E., and P. W. Flint, *Qumran Cave 1: II, The Isaiah Scrolls* (DJD 32 [2 vols.]; Oxford: Clarendon, 2008): Part 1, Introductions, Notes, and Variants; Part 2, redigitized plates with transcriptions on facing pages.

1QIsa[b]

Sukenik, E. L., **אוצר המגילות הגנוזות שבידי האוניברסיטה העברית** (Jerusalem: Bialik Foundation and the Hebrew University, 1954 [the title-page incorrectly reads 1956]). Two parts: Plates [1-15] and Transcription [1-15]. This publication also includes 1QM (1Q33) and 1QH[a]. It is a modern Hebrew version of the following edition.

(DSSHU)

Sukenik, E. L. (posthumously edited by N. Avigad and Y. Yadin), *The Dead Sea Scrolls of the Hebrew University* (Jerusalem: Hebrew University and Magnes Press, 1955). Two parts: Plates [1-15] and Transcription [1-15]. See also 1Q8 (D. Barthélemy, "8. Isaïe," DJD 1. 66-68 + pl. XII), which is part of this text. Cf. E. Puech, "Quelques aspects de la restauration du Rouleau des Hymnes (1QH)," *JJS* 39 (1988) 38-55, esp. 55 n. 40 (mention of a Shrine of the Book photograph [4287] that contains an unpublished frg. of four lines, part of Isa 44:23-25).

Ulrich, E. and P. W. Flint, Qumran *Cave 1: II, The Isaiah Scrolls* (DJD 32 [2 vols.]; Oxford: Clarendon, 2008): Part 1, Introductions, Notes, and Variants; Part 2, redigitized plates with transcriptions on facing pages.

Detailed Listing of Contents of 1QIsa[b]

Col. I	[not extant]
Col. II	[not extant]
Col. III (DJD I 1)	Isa 7:22–8:1
Col. IV (Jain 29)	Isa. 8:8 or 8:10
Col. V frg. a (*DSSHU* 1 i)	Isa 10:16-19
Col. V frg. b (DJD I 2)	Isa 12:3–13:8
Col. VI a-b (*DSSHU* 1 ii, 2 i)	Isa 13:16-19
Col. V c-d (DJD I 3)	Isa 15:3–16:3
Col. VII a-b (*DSSHU* 2 ii, 3 i)	Isa 16:5-11
Col. VV c (DJD 4)	Isa 19:7-17
Col. VIII a-b (*DSSHU* 3 ii, 4)	Isa 19:20–20:1
Col. VIII c-e (DJD XXXII 1 + DJD I 5)	Isa 22:9-20
Col. IX a (*DSSHU* 5)	Isa 22:23–23:5
Col. IX b (DJD I 6)	Isa 24:18–25:8
Col. X (*DSSHU* 6 i)	Isa 26:1-5

Col. XI a-c (*DSSHU* 6 ii)	Isa 28:15-21
Col. XI d-e (*DSSHU* 7)	Isa 29:1-8
Col. XII a-b (*DSSHU* 8)	Isa 30:10-15
Col. XII c-d (*DSSHU* 9)	Isa 30:21-26
Col. XIII (Jain 22)	Isa 32:17-20
Col. XIV (*DSSHU* 10)	Isa 35:4-7
Col. XV (DJD XXII 2-4 + *DSSHU* 11)	Isa 37:8-13
Col. XVI (*DSSHU* I)	Isa 38:12–40:4
Col. XVII (*DSSHU* II, Jain 24)	Isa 41:3-24
Col. XVIII (*DSSHU* III)	Isa 43:1-13, 20-27
Col. XIX (*DSSHU* IV, Jain 25)	Isa 44:21–45:1-13
Col. XX (*DSSHU* V)	Isa 46:3–47:14
Col. XXI (*DSSHU* VI)	Isa 48:17–49:15
Col. XXII (*DSSHU* VII)	Isa 50:7–51:11
Col. XXIII (*DSSHU* VIII, Jain 26)	Isa 52:7–54:6
Col. XXIV (*DSSHU* IX)	Isa 55:2–57:4
Col. XXV (*DSSHU* X, Jain 27)	Isa 57:17–59:8
Col. XXVI (*DSSHU* XI)	Isa 59:20–61:2
Col. XXVII (*DSSHU* XII)	Isa 62:2–64:8
Col. XXVIII (*DSSHU* XIII, Jain 28)	Isa 65:17–66:24

1QpHab

Burrows, M. (ed.), *The Dead Sea Scrolls of St. Mark's Monastery,* vol. 1, pls. LV-LXI (commentary on Hab 1:2-17; 2:1-20).

Cross, F. M. et al. (eds.), *Scrolls from Qumrân Cave I,* 149-163: Black-and white and colored photographs of 1QpHab cols. 1-13.

1QH^a

Sukenik, E. L., *DSSHU,* pls. XXXV-XLVII (upper), XLVIII-LVIII; transcription of cols. 1-18 and frgs. 1-66: The Thanksgiving Psalms *(Hôdāyôt).* The order of the columns and fragments of 1QH^a, as published by Sukenik, proved to be incorrect, and it was corrected by H. Stegemann in his unpublished Heidelberg dissertation, 1963; see now "The Material Reconstruction of 1QHodayot," *The Dead Sea Scrolls Fifty Years after Their Discovery* (ed. L. H. Schiffman et al; Jerusalem: Israel Exploration Society, 2000) 272-84. His reconstruction was confirmed by E. Puech, "Quelques aspects de la restauration du Rouleau des Hymnes (1QH)," *JJS* 39 (1988) 38-55; "Un hymne essénien en partie retrouvé et les béatitudes: *1QH* v 12-vi 18 (= col. xiii-xiv 7) et *4QBéat.,*" *RevQ* 13 (1988) 59-88. But see E. Schuller, "Table 1: Sections in 1QH^a Preserved in 1QH^b and 4QH^{a-f}," DJD 29. 72-73.

Stegemann, E., E. Schuller, and C. Newsom, *Qumran Cave 1: III, 1QHodayot a, with Incorporation of 4QHodayot a-f and 1QHodayat b* (DJD 40; Oxford: Clarendon, 2008). Pp. 410 + XXVI pls. Reconstructed text translated with commentary.

Stegemann & Schuller	*Sukenik Numbers*	*Equals All or Part of*
3:12-16	frg. 23 1-5	
3:24-32	frg. 16 1-9	
4:12-41	17:1-28 + frg. 14	4Q428 1?
5:12-40	13:1-21 + frgs. 15a, b i, 17, 20, 31, 33	4Q428 2?
6:12-41	14:1-28 + frgs. 15b ii, 18, 19, 22, 44	
7:11-41	15:1-28 + frgs. 10, 32, 34, 42	4Q427 8 I
8:8-38	16:1-20 + frgs. 12, 13	
9:2-41	1:1-39 + frg. 24	4Q432 frgs. 1 + 2
10:3-41	2:1-39	4Q428 3; 4Q432 3 + 4
11:2-41	3:1-39 + frg. 25	4Q428 4 + 5; 4Q432 5 + 6 + 7
12:2-41	4:1-40 + frg. 43	4Q428 6; 4Q430 1; 4Q432 7 + 8 + 9 + 10
13:3-41	5:1-39 + frg. 29	4Q428 7; 4Q429 1 I-ii + 2 + 3; 4Q432 11
14:4-41	6:1-36 + frg. 26	4Q428 8; 4Q429 4 I-ii
15:4-39	7:1-36	4Q428 9 + 10; 4Q432 12; 1QH^{b} 1
16:2-41	8:1-40	4Q428 10; 4Q432 13; 1QH^{b} 1 + 2
17:1-41	9:1-40	
18:3-41	10:1-39 + frg. 30	4Q428 11?
19:4-42	11:1-38 + frg. 60	4Q427 1; 4Q428 12 I
20:4-42	12:1-36 + frgs. 54, 60	4Q427 3 + 8 ii + 9; 4Q428 12 ii
21:2-38	18:16-33 + frg. 3	4Q427 10 + 11 + 12; 4Q428 13
22:4-39	19:8-10 + frgs. 1 i, 4, 47, 52	4Q428 15 + 16
23:2-39	18:1-16 + frgs. 2 i, 57 i	4Q428 14
24:4-39	19:1-7 + frgs. 2 ii, 6, 9, 45, 50, 57 ii	4Q428 15 + 16
25:3-37	frgs. 5, 7 i, 8, 46, 51, 55 i, 56 i, 63	4Q427 3; 4Q428 17 + 18 + 19 + 20

26:6-38	frgs. 7 ii, 46 ii, 55 ii, 56 ii	4Q427 7 i-ii; 4Q428 21; 4Q431 1 + 2
27:12-14	frgs. 61-62	
28:11-15	frg. 48	

New location not yet determined for frgs. 27-28, 35-41, 49, 53, 58, 64-66.

1QS

Burrows, M. (ed.), *The Dead Sea Scrolls of St. Mark's Monastery,* vol. 2, fasc. 2 ("The Manual of Discipline," 1951), cols. 1-11: The Rule of the Community *(Serek hay-yaḥad).*

Cross, F. M. et al. (eds.), *Scrolls from Qumrân Cave I,* 125-147: Black-and-white and colored photographs of 1QS 1-11.

Charlesworth, J. H. et al. (eds.), *The Dead Sea Scrolls: Rule of the Community, Photographic Multi-Language Edition* (Philadelphia, PA: American Interfaith Institute/World Alliance, 1996): Color photographs with transcription and translations of 1QS into English, French, German, Israeli Hebrew, Italian, and Spanish.

(ii) Numbered Texts

1Q1-72

Barthélemy, D. and J. T. Milik, *Qumran Cave I* (DJD 1; Oxford: Clarendon, 1955).

1Q1 1QGen

Barthélemy, "1. Genèse," DJD 1. 49-50 (+ pl. VIII): Gen 1:18-21; 3:11-14; 22:13-15; 23:17-19; 24:22-24; + 14 frgs.

1Q2 1QExod

Barthélemy, "2. Exode," DJD 1. 50-51 (+ pl. VIII): Exod 16:12-16; 19:24–20:2, 5-6, 25–21:1, 4-5; + six frgs.

1Q3 1QpaleoLev

Barthélemy, "3. Lévitique et autres fragments en écriture 'phénicienne,'" DJD 1. 51-54 (+ pls. VIII-IX): Lev 11:10-11; 19:30-34; 20:20-24; 21:24–22:6; 23:4-8; 27:30-31?; Num 1:48-50; 36:7-8?; + 14 frgs. See M. D. McLean, *The Use and Development of Paleo-Hebrew in the Hellenistic and Roman Period* (Cambridge, MA: Dissertation, Harvard University, 1982; Ann Arbor, MI: University Microfilms, 1982 [order #DA82-22670]). McLean distinguishes three different mss:

1QpaleoLev[a] (= frgs. 1-8, 10-15); 1QpaleoLev[b] (= frgs. 22-23); 1QpaleoNum (= frgs. 16-21).

Cf. E. C. Ulrich, "A Revised Edition of the *1QpaleoLev-Num[a]* and *1QpaleoLev[b]?* Fragments," *RevQ* 22 (2006) 341-47.

1Q4 1QDeut[a]

Barthélemy, "4. Deutéronome (premier exemplaire)," DJD 1. 54-57 (+ pl. IX): Deut 1:22-25; 4:47-49; 8:18-19?; 9:27-28; 11:27-30; 13:1-4, 4-6, 13-14; 14:21, 23-26; 16:4, 6-7; + 44 frgs.

1Q5 1QDeut[b]

Barthélemy, "5. Deutéronome (second exemplaire)," DJD 1. 57-62 (+ pl. X): Deut 1:9-13; 8:8-9; 9:10; 11:30-31; 15:14-15; 17:16; 21:8-9; 24:10-16; 25:13-18; 28:44-48; 29:9-11, 12-20; 30:19–31:6, 7-10, 12-13; 32:17-21, 21-22, 22-29, 24-25; 33:12-17, 18-19, 21-23, 24; + 27 frgs.

1Q6 1QJudg

Barthélemy, "6. Juges," DJD 1. 62-64 (+ pl. XI): Judg 6:20-22; 8:1?; 9:1-4, 4-6, 28-31, 40-42, 42-43, 48-49; + 31 frgs.

1Q7 1QSam

Barthélemy, "7. Livres de Samuel," DJD 1. 64-65 (+ pl. XI): 1 Sam 18:17-18; 2 Sam 20:6-10; 21:16-19; 23:9-12.

1Q8 1QIsa[b]

See *DSSHU,* pp. 15-16 above.

1Q9 1QEzek

Barthélemy, "9. Ézéchiel," DJD 1. 68-69 (+ pl. XII): Ezek 4:16–5:1.

1Q10 1QPs[a]

Barthélemy, "10. Psautier (premier exemplaire)," DJD 1. 69-70 (+ pl. XIII): Ps 86:5-8; 92:12-14; 94:16; 95:11–96:2; 119:31-34, 43-48, 77-79; 119:77-80; + 11 frgs.

1Q11 1QPs[b]

Barthélemy, "11. Psautier (second exemplaire)," DJD 1. 71 (+ pl. XIII): Ps 126:6; 127:1-5; 128:2-3.

1Q12 1QPs[c]

Barthélemy, "12. Psaume 44," DJD 1. 71-72 (+ pl. XIII): Ps 44:3-6, 7, 9, 23-25; + two frgs.

1Q13 1QPhyl

Barthélemy, "13. Phylactère," DJD 1. 72-76 (+ pl. XIV): Deut 5:1, 3, 5, 7, 9, 14, 21, 23-27; 10:17-18; 10:21–11:1, 8-11, 12; Exod 13:2-3, 7-9, 15-16?; + 26 frgs.

1Q14 1QpMic

Milik, "14. Commentaire de Michée," DJD 1. 77-80 (+ pl. XV): Pesher on Mic 1:2-5, 5-7, 8-9; 4:13?; 6:14-16; 7:6?, 8-9?, 17.

1Q15 1QpZeph

Milik, "15. Commentaire de Sophonie," DJD 1. 80 (+ pl. XVI): Pesher on Zeph 1:18–2:2.

1Q16 1QpPs

Milik, "16. Commentaire de Psaumes," DJD 1. 81-82 (+ pl. XVI): Pesher on Ps 57:1, 4; 68:12-13, 26-27, 30-31; + eight frgs.

1Q17-18 1QJub[a,b]

Milik, "17-18. Livre des Jubilés," DJD 1. 82-84 (+ pl. XVI): *Jub.* 27:19-20; 35:8-10; + three frgs. On 1Q17, see R. de Vaux, "La grotte des manuscrits hébreux," *RB* 56 (1949) 602-5 (+ pl. XVIa). Cf. J. C. VanderKam, "The Jubilees Fragments from Qumran Cave 4," *The Madrid Qumran Congress: Proceedings of the International Congress on the Dead Sea Scrolls,* ed. J. Trebolle Barrera and L. Vegas Montaner; *Madrid 18-21 March, 1991* (STDJ 11/2; Leiden: Brill; Madrid: Editorial Complutense, 1992) 635-48, esp. 636-37.

1Q19 1QNoah

Milik, "19. 'Livre de Noé,'" DJD 1. 84-86 (+ pl. XVI): Book of Noah (frgs. 1, 3 related to *1 Enoch* 8:4–9:4; 106:9-10; and 1QapGen 5:29; cf. Milik, *BE,* 55-60); + 18 frgs.

1Q19bis 1QNoah[bis]

Milik, "19bis. 'Livre de Noé,'" DJD 1. 152 (no pl.): = frg. 2 of the same text as 1Q19. For a photograph, see J. C. Trever, "Completion of the Publication of Some Fragments from Qumran Cave 1," *RevQ* 5 (1964-66) 323-44 (+ pls. I-VII, esp. pl. VIIb). Cf. *Jub.* 10:13; 21:10.

1Q20 1QapGen ar

Avigad, N. and Y. Yadin, *A Genesis Apocryphon: A Scroll from the Wilderness of Judaea: Description and Contents of the Scroll, Facsimiles, Transcription and Translation of Columns II, XIX-XXII* (Jerusalem: Magnes Press of the Hebrew

University and Heikhal ha-Sefer, 1956). See also what Milik had called 1Q20 in DJD 1. 86-87, "20. Apocalypse de Lamech." These frgs. 1-4 now are recognized as part of cols. 0 and 1 of 1QapGen, which was originally unnumbered but now has become 1Q20. It is an Aramaic extended paraphrase of Gen 5:18, 28-29; 6:8-9; 8:4, 13, 18; 9:2-4, 13, 20; 10:6, 20, 22, 25; 12:8–15:4. [N.B. Fascicle 1 of vol. 2 of Burrows, *The Dead Sea Scrolls of St. Mark's Monastery* (see above), was reserved originally for this text, but it was published separately in Israel in 1956.] See J. A. Fitzmyer, *The Genesis Apocryphon of Qumran Cave 1 (1Q20): A Commentary, Third Edition* (BibOr 18B; Rome: Editrice Pontificio Istituto Biblico, 2004), for the columns of this text that have been read subsequently to the preliminary edition of 1956. Cf. J. C. Greenfield and E. Qimron, "The Genesis Apocryphon Col. XII," *Studies in Qumran Aramaic* (Abr-NSup 3; ed. T. Muraoka; Louvain: Peeters, 1992) 70-77 (with a photograph); repr. in *'Al Kanfei Yonah: Collected Studies of Jonas C. Greenfield on Semitic Philology* (2 vols.; ed. S. M. Paul et al.; Leiden: Brill; Jerusalem: Hebrew University Magnes Press, 2001), 2. 646-52. Also M. Morgenstern, E. Qimron, and D. Sivan, "The Hitherto Unpublished Columns of the Genesis Apocryphon," *Abr-N* 33 (1995) 30-54 (without photographs, but with the Trever fragment as part of col. 1). A new edition of 1QapGen is being prepared by M. Bernstein and E. Eshel, which may appear in the DJD series.

1Q21 1QLevi ar (olim 1QTLevi ar)

Milik, "21. Testament de Lévi," DJD 1. 87-91 (+ pl. XVII): *T. Levi* 8:11? (possibly older form of Bodleian CLeviOxf ar). See Milik, "Le Testament de Lévi en araméen: Fragment de la grotte 4 de Qumrân," *RB* 62 (1955) 398-406. Cf. Beyer, *ATTM*, 195-97.

1Q22 1QDM

Milik, "22. 'Dires de Moïse,'" DJD 1. 91-97 (+ pls. XVIII-XIX): Sayings of Moses *(Dibrê Môšeh)*. See now 4QDM (DJD 31. 200-201, PAM 43.686, frg. 30); cf. E. Tigchelaar, "A Cave 4 Fragment of Divre Moshe (4QDM) and the Text of 1Q22 1:7-20 and Jubilees 1:9, 14," *DSD* 12 (2005) 303-12.

1Q23-24 1QEnGiants^{a,b} ar

Milik, "23-24. Deux apocryphes en araméen," DJD 1. 97-99 (+ pls. XIX-XX): Enoch, Book of Giants. See now L. Stuckenbruck, "23. 1QEnochGiants^{a} ar (Re-edition)," DJD 36. 49-66; "24. 1QEnochGiants^{b}? ar (Re-edition)," DJD 36. 67-72. Cf. Milik, "Turfan et Qumran: Livre des Géants juif et manichéen," *Tradition und Glaube: Das frühe Christentum in seiner Umwelt: Festgabe für Karl*

Georg Kuhn . . . (ed. G. Jeremias et al.; Göttingen: Vandenhoeck & Ruprecht, 1971) 117-27, esp. 120-21; Beyer, *ATTM*, 262-68.

1Q25 1QApocryphal Prophecy

Milik, "25. Une prophétie apocryphe (?)," DJD 1. 100-101 (+ pl. XX): Apocryphal Prophecy.

1Q26 1QInstruction (olim 1QapWis)

Milik, "26. Un apocryphe," DJD 1. 101-2 (+ pl. XX): Wisdom Apocryphon. See now J. Strugnell and D. Harrington, "1Q26. 1QInstruction (Re-edition)," DJD 34. 535-39. Frg. 2:2-4 overlaps with 4QInstruction[g] (4Q423) frgs. 3 and 4 (see T. Elgvin, "423. 4QInstruction[g] *(Mûsār l[e]Mēvîn[g])*," DJD 34. 513-18).

1Q27 1QMyst

Milik, "27. 'Livre des Mystères,'" DJD 1. 102-7 (+ pls. XXI-XXII): Book of Mysteries. Cf. R. de Vaux, *RB* 56 (1949) 605-9 (+ pl. XVII); Milik, *VDom* 39 (1952) 42-43; idem, *RB* 63 (1956) 61. Cf. 4Q299, 4Q300.

1Q28 1QStitle

Milik, "28. Annexes à la Règle de la Communauté," DJD 1. 107-8 (+ pls. XXII-XXIX): Title and Appendices to 1QS.

1Q28a 1QSa

Barthélemy, "28a. Règle de la Congrégation (1QSa)," DJD 1. 108-18 (+ pls. XXIII-XXIV): Rule of the Congregation, two cols. *(Serek hā-ʿĒdāh).*

1Q28b 1QSb

Milik, "28b. Recueil des Bénédictions," DJD 1. 118-30 (+ pls. XXV-XXIX): Collection of Blessings to be uttered over the faithful, the Priest, the priests, and the Prince of the Congregation. See also G. Brooke, "1Q28b. 1QSerekh ha-Yaḥad b (fragment)," DJD 26. 227-33 (+ pl. XXIV); this frg. supplies words for 1QSb 5:22-25.

1Q29 1QLiturgy of the Three Tongues of Fire

Milik, "29. Liturgie des 'Trois Langues de Feu,'" DJD 1. 130-32 (+ pl. XXX): Liturgy of 'Three Tongues of Fire'; see *RB* 63 (1956) 64.

1Q30-31 1QLitA-B

Milik, "30-31. Textes liturgiques (?)," DJD 1. 132-34 (+ pl. XXX): Liturgical Texts A and B.

1Q32 1QNJ ar

Milik, "32. 'Description de la Jérusalem Nouvelle' (?)," DJD 1. 134-35 (+ pl. XXXI): New Jerusalem. Cf. Beyer, *ATTM,* 214-22.

1Q33 1QM

Sukenik, E. L., *DSSHU,* pls. 16-34, 47 (lower); transcription, 1-19. What was called 1Q33 in DJD 1. 135-36 (+ pl. XXXI), "'La guerre des fils de lumière contre les fils de ténèbres' (1QM)," fragments that Milik thought were part of col. 5 of 1QM, which was originally unnumbered, but now is 1Q33, War Scroll *(Milḥāmāh):* 19 cols. and 10 frgs.

1Q34 1QLitPr^{a}

Milik, "34. Recueil de prières liturgiques," DJD 1. 136 (+ pl. XXXI): Liturgical Prayers, probably related to 4QPrFêtes (4Q507-9) and to the following text.

1Q34bis 1QLitPr^{b}

Milik, "34bis. Recueil de prières liturgiques," DJD 1. 152-55: Liturgical Prayers. See Trever, "Completion," *RevQ* 5 (1964-66) 323-44, esp. 328-29 (+ pls. II-IV).

1Q35 1QH^{b}

Milik, "35. Recueil de cantiques d'action de grâces (1QH)," DJD 1. 136-38 (+ pl. XXXI): Text related to 1QH^{a} 15(old 7):27–8:13]). See J. Carmignac, "Remarques sur le texte des Hymnes de Qumrân," *Bib* 39 (1958) 139-55; E. Puech, "Quelques aspects de la restauration du Rouleau des Hymnes (1QH)," *JJS* 39 (1988) 38-55; "Restauration d'un texte hymnique à partir de trois manuscrits fragmentaires: *1QH^{a}* xv 37–xvi 4 (vii 34–viii 3), *1Q35 (H^{b})* 1, 9-14, *4Q428 (H^{b})* 7," *RevQ* 16 (1993-95) 543-58 (with facsimile of reconstructed text). For a photograph of 1Q35, see G. L. Harding, "The Dead Scrolls: Excavations Which Establish the Authenticity and Pre-Christian Date of the Oldest Bible Manuscripts," *ILN* (1 October 1949) 493-95. Cf. E. M. Schuller and L. Di Tommaso, "A Bibliography of the Hodayot, 1948-1996," *DSD* 4 (1997) 55-101, esp. 89-90.

1Q36 1QHymns

Milik, "36. Recueil d'hymnes," DJD 1. 138-41 (+ pl. XXXII): Frgs. of hymns.

1Q37-40 1QHymComp

Milik, "37-40. Compositions hymniques (?)," DJD 1. 141-43 (+ pls. XXXII-XXXIII): Frgs. of hymnic compositions.

1Q41-62 1QUncA

Milik, "41-62. Groupes non caractérisés, en hébreu," DJD 1. 144-47 (+ pls. XXXIII-XXXV): Unclassified Hebrew frgs.

1Q63-67 1QUncB ar

Milik, "63-67. Groupes non caractérisés, en araméen," DJD 1. 147 (+ pl. XXXV): Unclassified Aramaic frgs.

1Q68-69 1QUncC

Milik, "68-69. Fragments non classifiés, araméens et hébreux," DJD 1. 147-48 (+ pls. XXXV-XXXVI): Unclassified Aramaic and Hebrew frgs.

1Q70 1QpapUncA

Milik, "70. Fragments de papyrus," DJD 1. 148-49 (+ pl. XXXVII): Tiny papyrus frgs. See Trever, "Completion," *RevQ* 5 (1964-66) 323-44, esp. 331 (+ pl. VII); cf. Beyer, *ATTM*, 271-72.

1Q70bis 1QpapUncB

Milik, "70bis. Fragment de papyrus," DJD 1. 155 (no pl.): Papyrus frg., possibly related to 1Q70.

1Q71 1QDan^{a}

Barthélemy, "71. Daniel (premier exemplaire)," DJD 1. 150-51 (no pl.): Dan 1:10-17; 2:2-6. See Trever, "Completion," *RevQ* 5 (1964-66) 329-30 (+ pl. V). Cf. Beyer, *ATTM*, 301-3.

1Q72 1QDan^{b}

Barthélemy, "72. Daniel (second exemplaire)," DJD 1. 151-52 (no pl.): Dan 3:22-28, 27-30. See Trever, "Completion," *RevQ* 5 (1964-66) 330-32 (+ pl. VI). Cf. Beyer, *ATTM*, 301-3. An added fragment, related to Dan 3:26, is reported to be found in Schøyen MS 1926/4c (see *NCAL* 12 [1996] 1-2).

b. Cave 2

2Q1-33

Baillet, M., J. T. Milik, and R. de Vaux, *Les 'Petites Grottes' de Qumrân: Exploration de la falaise, Les grottes 2Q, 3Q, 5Q, 6Q, 7Q à 10Q; Le rouleau de cuivre* (DJD 3; Oxford: Clarendon, 1962). Two parts: 1. Textes; 2. Planches. All Cave 2 texts have been edited by M. Baillet.

2Q1 2QGen
"1. Genèse," 48-49 (+ pl. X): Gen 19:27-28; 36:6, 35-37.

2Q2 2QExod[a]
"2. Exode (premier exemplaire)," 49-52 (+ pl. X): Exod 1:11-14; 7:1-4; 9:27-29; 11:3-7; 12:32-41; 21:18-20?; 26:11-13; 30:21?, 23-25; 32:32-34; + three frgs.

2Q3 2QExod[b]
"3. Exode (deuxième exemplaire)," 52-55 (+ pl. XI): Exod 4:31; 12:26-27?; 18:21-22; 21:37–22:2, 15-19; 27:17-19; 31:16-17; 19:9; 34:10; + six frgs.

2Q4 2QExod[c]
"4. Exode (troisième exemplaire)," 56 (+ pl. XII): Exod 5:3-5.

2Q5 2QpaleoLev
"5. Lévitique en écriture paléo-hébraïque," 56-57 (+ pl. XII): Lev 11:22-29.

2Q6 2QNum[a]
"6. Nombres (premier exemplaire)," 57-58 (+ pl. XII): Num 3:38-41, 51–4:3.

2Q7 2QNum[b]
"7. Nombres (deuxième exemplaire)," 58-59 (+ pl. XII): Num 33:47-53.

2Q8 2QNum[c]
"8. Nombres (troisième exemplaire)," 59 (+ pl. XII): Num 7:88.

2Q9 2QNum[d?]
"9. Nombres (quatrième exemplaire ?)," 59-60 (+ pl. XII): Num 18:8-9 (this frg. may belongs to 2Q7; possibly = Lev 23:1-3).

2Q10 2QDeut[a]
"10. Deutéronome (premier exemplaire)," 60 (+ pl. XII): Deut 1:7-9.

2Q11 2QDeut[b]
"11. Deutéronome (deuxième exemplaire)," 60-61 (+ pl. XII): Deut 17:12-15.

2Q12 2QDeut[c]
"12. Deutéronome (troisième exemplaire)," 61-62 (+ pl. XII): Deut 10:8-12.

2Q13 2QJer

"13. Jérémie," 62-69 (+ pl. XIII): Jer 42:7-11, 14; 43:8-11; 44:1-3, 12-14; 46:27–47:7; 48:7, 25-39, 43-45; 49:10; + (doubtfully identified) frgs.: 13:22; 32:24-25; 48:2-4, 41-42); + 10 frgs. Also Tov, "Some Aspects of the Textual and Literary History of the Book of Jeremiah," *Le Livre de Jérémie* (BETL 54; ed. P.-M. Bogaert; Leuven: Leuven University, 1981) 145-67.

2Q14 2QPs

"14. Psautier," 69-71 (+ pl. XIII): Ps 103:2-11; 104:6-11.

2Q15 2QJob

"15. Job," 71 (+ p1. XIII): Job 33:28-30.

2Q16 2QRuth[a]

"16. Ruth (premier exemplaire)," 71-74 (+ pl. XIV): Ruth 2:13-14, 14-19, 19-22; 2:22–3:3, 4-8; 4:3-4.

2Q17 2QRuth[b]

"17. Ruth (second exemplaire)," 74-75 (+ pl. XV): Ruth 3:13-18; + one frg.

2Q18 2QSir

"18. Ecclésiastique (texte hébreu)," 75-77 (+ pl. XV): Sir 6:14-15 (or 1:19-20); 6:20-31.

2Q19 2QJub[a]

"19. Livre des Jubilés (premier exemplaire)," 77-78 (+ pl. XV): *Jub.* 23:7-8 (cf. Gen 25:9, 7-8).

2Q20 2QJub[b]

"20. Livre des Jubilés (second exemplaire)," 78-79 (+ pl. XV): *Jub.* 46:1-3 (cf. Exod 1:7; Gen 50:26, 22); + two frgs.

2Q21 2QapocrMoses

"21. Un apocryphe de Moïse(?)," 79-81 (+ pl. XV): Apocryphal writing about Moses.

2Q22 2QapocrDavid

"22. Un apocryphe de David (?)," 81-82 (+ pl. XV): Apocryphal writing about David. See now E. M. Schuller, *Non-Canonical Psalms from Qumran: A Pseud-*

epigraphic Collection (HSS 28; Atlanta, GA: Scholars, 1986); but also C. Newsom, *JJS* 39 (1988) 56-73. This text overlaps with 4Q373 1:6-8.

2Q23 2QapocrProph

"23. Une prophétie apocryphe," 82-84 (+ pl. XV): Apocryphal prophetic text in six tiny frgs.

2Q24 2QNJ ar

"24. Description de la Jérusalem nouvelle," 84-89 (+ pl. XVI): Description of the New Jerusalem. See Baillet, *RB* 62 (1955) 225-45 (+ pls. II-III); *ATTM*, 214-22.

2Q25 2QJuridical text

"25. Document juridique," 90 (+ pl. XVII): A juridical text.

2Q26 2QEnGiants

"26. Fragment de rituel (?)," 90-91 (+ pl. XVII): Now known as part of the "Book of Giants" (see Milik, *BE*, 309, 334-35; cf. *ATTM*, 258-68). See now the re-edition by L. Stuckenbruck, "26. 2QEnochGiants ar (Re-edition)," DJD 36. 73-75.

2Q27-33 2QUnc

"[27-33] Textes de caractère mal défini," 91-93 (+ pl. XVII): Tiny, unidentified frgs.

2QX1

Debris in a box

c. Cave 3

3Q1-15

Baillet, M., J. T. Milik, and R. de Vaux, *Les 'Petites Grottes' de Qumrân: Exploration de la falaise, Les grottes 2Q, 3Q, 5Q, 6Q, 7Q à 10Q; Le rouleau de cuivre* (DJD 3; Oxford: Clarendon, 1962). Two parts: 1. Texte; 2. Planches. All Cave 3 texts have been edited by M. Baillet, apart from 3Q15.

3Q1 3QEzek

"1. Ezéchiel," 94 (+ pl. XVIII): Ezek 16:31-33.

3Q2 3QPs
"2. Psaume 2," 94 (+ pl. XVIII): Ps 2:6-7.

3Q3 3QLam
"3. Lamentations," 95 (+ pl. XVIII): Lam 1:10-12; 3:53-62.

3Q4 3QpIsa
"4. Commentaire d'Isaïe," 95-96 (+ pl. XVIII): Pesher on Isa 1:1; cf. R. de Vaux, *RB* 60 (1953) 555-56.

3Q5 3QJub (olim 3QapProph)
"5. Une prophétie apocryphe," 96-98 (+ pl. XVIII): It is now known as a fragment of *Jubilees* (= *Jub.* 23:6-7, 12-13, 23; cf. R. Deichgräber, "Fragmente einer Jubiläen-Handschrift aus Höhle 3 von Qumran," *RevQ* 5 (1964-65) 415-22; A. Rofé, "קטעים מכתב יד נוסף של ס׳ היובל במערב מס׳ 3 של קומראן (Further Manuscript Fragments of the Jubilees in the Third Cave of Qumran)," *Tarbiz* 34 (1964-65) 333-36. See M. Baillet, "Remarques sur le manuscrit des Jubilés de la Grotte 3 de Qumran," *RevQ* 5 (1964-65) 423-33.

3Q6 3QHymn
"6. Hymne de louange," 98 (+ pl. XVIII): Hymn of Praise.

3Q7 3QTJudah
"7. Un apocryphe mentionnant l'ange de la présence," 99 (+ pl. XVIII): Text about an Angel of the Presence. See Milik, "Ecrits préesséniens de Qumrân: D'Hénoch à Amram," *Qumrân: Sa piété, sa théologie et son milieu* (BETL 46; ed. M. Delcor; Gembloux: Duculot, 1978) 91-106, esp. 98-99. Milik thinks that frgs. 6 and 5 joined with 3 are part of a Hebrew text, "Testament of Judah." (Milik's impossible siglum: 3QHJu 6 and 5+3).

3Q8 3QUnid
"8. Un texte mentionnant un ange de paix (?)," 100 (+ pl. XIX): Text about an Angel of Peace.

3Q9 3QSectarian text?
"9. Un texte de la secte," 100-101 (+ pl. XIX): Sectarian text.

3Q10-11 3QUnc
"10-11. Groupes en hébreu," 101-2 (+ pl. XIX): Tiny, unclassified Hebrew frgs.

3Q12-13 3QUncA-B ar

"12-13. Groupes en araméen," 102 (+ pl. XIX): Tiny, unidentified Aramaic frgs.

3Q14 3QUncC

"14. Fragments isolés," 102-4 (+ pl. XIX): 21 frgs. See Milik, *BE*, 61.

3Q15 3QCopScr

Milik, "Le rouleau de cuivre provenant de la grotte 3Q (3Q15)," 199-302 (+ pls. XLVIII-LXXI): Copper plaque mentioning buried treasures; see section XI below.

d. Cave 4

4Q1 4QGen-Exod[a] (olim 4QGen[a], 4QEx[b])

Davila, J. R., "1. 4QGen-Exod[a]," *Qumran Cave 4: VII, Genesis to Numbers* (DJD 12; ed. E. Ulrich et al.; Oxford: Clarendon, 1994) 7-30 (+ pls. I-V): Gen 22:14; 27:38-39, 42-43; 34:17-21; 35:17–36:13, 19-27; 37:5-6, 22-27; 39:11–40:1; 45:23; 47:13-14; 48:2-4, 15-17, 18-22; 49:1-5; Exod 1:3-17, 22–2:5; 3:8-16, 18-21; 4:4-7, 8-9, 26–5:1, 3-17; 6:4-21, 25; 7:5-13, 15-20; 8:20-22; 9:8?; + 23 frgs.

4Q2 4QGen[b]

Davila, "2. 4QGen[b]," DJD 12. 31-38 (+ pls. VI-VIII); a text possibly not from Qumran: Gen 1:1-25, 25-28; 2:14-19; 4:2-11; 5:13 (or 14); + one frg.

4Q3 4QGen[c]

Davila, "3. 4QGen[c]," DJD 12. 39-42 (+ pl. IX): Gen 40:12-13, 18–41:11.

4Q4 4QGen[d]

Davila, "4. 4QGen[d]," DJD 12. 43-45 (+ pl. IX): Gen 1:18-27.

4Q5 4QGen[e]

Davila, "5. 4QGen[e]," DJD 12. 47-52 (+ pl. X): Gen 36:43–37:2, 27-30; 40:18–41:8, 35-44; 42:17-19; 43:8-14; 49:6-8; + one frg.

4Q6 4QGen[f]

Davila, "6. 4QGen[f]," DJD 12. 53-55 (+ pl. XI): Gen 48:1-11. See Eshel, E. and H. Eshel, *DSD* 12 (2005) 135-37: frg. 1a = Gen 33:19–34:2.

4Q7 4QGen[g]

Davila, "7. 4QGen[g]," DJD 12. 57-60 (+ pl. XII): Gen 1:1-11, 13-22; 2:6-7 (or 18-19).

4Q8 4QGen^{h}

Davila, "8. 4QGen^{h}," DJD 12. 61-64 (+ pl. XII): 4QGen^{h} is subdivided into four very small frgs. of Genesis. 4QGen^{h1} has a few words of Gen 1:8-10; 4QGen^{h2} a few words of Gen 2:17-18; 4QGen$^{h\text{-}para}$ is a paraphrase of Gen 12:4-5; and 4QGen$^{h\text{-}title}$ has only the word בראשית *(bĕrēšît),* "in the beginning."

4Q9 4QGen^{j}

Davila, "9. 4QGen^{j}," DJD 12. 65-73 (+ pl. XIII): Gen 41:15-18, 23-27, 29-36, 38-43; 42:15-22, 37–43:2, 5-8; 45:13-22, 25-28; + three frgs.

4Q10 4QGen^{k}

Davila, "10. 4QGen^{k}," DJD 12. 75-78 (+ pl. XII): Gen 1:9, 14-16, 27-28; 2:1-3; 3:1-2.

4Q11 4QpaleoGen-Exod^{l}

Skehan, P. W., E. Ulrich, and J. E. Sanderson, "11. 4QpaleoGenesis-Exodus^{l}," *Qumran Cave 4: IV, Palaeo-Hebrew and Greek Biblical Manuscripts* (DJD 9; ed. P. W. Skehan et al.; Oxford: Clarendon, 1992) 17-50 (+ pls. I-VI): Gen 50:26?; Exod 1:1-7; 2:10, 22–3:4, 17-21; 8:13-15, 19-21; 9:25-29, 33–10:5; 11:4–12:12, 42-46; 14:15-24; 16:2-6, 7, 13-14, 18-20, 23-25, 26-31, 33–17:3, 5-11; 18:17-24; 19:24–20:2; 22:23-24; 23:5-16; 25:7-20; 26:29–27:1, 6-14; 28:33-35, 40-42; 36:34-36; 1:1-5?; 27:4?; 40:15?; + nine frgs.

4Q12 4QpaleoGen^{m}

Skehan-Ulrich-Sanderson, "12. 4QpaleoGenesis^{m}," DJD 9. 51-52 (+ pl. VI): Gen 26:21-28.

4Q13 4QExod^{b}

Cross, F. M., "13. 4QExod^{b}," DJD 12. 79-95 (+ pls. XIV-XV): Exod 1:1-6, 16-21; 2:2-18; 3:13–4:8; 5:3-14. Cf. E. Tigchelaar, *RevQ* 21 (2003-4) 477-85.

4Q14 4QExod^{c}

Sanderson, J. E., "14. 4QExod^{c}," DJD 12. 97-125 (+ pls. XVI-XX): Exod 7:17-19, 20-23, 26–8:1, 5-14, 16-18; 8:22; 9:10-12, 15-20, 22-25, 27-35; 10:1-5, 7-9, 12-19, 23-24; 11:9-10; 12:12-16, 31-48; 13:18–14:3, 3-13; 15:9-21; 17:1–18:12; + nine frgs.

4Q15 4QExod^{d}

Sanderson, "15. 4QExod^{d}," DJD 12. 127-28 (+ pl. XXI): Exod 13:15-16; 15:1.

4Q16 4QExod^{e}

Sanderson, "16. 4QExod^{e}," DJD 12. 129-31 (+ pl. XXI): Exod 13:3-5.

4Q17 4QExod-Lev[f]
Cross, "17. 4QExod-Lev[f]," DJD 12. 133-44 (+ pl. XXII): Exod 38:18-22; 39:3-19, 20-24; 40:8-27; Lev 1:13-15, 17–2:1; + one frg.

4Q18 4QExod[g]
Sanderson, "18. 4QExod[g]," DJD 12. 145-46 (+ pl. XXI): Exod 14:21-27.

4Q19 4QExod[h]
Sanderson, "19. 4QExod[h]," DJD 12. 147 (+ pl. XXI): Exod 6:3-6.

4Q20 4QExod[j]
Sanderson, "20. 4QExod[j]," DJD 12. 149-50 (+ pl. XXI): Exod 7:28–8:2; + five frgs.

4Q21 4QExod[k]
Sanderson, "21. 4QExod[k]," DJD 12. 151 (+ pl. XXI): Exod 36:9-10.

4Q22 4QpaleoExod[m] (olim 4QExα)
Skehan-Ulrich-Sanderson, "22. 4QpaleoExodus[m]," DJD 9. 53-130 (+ pls. VII-XXXIII): Exod 6:25–7:16, 16-19, 29–8:1, [5], 12-18, [16-22], 19-22; 9:5-16, 19-21, 35; 10:1, 2-5, 5-12, 19-24, 25-28; 11:8–12:2, 6-8, 13-15, 17-22, 31-32, 34-39; 13:3-8, 12-13; 14:3-5, 8-9, 25-26; 15:23–16:1, 4-5, 7-8, 31-32, 32–17:16, 16–18:21, 21–19:1, 7-17, 23–20:1, 18-19; 21:5-6, 13-14, 22-32; 22:3-4, 6-7, 11-13, 16-19, 20-30; 23:14-16, 29-31; 24:1-4, 6-11; 25:11-12, 20-22, 22-29, 31-34; 26:8-15, 21-30; 30:10; 27:1-3, 9-14, 18-19; 28:3-4, 8-12, 22-24, 26-28, 30-39, 39–29:5, 20, 22-25, 31-34, 34-41; 30:12-18, 29-31, 34–31:7, 7-8, 13-15; 32:2-9, 10-19, 25-30; 33:12-15, 16–34:3, 10-13, 15-18, 20-24, 27-28; 35:1; 36:21-24; 37:9-16; + frgs. See Sanderson, J. E., *An Exodus Scroll from Qumran: 4QpaleoExod[m] and the Samaritan Tradition* (HSS 30; Atlanta, GA: Scholars, 1986); and the photograph in *BA* 28 (1965) 98; *SWDS*, 16, 26 (= Exod 6:25–7:19).

4Q23 4QLev-Num[a]
Ulrich, E., "23. 4QLev-Num[a]," DJD 12. 153-76 (+ pls. XXIII-XXX): Lev 13:32-33; 14:22-34, 40-50, 51-54; 15:10-11, 19-24; 16:15-29; 18:16-21; 19:3-8; 24:11-12; 26:26-33; 27:5-13, 14-22; Num 1:1-5, 21-22, 36-40; 2:18-20, 31-32; 3:3-19, 51; 4:1-12, 40-49; 5:1-9; 8:7-12, 21-22; 9:3-10, 19-20; 10:13-23; 11:4-5, 16-22; 12:3-11; 13:21; 22:5-6, 22-24; 26:5-7; 30:3-4?, 7?; 32:8-15, 23-42; 33:5-9, 22-34, 52-54; 35:4-5; + 30 frgs.

4Q24 4QLev[b]
Ulrich, "24. 4QLev[b]," DJD 12. 177-87 (+ pls. XXXI-XXXIV): Lev 1:11-17; 2:1-15;

3:1, 8-14; 21:17-20, 24; 22:1-33; 23:1, 2-25, 40; 24:2-23; 25:28-29, 45-49, 51-52; + two frgs.

4Q25 4QLev[c]

Tov, E., "25. 4QLev[c]," DJD 12. 189-92 (+ pl. XXXV): Lev 1:1-7; 3:16–4:6, 12-14, 23-28; 5:12-13; 8:26-28; + three frgs.

4Q26 4QLev[d]

Tov, "26. 4QLev[d]," DJD 12. 193-95 (+ pl. XXXVI): Lev 14:27-29, 33-36; 15:20-24; 17:2-11; + seven frgs.

4Q26a 4QLev[e]

Tov, "26a. 4QLev[e]," DJD 12. 197-201 (+ pl. XXXVII): Lev 2:4-6, 11-18; 3:2-4, 5-8; 19:34-37; 20:1-3, 27–21:4, 9-12, 21-24; 22:4-6, 11-17.

4Q26b 4QLev[g]

Tov, "26b. 4QLev[g]," DJD 12. 203-4 (+ pl. XXXVII): Lev 7:19-26.

4Q27 4QNum[b]

Jastram, N., "27. 4QNum[b]," DJD 12. 205-67 (+ pls. XXXVIII-XLIX): Num 11:31–12:11; 13:7-24; 15:41–16:11, 14-16; 17:12-17; 18:25–19:6; 20:12-13, 16–21:2, 12-13, 20-21; 22:5-7, 7-21, 31-34, 37-38, 41–23:6, 13-15, 21-22, 27–24:10; 25:4-8, 16–26:3, 4-34, 62-64, 64–27:10, 18-19, 21-23; 28:13-17, 28-31; 29:10-13, 16-18, 26-30; 30:1-3, 5-9, 15–31:6, 21-25, 30-38, 43-47, 48–32:1, 4-10, 13-19, 21-30, 35-39, 41–33:4, 23-31, 45-48, 50-52; 34:4-9, 19-23; 35:3-5, 11-15, 18-25, 27-28, 33–36:2, 4-7; + 25 frgs. A few lines in this text are written in red ink: 20:22-23; 21:21a; 22:21; 23:13, 27; 31:25, 37?-38, 48; 32:25; 33:1 (see DJD 12. 210-11 + pl. XLIX).

4Q28 4QDeut[a]

White Crawford, S., "28. 4QDeut[a]," *Qumran Cave 4: IX, Deuteronomy, Joshua, Judges, Kings* (DJD 14; ed. E. Ulrich et al.; Oxford: Clarendon, 1995) 7-8 (+ pl. I): Deut 23:26–24:8.

4Q29 4QDeut[b]

Duncan, J. A., "29. 4QDeut[b]," DJD 14. 9-14 (+ pl. II): Deut 29:24-27; 30:3-14; 31:9-17, 24-30; 32:1-3.

4Q30 4QDeut[c]

White Crawford, "30. 4QDeut[c]," DJD 14. 15-34 (+ pls. III-IX): Deut 3:25-26; 4:13-17, 31-32; 7:3-4; 8:1-5; 9:11-12, 17-19, 29; 10:1-2, 5-8; 11:3, 9-13, 18; 12:18-19, 26,

31; 13:5, 7, 11-12, 16; 15:1-4, 15-19; 16:2-3, 6-11, 21-22; 17:1-5, 7, 15-20; 18:1; 26:19; 27:1-2, 24-26; 28:1-7, 8-11, 12-14, 20, 22-25, 29-30, 48-50, 61; 29:17-19; 31:16-19; 32:3; + 11 frgs.

4Q31 4QDeut[d]

White Crawford, "31. 4QDeut[d]," DJD 14. 35-38 (+ pl. X): Deut 2:24-36; 3:14–4:1.

4Q32 4QDeut[e]

Duncan, "32. 4QDeut[e]," DJD 14. 39-44 (+ pl. XI): Deut 3:24; 7:12-16, 21-26; 8:1-4, 5-7, 10-11, 15-16; + three frgs.

4Q33 4QDeut[f]

White Crawford, "33. 4QDeut[f]," DJD 14. 45-54 (+ pls. XII-XV): Deut 4:24-26; 7:22-25; 8:2-14; 9:6-7; 17:17-18; 18:6-10, 18-22; 19:17-21; 20:1-6; 21:4-12; 22:12-19; 23:21-26; 24:2-7; 25:3-9; 26:18-19; 27:1-10; + six frgs.

4Q34 4QDeut[g]

White Crawford, "34. 4QDeut[g]," DJD 14. 55-59 (+ pl. XVI): Deut 9:12-14; 23:18-20; 24:16-22; 25:1-5, 14-19; 26:1-5; 28:21-25, 27-29.

4Q35 4QDeut[h]

Duncan, "35. 4QDeut[h]," DJD 14. 61-70 (+ pls. XVII-XVIII): Deut 1:1-17, 22-24, 29-39, 41, 43-46; 2:1-6, 28-30; 4:31-34; 19:21?; 31:9-11; 33:8-22.

4Q36 4QDeut[i]

White Crawford, "36. 4QDeut[i]," DJD 14. 71-74 (+ pl. XIX): Deut 20:9-13; 21:23; 22:1-9; 23:6-8, 12-16, 23-26; 24:1; + two frgs.

4Q37 4QDeut[j]

Duncan, "37. 4QDeut[j]," DJD 14. 75-91 (+ pls. XX-XXIII): Deut 5:1-11, 13-15, 21, 22-28, 29-33; 6:1-3; 8:5-10; 11:6-13, 21? (with Exod 12:43-44; 12:46-51; 13:1-5); 32:7-8; + 13 frgs.

4Q38 4QDeut[k1]

Duncan, "38. 4QDeut[k1]," DJD 14. 93-98 (+ pl. XXIV): Deut 5:28-32; 11:6-13; 32:17-18, 22-23, 25-27.

4Q38a 4QDeut[k2]

Duncan, "38a. 4QDeut[k2]," DJD 14. 99-105 (+ pl. XXV): Deut 19:8-16; 20:6-19; 23:22-26; 24:1-3; 25:19; 26:1-5, 18-19; 27:1?; + five frgs.

4Q38b 4QDeut[k3]

Duncan, "38b. 4QDeut[k3]," DJD 14. 107 (+ pl. XXV): Deut 30:16-18.

4Q39 4QDeut[l]

Duncan, "39. 4QDeut[l]," DJD 14. 109-12 (+ pl. XXVI): Deut 10:12-15: 28:67-68; 29:2-5; 31:12; 33:1-2; 34:4-6, 8?

4Q40 4QDeut[m]

Duncan, "40. 4QDeut[m]," DJD 14. 113-16 (+ pl. XXVII): Deut 3:18-22; 4:32-33; 7:18-22.

4Q41 4QDeut[n]

White Crawford, "41. 4QDeut[n]," DJD 14. 117-28 (+ pls. XXVIII-XXIX): Deut 8:5-10; 5:1-6, 6-14, 14-21, 22-28, 28-33; 6:1. Often called the "All Souls Deuteronomy" text, it is not a copy of the complete Book of Deuteronomy but of excerpts in a diverse order, which include the Decalogue.

4Q42 4QDeut[o]

White Crawford, "42. 4QDeut[o]," DJD 14. 129-33 (+ pl. XXX): Deut 2:8; 4:30-34; 5:1-5, 8-9; 28:15-18, 33-36, 47-52, 58-62; 29:22-25.

4Q43 4QDeut[p]

White Crawford, "43. 4QDeut[p]," DJD 14. 135-36 (+ pl. XXXI): Deut 6:4-11.

4Q44 4QDeut[q]

Skehan, P. W. and E. Ulrich, "44. 4QDeut[q]," DJD 14. 137-42 (+ pl. XXXI): Deut 32:9-10?, 37-41, 41-43.

4Q45 4QpaleoDeut[r]

Skehan-Ulrich-Sanderson, "45. 4QpaleoDeuteronomy[r]," DJD 9. 131-52 (+ pls. XXXIV-XXXVI): Deut 1:8?; 7:2-5, 6-7, 16-21, 21-25; 10:11-12; 11:28, 30-32; 12:1, 2-5, 11-12, 22-23; 13:19; 14:1, 2-4, 19-22, 26-29; 15:5-6, 8-10; 19:2-3; 22:3-6; 23:7, 12-15; 28:15-18, 20; 31:29; 32:6-8, 10-11, 13-14, 33-35; 33:2-8, 29; 34:1-2; + 21 frgs.

4Q46 4QpaleoDeut[s]

Skehan-Ulrich-Sanderson, "46. 4QpaleoDeuteronomy[s]," DJD 9. 153-54 (+ pl. XXXVII): Deut 26:14-15.

4Q47 4QJosh[a]

Ulrich, "47. 4QJosh[a]," DJD 14. 143-52 (+ pls. XXXII-XXXIV): Josh 8:34-35; 5:?, 2-7; 6:5-10; 7:12-17; 8:3-14, 18?; 10:2-5, 8-11.

4Q48 4QJosh[b]

Tov, E., "48. 4QJosh[b]," DJD 14. 153-60 (+ pl. XXXV): Josh 2:11-12; 3:15–4:3; 17:1-5, 11-15; + one frg.

4Q49 4QJudg[a]

Trebolle Barrera, J., "49. 4QJudg[a]," DJD 14. 161-64 (+ pl. XXXVI): Judg 6:2-6, 11-13.

4Q50 4QJudg[b]

Trebolle Barrera, "50. 4QJudg[b]," DJD 14. 165-69 (+ pl. XXXVI): Judg 19:5-7; 21:12-25.

4Q51 4QSam[a]

Cross, F. M. et al., "51. 4QSam[a]," *Qumran Cave 4: XII, 1-2 Samuel* (DJD 17; Oxford: Clarendon, 2005) 1-216 (+ pls. I-XXIII): 1 Sam 1:9, 11-13, 17-18, 22-26, 28; 2:1-10, 16–3:4, 18-21; 4:3-4, 9-10, 12; 5:8-10, 10–6:9, 10-11, 12-13, 16-18, 20–7:1; 8:7, 9-14, 16-20; 9:6-8, 10-12, 16-24; 10:3-12, 14, 16, 18, 24–11:2, 7-11, 11-12; 12:7-8, 10-11, 12-19; 14:24-25, 28-34, 47-51; 15:20-21, 24-32; 17:3-8, 40-41; 18:4-5; 20:37-40; 22:10-11; 24:3-5, 8-10, 14-23; 25:3-12, 20-21, 25-27, 38-40; 26:9-12, 21-24; 27:1-2, 8–28:3, 22–29:1; 30:22-26, 27-31; 31:1-4; 2 Sam 1:4-5, 10-13; 2:5-16, 25-28, 29–3:15, 17, 21, 23–4:4, 9–5:3, 6-16, 18-19; 6:2-18; 7:6-7, 22-29; 8:1-8; 9:8-10; 10:4-5, 6-7, 18-19; 11:2-12, 15-20; 12:1-2, 3, 4-6, 8-9, 13-14, 14-20, 29–13:6, 13-34, 36–14:3, 14, 18-19, 33; 15:1-7, 20-23, 26-31, 37–16:2, 6-8, 10-13, 17-18, 20-23; 17:2-3, 23-25, 28–18:11, 28-29; 19:6-12, 14-16, 25, 27-29, 38; 20:1-2, 4, 9-14, 19, 21-25; 21:1, 3-6, 8-9, 12, 15-17; 22:17, 19, 21, 24, 26-28, 30-31, 33–23:6, 14-16, 21-22, 38-39; 24:16-22; + frgs.

4Q51a 4QpapUncFrgs

Cross et al., "51a. 4QpapUnclassified Fragments," DJD 17. 217 (+ pl. XXIII).

4Q52 4QSam[b]

Cross et al., "52. 4QSam[b]," DJD 17. 219-46 (+ pls. XXIV-XXV): 1 Sam 12:4-6; 14:41-42; 15:16-18; 16:1-11; 19:10-13, 15-17; 20:26–21:3, 5-7, 8-10; 22:8-9; 23:8-23.

4Q53 4QSam[c]

Ulrich, E., "53. 4QSam[c]," DJD 17. 247-67 (+ pls. XXVI-XXVII): 1 Sam 25:30-32; 2 Sam 14:7-21, 22–15:4, 4-15; + three frgs.

4Q54 4QKgs

Trebolle Barrera, "54. 4QKgs," DJD 14. 171-83 (+ pl. XXXVII): 1 Kgs 7:20-21, 25-27, 29-31, 31-42, 51–8:9, 16-18; + one frg.

4Q55 4QIsa[a]

Skehan, P. W. and E. Ulrich, "55. 4QIsa[a]," *Qumran Cave 4: X, The Prophets* (DJD 15; ed. E. Ulrich et al.; Oxford: Clarendon, 1997) 7-18 (+ pls. I-II): Isa 1:1-3; 2:7-10; 4:5–5:1; 6:4-8; 11:11-15; 12:4–13:16; 17:9-14; 19:24–21:16; 22:13–23:12; 33:16-17?; + frgs.

4Q56 4QIsa[b]

Skehan-Ulrich, "56. 4QIsa[b]," DJD 15. 19-43 (+ pls. III-VI): Isa 1:1-6; 2:3-16; 3:14-22; 5:15-28; 9:10-11; 11:7-9; 12:2; 13:3-18; 17:8-14; 18:1, 5-7; 19:1-25; 20:1-4; 21:11-14; 22:24-25; 24:2, 4; 26:1-5, 7-19; 35:9-10; 36:1-2; 37:29-32; 39:1-8; 40:1-4, 22-26; 41:8-11; 42:2-7, 9-12; 43:12-15; 44:19-28; 45:20-25; 46:1-3; 48:6-8; 49:21-23; 51:1-2, 14-16; 52:2, 7; 53:11-12; 61:1-3; 64:5-11; 65:1; 66:24; + frgs. See Eshel, *DSD* 12 (2005) 137-42: frgs. 16a (24:16-17), 20a (26:19–27:1).

4Q57 4QIsa[c]

Skehan-Ulrich, "57. 4QIsa[c]," DJD 15. 45-74 (+ pls. VII-XII): Isa 9:3-12; 10:23-33; 11:4-11, 14-16; 12:1; 14:1-5, 13?; 22:10-14, 23; 23:8-18; 24:1-15, 19-23; 25:1-2, 8-12; 26:1-9; 28:6-14; 30:8-17; 33:2-8, 16-23; 44:3-7, 23; 45:1-4, 6-8; 46:8-13; 48:10-11, 12-13, 14-15, 17-19; 49:22; 51:8-16; 52:10-15; 53:1-3, 6-8; 54:3-5, 7-8, 9, 9-17; 55:1-7; 66:20-24 (see "Recently Identified Fragments" on pp. 72-74).

4Q58 4QIsa[d]

Skehan-Ulrich, "58. 4QIsa[d]," DJD 15. 75-88 (+ pls. XIII-XV): Isa 45:20; 46:10-13; 47:1-6, 8-9; 48:8-16, 17-22; 49:1-15; 52:4-7; 53:8-12; 54:1-2, 2-11; 57:9-17, 18-21; 58:1-3, 5-7; + one frg.

4Q59 4QIsa[e]

Skehan-Ulrich, "59. 4QIsa[e]," DJD 15. 89-97 (+ pls. XVI-XVII): Isa 2:1-4; 7:17-20; 8:2-14; 9:17-20; 10:1-10; 11:14-15; 12:1-6; 13:1-4; 14:1-13, 20-24; 59:15-16.

4Q60 4QIsa[f]

Skehan-Ulrich, "60. 4QIsa[f]," DJD 15. 99-111 (+ pls. XVIII-XX): Isa 1:10-16, 18-31; 2:1-3; 5:13-14, 25; 6:3-8, 10-13; 7:16-18, 23-25; 8:1, 4-11; 20:4-6; 22:14-22, 25; 24:1-3; 27:1, 5-6, 8-10, 11-12; 28:6-9, 16-17?, 18?, 22, 24?; 29:8?; + three frgs.

4Q61 4QIsa[g]

Skehan-Ulrich, "61. 4QIsa[g]," DJD 15. 113-15 (+ pl. XXI): Isa 42:14-25; 43:1-4, 17-24.

4Q62 4QIsa^{h}
Skehan-Ulrich, "62. 4QIsa^{h}," DJD 15. 117-19 (+ pl. XXI): Isa 42:4-11.

4Q62a 4QIsa^{i}
Skehan-Ulrich, "62a. 4QIsa^{i}," DJD 15. 121-22 (+ pl. XXI): Isa 56:7-8; 57:5-8.

4Q63 4QIsa^{j}
Skehan-Ulrich, "63. 4QIsa^{j}," DJD 15. 123 (+ pl. XXII): Isa 1:1-6.

4Q64 4QIsa^{k}
Skehan-Ulrich, "64. 4QIsa^{k}," DJD 15. 125-27 (+ pl. XXII): Isa 28:26–29:9.

4Q65 4QIsa^{l}
Skehan-Ulrich, "65. 4QIsa^{l}," DJD 15. 129-30 (+ pl. XXII): Isa 7:14-15; 8:11-14.

4Q66 4QIsa^{m}
Skehan-Ulrich, "66. 4QIsa^{m}," DJD 15. 131-32 (+ pl. XXII): Isa 60:20–61:1, 3-6.

4Q67 4QIsa^{n}
Skehan-Ulrich, "67. 4QIsa^{n}," DJD 15. 133-34 (+ pl. XXIII): Isa 58:13-14.

4Q68 4QIsa^{o}
Skehan-Ulrich, "68. 4QIsa^{o}," DJD 15. 135-37 (+ pl. XXIII): Isa 14:28–15:2; + one frg.

4Q69 pap4QIsa^{p}
Skehan-Ulrich, "69. 4QIsa^{p}," DJD 15. 139 (+ pl. XXIII): Isa 5:28-30.

4Q69a 4QIsa^{q}
Skehan-Ulrich, "69a. 4QIsa^{q}," DJD 15. 141 (+ pl. XXIII): Isa 54:10-13.

4Q69b 4QIsa^{r}
Skehan-Ulrich, "69b. 4QIsa^{r}," DJD 15. 143 (+ pl. XXIII): Isa 30:23.

4Q70 4QJer^{a}
Tov, E., "70. 4QJer^{a}," DJD 15. 145-70 (+ pls. XXIV-XXIX): Jer 6:30?; 7:1-2, 15-19, 28–9:2, 7-15; 10:9-14, 23; 11:3-6, 19-20; 12:3-7, 13-16, 17; 13:1-7, 22-23? [or 22:3], 27; 14:4-7; 15:1-2; 17:8-26; 18:15-23; 19:1; 20:14-18; 21:1?; 22:3-16; 26:10?; + 14 frgs.

4Q71 4QJer[b]

Tov, "71. 4QJer[b]," DJD 15. 171-76 (+ pl. XXIX): Jer 9:22-25; 10:1-21.

4Q72 4QJer[c]

Tov, "72. 4QJer[c]," DJD 15. 177-201 (+ pls. XXX-XXXVI): Jer 4:5, 13-16; 8:1-3, 21-23; 9:1-5; 10:12-13; 19:8-9; 20:2-5, 7-9, 13-15; 21:7-10; 22:4-6, 10-17, 17-28; 25:7-8, 15-17, 24-26; 26:10-13; 27:1-3, 13-15; 30:6-9, [10-17], 17-24; 31:1-4, 4-14, 19-26; 33:?, 16-20; + 17 frgs.

4Q72a 4QJer[d] (olim 4QJer[b])

Tov, "72a. 4QJer[d]," DJD 15. 203-5 (+ pl. XXXVII): Jer 43:2-10.

4Q72b 4QJer[e] (olim 4QJer[b])

Tov, "72b. 4QJer[e]," DJD 15. 207 (+ pl. XXXVII): Jer 50:4-6.

4Q73 4QEzek[a]

Sanderson, J. E., "73. 4QEzek[a]," DJD 15. 209-14 (+ pl. XXXVIII): Ezek 10:5-16, 17-22; 11:1-11; 23:14-15, 17-18, 44-47; 41:3-6.

4Q74 4QEzek[b]

Sanderson, "74. 4QEzek[b]," DJD 15. 215-18 (+ pl. XXXIX): Ezek 1:10-13, 16-17, 19, 20-24.

4Q75 4QEzek[c]

Sanderson, "75. 4QEzek[c]," DJD 15. 219-10 (+ pl. XXXIX): Ezek 24:2-3.

4Q76 4QXII[a]

Fuller, R. E., "76. 4QXII[a]," DJD 15. 221-32 (+ pls. XL-XLII): Zech 14:18; Mal 2:10-14, 15–3:4, 5-14, 14-24; Jon 1:1-5, 7-8, 9–2:1, 7; 3:2; + one frg.

4Q77 4QXII[b]

Fuller, "77. 4QXII[b]," DJD 15. 233-36 (+ pl. XLIII): Zeph 1:1-2; 2:13-15; 3:19-20; Hag 1:1-2; 2:2-4; + one frg.

4Q78 4QXII[c]

Fuller, "78. 4QXII[c]," DJD 15. 237-51 (+ pls. XLIV-XLVI): Hos 2:13-15; 3:2-4; 4:1-19; 5:1; 7:12-13; 13:3-10, 15; 14:1-6; Joel 1:10-20; 2:1, 8-10, 10-23; 4:6-21; Amos 1:1?; 2:11-16; 3:1-7, 8-15; 4:1-2; 6:13-14; 7:1-16; Zeph 2:15; 3:1-2; + 17 frgs. — From other mss: Mal 3:6-7?; Ps 38:4-6 (p. 251); part of 4QPs[a] (4Q83).

4Q79 4QXII[d]

Fuller, "79. 4QXII[d]," DJD 15. 253-56 (+ pl. XLVI): Hos 1:6–2:5.

4Q80 4QXII[e]

Fuller, "80. 4QXII[e]," DJD 15. 257-65 (+ pl. XLVII): Hag 2:18-19, 20-21; Zech 1:4-6, 8-10, 13-15; 2:10-14; 3:2-10; 4:1-4; 5:8–6:5; 8:2-4, 6-7; 12:7-12; + seven frgs.

4Q81 4QXII[f]

Fuller, "81. 4QXII[f]," DJD 15. 267-70 (+ pl. XLVIII): Jon 1:6-8, 10-16; Mic 5:1-2 (2-3).

4Q82 4QXII[g]

Fuller, "82. 4QXII[g]," DJD 15. 271-318 (+ pls. XLIX-LXIV): Hos 2:1-5, 14-19, 22-25; 3:1-5; 4:1, 10-11, 13-14; 6:3-4, 8-11; 7:1, 12-13, 13-16; 8:1; 9:1-4, 9-17; 10:1-14; 11:2-5, 6-11; 12:1-15; 13:1, 6-8?, 11-13; 14:9-10; Joel 1:12-14; 2:2-13; 4:4-9, 11-14, 17, 19-20; Amos 1:3-15; 2:1, 7-9, 15-16; 3:1-2; 4:4-9; 5:1-2, 9-18; 6:1-4, 6-14; 7:1, 7-12, 14-17; 8:1-5, 11-14; 9:1, 5-6, 14-15; Obad 1-5, 8-12, 14-15; Jon 1:1-9; 2:3-11; 3:1-3; 4:5-11; Mic 1:7, 12-15; 2:3-4; 3:12; 4:1-2; 5:6-7 (7-8); 7:2-3, 20; Nah 1:7-9; 2:9-11; 3:1-3, 17; Hab 2:4?; Zeph 3:3-5; Zech 10:11-12; 11:1-2; 12:1-3; + many frgs.

4Q83 4QPs[a]

Skehan, P. W., E. Ulrich, and P. W. Flint, "83. 4QPs[a]," *Qumran Cave 4: XI, Psalms to Chronicles* (DJD 16; ed. E. Ulrich et al.; Oxford: Clarendon, 2000) 7-22 (+ pls. I-II): Ps 5:9–6:4; 25:8-12, 15; 31:23-25 → 33:1-12; 34:21-22; 35:1-2, 13-20, 26-28; 36:1-9; 38:2-12, 16-23 → 71:1-14; 47:2; 53:2-7; 54:1-6; 56:4; 62:13; 63:1-4; 66:16-20; 67:1-8; 69:1-19. See Fuller, DJD 15. 251 (+ pl. XLVI) for frg. 38 of 4QXII[c], subsequently identified as belonging to 4QPs[a], = Ps 38:4-6.

4Q84 4QPs[b]

Skehan-Ulrich-Flint, "84. 4QPs[b]," DJD 16. 23-48 (+ pls. III-VI): Ps 91:5-8, 12-15; 92:4-8, 13-15; 93:5; 94:1-4, 7-9, 10-14, 16-18, 21-22; 96:2; 98:4-5; 99:5-6; 100:1-2; 102:5?, 10-17, 18-25, 26-29; 103:1-3, 4-6, 9-11, 12-14, 20-21; 112:4-5; 113:1; 115:2-3; 116:17-19; 118:1-3, 5-10, 12, 18-20, 23-26, 29; + three frgs.

4Q85 4QPs[c]

Skehan-Ulrich-Flint, "85. 4QPs[c]," DJD 16. 49-61 (+ pls. VII-IX): Ps 16:7-10; 17:1?; 18:1-14, 16-18, 32-36, 39-41; 27:12–28:5; 35:27-28; 37:18-19; 42:5; 44:8-9?; 45:8-11; 49:1-17; 50:14-23; 51:1-5; 52:5-11; 53:1; 46:8? (or 12?); + eight frgs.

4Q86 4QPs^{d}

Skehan-Ulrich-Flint, "86. 4QPs^{d}," DJD 16. 63-71 (+ pl. X): Ps 106:48?; 147:1-4, 13-17, 20; 104:1-5, 8-11, 14-15, 22-25, 33-35.

4Q87 4QPs^{e}

Skehan-Ulrich-Flint, "87. 4QPs^{e}," DJD 16. 73-84 (+ pls. XI-XII): Ps 76:10-12; 77:1; 78:6-7, 31-33; 81:2-3; 86:10-11; 88:1-5; 89:44-48, 50-53; 103:22? → 109:1?, 8?, 13; 114:5; 115:15-18; 116:1-4; 118:29; 104:1-3, 20-22; 105:1-3, 23-25, 36-45; 146:1?; 120:6-7; 125:2-5; 126:1-5; 129:8; 130:1-6; + 18 frgs.

4Q88 4QPs^{f}

Skehan-Ulrich-Flint, "88. 4QPs^{f}," DJD 16. 85-106 (+ pls. XIII-XIV): Ps 22:14-17; 107:2-5, 8-16, 18-19, 22-30, 35-42; 109:4-7?, 24-28; ApostrZion 1-2, 11-18 [cf. DJD 4. 43, 85-89]; EschatHymn; ApostrJudah; + one frg. This text has parts of three apocryphal writings, "written in the same hand, on the same type of leather, and are in the same basic format."

4Q89 4QPs^{g}

Skehan-Ulrich-Flint, "89. 4QPs^{g}," DJD 16. 107-12 (+ pl. XV): Ps 119:37-43, 44-46, 49-50, 73-74, 81-83, 89-92. Psalm 119 is arranged stichometrically by the full line, with a blank line left after each stanza of eight verses.

4Q90 4QPs^{h}

Skehan-Ulrich-Flint, "90. 4QPs^{h}," DJD 16. 113-15 (+ pl. XV): Ps 119:10-21. Again, the psalm is arranged stichometrically, with a blank line left after each stanza of eight verses.

4Q91 4QPs^{j}

Skehan-Ulrich-Flint, "91. 4QPs^{j}," DJD 16. 117-21 (+ pl. XVI): Ps 48:1-9; 49:9-12, 15, 17; 51:2-6; + two frgs.

4Q92 4QPs^{k}

Skehan-Ulrich-Flint, "92. 4QPs^{k}," DJD 16. 123-25 (+ pl. XVII): Ps 135:6-8, 10-13, 15-16; 99:1-2, 5. The order of the psalms differs from that of the MT.

4Q93 4QPs^{l}

Skehan-Ulrich-Flint, "93. 4QPs^{l}," DJD 16. 127-29 (+ pl. XVII): Ps 104:3-5, 11-12.

4Q94 4QPs^{m}

Skehan-Ulrich-Flint, "94. 4QPs^{m}," DJD 16. 131-33 (+ pl. XVII): Ps 93:3-5; 95:3-7; 97:6-9; 98:4-8.

4Q95 4QPs^{n}

Skehan-Ulrich-Flint, "95. 4QPs^{n}," DJD 16. 135-37 (+ pl. XVIII): Ps 135:6-9, 11-12; 136:23-24.

4Q96 4QPs^{o}

Skehan-Ulrich-Flint, "96. 4QPs^{o}," DJD 16. 139-41 (+ pl. XVIII): Ps 114:7; 115:1-2, 4; 116:3, 5, 7-10.

4Q97 4QPs^{p} (olim 4Q237)

Skehan-Ulrich-Flint, "97. 4QPs^{p}," DJD 16. 143-44 (+ pl. XVIII): Ps 143:2-4, 6-8.

4Q98 4QPs^{q}

Skehan-Ulrich-Flint, "98. 4QPs^{q}," DJD 16. 145-49 (+ pl. XIX): Ps 31:24-25 → 33:1-18; 35:4-20. Of doubtful provenience; possibly related to psalms of Naḥal Ḥever.

4Q98a 4QPs^{r}

Skehan-Ulrich-Flint, "98a. 4QPs^{r}," DJD 16. 151-52 (+ pl. XIX): Ps 26:7-12; 27:1; 30:9-13.

4Q98b 4QPs^{s}

Skehan-Ulrich-Flint, "98b. 4QPs^{s}," DJD 16. 153-54 (+ pl. XIX): Ps 5:8-13; 6:1.

4Q98c 4QPs^{t}

Skehan-Ulrich-Flint, "98c. 4QPs^{t}," DJD 16. 155 (+ pl. XIX): Ps 88:15-17.

4Q98d 4QPs^{u}

Skehan-Ulrich-Flint, "98d. 4QPs^{u}," DJD 16. 157 (+ pl. XX): Ps 42:5.

4Q98e 4QPs^{v} (olim 4QPs^{u} frg. 2)

Skehan-Ulrich-Flint, "98e. 4QPs^{v}," DJD 16. 159 (+ pl. XX): Ps 99:1.

4Q98f 4QPs^{w}

Fitzmyer, J. A., "98f. 4QPs^{w}," DJD 16. 161-62 (+ pl. XX): Ps 112:1-9.

4Q98g 4QPs^{x} (olim 4Q236)

Skehan-Ulrich-Flint, "98g. 4QPs^{x}," DJD 16. 163-67 (+ pl. XX): Ps 89:20-22, 26, 23, 27-28, 31.

4Q99 4QJob[a]

Ulrich, E. and S. Metso, "99. 4QJob[a]," DJD 16. 171-78 (+ pl. XXI): Job 31:14-19; 32:3-4; 33:10-11, 24-26, 28-30; 35:16; 36:7-11, 13-24, 25-27, 32-33; 37:1-5, 14-15; + four frgs.

4Q100 4QJob[b]

Ulrich-Metso, "100. 4QJob[b]," DJD 16. 179-80 (+ pl. XXII): Job 8:15-17; 9:27; 13:4; 14:4-6; 31:20-21.

4Q101 4QpaleoJob[c]

Skehan-Ulrich-Sanderson, "101. 4QpaleoJob[c]," DJD 9. 155-57 (+ pl. XXXVII): Job 13:18-20, 23-27; 14:13-18.

4Q102 4QProv[a]

Skehan-Ulrich, "102. 4QProv[a]," DJD 16. 181-82 (+ pl. XXII): Prov 1:27-33; 2:1.

4Q103 4QProv[b]

Skehan-Ulrich, "103. 4QProv[b]," DJD 16. 183-86 (+ pl. XXIII): Prov 13:6-9; 14:5-10, 12-13, 31-35; 15:1-8, 19-31; 7:9, 11? possibly preserved on frg. 15.

4Q104 4QRuth[a]

Ulrich, E. and C. M. Murphy, "104. 4QRuth[a]," DJD 16. 187-89 (+ pl. XXIV): Ruth 1:1-12.

4Q105 4QRuth[b]

Ulrich-Murphy, "105. 4QRuth[b]," DJD 16. 191-94 (+ pl. XXIV): Ruth 1:1-6, 12-15.

4Q106 4QCant[a]

Tov, E., "106. 4QCant[a]," DJD 16. 199-204 (+ pl. XXIV): Cant 3:4-5, 7-11; 4:1-6, 7; 6:11?-12; 7:1-7; + frg. An Introduction to 4QCant[a-c] precedes the discussion of 4QCant[a], pp. 195-98.

4Q107 4QCant[b]

Tov, "107. 4QCant[b]," DJD 16. 205-18 (+ pl. XXV): Cant 2:9-17; 3:1-2, 5, 9-11; 4:1, 1b-3, 8-11, 14-16; 5:1.

4Q108 4QCant[c]

Tov, "108. 4QCant[c]," DJD 16. 219 (+ pl. XXV): Cant 3:7-8.

4Q109 4QQoh[a]

Ulrich, "109. 4QQoh[a]," DJD 16. 221-26 (+ pl. XXVI): Qoh 5:13-17; 6:1?, 3-8, 12; 7:1-6, 7-10, 19-20.

4Q110 4QQoh[b]

Ulrich, "110. 4QQoh[b]," DJD 16. 227 (+ pl. XXVI): Qoh 1:10-15.

4Q111 4QLam

Cross, F. M., "111. 4QLam," DJD 16. 229-37 (+ pls. XXVII-XXVIII): Lam 1:1-6, 6-10, 10-15, 17, 16, 18; 2:5.

4Q112 4QDan[a]

Ulrich, "112. 4QDan[a]," DJD 16. 239-54 (+ pls. XXIX-XXXI): Dan 1:16-20; 2:9-11, 19-33, 33-46, 47-49; 3:1-2; 4:29-30; 5:5-7, 12-14, 16-19; 7:5-7, 25-28; 8:1-5; 10:16-20; 11:13-16; + one frg.

4Q113 4QDan[b]

Ulrich, "113. 4QDan[b]," DJD 16. 255-67 (+ pls. XXXII-XXXIII): Dan 5:10-12, 14-16, 19-22; 6:8-13, 13-22, 27-29; 7:1-4, 5-6, 11?, 26-28; 8:1-8, 13-16; + one frg.

4Q114 4QDan[c]

Ulrich, "114. 4QDan[c]," DJD 16. 269-77 (+ pls. XXXIV-XXXV): Dan 10:5-9, 11-13, 13-16, 21; 11:1-2, 13-17, 25-29.

4Q115 4QDan[d]

Ulrich, "115. 4QDan[d]," DJD 16. 279-86 (+ pls. XXXVI-XXXVII): Dan 3:8-10?, 23-25; 4:5-9, 12-16; 7:15-23; + seven frgs.

4Q116 4QDan[e]

Ulrich, "116. 4QDan[e]," DJD 16. 287-89 (+ pl. XXXVIII): Dan 9:12-14, 15-17.

4Q117 4QEzra

Ulrich, "117. 4QEzra," DJD 16. 291-93 (+ pl. XXXVIII): Ezra 4:2-6, 9-11; 5:17; 6:1-5. Some of the fragments are parallel to 1 Esdras 5:66-70; 6:20-25.

4Q118 4QChr

Trebolle Barrera, J., "118. 4QChr," DJD 16. 295-97 (+ pl. XXXVIII): 2 Chr 28:27; 29:1-3.

4Q119 4QLXXLev[a] gr

Skehan, P. W. and E. Ulrich, "119. 4QLXXLeviticus[a]," DJD 9. 161-65 (+ pl. XXXVIII): Lev 26:2-16.

4Q120 pap4QLXXLev[b] gr

Skehan-Ulrich, "120. pap4QLXXLeviticus[b]," DJD 9. 167-86 (+ pls. XXXIX-XLI): Lev 1:11; 2:3-5, 7-8?; 3:4, 7, 9-13, 13-14; 4:3-4, 4, 6-8, 10-11, 18-19, 26, 26-28, 30; 5:6, 8-10, 16-17, 18-19, 20-24 [6:1-5]; + 66 frgs. God's name is written as Ιαω.

4Q121 4QLXXNum gr

Skehan-Ulrich, "121. 4QLXXNumbers," DJD 9. 187-94 (+ pls. XLII-XLIII): Num 3:40-43, 50-51?; 4:1?, 5-9, 11-16; 3:39?

4Q122 4QLXXDeut gr

Skehan-Ulrich, "122. 4QLXXDeuteronomy," DJD 9. 195-97 (+ pl. XLIII): Deut 11:4; + four frgs.

4Q123 4QpaleoParaJosh

Skehan-Ulrich-Sanderson, "123. 4QpaleoParaJoshua," DJD 9. 201-3 (+ pl. XLVI): "The text is reminiscent of, but not identical with, the received form of Joshua 21" (201).

4Q124 4QpaleoUnid 1

Skehan-Ulrich-Sanderson, "124. 4QpaleoUnidentified(1)," DJD 9. 205-14 (+ pls. XLIV-XLV): 36 frgs.

4Q125 4QpaleoUnid 2

Skehan-Ulrich-Sanderson, "125. 4QpaleoUnidentified(2)," DJD 9. 215 (+ pl. XLVI): one frg.

4Q126 4QUnid gr

Skehan-Ulrich, "126. 4QUnidentified gr," DJD 9. 219-21 (+ pl. XLVI): eight frgs.

4Q127 pap4QParaExod gr

Skehan-Ulrich, "127. pap4QParaExodus gr," DJD 9. 223-42 (+ pl. XLVII): 86 frgs. mentioning persons or places known from the Book of Exodus (Moses, Pharaoh, Egypt, Aaron?, Miriam?).

4Q128 4Qphyl[a] (olim 4Qphyl[c])

Vaux, R. de and J. T. Milik, *Qumrân Grotte 4: II, i. Archéologie; ii. Tefillin, mezuzot et targums (4Q128-4Q157)* (DJD 6; Oxford: Clarendon, 1977): "128. Phylactère A," 48-51 (+ pls. VII-VIII). See also K. G. Kuhn, *Phylakterien aus Höhle 4 von Qumran* (Abhandlungen der Heidelberger Akademie der Wissenschaften, Philos.-hist. Kl., 1957/1; Heidelberg: Winter, 1957) 15-16: Deut 5:1-14; 5:27–6:3; 10:12–11:17 (recto); Deut 11:18-21; Exod 12:43–13:7 (verso).

4Q129 4Qphyl[b]
"129. Phylactère B," DJD 6. 51-53 (+ pl. IX); also Kuhn, *Phylakterien,* 11-15: Deut 5:1–6:5 (recto); Exod 13:9-16 (verso).

4Q130 4Qphyl[c]
"130. Phylactère C," DJD 6. 53-55 (+ pls. X-XI): Exod 13:1-16; Deut 6:4-9; 11:13-21.

4Q131 4Qphyl[d]
"131. Phylactère D," DJD 6. 56 (+ pl. XII): Deut 11:13-21.

4Q132 4Qphyl[e]
"132. Phylactère E," DJD 6. 56-57 (+ pl. XIII): Exod 13:1-10.

4Q133 4Qphyl[f]
"133. Phylactère F," DJD 6. 57 (+ pl. XIV): Exod 13:11-16.

4Q134 4Qphyl[g]
"134. Phylactère G," DJD 6. 58-60 (+ pl. XV): Deut 5:1-21 (recto); Exod 13:11-12 (verso).

4Q135 4Qphyl[h]
"135. Phylactère H," DJD 6. 60-62 (+ pl. XVI); see also Kuhn, *Phylakterien,* 16-20: Deut 5:22–6:5 (recto); Exod 13:14-16 (verso).

4Q136 4Qphyl[i]
"136. Phylactère I," DJD 6. 62-63 (+ pl. XVII); see also Milik, "Fragment d'une source du Psautier (4QPs 89) et fragments des *Jubilés,* du *Document de Damas,* d'un phylactère dans la grotte 4 de Qumrân," *RB* 73 (1966) 94-106, esp. 106 (+ pl. IIb): Deut 11:13-21; Exod 12:43–13:10 (recto); Deut 6:6-7? (verso).

4Q137 4Qphyl[j] (olim 4Qphyl[a])
"137. Phylactère J," DJD 6. 64-67 (+ pls. XVIII-XIX); see also Kuhn, *Phylakterien,* 5-11: Deut 5:1-24 (recto); Deut 5:24-32; 6:2-3 (verso).

4Q138 4Qphyl[k]
"138. Phylactère K," DJD 6. 67-69 (+ pl. XX): Deut 10:12–11:7 (recto); Deut 11:7-12 (verso).

4Q139 4Qphyl[l]
"139. Phylactère L," DJD 6. 70 (+ pl. XXII): Deut 5:7-24.

4Q140 4Qphyl[m]
"140. Phylactère M," DJD 6. 71-72 (+ pl. XXI): Exod 12:44–13:10 (recto); Deut 5:33–6:5 (verso).

4Q141 4Qphyl[n]
"141. Phylactère N," DJD 6. 72-74 (+ pl. XXII): Deut 32:14-20, 32-33.

4Q142 4Qphyl[o]
"142. Phylactère O," DJD 6. 74-75 (+ pl. XXII): Deut 5:1-16 (recto); Deut 6:7-9 (verso).

4Q143 4Qphyl[p]
"143. Phylactère P," DJD 6. 75-76 (+ pl. XXII): Deut 10:22–11:3 (recto); Deut 11:18-21 (verso).

4Q144 4Qphyl[q]
"144. Phylactère Q," DJD 6. 76 (+ pl. XXIII): Deut 11:4-18 (recto); Exod 13:4-9 (verso).

4Q145 4Qphyl[r]
"145. Phylactère R," DJD 6. 77-78 (+ pl. XXIII): Exod 13:1-7 (recto); Exod 13:7-10 (verso).

4Q146 4Qphyl[s]
146. "Phylactère S," DJD 6. 78 (+ pl. XXIII): Deut 11:19-21.

4Q147 4Qphyl[t]
"147. Phylactère T," DJD 6. 79 (+ pl. XXIV): could not be deciphered.

4Q148 4Qphyl[u]
"148. Phylactère U," DJD 6. 79 (+ pl. XXV): could not be deciphered.

4Q149 4Qmez[a]
"149. Mezuza A," DJD 6. 80-81 (+ pl. XXVI): Exod 20:7-12; cf. Deut 5:11-16.

Q150 4Qmez[b]
"150. Mezuza B," DJD 6. 81 (+ pl. XXVI): Deut 6:5-6; 10:14–11:2.

4Q151 4Qmez[c]
"151. Mezuza C," DJD 6. 82-83 (+ pl. XXVII): Deut 5:27–6:9; 10:12-20.

4Q152 4Qmez[d]
"152. Mezuza D," DJD 6. 83 (+ pl. XXVI): Deut 5:6-7.

4Q153 4Qmez[e]
"153. Mezuza E," DJD 6. 83 (+ pl. XXVI): Deut 11:17-18.

4Q154 4Qmez[f]
"154. Mezuza F," DJD 6. 83-84 (+ pl. XXVI): Exod 13:1-4.

4Q155 4Qmez[g]
"155. Mezuza G," DJD 6. 84-85 (+ pl. XXV): Exod 13:11-16.

4Q156 4QtgLev
"156. Targum du Lévitique," DJD 6. 86-89 (+ pl. XXVIII); see also appendix (M. M. Kasher), 92-93: Lev 16:12-15, 18-21.

4Q157 4QtgJob
"157. Targum de Job," DJD 6. 90 (+ pl. XXVIII): Job 3:5-9; 4:16–5:4; + one frg.

4Q158-186

Allegro, J. M. (with the collaboration of A. A. Anderson), *Qumrân Cave 4: I (4Q158-4Q186)* (DJD 5; Oxford: Clarendon, 1968). This publication must be used with caution. Some frgs. have not been properly identified or joined; many readings are questionable; the numbering of plates is confusing at times; the secondary literature on the fifteen texts in it that were previously published in partial or preliminary form has normally been neglected. Essential for further work on these texts are the following: J. Strugnell, "Notes en marge du volume V des 'Discoveries in the Judaean Desert of Jordan,'" *RevQ* 7 (1969-71) 163-276; J. A. Fitzmyer, "A Bibliographical Aid to the Study of Qumrân Cave IV Texts 158-86," *CBQ* 31 (1969) 59-71. Criticism of this volume has been severe: "Überhaupt ist DJD V die schlechteste und unzuverlässigste Q-Edition, die seit dem Beginn der Funde dem Leser zugemutet wurde" (K. Müller, "Die Handschriften" [see section V below] 310). "'R' habet italicum liber hic, habet atque Pelasgum, Necnon hebraeum, praetereaque nihil!" (J. Strugnell, *RevQ* 7 [1969-71] 276; cf. *America* 123 [26 Sept. 1970] 207). Vol. 5 is presently undergoing revision under the editorship of M. Bernstein and G. J. Brooke with the assistance of J. Høgenhaven; scheduled for publication in 2010.

4Q158 4QRP[a] (olim 4QBibPar)

Allegro, "158. Biblical Paraphrase: Genesis, Exodus," DJD 5. 1-6 (+ pl. I): A reworking of Gen 32:25-32; Exod 4:27-28; Gen 32:31?; Exod 3:12; 24:4-6; 19:17-23; 20:19-22; Deut 5:29; 8:18-20, 22; Exod 20:12, 16, 17; Deut 5:30, 31; Exod 20:22-26; 21:1, 3, 4, 6, 8, 10; 21:15, 16, 18, 20, 22, 25, 32, 34, 35-37; 22:1-11, 13; 30:32, 34; + two frgs. This text is now called "Reworked Pentateuch[a]," because it resembles others that do the same (see 4Q364, 4Q365, 4Q366, 4Q367). Cf. M. Segal, "4QReworked Pentateuch or 4QPentateuch?" *The Dead Sea Scrolls Fifty Years after Their Discovery* (ed. L. H. Schiffman et al.; Jerusalem: Israel Exploration Society, 2000) 391-99. Also E. Tov, "Biblical Texts as Reworked," *The Community of the Renewed Covenant* (eds. E. C. Ulrich and J. C. VanderKam; Notre Dame, IN: University of Notre Dame, 1994) 123-39. Tov has recently changed his position on RP and has now designated it "4QPentateuch."

4Q159 4QOrd[a] (olim 4QOrd)

Allegro, "159. Ordinances," DJD 5. 6-9 (+ pl. II): A halakhic writing; related to 4Q334?, 4Q513, 4Q514. Cf. Allegro, *JSS* 6 (1961) 71-73.

4Q160 4QVisSam

Allegro, "160. The Vision of Samuel," DJD 5. 9-11 (+ pl. III): Related to 1 Sam 3:14-17.

4Q161 4QpIsa[a]

Allegro, "161. Commentary on Isaiah (A)," DJD 5. 11-15 (+ pls. IV-V): Pesher on Isa 10:20-21, 22, 24-27, 28-32, 33-34; 11:1-5. Cf. Allegro, *JBL* 75 (1956) 177-82.

4Q162 4QpIsa[b]

Allegro, "162. Commentary on Isaiah (B)," DJD 5. 15-17 (+ pl. VI): Pesher on Isa 5:5-6, 11-14, 24-25, 29-30; 6:9? Cf. Allegro, *JBL* 77 (1958) 215-18.

4Q163 4QpIsa[c]

Allegro, "163. Commentary on Isaiah (C)," DJD 5. 17-27 (+ pls. VII-VIII): Pesher on Isa 8:7-8, 9?; 9:11?, 14-20; 10:12-13, 19?, 20-24; 14:8, 26-30; 19:9-12;

29:10-11, 15-16, 19-23; Zech 11:11; Isa 30:1-5, 15-18; Hos 6:9; Isa 30:19-21; 31:1; 32:5-6; + 31 frgs. Cf. Allegro, *JBL* 77 (1958) 218-20.

4Q164 4QpIsa[d]

Allegro, "164. Commentary on Isaiah (D)," DJD 5. 27-28 (+ pl. IX): Pesher on Isa 54:11-12; + two frgs. Cf. Allegro, *JBL* 77 (1958) 220-21.

4Q165 4QpIsa[e]

Allegro, "165. Commentary on Isaiah (E)," DJD 5. 28-30 (+ pl. IX): Pesher on Isa 1:1?; 40:12; 14:19; 15:4-6; 21:2?, 11-15; 32:5-7; + four frgs.

4Q166 4QpHos[a] (olim 4QpHos[b])

Allegro, "166. Commentary on Hosea (A)," DJD 5. 31-32 (+ pl. X): Pesher on Hos 2:8-9, 10-14. Cf. Allegro, *JBL* 78 (1959) 142-47.

4Q167 4QpHos[b] (olim 4QpHos[a])

Allegro, "167. Commentary on Hosea (B)," DJD 5. 32-36 (+ pls. X-XI): Pesher on Hos 5:13-15; 6:4, 7, 9-10; 8:6-7, 13-14; + 23 frgs. Cf. Allegro, *JBL* 75 (1956) 93.

4Q168 4QpMic(?)

Allegro, "168. Commentary on Micah (?)," DJD 5. 36 (+ pl. XII): Pesher on Mic 4:8-12; + three frgs.

4Q169 4QpNah

Allegro, "169. Commentary on Nahum," DJD 5. 37-42 (+ pls. XII-XIV): Pesher on Nah 1:3-6; 2:12-14; 3:1-5, 6-9, 10-12, 14. Cf. Allegro, *JBL* 75 (1956) 90-93; *JSS* 7 (1962) 304-8; *SWDS*, 17, 26-27. Berrin, S., *The Pescher Nahum Scroll from Qumran: An Exegetical Study of 4Q169* (STDJ 53; Leiden: Brill, 2004).

4Q170 4QpZeph

Allegro, "170. Commentary on Zephaniah," DJD 5. 42 (pl. XIV): Pesher on Zeph 1:12-13.

4Q171 4QpPs[a] (olim 4QpPs37)

Allegro, "171. Commentary on Psalms (A)," DJD 5. 42-50 (+ pls. XIV-XVII): Pesher on Ps 37:7, 8-19, 19-26, 28-40; 45:1-2; 60:8-9 (108:8-9). Cf. H. Stegemann, "Der Pešer Psalm 37 aus Höhle 4 von Qumran (4Q p Ps 37)," *RevQ* 4 (1963-64) 235-70; "Weitere Stücke von 4QpPsalm 37 . . . ," *RevQ* 6 (1967-69) 193-210.

4Q172 4QpUnid

Allegro, "172. Commentaries on Unidentified Texts," DJD 5. 50-51 (+ pl. XVIII): 14 frgs. of unidentified pesher(s). Cf. M. P. Horgan, *Pesharim: Qumran Interpretations of Biblical Books* (CBQMS 8; Washington, DC: Catholic Biblical Association, 1979).

4Q173 4QpPs[b]

Allegro, "173. Commentary on Psalms (B)," DJD 5. 51-53 (+ pl. XVIII): Pesher on Ps 127:2-3, 5; 129:7-8; 118:26-27?

4Q174 4QFlor (or 4QEschMidr)

Allegro, "174. Florilegium," DJD 5. 53-57 (+ pls. XIX-XX): Quotations from 2 Sam 7:10-14 (1 Chr 17:9-13); Exod 15:17-18; Amos 9:11; Ps 1:1; Isa 8:11; Ezek 37:23?; Ps 2:1; Dan 12:10; 11:32; Deut 33:8-11, 12, 19-21; + 16 frgs.: with midrashic commentary. Cf. Allegro, *JBL* 75 (1956) 176-77; 77 (1958) 350-54.

4Q175 4QTestim (or 4QTest)

Allegro, "175. Testimonia," DJD 5. 57-60 (+ pl. XXI): Contains a proto-Samaritan text of Exod 20:21, which conflates Deut 5:28-29 and 18:18-19 (see P. W. Skehan, *CBQ* 19 [1957] 435-40); then quotes Num 24:15-17; Deut 33:8-11; Josh 6:26, and Apocryphon of Joshua (see 4Q379). Cf. Allegro, *JBL* 75 (1956) 182-87.

4Q176 4QTanh

Allegro, "176. Tanḥûmîm," DJD 5. 60-67 (+ pls. XXII-XXIII): Quotations from Ps 79:2-3; Isa 40:1-5; 41:8-9; 49:7, 13-17; 43:1-2, 4-6; 51:22-23; 51:23; 52:1-3; 54:4-10; 52:1-2; Zech 13:9; + 42 frgs., with commentary. Frgs. 19-21 are part of *Jubilees* [4Q176a Jubi?], as M. Kister recognized (*RevQ* 12 [1985-87] 529-36).

4Q177 4QCatena[a]

Allegro, "177. Catena (A)," DJD 5. 67-74 (+ pls. XXIV-XXV): Apocalyptic vision of a victory of the community on 30 frgs.

4Q178 4QUnid[a]

Allegro, "178.," DJD 5. 74-75 (+ pl. XXV): 13 unidentified frgs.

4Q179 4QapocrLam[a]

Allegro, "179. Lamentations," DJD 5. 75-77 (+ pl. XXVI): This is not a copy of the canonical Lamentations; it is an apocryphal writing, like 4Q501.

4Q180 4QAgesCreat[a]

Allegro, "180. The Ages of Creation," DJD 5. 77-79 (+ pl. XXVII): This text describes periods of human history; see Milik, *BE,* 248-52. Cf. Allegro, *ALUOS* 4 (1962-63) 3-5.

4Q181 4QAgesCreat[b]

Allegro, "181.," DJD 5. 79-80 (+ pl. XVIII): Although Allegro did not entitle this text, it is clearly related to 4Q180 and so bears the same title as a different copy of it; see Milik, *BE,* 248-52. Cf. Allegro, *ALUOS* 4 (1962-63) 3-5.

4Q182 4QCatena[b]

Allegro, "182. Catena[b]," DJD 5. 80-81 (+ pl. XXVII): Eschatological text with introductory formula of quotation from Jeremiah.

4Q183 4QmidrEschat[e]?

Allegro, "183.," DJD 5. 81-82 (+ pl. XXVI): Three unidentified frgs. of a writing that seems to recount some historical event.

4Q184 4QWiles

Allegro, "184.," DJD 5. 82-85 (+ pl. XXVIII): This unentitled work is called by Allegro, "The Wiles of the Wicked Woman," in *PEQ* 96 (1964) 53-55. Frg. 2, which is said to be "in private hands," is found in the Museum of the Oriental Institute of the University of Chicago (# A30303; Photo 47799).

4Q185 4QSapiential Work

Allegro, "185.," DJD 5. 85-87 (+ pls. XXIX-XXX): This unentitled text of six frgs. is a wisdom text related to several others (e.g., 1Q26, 4Q415-4Q418, 4Q423-4Q424). Cf. *EDSS,* 976-80.

4Q186 4QHoroscope (olim 4QCryptic)

Allegro, "186.," DJD 5. 88-91 (+ pl. XXXI): This is an astrological text with some words or lines written in a cryptic script. Some relate it to 4QElectofGod (4Q534) and 4QPhysHor ar (4Q561), but it is questionable that the literary genre is the same. Cf. *EDSS,* 370-73; Milik, *BE,* 56; Allegro, "An Astrological Cryptic Document from Qumran," *JSS* 9 (1964) 291-94 (+ pl. I).

4Q187-195

No manuscripts have been assigned to these numbers.

4Q196 4QpapTob[a] ar

Fitzmyer, J. A., "196. 4QpapTobit[a] ar," *Qumran Cave 4: XIV, Parabiblical Texts, Part 2* (DJD 19; ed. M. Broshi et al.; Oxford: Clarendon, 1995) 7-39 (+ pls. I-V): Tob 1:17, 19-22; 2:1-2, 3, 10-11; 3:5, 9-15, 17; 4:2, 5, 7, 21; 5:1, 9; 6:6-8, 13-18, 19; 7:1-6, 13; 12:1, 18-21; 13:1-6, 6-12, 12-19; 14:1-3, 7; + 30 frgs. This text is preceded by an Introduction to 4Q196-4Q200, ibid., 1-6. Cf. Fitzmyer, "The Qumran Texts of Tobit," *DSSCO,* 159-235; *Tobit* (Commentaries on Early Jewish Literature; Berlin: de Gruyter, 2003).

4Q197 4QTob[b] ar

Fitzmyer, "197. 4QTobit[b] ar," DJD 19. 41-56 (+ pls. VI-VII): Tob 3:6-8; 4:21; 5:1, 12-14, 19-22; 6:1-12, 12-18, 18; 7:1-10; 8:17-21; 9:1-4; + two frgs.

4Q198 4QTob[c] ar

Fitzmyer, "198. 4QTobit[c] ar," DJD 19. 57-60 (+ pl. VIII): Tob 14:2-6, 10?

4Q199 4QTob[d] ar

Fitzmyer, "199. 4QTobit[d] ar," DJD 19. 61-62 (+ pl. VIII): Tob 7:11; 14:10.

4Q200 4QTob[e]

Fitzmyer, "200. 4QTobit[e]," DJD 19. 63-76 (+ pls. IX-X): Tob 3:6, 10-11; 4:3-9; 5:2; 10:7-9; 11:10-14; 12:20-21; 13:1-4, 13-14, 18; 14:1-2; + two frgs.

4Q201 4QEn[a] ar

Milik, J. T., "First Copy (4QEn[a], Pls. I-V)," *BE,* 139-63, 340-43: *1 Enoch* 1:1-6; 2:1–5:6; 6:4–8:1; 8:3–9:3, 6-8; 10:3-4, 21–11:1 + 12:4-6. See also L. Stuckenbruck, "201 2-8. 4QEnoch[a] ar," *Qumran Cave 4: XXVI, Cryptic Texts and Miscellanea, Part 1* (DJD 36; ed. S. J. Pfann et al.; Oxford: Clarendon, 2000) 3-7 (+ pl. I): Publication of frgs. 2-8, which Milik did not include in *BE* (= recto of 4Q338).

4Q202 4QEn[b] ar

Milik, "Second Copy (4QEn[b], Pls. VI-IX)," *BE,* 164-78, 344-46: *1 Enoch* 5:9–6:4 + 6:7–8:1; 8:2–9:4; 10:8-12; 14:4-6.

4Q203 4QEnGiants[a] ar

Milik, "First Copy (4QEnochGiants[a], Pls. XXX-XXXII)," *BE,* 57-58, 298-339, esp. 310-17 (13 frgs., originally the second part of the same scroll as 4QEn[c]). See now L. Stuckenbruck, "203. 4QEnochGiants[a] ar," DJD 36. 8-41 (+ pls. I-II): A new study of frgs. 2-13, bringing Milik's work to a better interpretation. Cf. 4Q530-4Q533 and E. Puech's new treatment of 4Q203 frg. 1 in "4Q203 1.

4QLivre des Géants^{a} ar," DJD 31. 17-18 (+ pl. I). See Milik, "Turfan et Qumran: Livre des Géants juif et manichéen," *Tradition und Glaube: Das frühe Christentum in seiner Umwelt: Festgabe für Karl Georg Kuhn . . .* (ed. G. Jeremias et al.; Göttingen: Vandenhoeck & Ruprecht, 1971) 117-27 (+ pl. I); also L. T. Stuckenbruck, *The Book of Giants from Qumran: Texts, Translation, and Commentary* (TSAJ 63; Tübingen: Mohr Siebeck, 1997) 66-100.

4Q204 4QEn^{c} ar (olim 4QHen^{b})

Milik, "Third Copy (4QEn^{c}, Pls. IX-XV)," *BE*, 178-217, 346-53: *1 Enoch* 1:9–5:1; 6:7; 10:13-19 + 12:3; 13:6–14:16, 18-20 + 15:11?; 18:8-12; 30:1–32:1; 35 + 36:1-4; 89:31-37; 104:13–106:2, 13–107:2. Frgs. 2-3 = 4QEnGiants^{a} 9-10 (see *BE*, 316-17). Cf. J. T. Milik, "Hénoch au pays des aromates (ch. xxvii à xxxii): Fragments araméens de la grotte 4 de Qumran," *RB* 65 (1958) 70-77, esp. 70-73, 77 (what appears there as 4QHen^{b} 1:1-8 is now 4QEn^{c} ar 1 xii 23-30; and what was 4QHen^{b} 2:1-8 is now 4QEn^{c} 1 xiii 23-30).

4Q205 4QEn^{d} ar

Milik, "Fourth Copy (4QEn^{d}, Pls. XVI-XVII)," *BE*, 217-25, 353-55: *1 Enoch* 22:13–24:1; 25:7–27:1; 89:11-14, 29-31, 43-44.

4Q206 4QEn^{e} ar (olim 4QHen^{d})

Milik, "Fifth Copy (4QEn^{e}, Pls. XVIII-XXI)," *BE*, 225-44, 355-59: *1 Enoch* 18:15?; 21:2-4; 22:3-7; 28:3–29:2 + 31:2–32:3, 6 + 33:3–34:1; 88:3–89:6, 7-16, 26-30. Frgs. 2-3 may contain a text which = 4QEnGiants^{f}; see *BE*, 236-38, but now also Stuckenbruck, "206 2-3. 4QEnochGiants^{f} ar," DJD 36. 42-48 (+ pl. II): A new study of frgs. 2 and 3, bringing Milik's work to a better interpretation. Cf. Milik, *RB* 65 (1958) 70-77 (4QHen^{d} 1:1-8 is now 4QEn^{e} ar 1 xxvi 14-21).

4Q207 4QEn^{f} ar

Milik, "Sixth Copy (4QEn^{f}, Pl. XXI)," *BE*, 244-45, 359: *1 Enoch* 86:1-3.

4Q208 4QEnastr^{a} ar (olim 4QHen astr^{b})

Milik, *BE*, 7-22, 273-78: Description only of the Astronomical Book; no text of the 36 frgs. supplied. See now E. J. C. Tigchelaar and F. García Martínez, "208. 4QAstronomical Enoch^{a} ar," DJD 36. 104-31 (+ pls. III-IV): The 37 frgs. contain the "synchronistic calendar" in *1 Enoch* 72-75, which give the basic patterns of the rising of the moon. Cf. "208-209. 4QAstronomical Enoch$^{a\text{-}b}$ ar: Introduction," ibid., 95-103. Also Milik, "Problèmes de la littérature hénochique," *HTR* 64 (1971) 333-78; M. Black, "The Fragments of the Aramaic Enoch from

Qumran," *La littérature juive entre Tenach et Mischna: Quelques problèmes* (RechBib 9; ed. W. C. van Unnik; Leiden: Brill, 1974) 15-28.

4Q209 4QEnastr[b] ar (olim 4QHen astr[a])

Milik, *BE*, 7-22, 273-74, 278-84, 287-91, 293-96 (+ pls. XXV-XXVII, XXX): Publication of frgs. 6:4-10, 7, 23, 25, 26, 28. See now Tigchelaar-García Martínez, "209. 4QAstronomical Enoch[b] ar," DJD 36. 132-71 (+ pls. V-VII): Publication of 41 frgs.; a few of them = *1 Enoch* 76:13–77:4; 74:1-2 (or 78:9-12?); 79:3-5; 78:17–79:2; 82:9-13. Cf. Milik, *RB* 65 (1958) 70-77, esp. 76 (what was published there as 4QHen astr[a] is now 4QEnastr[b] ar 23:6-9); also *HTR* 64 (1971) 338-39, 342.

4Q210 4QEnastr[c] ar

Milik, *BE*, 7-22, 274, 284-88, 292-93 (+ pls. XXVIII, XXX): *1 Enoch* 76:3-10; 76:13–77:4; 78:6-8. Cf. *RB* 65 (1958) 70-77, esp. 76 (what was published there as 4QHen astr[c] 6-9 is now 4QEnastr[a] ar l ii 16-18).

4Q211 4QEnastr[d] ar

Milik, *BE*, 7-22, 274, 296-97 (+ pl. XXIX). The frgs. follow after *1 Enoch* 82:20.

4Q212 4QEn[g] ar

Milik, "Seventh Copy (4QEn[g], Pls. XXI-XXIV)," *BE*, 245-48, 52-72, 360-62: *1 Enoch* 91:10? + 91:18-19 + 92:1-2, 5–93:4, 9-10 + 91:11-17; 93:11–94:2. This is also known as the "Letter of Enoch." Cf. Milik, "Problèmes de la littérature hénochique," *HTR* 64 (1971) 333-78.

4Q213 4QLevi[a] ar

Stone, M. E. and J. C. Greenfield, "213. 4QLevi[a] ar," *Qumran Cave 4: XVII, Parabiblical Texts, Part 3* (DJD 22; ed. G. Brooke et al.; Oxford: Clarendon, 1996) 1-24 (+ pl. I): This Aramaic text and the five that follow are an early form of texts found in the Cairo Genizah and housed today in the Bodleian Library, Oxford, and the Cambridge University Library. It is also related to 1Q21 (1QLevi ar). As the fragments were being studied, different names and sigla were applied to them, and they were misnamed as the "Testament of Levi," but the editors of this text now recognize that "there are no characteristics within this document which mark it as a testament" (pp. 1-2), agreeing with others who had determined that earlier. It is now known simply as "Aramaic Levi Document" (ALD). See Fitzmyer, "The Aramaic Levi Document," *DSSCO*, 237-48.

4Q213a 4QLevi[b] ar
Stone-Greenfield, "213a. 4QLevi[b] ar," DJD 22. 25-36 (+ pl. II) (olim 4QTLevi[a] [sic Milik, *RB* 62 (1955) 398-406]).

4Q213b 4QLevi[c] ar
Stone-Greenfield, "213b. 4QLevi[c] ar," DJD 22. 37-41 (+ pl. III).

4Q214 4QLevi[d] ar
Stone-Greenfield, "214. 4QLevi[d] ar," DJD 22. 43-51 (+ pl. III).

4Q214a 4QLevi[e] ar
Stone-Greenfield, "214a. 4QLevi[e] ar," DJD 22. 53-60 (+ pl. IV).

4Q214b 4QLevi[f] ar
Stone-Greenfield, "214b. 4QLevi[f] ar," DJD 22. 61-72 (+ pl. IV).

4Q215 4QTNaph
Stone, M. E., "215. 4QTestament of Naphtali," DJD 22. 73-82 (+ pl. V).

4Q215a 4QTimeRight (olim 4QTNaph)
Chazon, E. and M. Stone, "215a. 4QTime of Righteousness," DJD 36. 172-84 (+ pl. VIII): Four frgs. describe the elect of righteousness, the time of righteousness, the period of peace, the period of wickedness, etc., themes found in other texts such as *1 Enoch* 1-11, 4QApocWeeks, etc.

4Q216 4QJub[a]
VanderKam, J. C. and J. T. Milik, "216. 4QJubilees[a]," *Qumran Cave 4: VIII, Parabiblical Texts, Part 1* (DJD 13; ed. H. Attridge et al.; Oxford: Clarendon, 1994) 1-22 (+ pls. I-II): *Jub.* Prologue + 1:1-2, 4-7, 7-15, 26-28; 2:1-4, 7-12, 13-24. Cf. J. C. VanderKam, "The Jubilees Fragments from Qumran Cave 4," *The Madrid Qumran Congress: Proceedings of the International Congress on the Dead Sea Scrolls, Madrid 18-21 March, 1991* (STDJ 11/1-2; ed. J. Trebolle Barrera and L. Vegas Montaner; Leiden: Brill; Madrid: Editorial Complutense, 1992) 635-48.

4Q217 4QpapJub[b]
VanderKam-Milik, "217. 4QpapJubilees[b]?," DJD 13. 23-33 (+ pl. III): *Jub.* 1:29?; 2:1?; + 13 frgs.

4Q218 4QJub[c]

VanderKam-Milik, "218. 4QJubilees[c]," DJD 13. 35-38 (+ pl. IV): *Jub.* 2:26-27.

4Q219 4QJub[d]

VanderKam-Milik, "219. 4QJubilees[d]," DJD 13. 39-53 (+ pl. IV): *Jub.* 21:1-2, 7-10, 12-16, 18-26; 22:1.

4Q220 4QJub[e]

VanderKam-Milik, "220. 4QJubilees[e]," DJD 13. 55-61 (+ pl. V): *Jub.* 21:5-10.

4Q221 4QJub[f]

VanderKam-Milik, "221. 4QJubilees[f]," DJD 13. 63-85 (+ pl. VI): *Jub.* 21:22-24; 22:22, 30?; 23:10-13; 33:12-15; 37:11-15; 38:6-8; 39:4-9; + 12 frgs.

4Q222 4QJub[g]

VanderKam-Milik, "222. 4QJubilees[g]," DJD 13. 87-94 (+ pl. V): *Jub.* 25:9-12; 27:6-7; 48:5?; + three frgs.

4Q223-224 4QpapJub[h]

VanderKam-Milik, "223-224. 4QpapJubilees[h]," DJD 13. 95-140 (+ pls. VII-IX): *Jub.* 32:18-21; 34:4-5; 35:7-12, 12-22; 36:7-10, 10-23; 37:17-24; 38:1-13; 39:9-18; 40:1-7; 41:7-10; + 27 frgs.

4Q225 4QpsJub[a]

VanderKam-Milik, "225. 4QPseudo-Jubilees[a]," DJD 13. 141-55 (+ pl. X): This and the two following fragmentary texts use language that is similar to *Jubilees,* but are not copies of any text that can be identified as *Jubilees.*

4Q226 4QpsJub[b]

VanderKam-Milik, "226. 4Qpseudo-Jubilees[b]," DJD 13.157-69 (+ pl. XI). See Eshel, *DSD* 12 (2005) 142-44: frg. 6a.

4Q227 4QpsJub[c]?

VanderKam-Milik, "227. 4Qpseudo-Jubilees[c]," DJD 13. 171-75 (+ pl. XII).

4Q228 4QcitJub

VanderKam-Milik, "228. Text with a Citation of *Jubilees,*" DJD 13. 177-85 (+ pl. XII): This text quotes *Jubilees* 1 as authoritative writing, כי כן כתוב במחלקות, "for so it is written in the divisions [of time]."

4Q229

??? (A text said to be a "pseudepigraphic work in mishnaic Hebrew"); cannot be located.

4Q230 4QCatSpir[a]

??? ("Catalogue of Spirits[a]"); cannot be located.

4Q231 4QCatSpir[b]

??? ("Catalogue of Spirits[b]"); cannot be located

4Q232 4QNJ?

??? ("New Jerusalem ?"); cannot be located.

4Q233 4QPlaces

??? ("Frgs. with place names"); cannot be located.

4Q234 4QExerCal A

Yardeni, A., "234. 4QExercitium Calami A," DJD 36. 185-86 (+ pl. IX): A frg. used for a writing exercise with Gen 27:19-21.

4Q235

Cancelled; now classified as UnidText nab (appendix to 4Q343). Yardeni, A., "343. 4QLetter nab," DJD 27. 288 (+ fig. 28, pl. XV).

4Q236

Cancelled; now = 4Q98g (4QPs[x]).

4Q237

Cancelled; now = 4Q97 (4QPs[p]).

4Q238 4QWordJudg

Flint, P., "238. 4QWords of Judgement," *Qumran Cave 4: XXVIII, Miscellanea, Part 2* (DJD 28; ed. M. Bernstein et al.; Oxford: Clarendon, 2001) 119-23 (+ pl. XL): Difficult text.

4Q239 4QpTrueIsr

??? (Pesher on the True Israel; see *EDSS*, 646); cannot be located.

4Q240 4QpCant?

??? (Commentary on Canticles?); cannot be located.

4Q241

Cancelled; now = 4Q282 frgs. h and i.

4Q242 4QprNab ar (olim 4QsNab)

Collins, J., "242. 4QPrayer of Nabonidus ar," DJD 22. 83-93 (+ pl. VI): A text related somehow to the account of Nebuchadnezzar's madness in Daniel 4. See J. T. Milik, "'Prière de Nabonide' et autres écrits d'un cycle de Daniel, fragments de Qumrân 4," *RB* 63 (1956) 407-15, esp. 407-11; F. M. Cross, "Fragments of the Prayer of Nabonidus," *IEJ* 34 (1984) 260-64.

4Q243 4QpsDan[a] ar

Collins, J. and P. Flint, "243. 4QPseudo-Daniel[a] ar," DJD 22.97-121 (+ pls. VII-VIII): 40 fragments of an account related to that in the Book of Daniel, as the names "Daniel" and "Belshazzar" reveal; but it is difficult to get much sense of the text, because so few words are preserved on many of the frgs. This text is preceded by a general introduction to 4Q243-4Q245 (p. 95).

4Q244 4QpsDan[b] ar

Collins-Flint, "244. 4Qpseudo-Daniel[b] ar," DJD 22. 123-31 (+ pl. IX): Another copy of the text of 4Q243; frg. 12 overlaps with frg. 13 of 4Q243. On pp. 133-51 one finds "4Q243-244: The Combined Text" and a discussion of it.

4Q245 4QpsDan[c] ar

Collins-Flint, "245. 4Qpseudo-Daniel[c] ar," DJD 22. 153-64 (+ pl. X): Four frgs. related to, but not part of, 4Q243-4Q244. Frg. 1 has many names but little context in which to place them.

4Q246 4QapocrDan ar (olim 4QpsDan[d])

Puech, E., "246. 4QApocryphe de Daniel ar," DJD 22.165-84 (+ pl. XI): This text is often called "4QSon of God" or "4QAramaic Apocalypse" (Milik, *BE*, 60, 213, 261); various sigla have been used for it at times (4Q243; 4QpsDan ar[a]; 4QpsDan A). Its interpretation is highly controverted; for a survey, see Puech's introduction and commentary; cf. J. A. Fitzmyer, "The Aramaic 'Son of God' Text from Qumran Cave 4 (4Q246)," *DSSCO*, 41-61.

4Q247 4QApocWeeks

Broshi, M., "247. 4QPesher on the Apocalypse of Weeks," DJD 36. 187-91 (+ pl. IX): The text is misnamed; it is not a pesher. It is a composition that comments on the ten periods of the so-called Apocalypse of Weeks in *1 Enoch* 93:1-10; 91:11-17. See also Milik, *BE*, 256; J. C. VanderKam, *Enoch and the Growth of an*

Apocalyptic Tradition (CBQMS 16; Washington, DC: Catholic Biblical Association, 1984) 142-60.

4Q248 4QHistTextA

Broshi, M. and E. Eshel, "248. 4QHistorical Text A," DJD 36. 192-200 (+ pl. IX): This text has been known as "Acts of a Greek King" (in protomishnaic Hebrew) or "Pseudo History E," but the editors now maintain that it is "a genuine historical composition which is part of an apocalyptic work." They think that the Greek king to whom it refers is Antiochus IV Epiphanes.

4Q249 4QpapcryptAMSM

Pfann, S. J., "249. 4Qpap cryptA Midrash Sefer Moshe," *Qumran Cave 4: XXV, Halakhic Texts* (DJD 35; ed. J. Baumgarten et al.; Oxford: Clarendon, 1999) 1-24 (+ pls. I-II): The title *midraš sēpher Môšeh* is inscribed on the back of the first turn of the papyrus scroll, the text of which is written in an esoteric script called "Cryptic A." See DJD 36, pl. XLIX for a photograph.

4Q249a 4QpapcryptA[a]

Pfann, S. J., "249a. 4Qpap cryptA Serekh ha-ʿEdah[a]," DJD 36. 547-49 (+ pl. XXXV; see also DJD 35, pl. II, where frg. 46 is shown): Papyrus frgs. parallel to 1QSa (1Q28a) 1:4-8. This text and some of the following copies have also been known as 4QpapCrypt AMSM (4Q249), to which they are somehow related.

4Q249b 4QpapcryptA[b]

Pfann, "249b. 4Qpap cryptA Serekh ha-ʿEdah[b]," DJD 36. 550 (+ pl. XXXV): Parallel to 1QSa (1Q28a) 1:25-27.

4Q249c 4QpapcryptA[c]

Pfann, "249c. 4Qpap cryptA Serekh ha-ʿEdah[c]," DJD 36. 551-52 (+ pl. XXXV): Parallel to 1QSa (1Q28a) 1:13-17.

4Q249d 4QpapcryptA[d]

Pfann, "249d. 4Qpap cryptA Serekh ha-ʿEdah[d]," DJD 36. 553-54 (+ pl. XXXV): Parallel to 1QSa (1Q28a) 1:6-10, 13-14.

4Q249e 4QpapSE[e]

Pfann, "249e. 4Qpap cryptA Serekh ha-ʿEdah[e]," DJD 36. 555-59 (+ pl. XXXV): Parallel to 1QSa (1Q28a) 1:5-10, 12, 24-26.

4Q249f 4QpapcryptA[f]

Pfann, "249f. 4Qpap cryptA Serekh ha-ʿEdah[f]," DJD 36. 560-62 (+ pl. XXXVI): Parallel to 1QSa (1Q28a) 2:3-18.

4Q249g 4QpapcryptA[g]

Pfann, "249g. 4Qpap cryptA Serekh ha-ʿEdah[g]," DJD 36. 563-68 (+ pl. XXXVI): Parallel to 1QSa (1Q28a) 1:1-4; 2:3-18.

4Q249h 4QpapcryptA[h]

Pfann, "249h. 4Qpap cryptA Serekh ha ʿEdah[h]," DJD 36. 569-71 (+ pl. XXXVII): Parallel to 1QSa (1Q28a) 2:7-12, 17-18.

4Q249i 4QpapcryptA[i]

Pfann, "249i. 4Qpap cryptA Serekh ʿEdah[i]?," DJD 36. 572-74 (+ pl. XXXVII): Parallel to 1QSa (1Q28a) 2:11-15.

4Q249j 4QpapcryptA[j]

Pfann, "249j. 4Qpap cryptA Leviticus[h]?," DJD 36. 575-77 (+ pl. XXXVII): Quotes Lev 26:14-16.

4Q249k 4QpapcryptA[k]

Pfann, "249k. 4Qpap cryptA Text Quoting Leviticus A," DJD 36. 578-80 (+ pl. XXXVIII): Quotes Lev 26:16-17.

4Q249l 4QpapcryptA[l]

Pfann, "249l. 4Qpap cryptA Text Quoting Leviticus B," DJD 36. 581-82 (+ pl. XXXVIII): Quotes Lev 26:33-34.

4Q249m 4QpapcryptAHE

Pfann, "249m. 4Qpap cryptA Hodayot-like Text E," DJD 36. 583-84 (+ pl. XXXVIII).

4Q249n 4QpapcryptALitE

Pfann, "249n. 4Qpap cryptA Liturgical Work E," DJD 36. 585-86 (+ pl. XXXVIII).

4Q249o 4QpapcryptALitF

Pfann, "249o. 4Qpap cryptA Liturgical Work F?," DJD 36. 587 (+ pl. XXXVIII).

4Q249p 4QpapcryptAProph

Pfann, "249p. 4Qpap cryptA Prophecy?," DJD 36. 588-89 (+ pl. XXXIX; see also DJD 35, pls. I-II, where frgs. 5-6 are shown but wrongly labelled "249k," instead of 249p).

4Q249q 4QpapcryptAPlant

Pfann, "249q. 4Qpap cryptA Fragment Mentioning a Planting," DJD 36. 590-91 (+ pl. XXXIX; see also DJD 35, pl. II, where the verso of frg. 41 is shown, but wrongly labelled "249l" instead of 249q).

4Q249r-y 4QpapcryptAUnidA-H

Pfann, "249r-y. 4Qpap cryptA Unidentified Text A-H," DJD 36. 592-602 (+ pls. XXXIX-XL).

4Q249z 4QpapcryptAMiscA

Pfann, "249z. 4Qpap cryptA Miscellaneous Texts A," DJD 36. 603-77 (+ pls. XLI-XLV).

4Q250 4QpapcryptACultA

Pfann, "250. 4Qpap cryptA Text Concerning Cultic Service A," DJD 36. 678-79 (+ pl. XLVI).

4Q250a 4QpapcryptACultB

Pfann, "250a. 4Qpap cryptA Text Concerning Cultic Service B?," DJD 36. 680-81 (+ pl. XLVI).

4Q250b 4QpapcryptAIsa

Pfann, "250b. 4Qpap cryptA Text Related to Isaiah 11," DJD 36. 682 (+ pl. XLVI). Possibly a variant of Isa 11:6-7.

4Q250c-i 4QpapcryptAUnidI-O

Pfann, "250c-i. 4Qpap cryptA Unidentified Text I-O," DJD 36. 683-93 (+ pls. XLVII-XLVIII).

4Q250j 4QpapcryptAMiscB

Pfann, "250j. 4Qpap cryptA Miscellaneous Texts B," DJD 36. 694-96 (+ pl. XLVIII).

4Q251 4QHlkA

Larson, E., M. R. Lehmann, and L. Schiffman, "251. 4QHalakha A," DJD 35. 25-51 (+ pls. III-IV): 18 frgs. of coherent text; + eight frgs.

4Q252 4QCommGenA (olim 4QpGen[a])

Brooke, G., "252. 4QCommentary on Genesis A," DJD 22. 185-207 (+ pls. XII-XIII): This fragmentary text interprets various passages of Genesis in different ways, sometimes in the manner of a pesher. Comments are made on Gen 6:3; 7:10–8:18; 9:24-27 (with 9:1 + 2 Chr 20:7); 11:31; 15:9, 17; 17:20?; 18:31-32 (with Deut 13:16, 17; 20:11, 14); 22:10-12; 28:3-4; 36:12 (with Deut 25:19); 49:3-4, 10 (with Jer 33:17), 20-21. (Col. 5, frg. 6 was published originally by Allegro as 4QPBless [Patriarchal Blessings] in *JBL* 75 [1956] 174-76.)

4Q253 4QCommGenB (olim 4QpGen[b])

Brooke, "253. 4QCommentary on Genesis B," DJD 22. 209-12 (+ pl. XIV): The frgs. may deal with Noah and the flood, but the sense of the comments is far from clear.

4Q253a 4QCommMal (olim 4QCommGen[b])

Brooke, "253a. 4QCommentary on Malachi," DJD 22. 213-15 (+ pl. XIV): Interpretation of Mal 3:16-18, which is quoted in frg. 1 i 1-4.

4Q254 4QCommGenC

Brooke, "254. 4QCommentary on Genesis C," DJD 22. 217-32 (+ pl. XV): Frgs. 1-7 reflect somewhat Gen 9:24-25; 22:5?, 17?; Zech 4:14; Gen 49:15, 24-26?; + 10 frgs.

4Q254a 4QCommGenD (olim 4QpGen[c])

Brooke, "254a. 4QCommentary on Genesis D," DJD 22. 233-36 (+ pl. XVI): The commentary seems to interpret Gen 8:8; 6:15; 8:18-19. Frg. 3 seems to parallel 4Q252 2:1-5. The role of the raven is described, but the text unfortunately breaks off at a crucial point.

4Q255 4QpapS[a]

Alexander, P. S. and G. Vermes, "255. 4QpapSerekh ha-Yaḥad[a]," *Qumran Cave 4: XIX, Serekh Ha-Yaḥad and Two Related Texts* (DJD 26; ed. P. S. Alexander and G. Vermes; Oxford: Clarendon, 1998) 27-38 (+ pl. I): Fragments of the Rule of the Community parallel to 1QS 1:1-5; 3:7-12; + two frgs. Compare 4QpapS[c] (4Q257) 1:1-2; 3:10-14. See "4Q255-264. General Introduction," ibid., 1-25.

4Q256 4QS[b]

Alexander-Vermes, "256. 4QSerekh ha-Yaḥad[b]," DJD 26. 39-64 (+ pls. II-V): Frgs. 1 and 8 are not certainly identified as part of this 4Q text, which is otherwise parallel to 1QS 1:10?, 15-19, 21-23; 2:4-5, 6-11; 5:1-20; 6:10-13, 16-18; 9:18-23; 10:3-7, 13-18; 11:22; + additional text not in 1QS.

4Q257 4QpapS[c]

Alexander-Vermes, "257. 4QSerekh ha-Yaḥad[c]," DJD 26. 65-82 (+ pls. VI-IX): Parallel to 1QS 1:1-3; 2:4-11, 26; 3:1-10; 4:4-10, 13-15, 23-25; + one frg.

4Q258 4QS[d]

Alexander-Vermes, "258. 4QSerekh ha-Yaḥad[d]," DJD 26. 83-128 (+ pls. X-XIII): Parallel to 1QS 5:1-20, 21-26; 6:1-7, 9-12; 8:6-21, 24-26; 9:1-10, 15-26; 10:1-3, 4-12, 12-18; 11:7-8, 14-15.

4Q259 4QS[e]

Alexander-Vermes, "259. 4QSerekh ha-Yaḥad[e]," DJD 26. 129-52 (+ pls. XIV-XVI): Parallel to 1QS 7:8-15, 20-25; 8:1-10, 10-15; 9:12-20, 20-24 (+ 4QOtot [4Q319], which is not part of 1QS). This is the text that lacks the equivalent of 1QS 8:15 to 9:12, the passage where the coming of "a prophet and the Messiahs of Aaron and Israel" is mentioned; see col. 3, line 6 (p. 144).

4Q260 4QS[f]

Alexander-Vermes, "260. 4QSerekh ha-Yaḥad[f]," DJD 26. 153-67 (+ pl. XVII): Parallel to 1QS 9:23-24; 10:1-5, 9-11, 15-20, 20-24.

4Q261 4QS[g]

Alexander-Vermes, "261. 4QSerekh ha-Yaḥad[g]," DJD 26. 169-87 (+ pls. XVIII-XIX): Parallel to 1QS 5:22-24; 6:3-5, 22-25, 27; 7:1-4, 9-14, 15-18; + three frgs.

4Q262 4QS[h]

Alexander-Vermes, "262. 4QSerekh ha-Yaḥad[h]," DJD 26. 189-95 (+ pl. XX): Parallel to 1QS 3:4-5; two unidentified additional frgs. not part of 1QS. Three frgs. of this text may come from two different scrolls; see n. 1 on p. 1.

4Q263 4QS[i]

Alexander-Vermes, "263. 4QSerekh ha-Yaḥad[i]," DJD 26. 197-200 (+ pl. XXI): Parallel to 1QS 6:1-4.

4Q264 4QS[j]

Alexander-Vermes, "264. 4QSerekh ha-Yaḥad[j]," DJD 26. 201-6 (+ pl. XXI): Parallel to 1QS 11:14-22.

4Q264a 4QHlkB

Baumgarten, J., "264a. 4QHalakha B," DJD 35. 53-56 (+ pl. V): Regulations for the observance of the Sabbath, related to 4Q421, with which it has some overlaps.

4Q265 4QMiscRules (olim 4QSD)

Baumgarten, "265. 4QMiscellaneous Rules," DJD 35. 57-78 (+ pls. V-VIII): A diverse collection of regulations based on Sabbath rules, grazing animals on the Sabbath, eschatological communal council, Adam and Eve in Paradise, and purification after childbirth. The rules seem to be related to 4QOrd[a] (4Q159) frg. 5.

4Q266 4QD[a] (olim 4QD[b])

Baumgarten, J. M., "266. 4QDamascus Document[a]," *Qumran Cave 4: XIII, The Damascus Document (4Q266-273)* (DJD 18; ed. J. M. Baumgarten et al.; Oxford: Clarendon, 1996) 23-93 (+ pls. I-XVII): Parallel to CD 0; 1:1-21; 2:1-21; 3:1-3, 8; 4:1-3, 7-14; 5:13-21; 6:1-18; 7:3-5, 17-21; 8:1-3, 3-9; 20:33-34; 15:10-17; 16:17-20; 9:1-2; 10:3-12; 11:15-18; 12:6-7, 14-22; 13:4-9, 15-21; 14:1-2, 8-20; 7:7-15. There are also frgs. with no parallels in CD, but with other 4QD texts; and many tiny frgs. with only a few words on them. Overlapping words with other 4QD texts are underlined or otherwise marked. See "4Q266-273. Introduction," ibid., 1-22.

4Q267 4QD[b] (olim 4QD[d])

Baumgarten, "267. 4QDamascus Document[b]," DJD 18. 95-113 (+ pls. XVIII-XXI): Parallel to CD 5:17-21; 6:1-7; 20:25-28; 9:6-14; 11:5-6, 14; 12:6-9; 13:5-14, 22-23; 14:1-10. There are also frgs. with no parallels in CD, but with other 4QD texts; and nine tiny frgs. with only a few words on them.

4Q268 4QD[c] (olim 4QD[a])

Baumgarten, "268. 4QDamascus Document[c]," DJD 18. 115-21 (+ pl. XXII): Parallel to CD 0; 1:1-10; 14:5-6; + one frg.

4Q269 4QD[d] (olim 4QD[f])

Baumgarten, "269. 4QDamascus Document[d]," DJD 18. 123-36 (+ pls. XXIII-XXV); see now H. Stegemann, "269. 4QDamascus Document[d] frgs. 10, 11 (Re-edition), 15, 16," DJD 36. 201-11 (+ pl. IX): Parallel to CD 2:4-6; 3:7-11; 4:19-20; 5:21; 6:1-2, 19-20; 7:1-3, 14-18, 17-20; 8:5-6; 13:2-5, 16-23; 14:1-7, 18-22. There are also frgs. with no parallels in CD. Stegemann re-edits frgs. 10 i-ii and 11 ii and presents the *editio princeps* of frgs. 15-16, which had not been available to Baumgarten. Cf. E. Tigchelaar, *RevQ* 21 (2003-4) 477-85.

4Q270 4QD[e]

Baumgarten, "270. 4QDamascus Document[e]," DJD 18. 137-68 (+ pls. XXVI-XXXVI): Parallel to CD 2:16-18; 4:2-3, 7-8; 20:32-33?; 15:4-5, 12-18; 16:3-8, 19-22; 9:1-7, 7-12, 21-22; 10:1-12, 15-19; 11:6-18; 7:12-21. There are also frgs. with no parallels in CD, but with other QD texts; and five tiny frgs. with only a few words on them.

4Q271 4QD[f] (olim 4QD[c])

Baumgarten, "271. 4QDamascus Document[f]," DJD 18. 169-83 (+ pls. XXXVII-XXXIX): Parallel to CD 5:18-20; 15:2-10, 20; 16:1-18; 11:4-23; 12:1-6, 8-12, 16; 13:5-6.

4Q272 4QD[g]

Baumgarten, "272. 4QDamascus Document[g]," DJD 18. 185-91 (+ pl. XL): No parallels to CD, but to other 4QD texts.

4Q273 4QD[h]

Baumgarten, "273. 4QDamascus Document[h]," DJD 18. 193-98 (+ pls. XLI-XLII): No parallels to CD, but to other 4QD texts.

4Q274 4QTohorotA

Baumgarten, "274. Tohorot A," DJD 35. 99-109 (+ pl. VIII): Regulations about purity derived from Leviticus, esp. Lev 13:45-46, as applied to one who is *zāb*, "gonorrheic." See the introductory essay, "274-278. 4QTohorot A-C," ibid., 79-97.

4Q275 4QComCer (olim 4QTohorot B[a])

Alexander-Vermes, "275. 4QCommunal Ceremony," DJD 26. 209-16 (+ pl. XXII): A text difficult to analyze, but with "little to commend its older classification as 'Tohorot B[a]' . . . following Milik, *JJS* 23 [1972] 129." Possibly it alludes to *Šābûʿôt*, "(Feast of) Weeks," or the Qumran feast of the renewal of the covenant.

4Q276 4QTohorotB[a] (olim 4QTohorot B[b])

Baumgarten, "276. 4QTohorot B[a]," DJD 35. 111-13 (+ pl. IX): Regulations for the priest who slaughters the red cow (see Numbers 19).

4Q277 4QTohorotB[b] (olim 4QTohorot B[c])

Baumgarten, "277. 4QTohorot B[b]," DJD 35. 115-19 (+ pl. IX): Further regulations for the priest who slaughters the red cow.

4Q278 4QTohorotC

Baumgarten, "278. 4QTohorot C," DJD 35. 121-22 (+ pl. IX).

4Q279 4QFourLots (olim 4QTohorot D)

Alexander-Vermes, "279. 4QFour Lots," DJD 26. 217-23 (+ pl. XXIII): A text difficult to analyze, but with "little to commend its older classification as (4QTohorot D) . . . following Milik, *JJS* 23 (1972) 129." Frg. 5 seems to refer to rewards for priests, Levites, Israelites, and proselytes; hence the new title.

4Q280 4QCurses (olim 4QBrk[z] and 4QTohorot D[b])

Nitzan, B., "280. 4QCurses," *Qumran Cave 4: XX, Poetical and Liturgical Texts, Part 2* (DJD 29; ed. E. Chazon et al.; Oxford: Clarendon, 1999) 1-8 (+ pl. I): A text containing a series of covenantal curses related to those in 1QS 2, but not identical with them or in the same order as those. Some of the curses in this text are related to 4QBer[a] 7 ii (= 4QBer[b] 6).

4Q281a-f 4QUnidAa-f (olim 4QTohorot E[a])

Fitzmyer, J. A. "281a-f. 4QUnidentified Fragments A, a-f," DJD 36. 212-15 (+ pl. X).

4Q282a-t 4QUnidBa-t

Fitzmyer, "282a-t. 4QUnidentified Fragments B, a-t," DJD 36. 216-27 (+ pls. X-XI): Frg. a was known earlier as 4QUnidC and also as 4QTohorot E[b].

4Q283

Cancelled.

4Q284 4QPurLit (olim 4QSndt)

Baumgarten, "284. 4QPurification Liturgy," DJD 35. 123-29 (+ pl. X): This text mentions purification with "water of impurity" *(mê niddāh)* and feast days; it resembles 4Q512 (4QpapRitPur).

4Q284a 4QHarvest (olim 4QTohorot G, 4QLeqet)

Baumgarten, "284a. 4QHarvesting," DJD 35. 131-33 (+ pl. XI).

4Q285 4QSefM

Alexander-Vermes, "285. 4QSefer ha-Milḥamah," DJD 36. 228-46 (+ pls. XII-XIII): This is a fragmentary text related to the War Scroll, but without any overlapping with 1QM or 4QM; but frg. 8 is parallel to 11QSefM (11Q14) 1 ii 2-15.

4Q286 4QBer[a]

Nitzan, B., "286. 4QBerakhot[a]," *Qumran Cave 4: VI, Poetical and Liturgical Texts, Part 1* (DJD 11; ed. E. Eshel et al.; Oxford: Clarendon, 1998) 7-48 (+ pls. I-IV): The text declares that the council and the community will invoke all things, earthly and angelic, to bless God's holy name, and it lists them in great detail. It also curses Belial, the Angel of the Pit, and the Spirit of Abaddon. See also the introductory essay, "286-290. 4QBerakhot[a-c]," ibid., 1-5.

4Q287 4QBer[b]

Nitzan, "287. 4QBerakhot[b]," DJD 11. 49-60 (+ pls. V-VI): This text overlaps 4QBer[a] in several places.

4Q288 4QBer[c]

Nitzan, "288. 4QBerakhot[c]," DJD 11. 61-65 (+ pl. VII): This text provides regulations for the covenantal ceremony of 1QS 1-2.

4Q289 4QBer[d]

Nitzan, "289. 4QBerakhot[d]," DJD 11. 67-71 (+ pl. VII): Holy angels are present to the community as it thanks God.

4Q290 4QBer[e]

Nitzan, "290. 4QBerakhot[e]," DJD 11. 73-74 (+ pl. VII).

4Q291 4QWCPrA

Nitzan, "291. 4QWork Containing Prayers A," DJD 29. 9-14 (+ pl. I): Perhaps a liturgical text with a prayer blessing the name of God Most High *('ēl 'elyôn)*.

4Q292 4QWCPrB

Nitzan, "292. 4QWork Containing Prayers B," DJD 29. 15-18 (+ pl. I): The text seems to be the ending of a prayer for Israel, which mentions God's mercy toward it.

4Q293 4QWCPrC

Nitzan, "293. 4QWork Containing Prayers C," DJD 29. 10-22 (+ pl. I): Liturgical praise of the Lord.

4Q294 4QSapDidC

Tigchelaar, E. J. C. "294. 4QSapiential-Didactic Work C," DJD 36. 247-48 (+ pl. XIV).

4Q295-297

Cancelled.

4Q298 4QDibMask

Pfann, S. J. and M. Kister, "298. 4QCryptA Words of the Maskil to All Sons of Dawn," *Qumran Cave 4: XV, Sapiential Texts, Part 1* (DJD 20; ed. T. Elgvin et al.; Oxford: Clarendon, 1997) 1-30 (+ pls. I-II): A sapiential text written in an esoteric script called Cryptic A that gives the words of wisdom as an instruction to neophytes of the community, here called "sons of dawn." Eight frgs., only half of which have a somewhat extended text.

4Q299 4QMyst[a]

Schiffman, L., "299. 4QMysteries[a]," DJD 20. 33-97 (+ pls. III-VII): A sapiential text mentioning *rāzîm*, "mysteries," a copy of the same composition found in 1QMyst (1Q27) and 4QMyst[b] (4Q300), with which it has overlaps. See also the introductory essay, "299-301. 4QMysteries[a-b,c?]," ibid., 31-32.

4Q300 4QMyst[b]

Schiffman, "300. 4QMysteries[b]," DJD 20. 99-112 (+ pl. VIII): Another copy of "Mysteries."

4Q301 4QMyst[c]?

Schiffman, "301. 4QMysteries[c]?," DJD 20. 113-23 (+ pl. IX): A sapiential text, which is not the same as 1Q27 or 4QMyst[a-b] and has no overlaps with them, but it has close parallels with later hekhalot literature. It is not certain that it should be called "Mysteries"; the word occurs only once in frg. 1 and is partially restored even there.

4Q302 4QpapAdmonPar (olim 4Q302-302a, 4QSap[a])

Nitzan, B., "302. 4QpapAdmonitory Parable," DJD 20. 125-49 (+ pls. X-XII): 23 papyrus frgs. preserve part of an admonition and a sapiential tree-parable; the two parts of this composition were thought at first to be separate works.

4Q303 4QMedCreatA (olim 4QSap[c])

Lim. T., "303. 4QMeditation on Creation A," DJD 20. 151-53 (+ pl. XIII): A meditative text based on the opening chapters of Genesis.

4Q304 4QMedCreatB

Lim, "304. 4QMeditation on Creation B," DJD 20. 155 (+ pl. XIII).

4Q305 4QMedCreatC

Lim, "305. 4QMeditation on Creation C," DJD 20. 157-58 (+ pl. XIII).

4Q306 4QPeopErr (olim 4QSap[b])

Lim, "306. 4QMen of the People Who Err," DJD 36. 249-54 (+ pl. XIV): Three frgs. of a sapiential text about transgressors of the Torah and other regulations.

4Q307 4QTemple (olim 4QSap[f])

Lim, T. "307. 4QText Mentioning Temple," DJD 36. 255-58 (+ pl. XIV): Nine frgs. that may not all be part of the same text; *miqdāš*, "temple," occurs on frg. 2. Otherwise it is difficult to say what the text is about.

4Q308-312

Missing texts, cited in Milik's list, but never located: 4Q308 Sapiental fragment; 4Q309 Cursive Work; 4Q310 Unc; 4Q311 papUnc; 4Q312 Hebrew text in Phoenician cursive.

4Q313 4QcryptAMMT[g]

Pfann, "313. 4QcryptA Miqṣat Maʿaśeh ha-Torah[g]?," DJD 36. 697-99 (+ pl. XLIX): Two frgs. parallel to 4Q394, 4Q396, 4Q397, written in cryptic script.

4Q313a 4QcryptAUnidP

Pfann, "313a. 4QcryptA Unidentified Text P," DJD 36. 700 (+ pl. XLIX).

4Q313b 4QcryptAUnidQ

Pfann, "313b. 4QcryptA Unidentified Text Q," DJD 36. 701 (+ pl. XLIX).

4Q313c 4QcryptACalDocB

Pfann, S. J. "313c. 4QcryptA Calendrical Document B," *Wadi Daliyeh II: The Samaria Papyri from Wadi Daliyeh and Qumran Cave 4: XXVIII, Miscellanea, Part 2* (DJD 28; ed. D. M. Gropp et al.; Oxford: Clarendon, 2001) pl. LII (photograph only); see p. ix.

4Q314-316

Cancelled.

4Q317 4QAstrCrypt

Pfann, "317. 4QcryptA Lunisolar Calendar," DJD 28, pls. LII-LVIII (photograph only); see p. ix.

4Q318 4QZodBront ar

Greenfield, J. C. and M. Sokoloff, "318. 4QZodiology and Brontology ar," DJD 36. 259-74 (+ pls. XV-XVI): Fragments of the end of a zodiacal calendar and the beginning of a brontologion, which describe the movement of the moon across the sky in the various signs of the zodiac. It was supposed to determine the days of good luck for various planned activity. The brontologion would tell when, if it would thunder in a certain sign, it would be a good omen or not. Many of the omen predictions, however, have not been preserved.

4Q319 4QOtot

Ben-Dov, J., "319. 4QOtot," *Qumran Cave 4: XVI, Calendrical Texts* (DJD 21; ed. S. Talmon et al.; Oxford: Clarendon, 2001) 195-244 (+ pls. X-XIII): *'ôtôt* means "signs," and it denotes the various names of priestly families and their rounds of duty in the Temple. Thus every sabbath, month, and year was determined by the "sign" of a priestly family.

4Q320 4QCalDocMA

Talmon, S. and J. Ben-Dov, "320. 4QCalendrical Document/Mishmarot A," DJD 21. 37-63 (+ pls. I-II): This fragmentary text is a compendium of calendar-related compositions, giving dates in lunar months. See also "320-330, 337, 394 1-2: Introduction," ibid., 1-36.

4Q321 4QCalDocMB

Talmon-Ben-Dov, "321. 4QCalendrical Document/Mishmarot B," DJD 21. 65-79 (+ pls. III-IV).

4Q321a 4QCalDocMC

Talmon-Ben-Dov, "321a. 4QCalendrical Document/Mishmarot C," DJD 21. 81-91 (+ pl. V).

4Q322 4QMišmarotA

Talmon-Ben-Dov, "322. 4QMishmarot A," DJD 21. 93-97 (+ pl. V).

4Q322a 4QHistTextH (olim 4QMishmarot C^{b})

Tigchelaar, E. J. C., "322a. 4QHistorical Text H?," DJD 28. 125-28 (+ pl. XL).

4Q323 4QMišmarotB

Talmon-Ben-Dov, "323. 4QMishmarot B," DJD 21. 99-101 (+ pl. V).

4Q324 4QMišmarotC

Talmon-Ben-Dov, "324. 4QMishmarot C," DJD 21. 103-6 (+ pl. VI). The verso of two frgs. bear the unintelligible text of 4Q355.

4Q324a 4QMišmarotD

Talmon-Ben-Dov, "324a. 4QMishmarot D," DJD 21. 107-11 (+ pl. VI).

4Q324b 4QpapCalDocA

Talmon-Ben-Dov, "324b. 4QpapCalendrical Document A?," DJD 21. 113-17 (+ pl. VI).

4Q324c 4QMišmarotE

Talmon-Ben-Dov, "324c. 4QMishmarot E," DJD 21. 119-22 (+ pl. VI).

4Q324d-f 4QcryptALitCal^{a-c}

Pfann, "324d-f. 4Qcrypt A Liturgical Calendar^{a-c}," DJD 28, pls. LIX-LXI (photograph only; no discussion).

4Q324g-h 4QcryptACalDocFG

Pfann, DJD 28, pl. LXII (photograph only).

4Q324i 4QcryptAMišmarotJ

Pfann, DJD 28, pl. LXII (photograph only).

4Q325 4QCalDocDM

Talmon-Ben-Dov, "325. 4QCalendrical Document/Mishmarot D," DJD 21. 123-31 (+ pl. VII).

4Q326 4QCalDocC

Talmon-Ben-Dov, "326. 4QCalendrical Document C," DJD 21. 133-38 (+ pl. VII).

4Q327

Cancelled; see now 4Q394.

4Q328 4QMišmarotF

Talmon-Ben-Dov, "328. 4QMishmarot F," DJD 21. 139-41 (+ pl. VII).

4Q329 4QMišmarotG

Talmon-Ben-Dov, "329. 4QMishmarot G," DJD 21. 143-46 (+ pl. VII).

4Q329a 4QMišmarotH

Talmon-Ben-Dov, "329a. 4QMishmarot H," DJD 21. 147-50 (+ pl. VII).

4Q330 4QMišmarotI

Talmon-Ben-Dov, "330. 4QMishmarot I," DJD 21. 151-54 (+ pl. VIII).

4Q331 4QpapHistTextC

Fitzmyer, "331. 4QpapHistorical Text C," DJD 36. 275-80 (+ pl. XVII): The text mentions names of rulers in the Hasmonean dynasty associated with events in ancient Judea, e.g., Hyrcanus and Salome Alexandra.

4Q332 4QHistTextD

Fitzmyer, "332. 4QHistorical Text D," DJD 36. 281-86 (+ pl. XVII): The text mentions Arabs, Salome, Hyrcanus, the Kittim, and Jedaiah.

4Q332a 4QUnidText

Tigchelaar, "332a. 4QUnidentifed Text," DJD 28. 129 (+ pl. XLI).

4Q333 4QHistTextE

Fitzmyer, "333. 4QHistorical Text E," DJD 36. 287-89 (+ pl. XVIII): The text mentions Jehezkel, Aemilius, and Gamul.

4Q334 4QOrdo

Glessmer, U., "334. 4QOrdo," DJD 21. 167-94 (+ pl. IX): The text mentions "songs" and "words of praise" to be uttered each day in a sequential listing that marks days and nights. The text seems to be related to 4Q326 and 4Q394.

4Q335-336

Missing texts.

4Q337 4QCalDocE

Talmon-Ben-Dov, "337. 4QCalendrical Document E?," DJD 21. 155-56 (+ pl. VIII): A tiny text mentioning the Sabbath twice; doubtfully related to the calendrical texts.

4Q338 4QGenealogy

Tov, E., "338. 4QGenealogical List?," DJD 36. 290 (+ pl. XIX): The ink of the text has faded and the contents have been completely lost; no transcription, but only photograph. It is said to be the verso of 4QEn[a] ar (4Q201). See Milik, *BE*, 139.

4Q339 4QFalProph ar

Broshi, M. and A. Yardeni, "339. 4QList of False Prophets ar," DJD 19. 77-79 (+ pl. XI): Names of eight false prophets who arose in Israel.

4Q340 4QNetinim

Broshi-Yardeni, "340. 4QList of Netinim," DJD 19. 81-84 (+ pl. XI): The Nethinim (*nĕtînîm*, "those given [to the service of the Temple]") are listed in Ezra 2:43-54; Neh 10:28 as persons appointed for the lowest menial tasks in the sanctuary (RSV calls them "temple servants").

4Q341 4QExerCalC

Naveh, J., "341. 4QExercitium Calami C," DJD 36. 291-93 (+ pl. XVIII): This text was called by Allegro "4QTherapeia," since he believed its strange mixture of words were an attempt at the "obscurantism, not entirely unfamiliar in medical writing" (*The Dead Sea Scrolls and the Christian Myth* [Buffalo, NY: Prometheus Books, 1984] 235-40). Cf. J. H. Charlesworth, *The Discovery of a Dead Sea Scroll (4Q Therapeia): Its Importance in the History of Medicine and Jesus Research* (ICASALS Publ. 85/1; Lubbock, TX: Texas Tech University, 1985). Later it came to be known as "4QList of Proper Names," but it was finally recognized by J. Naveh to be nothing more than a writing exercise (*IEJ* 36 [1986] 52-55 [+ pl. II]).

4Q342-346a

See 2.B.1.i below, *Alleged Qumran Texts* (pp. 117-20).

4Q347

See XḤev/Se 32 (XḤev/SepapDeedF ar).

4Q348

See 2.B.1.i below, *Alleged Qumran Texts* (pp. 117-20).

4Q349

Cancelled.

4Q350 4QAcc gr

Cotton, H., "350. 4QAccount gr," DJD 36. 294-95 (+ pl. XX): A few Greek letters of a list of cereals inscribed on the verso of frg. 9 of 4Q460.

4Q351-354

See 2.B.1.i below, *Alleged Qumran Texts* (pp. 117-20).

4Q355 4QAccC

Yardeni, "355. 4QAccount C ar or heb," DJD 36. 296 (+ pl. XX): The unintelligible text is written on the verso of two frgs. of 4Q324.

4Q356-359

See 2.B.1.i below, *Alleged Qumran Texts* (pp. 117-20).

4Q360 4QExerCalB

Yardeni, "360. 4QExercitium Calami B," DJD 36. 297 (+ pl. XX).

4Q360a-361

See 2.B.1.i below, *Alleged Qumran Texts* (pp. 117-20).

4Q362 4QcryptBUnidA

Pfann, "362. 4QcryptB Unidentified Text A," DJD 28, pl. XLI: No transcription; photograph only.

4Q363 4QcryptBUnidB

Pfann, "363. 4QcryptB Unidentified Text B," DJD 28, pl. XLII: No transcription; photograph only.

4Q363a 4QcryptCUnid

Pfann, "363a. 4QcryptC Unidentified Religious Text," DJD 28, pl. XLIII: No transcription; photograph only.

4Q363b 4QcryptMisc

Pfann, "363b. 4Qcrypt Miscellaneous Texts," DJD 28, pl. XLIII: No transcription; photograph only.

4Q364 4QRP[b]

Tov, E., "364. 4QReworked Pentateuch[b]," DJD 13. 197-254 (+ pls. XIII-XXI): Reworking of Gen 25:18-21; 26:7-8; 27:39 (or 41?); 28:6; 29:32-33?; 30:8-14, 26-36; 31:47-53; 32:18-20, 26-30; 34:2?; 35:28; 37:7-8; 38:14-21; 44:30-34; 45:1, 21-27; 48:14-15?; Exod 21:14-22; 19:17?; 24:12-14, 18; 25:1-2; 26:1, 33-35; Num 14:16-20; 33:31-49; Deut 1:1-6, 17-33, 45-46; Num 20:17-18; Deut 2:8-14, 30-37; 3:2, 18-23; 9:6-7, 12-18, 22-24, 27-29, 21?, 25?; 10:1-4, 6-7?, 10-13, 22; 11:1-2, 6-9, 23-24; 14:24-26; + 35 frgs. There also are words added in many of these passages. See the introductory essay, "364-367. 4QReworked Pentateuch[b-e] and 365a. 4QTemple?," ibid., 187-96.

4Q365 4QRP[c]

Tov, "365. 4QReworked Pentateuch[c]," DJD 13. 255-318 (+ pls. XXII-XXXII): Reworking of Gen 21:9-10; Exod 8:13-19; 9:9-12; 10:19?-20; 14:10, 12-21; 15:16-[21], 22-26; 17:3-5; 18:13-16; 26:34-36; 28:16-20; 29:20-22; 30:37-38; 31:1-2; 35:[2]-5; 36:32-38; 37:29; 38:1-7; 39:1-16, 17-19; Lev 11:1-[3], 17-[25], 32-[33], [39]-[46]; 13:6-8, 15-[19], 51-52; 16:6-7 (or 11-12 or 17-18); 18:[25]-[29]; 23:42-44; 24:1-2; 25:7-9; 26:17-32; 27:34?; Num 1:1-5; 3:26-30; 4:47-49; 7:1, 78-80; 8:11-12; 9:15-23; 10:1-[4]; 13:[11]-25, [28]-30; 15:26-[29]; 17:20-24; 27:11; 36:1-2; Deut 2:24 (or 36?); 19:20-21; 20:1; + 24 frgs. There are added words at times in these passages.

4Q365a 4QTemple[a]

White, S., "365a. 4QTemple?," DJD 13. 319-33 (+ pls. XXXIII-XXXIV): Five frgs., written by the same hand as that of 4Q365, but frgs. 2, 3, and frg. 23 of 4Q365 are copies of 11QTemple[a] (11Q19).

4Q366 4QRP[d]

Tov, "366. 4QReworked Pentateuch[d]," DJD 13. 335-43 (+ pl. XXXV): Reworking of Exod 21:35-37; 22:1-5; Lev 24:20-22?; 25:39-43; Num 29:14-[25], 32-39; 30:1; Deut 16:13-14; 14:[13]-21.

4Q367 4QRP[e]

Tov, "367. 4QReworked Pentateuch[e]," DJD 13. 345-51 (+ pl. XXXVI): Reworking of Lev 11:47; 12:1-8; 13:1; 15:14-15; 19:1-4, 9-15; 20:13; 27:30-34; + one frg.

4Q368 4QapocrPentA

VanderKam, J. C. and M. Brady, "368. 4QApocryphal Pentateuch A," DJD 28. 131-49 (+ pls. XLIV-XLV): A fragmentary text about Moses, which is related to Exod 33:11-13; 34:11-24, 29-35; Num 20:25-28. It is similar to 1Q22 (1QDM = *Dibrê Môšeh*).

4Q369 4QprEnosh

Attridge, H. and J. Strugnell, "369. 4QPrayer of Enosh," DJD 13. 353-62 (+ pl. XXXVII): This fragmentary text seems to have a prayer addressed to God by a patriarch, with a few lines of a genealogy inserted, which mentions Mehalalel as the fifth generation and Enoch as the seventh. From these indications one may conclude that it is a prayer of Enosh, who is not mentioned. See Gen 4:26; 5:10; *Jub.* 4:11-15.

4Q370 4QAdmonFlood

Newsom, C., "370. 4QAdmonition Based on the Flood," DJD 19. 85-97 (+ pl.

XII): Column 1 of this frg. has a narrative about the deluge similar to Genesis 6–9, and col. 2 seems to formulate warnings about it. This text may be related to 4Q185.

4Q371 4QNPC[a]

Schuller, E. and M. Bernstein, "371. 4QNarrative and Poetic Composition[a]," DJD 28. 155-63 (+ pl. XLVI): A text that mentions Joseph but is difficult to analyze, because it deals with much more than him. It is related to 4Q372, 4Q373, and 2Q22 (2QapDavid), with all of which it has some overlaps. See also "371-373. 4QNarrative and Poetic Composition[a-c]: Introduction," ibid., 151-54.

4Q372 4QNPC[b]

Schuller-Bernstein, "372. 4QNarrative and Poetic Composition[b]," DJD 28. 165-97 (+ pls. XLVII-XLIX).

4Q373 4QNPC[c]

Schuller-Bernstein, "373. 4QNarrative and Poetic Composition[c]," DJD 28. 199-204 (+ pl. XLIX). See annotation on 2Q22 (2QapDavid).

4Q374 4QExodConq (olim 4QapMosesA)

Newsom, "374. 4QDiscourse on the Exodus/Conquest Tradition," DJD 19. 99-110 (+ pl. XIII): The fragmentary text seems to refer to the exodus of the Hebrews from Egypt and their settlement in Canaan; God seems to be addressed in some frgs.

4Q375 4QapocrMoses[a]

Strugnell, J., "375. 4QApocryphon of Moses[a]," DJD 19. 111-19 (+ pl. XIV): Instructions of Moses to the people about God's anger, false prophets, and the ritual of the Day of Atonement. The text is similar to 1Q22 (1QDM).

4Q376 4QapocrMoses[b]

Strugnell, "376. 4QApocryphon of Moses[b]?," DJD 19. 121-36 (+ pl. XV): The text has some parallels with 1Q29 (1QLTLF) and 4Q408 (4QapMoses[c]).

4Q377 4QapocrPentB

VanderKam-Brady, "377. 4QApocryphal Pentateuch B," DJD 28. 205-17 (+ pls. L-LI): A text in which Moses plays a prominent role similar to that in Exodus and Numbers, especially in the events at Sinai and later during the wanderings in the desert; see Exod 24:10; 34:11; Numbers 12–13. Cf. E. Puech, "Le fragment 2 de *4Q377, Pentateuque apocryphe B:* L'exaltation de Moïse," *RevQ* 21 (2003-4) 469-75.

4Q378 4QapocrJosh[a]

Newsom, "378. 4QApocryphon of Joshua[a]," DJD 22. 241-62 (+ pls. XVII-XX): A text that sounds like Josh 1:6, 7, 9, 17-18; Exod 32:30-34; Num 14:13-19; Deut 8:8; 9:5.

4Q379 4QapocrJosh[b]

Newsom, "379. 4QApocryphon of Joshua[b]," DJD 22. 263-88 (+ pls. XXI-XXV): The first frg. mentions five sons of Jacob in a prayer addressed to God, and frg. 12 the crossing of the Jordan, but most of the 41 frgs. are difficult to interpret because they are so tiny. Some of them are a blessing or praise of God. Lines 7-15 of frg. 22 ii are parallel to 4Q175 21-30, with a partial quotation of Josh 6:26.

4Q380 4QNoncanPsA

Schuller, E., "380. 4QNon-Canonical Psalms A," DJD 11. 75-85 (+ pl. VIII): The text contains a series of psalm-like compositions attributed to an Obadiah and other (lost) OT figures.

4Q381 4QNoncanPsB

Schuller, "381. 4QNon-Canonical Psalms B," DJD 11. 87-172 (+ pls. IX-XV): A collection of psalm-like compositions attributed to Manasseh, a Man of God, and a king of Judah (name lost). There is no overlap with 4Q380.

4Q382 4QpapparaKgs

Olyan, S., "382. 4Qpap paraKings et al.," DJD 13. 363-416 (+ pls. XXXVIII-XLI): 154 papyrus frgs. that seem to paraphrase 1 Kgs 18:5; 19:3; 2 Kgs 2:3-4. Many of the frgs. are tiny and hard to read and interpret.

4Q383 4QapocrJerA

Dimant, D., "383. 4QApocryphon of Jeremiah A," *Qumran Cave 4: XXI, Parabiblical Texts, Part 4: Pseudo-Prophetic Texts* (DJD 30; ed. D. Dimant; Oxford: Clarendon, 2001) 117-27 (+ pl. IV): Fragments of a work mentioning Jeremiah and events in his prophetic career; he even speaks in the first person in some of them. See also "4QApocryphon of Jeremiah: Introduction," ibid., 91-116; and above all the "General Introduction," ibid., 1-3, because the naming and numbering of texts and their order in volume 30 are at times bewildering.

4Q384 4QpapapocrJerB

Smith, M., "384. 4QpapApocryphon of Jeremiah B?," DJD 19. 137-52 (+ pl. XVI): A fragmentary text possibly related to other 4QapJer texts; only the proper noun in frg. 7 indicates a relationship, which is not certain. Hence the question mark.

4Q385 4QpsEzek[a]

Dimant, "385. 4QPseudo-Ezekiel[a]," DJD 30. 17-51 (+ pl. I): Fragments that mention many of the themes of the Book of Ezekiel: resurrection of the dead, the future of the land of Israel, the *Merkabah* vision, and esp. the Vision of the Dry Bones and its sequel. There are parallels to 4Q386, 4Q388. See 4QPseudo-Ezekiel: Introduction," ibid., 7-16.

4Q385a 4QapocrJerC[a]

Dimant, "385a. 4QApocryphon of Jeremiah C[a]," DJD 30. 129-71 (+ pls. IV-VI): These frgs. contain a divine discourse that reviews past biblical history (e.g., David and Solomon) and then moves to events of the kingdoms of Israel and Judah, even of Second-Temple times (mention of the demise of Greece [the Seleucid dynasty?]). Toward the end, a third-person narrative about Jeremiah in the land of Tahpanhes is recounted in frg. 18. Allusion is made to Ezek 20:24; Nah 3:8-10. There are overlaps with 4Q387, 4Q389 in some of the frgs. See introductory remarks, ibid., 91-116 and 1-3. Cf. L. Doering, "Jeremia in Babylonien und Ägypten: Mündlichte und schriftliche Toraparänese für Exil und Diaspora nach 4QApocryphon of Jeremiah C," *Frühjudentum und Neues Testament im horizont Biblischer Theologie* (eds. W. Kraus and K.-W. Niebuhr; Tübingen: Mohr Siebeck, 2003) 50-79; also "Jeremiah and the 'Diaspora Letters' in Ancient Judaism," *Reading the Present in the Qumran Library* (ed. K. De Troyer and A. Lange; SBLSS 30; Atlanta: SBL, 2005) 44-72.

4Q385b 4QpsEzek[c]

Dimant, "385b. 4QPseudo-Ezekiel[c]," DJD 30. 71-75 (+ pl. II): The text mentions Ezekiel and reworks his prophecy against Egypt (Ezek 30:1-5), transposing it as a diatribe against Ptolemaic Egypt; it probably refers to the campaign of Antiochus IV Epiphanes against Egypt in 169 B.C.

4Q385c 4QpsEzek[?]

Dimant, "385c. 4QPseudo-Ezekiel: Unidentified Fragments," DJD 30. 85-88 (+ pl. III).

4Q386 4QpsEzek[b]

Dimant, "386. 4QPseudo-Ezekiel[b]," DJD 30. 53-69 (+ pl. II): The text presents a reworking of the Vision of the Dry Bones in Ezek 37:1-14, but includes a non-biblical vision of the desolation of the land of Israel. There is also a response of God to Ezekiel. Some of the frgs. have overlaps with 4Q385, 4Q388.

4Q387 4QapocrJerC[b]

Dimant, "387. 4QApocryphon of Jeremiah C[b]," DJD 30. 173-99 (+ pls. VII-VIII): The text begins with a reference to the last generations of the First-Temple period and then moves to parts of the Second-Temple era. A divine discourse complains about the defilement of the Temple and desecration of the Sabbath. Frg. 2 switches to the future and mentions the passing of the kingdom of Israel and the servitude of the people to "many nations" such as one knows from the Book of Daniel. There are overlaps with 4Q385a, 4Q388a, and 4Q389 in some frgs.

4Q387a 4QapocrJerC[f]

Dimant, "387a. 4QApocryphon of Jeremiah C[f]," DJD 30. 255-60 (+ pl. XII): The frgs. gathered under this number are only doubtfully part of the Apocryphon of Jeremiah C.

4Q388 4QpsEzek[d]

Dimant, "388. 4QPseudo-Ezekiel[d]," DJD 30. 77-84 (+ pl. III): Third copy of a reworking of the Vision of Dry Bones, related to 4Q385 frg. 2 and 4Q386 frg. 1 i.

4Q388a 4QapocrJerC[c]

Dimant, "388a. 4QApocryphon of Jeremiah C[c]," DJD 30. 201-17 (+ pls. VIII-IX): Some frgs. (1?, 2, 5) relate past events (entrance of Israel into Canaan, fall of Jerusalem), but most seem to recount those of the Second-Temple period. Some frgs. have overlaps with 4Q385a, 4Q387, 4Q389; nine frgs. have unidentified texts.

4Q389 4QapocrJerC[d]

Dimant, "389. 4QApocryphon of Jeremiah C[d]," DJD 30. 219-34 (+ pls. IX-X): Eight frgs. contain parts of a divine speech, similar to that of other copies of 4QapJerC. Some frgs. have parallels with 4Q385a, 4Q387, 4Q388a; five frgs. remain unidentified.

4Q390 4QapocrJerC[e]

Dimant, "390. 4QApocryphon of Jeremiah C[e]," DJD 30. 235-53 (+ pl. XI): Some frgs. speak of the returnees from Babylon and the desolation of the land in the seventh jubilee. This text precedes 4Q387 frg. 2 in its details. Frg. 2 of this text mentions a rift in Israel of a later period, having to do with cult in the Temple. Later frgs. recount details in the Second-Temple period.

4Q391 4QpappsEzek[e]

Smith, "391. 4QpapPseudo-Ezekiel[e]," DJD 19. 153-93 (+ pls. XVII-XXV): Some frgs. contain a first-person speech of Ezekiel, formulated in manner of the Book of Ezekiel, especially as in chaps. 40–48, or like the lament of Ezek 27:32. Most of the 78 frgs. are tiny and contain only a few letters.

4Q392 4QWorksGod (olim 4QLitWork)

Falk, D., "392. 4QWorks of God," DJD 29. 25-44 (+ pls. II-III): A poem, similar in style to the *Hôdāyôt,* reflects on the greatness of God in contrast to human insignificance. It is preserved on 11 frgs. See Introduction, ibid., 23-24.

4Q393 4QComConf (olim 4QLitWork)

Falk, "393. 4QCommunal Confession," DJD 29. 45-61 (+ pls. II-III): Nine frgs. of a penitential prayer, which admits the sins of ancestors, acknowledges God's justice and mercies, and asks for forgiveness.

4Q394 1-2 4QCalDocD (olim 4Q327, 4QMishE[b])

Talmon-Ben-Dov, "394 1-2. 4QCalendrical Document D (Re-edition)," DJD 21. 157-66 (+ pl. VIII): The two joined frgs. have a roster of the sequentially registered Sabbaths of the 364-day solar year and various feasts of the Qumran community. The text was earlier related to 4QMMT (see DJD 10. 3-6), but that proved to be incorrect. That also accounts for the peculiar numbering of these frgs.

4Q394 4QMMT[a] (olim 4QMishnique)

Qimron, E. and J. Strugnell, "4Q394 3-9," *Qumran Cave 4: V, Miqṣat Maʿaśe ha-Torah* (DJD 10; ed. E. Qimron and J. Strugnell; Oxford: Clarendon, 1994) 7-13 (+ pls. I-III): This text, "Some Deeds of the Law," is a sectarian polemical document in six fragmentary copies, with many overlaps. See the "Introduction," ibid., 1-2; and "Composite Text" and its important subdivisions (A-C), according to which it is often cited, ibid., 43-63. DJD 10 also has important discussions: The Language of the Text (pp. 65-108); Literary Character and Historical Setting (109-21); The Halakha (123); also three appendices: 1. The History of the Halakha and the Dead Sea Scrolls (Y. Sussmann); 2. Additional Textual Observations (E. Qimron); 3. Additional Observations (J. Strugnell).

4Q395 4QMMT[b]
Qimron-Strugnell, "4Q395," DJD 10. 14-15 (+ pl. III).

4Q396 4QMMT[c]
Qimron-Strugnell, "4Q396," DJD 10. 16-21 (+ pl. IV).

4Q397 4QMMT[d]
Qimron-Strugnell, "4Q397," DJD 10. 21-28 (+ pls. V-VI).

4Q398 4QMMT[e]
Qimron-Strugnell, "4Q398," DJD 10. 28-38 (+ pls. VII-VIII).

4Q399 4QMMT[f]
Qimron-Strugnell, "4Q399," DJD 10. 38-40 (+ pl. VIII).

4Q400 4QShirShabb[a]
Newsom, C., "400. 4QShirot ʿOlat HaShabbat[a]," DJD 11. 173-96 (+ pl. XVI): The first copy of "Songs of the Sabbath Sacrifice," which praise God as the holocaust is burnt on the dated Sabbaths. This text has overlaps with 4Q401.

4Q401 4QShirShabb[b]
Newsom, "401. 4QShirot ʿOlat HaShabbat[b]," DJD 11. 197-219 (+ pls. XVII-XVIII); see H. Eshel, "Another Fragment (3A) of *4QShirot ʿOlat HaShabbat[b]* (4Q401)," *Liturgical Perspectives* . . . (STDJ 48; ed. E. G. Chazon; Leiden: Brill, 2003) 89-94.

4Q402 4QShirShabb[c]
Newsom, "402. 4QShirot ʿOlat HaShabbat[c]," DJD 11. 221-37 (+ pl. XVIII).

4Q403 4QShirShabb[d]
Newsom, "403. 4QShirot ʿOlat HaShabbat[d]," DJD 11. 253-92 (+ pl. XX).

4Q404 4QShirShabb[e]
Newsom, "404. 4QShirot ʿOlat HaShabbat[e]," DJD 11. 293-305 (+ pl. XXI).

4Q405 4QShirShabb[f]
Newsom, "405. 4QShirot ʿOlat HaShabbat[f]," DJD 11. 307-93 (+ pls. XXII-XXX).

4Q406 4QShirShabb[g]
Newsom, "406. 4QShirot ʿOlat HaShabbat[g]," DJD 11. 395-98 (+ pl. XXXI).

4Q407 4QShirShabb[h]

Newsom, "407. 4QShirot ʿOlat HaShabbat[h]," DJD 11. 399-401 (+ pl. XXXI).

4Q408 4QapocrMoses[c]

Steudel, A., "408. 4QApocryphon of Moses[c]?," DJD 36. 298-315 (+ pl. XXI): Another copy of 1Q29 (1QLTLF) and 4Q376 (4QapMoses[b]), as overlaps suggest in some of the 16/17 frgs. Morning and evening prayers praise God as creator.

4Q409 4QLitWA

Qimron, E., "409. 4QLiturgical Work A," DJD 29. 63-67 (+ pl. IV) The text sings praise of God on various festivals (firstfruits: new wheat, new wine, new oil, etc.).

4Q410 4QVisInterp

Steudel, "410. 4QVision and Interpretation," DJD 36. 316-19 (+ pl. XXI): The text speaks of curses, and then of a vision (using the first person singular); and then apparently gives an interpretation of it.

4Q411 4QSapHymn

Steudel, A., "411. 4QSapiential Hymn," DJD 20. 159-62 (+ pl. XIV): A small frg. that seems to praise God's wisdom in creation. The tetragrammaton occurs in several lines.

4Q412 4QSapDidWA

Steudel, "412. 4QSapiential-Didactic Work A," DJD 20. 163-67 (+ pl. XIV): The text seems to give instructions for life and behavior.

4Q413 4QDivProv

Qimron, E., "413. 4QComposition concerning Divine Providence," DJD 20. 169-71 (+ pl. XIV): The text exhorts the reader to consider how God rewards those who do what God desires.

4Q414 4QRitPurA

Eshel, E., "414. 4QRitual of Purification A," DJD 35. 135-54 (+ pls. XI-XII): This is a halakhic-liturgical text that provides an immersion ritual and prayers for persons defiled by contamination from a corpse. It seems to be related to 11QT[a] 49 vii 17-20.

4Q415 4QInstruction[a] (olim 4QSapWork[a])

Strugnell, J. and D. J. Harrington, "415. 4QInstruction[a] *(Mûsār lĕMēvîn[a])*,"

Qumran Cave 4: XXIV, Sapiential Texts, Part 2 (DJD 34; ed. J. Strugnell et al.; Oxford: Clarendon, 1999) 41-71 (+ pls. I-II): This is the first copy of an important wisdom text related to 4Q416, 4Q417, 4Q418, 4Q418a, 4Q423, and 1Q26. As a group they constitute *Mûsār lĕMēvîn,* "Instruction for a Maven/Student." See "General Introduction" (to these wisdom texts), ibid., 1-40.

4Q416 4QInstruction[b]

Strugnell-Harrington, "416. 4QInstruction[b] *(Mûsār lĕMēvîn[b]),*" DJD 34. 73-141 (+ pls. III-VII).

4Q417 4QInstruction[c]

Strugnell-Harrington, "417. 4QInstruction[c] *(Mûsār lĕMēvîn[c]),*" DJD 34. 143-210 (+ pls. VIII-XI).

4Q418 4QInstruction[d]

Strugnell-Harrington, "418. 4QInstruction[d] *(Mûsār lĕMēvîn[d]),*" DJD 34. 211-474 (+ pls. XII-XXVII).

4Q418a 4QInstruction[e]

Strugnell-Harrington, "418a. 4QInstruction[e] *(Mûsār lĕMēvîn[e]),*" DJD 34. 475-95 (+ pls. XXVIII-XXIX).

4Q418b 4QQuoPs107

Strugnell-Harrington, "418b. 4QText with Quotation from Psalm 107?," DJD 34. 497-99 (+ pl. XXIX).

4Q418c 4QInstruction[f]

Strugnell-Harrington, "418c. 4QInstruction[f] ? *(Mûsār lĕMēvîn[f]?),*" DJD 34. 501-3 (+ pl. XXIX).

4Q419 4QInstrCompA

Tanzer, S., "419. 4QInstruction-like Composition A," DJD 36. 320-32 (+ pl. XXII): This text is vaguely paraenetic, with a section depicting God sitting on a throne, who presides over human beings.

4Q420 4QWaysRight[a]

Elgvin, T., "420. 4QWays of Righteousness[a]," DJD 20. 173-82 (+ pl. XV): These frgs. are part of a sapiential writing that is composite, with a part of it dealing with sectarian organization, and another part with wisdom sayings about righteous people, and another with Temple cult.

4Q421 4QWaysRight[b]

Elgvin, "421. 4QWays of Righteousness[b]," DJD 20. 183-202 (+ pl. XVI): Another copy of same text as 4Q420, with overlaps in one frg. Cf. 4Q264a (4QHlkB).

4Q422 4QparaGenExod

Elgvin, T. and E. Tov, "422. 4QParaphrase of Genesis and Exodus[1]," DJD 13. 417-41 (+ pls. XLII-XLIII): A paraphrase of the opening chaps. of Genesis (frgs. 1-9) and Exodus (frgs. 10a-e).

4Q423 4QInstruction[g]

Elgvin, T., "423. 4QInstruction[g] *(Mûsār lĕMēvîn[g])*," DJD 34. 505-33 (+ pls. XXX-XXXI): A text related to 4Q416, 4Q417, 4Q418, 4Q418a, and 1Q26.

4Q424 4QInstrCompB

Tanzer, "424. 4QInstruction-like Composition B," DJD 36. 333-45 (+ pl. XXIII): This text is a collection of sapiential sayings about two types of human beings, those who cannot be trusted and those of valued qualities.

4Q425 4QSapDidWB

Steudel, "425. 4QSapiential-Didactic Work B," DJD 20. 203-10 (+ pl. XVII): Six frgs. of a wisdom writing similar to the Book of Proverbs.

4Q426 4QSapHymWA

Steudel, "426. 4QSapiential-Hymnic Work A," DJD 20. 211-24 (+ pl. XVIII): A sapiential writing with a prayer and didactic advice.

4Q427 4QH[a]

Schuller, E., "427. 4QHodayot[a]," DJD 29. 77-123 (+ pls. IV-VI; Foldout pl. I): These psalms are related to and often parallel those of 1QH[a], but they appear at times in a different order. See "427-432. 4QHodayot[a-e] and 4QpapHodayot[f]: Introduction," ibid., 69-75.

4Q428 4QH[b]

Schuller, "428. 4QHodayot[b]," DJD 29. 125-75 (+ pls. VII-XI; Foldout pl. II): This text has many parallels with 1QH[a] (see Table 1 on pp. 126-27).

4Q429 4QH[c]

Schuller, "429. 4QHodayot[c]," DJD 29. 177-94 (+ pls. XI-XII; Foldout pl. II): This text has many parallels with 1QH[a] (see Table 1 on p. 178).

4Q430 4QH[d]

Schuller, "430. 4QHodayot[d]," DJD 29. 195-98 (+ pl. XII): This text overlaps 1QH[a] 12:14-20.

4Q431 4QH[e]

Schuller, "431. 4QHodayot[e]," DJD 29. 199-208 (+ pl. XII; Foldout pl. III): Some overlaps with 1QH[a].

4Q432 4QpapH[f]

Schuller, "432. 4QpapHodayot[f]," DJD 29. 209-32 (+ pls. XIII-XIV; Foldout pl. III): This text has many parallels with 1QH[a] (see Table 1 on pp. 209-10).

4Q433 4QH-likeA

Schuller, "433. 4QHodayot-like Text A," DJD 29. 233-36 (+ pl. XV): There is no overlapping with other Hodayot texts from either Cave 1 or Cave 4, but the hymn has a first-person speaker.

4Q433a 4QpapH-likeB

Schuller, "433a. 4QpapHodayot-like Text B," DJD 29. 237-45 (+ pl. XV): The four frgs. are inscribed on the verso of 4Q255 (4QpapS[a]). The text is similar to other Hodayot, but it has no overlaps with any of them.

4Q434 4QBarNaf[a]

Weinfeld, M. and D. Seely, "434. 4QBarki Nafshi[a]," DJD 29. 267-86 (+ pls. XVII-XIX): 15 frgs., which begin with "Bless the Lord, O my soul"(words borrowed from Psalms 103–104), praise God for his might and deliverance from distress and destruction. See "434-438. 4QBarki Nafshi[a-e]: Introduction," ibid., 255-65.

4Q435 4QBarNaf[b]

Weinfeld-Seely, "435. 4QBarki Nafshi[b]," DJD 29. 287-93 (+ pl. XX): This copy has parallels with 4Q434, 4Q436, 4Q437.

4Q436 4QBarNaf[c]

Weinfeld-Seely, "436. 4QBarki Nafshi[c]," DJD 29. 295-305 (+ pl. XXI): The praise is addressed to God in the second-person singular, not in the third, as in some other copies.

4Q437 4QBarNaf[d]

Weinfeld-Seely, "437. 4QBarki Nafshi[d]," DJD 29. 307-25 (+ pls. XXII-XXIII): God is again praised for deliverance and addressed in the second person.

4Q438 4QBarNaf[e]

Weinfeld-Seely, "438. 4QBarki Nafshi[e]," DJD 29. 327-34 (+ pls. XXIII-XXIV): 14 poorly preserved frgs. again contain the praise of God.

4Q439 4QLamLeader

Weinfeld-Seely, "439. 4QLament by a Leader," DJD 29. 335-41 (+ pl. XXIV): A community leader laments what is happening to "the righteous ones of my people."

4Q440 4QH-likeC

Schuller, "440. 4QHodayot-like Text C," DJD 29. 247-54 (+ pl. XVI): The psalmist speaks in the first-person singular and addresses God in the second, praising Him for the creation of light and darkness with calendaric and predestinarian emphasis.

4Q440a 4QH-likeD

Lange, A., "440a. 4QHodayot-like Text D," DJD 36. 347-48 (+ pl. XXIV): This frg. was thought earlier to be 4QH[a] (4Q427) 14.

4Q440b 4QCourt

Lange, "440b. 4QFragment Mentioning a Court," DJD 36. 349-50 (+ pl. XXIV).

4Q441 4QIndThanksA

Chazon, E., "441. 4QIndividual Thanksgiving A," DJD 29. 343-44 (+ pl. XXV).

4Q442 4QIndThanksB

Chazon, "442. 4QIndividual Thanksgiving B," DJD 29. 345 (+ pl. XXV).

4Q443 4QPersPr

Chazon, "443. 4QPersonal Prayer," DJD 29. 347-66 (+ pl. XXV): 13 tiny frgs., many of which have only a few letters.

4Q444 4QIncant

Chazon, "444. 4QIncantation," DJD 29. 367-78 (+ pl. XXVI): This two-part text of four frgs. begins with a hymn similar to 4QShir[a,b] (4Q510, 4Q511) and continues with curses.

4Q445 4QLamentA

Tigchelaar, E., "445. 4QLament A," DJD 29. 379-84 (+ pl. XXVI): Eight tiny frgs of a lament about bereavement.

4Q446 4QPoetTextA

Tigchelaar, "446. 4QPoetic Text A," DJD 29. 385-88 (+ pl. XXVI): Three small frgs. resembling the Hodayot.

4Q447 4QPoetTextB

Tigchelaar, "447. 4QPoetic Text B," DJD 29. 389-90 (+ pl. XXVI).

4Q448 4QapocrPsPr

Eshel, E., H. Eshel, and A. Yardeni, "448. 4QApocryphal Psalm and Prayer," DJD 11. 403-25 (+ pl. XXXII): A skin frg. with three columns of writing, one at the top and two below it. The upper column has part of an apocryphal psalm, and the lower columns have part of petitionary prayer for King Jonathan's welfare and for that of the people of Israel. The psalm has some parallels to Syriac Ps 154:17-20, known in a Hebrew form from 11Q5 ($11QPs^a$).

4Q449 4QPrA

Chazon, "449. 4QPrayer A?," DJD 29. 391-93 (+ pl. XXVII): In three frgs. a group, speaking in the first-person plural, addresses God.

4Q450 4QPrB

Chazon, "450. 4QPrayer B?," DJD 29. 395-97 (+ pl. XXVII).

4Q451 4QPrC

Chazon, "451. 4QPrayer C," DJD 29. 399-400 (+ pl. XXVII): The frg. contains a petition addressed to God that certain people be delivered into the hands of His "beloved ones."

4Q452 4QPrD

Chazon, "452. 4QPrayer D?," DJD 29. 401 (+ pl. XXVII): Possibly a prayer of praise addressed to God.

4Q453 4QLamentB

Chazon, "453. 4QLament B," DJD 29. 403 (+ pl. XXVII): A tiny frg. with two words, hard to identify.

4Q454 4QPrE

Chazon, "454. 4QPrayer E?," DJD 29. 405-6 (+ pl. XXVII): A tiny frg. that may refer to God's righteousness.

4Q455 4QDidWC (olim 4QPr[f])

Chazon, E., "455. 4QDidactic Work C," DJD 36. 351-52 (+ pl. XXIV): A tiny frg. with three lines of an apparently sapiential text.

4Q456 4QHalleluyah

Chazon, "456. 4QHalleluyah," DJD 29. 407-8 (+ pl. XXVII): *hllw yh* occurs on each of the two tiny frgs.

4Q457a 4QCreation
4Q457b 4QEschHymn

Chazon, "457a. 4QCreation? / 457b. 4QEschatological Hymn," DJD 29. 409-19 (+ pl. XXVII): Two frgs. of a palimpsest scroll; hence the double siglum. Little survives of the first writing, and the second refers to a holy war.

4Q458 4QNarrA

Larson, E., "458. 4QNarrative A," DJD 36. 353-65 (+ pl. XXV): The fragmentary narrative mentions "one anointed with the oil of kingship," who seems to be involved in some sort of battle against the uncircumcised.

4Q459 4QNarrLeb

Larson, "459. 4QNarrative Work Mentioning Lebanon," DJD 36. 366-68 (+ pl. XXIV).

4Q460 4QNarrWPr

Larson, "460. 4QNarrative Work and Prayer," DJD 36. 369-86 (+ pl. XXVI): 10 frgs. contain words of prayer, exhortation, and admonition, somewhat similar to the Hodayot, but frgs. 5 and 7 also have a narrative reminiscent of Israel's history similar to 4QapJosh[a,b] (4Q378, 4Q379).

4Q461 4QNarrB

Larson, "461. 4QNarrative B," DJD 36. 387-93 (+ pl. XXVII): Five frgs. of a narrative that recounts some of the Egyptian bondage of the Hebrews with a petition directed to God for deliverance.

4Q462 4QNarrC

Smith, "462. 4QNarrative C," DJD 19. 195-209 (+ pl. XXVI): Seven frgs. of a narrative text describing the exile and return of Israelites and the restoration of Jerusalem.

4Q463 4QNarrD

Smith, "463. 4QNarrative D," DJD 19. 211-14 (+ pl. XXVII): The narrative quotes Lev 26:44, God's words about remembering the Hebrews in the land of exile.

4Q464 4QExpoPatr

Eshel, E. and M. Stone, "464. 4QExposition on the Patriarchs," DJD 19. 215-30 (+ pl. XXVIII): 11 frgs. seem to recount incidents in the lives of Abraham and Jacob, as well as the deluge and the sacrifice of Isaac.

4Q464a 4QNarrE

Eshel-Stone, "464a. 4QNarrative E," DJD 19. 231-32 (+ pl. XXIX): The frg. seems to refer to Exodus 1.

4Q464b 4QUnc[a]

Eshel-Stone, "464b. 4QUnclassified Fragments," DJD 19. 233-34 (+ pl. XXIX).

4Q465 4QpapSamson

Larson, "465. 4QpapText Mentioning Samson?," DJD 36. 394-95 (+ pl. XXVII): Possibly a frg. of a letter addressed to Samson.

4Q466 4QCongLord

Pike, D., "466. 4QText Mentioning the Congregation of the Lord," DJD 36. 396-97 (+ pl. XXVII).

4Q467 4QLightJacob

Pike, "467. 4QText Mentioning 'Light to Jacob,'" DJD 36. 398-400 (+ pl. XXVII).

4Q468a-d 4QUnidCa-d

Broshi, M., "468a-d. 4QUnidentified Fragments C, a-d," DJD 36. 401-5 (+ pl. XXVIII).

4Q468e 4QHistTextF

Broshi, "468e. 4QHistorical Text F," DJD 36. 406-11 (+ pl. XXVIII): This fragmentary text mentions the name *Pwtl'ys,* apparently Potlais, which may be a Hebrew form of Greek *Ptollas,* known from Josephus, *Ant.* 17.9.3 §219.

4Q468f 4QHistTextG

Lange, "468f. 4QHistorical Text G," DJD 36. 412-13 (+ pl. XXVIII): The frg. mentions "sons of Gilead."

4Q468g 4QEschWA

Lange, "468g. 4QEschatological Work A?," DJD 36. 414-15 (+ pl. XXVIII): The frg. seems to refer to a war, perhaps at the end-time.

4Q468h

Cancelled.

4Q468i 4QSectText

Lange, "468i. 4QSectarian Text?," DJD 36. 416-17 (+ pl. XXIX): The frg. possibly is related to the founding of the community, as in CD 1; but other identifications have been suggested.

4Q468j 4QUnc[b]

Lange, "468j. 4QpapUnclassified Fragments," DJD 36. 418-19 (+ pl. XXIX).

4Q468k 4QHymB

Ernst, D. and A. Lange, "468k. 4QHymnic Text B?," DJD 36. 420-21 (+ pl. XXIX).

4Q468l 4QFrgQoh

Ernst-Lange, "468l. 4QFragment Mentioning Qoh 1:8-9," DJD 36. 422 (+ pl. XXIX).

4Q468m-bb 4QUnidD

Ernst-Lange, "468m-bb. 4QUnidentified Fragments D," DJD 36. 423-32 (+ pls. XXIX-XXX).

4Q468cc-dd 4QUnidCcc-dd

Tigchelaar, "468cc-dd. 4QUnidentified Fragments C, cc-dd," DJD 28. 219-22 (+ pl. LI).

4Q469 4QNarrI

Larson, "469. 4QNarrative I," DJD 36. 433-38 (+ pl. XXX): This text seems related to 4Q439 (4QLamLeader).

4Q470 4QZedekiah

Larson, E., L. Schiffman, and J. Strugnell, "470. 4QText Mentioning Zedekiah," DJD 19. 235-44 (+ pl. XXIX): The text seems to mention a covenant made between God and Zedekiah and also the events leading up to the establishment of the pact on Mt. Sinai.

4Q471 4QM-likeB

Eshel, E. and H. Eshel, "471. 4QWar Scroll-like Text B," DJD 36. 439-45 (+ pl. XXX): This text seems related to 1QM 2 and 4QM[d].

4Q471a 4QPolText

Eshel, E., and M. Kister, "471a. 4QPolemical Text," DJD 36. 446-49 (+ pl. XXXI): The frg. addresses the author's opponents in the second-person plural, accusing them of violating the covenant with God and transgressing His commandments.

4Q471b 4QSelfGH[a]

Eshel, E., "471b. 4QSelf-Glorification Hymn (= 4QH[e] frg. 1?)," DJD 29. 421-32 (+ pl. XXVIII): This text is a re-edition of what was called originally 4QM[a] (4Q491) frg. 11, col. i; it is also related to 4QH[a] (4Q427) 7 i and 12; 1QM 25-26; and possibly also 4QH[e] (4Q431) 1. See 4Q491c.

4Q471c 4QPrGodIsr

Eshel, "471c. 4QPrayer Concerning God and Israel," DJD 29. 433-35 (+ pl. XXVIII). A fragmentary text possibly related to 4QPrEnosh (4Q369).

4Q472 4QEschWB

Elgvin, T., "472. 4QEschatological Work B," DJD 36. 450-55 (+ pl. XXXI): Two frgs. of a text that speaks of a royal court, but it is difficult to determine whether it is heavenly or earthly. It could be a description of an end-time renewal of Israel, with God bringing redemption, peace, and joy to His chosen people.

4Q472a 4QHlkC

Elgvin, T., "472a. 4QHalakha C," DJD 35. 155-56 (+ pl. XII): A tiny frg. difficult to read and interpret.

4Q473 4QTwoWays

Elgvin, T., "473. 4QThe Two Ways," DJD 22. 289-94 (+ pl. XXVI): Two frgs. imitating admonitions from Deuteronomy in a style similar to 1QDM (1Q22)

4Q474 4QRachJos

Elgvin, "474. 4QText Concerning Rachel and Joseph," DJD 36. 456-63 (+ pl. XXXI): The fragmentary text may refer to Gen 30:24; 37:3; 48:22.

4Q475 4QRenewEarth

Elgvin, "475. 4QRenewed Earth," DJD 36. 464-73 (+ pl. XXXI): The frg. seems to tell of God's judgment of the earth and its subsequent peaceful renewal.

4Q476 4QLitWB

Elgvin, T., "476. 4QLiturgical Work B," DJD 29. 437-43 (+ pl. XXVIII): Three frgs. preserve the remnants of a hymnic or liturgical text that link the Sabbath to heavenly realms like the Songs of the Sabbath Sacrifice.

4Q476a 4QLitWC

Elgvin, "476a. 4QLiturgical Work C," DJD 29. 445-46 (+ pl. VIII): The text describes the liturgical worship of the heavenly temple.

4Q477 4QRebukes

Eshel, E., "477. 4QRebukes Reported by the Overseer," DJD 36. 474-83 (+ pl. XXXII): Five frgs. of this text list the community members (some named) who were rebuked by the Overseer for committing certain sinful deeds; see Lev 19:17 for the justification of the rebukes.

4Q478 4QpapFest

Larson, E. and L. Schiffman, "478. 4QpapFragment Mentioning Festivals," DJD 22. 295-96 (+ pl. XXVI).

4Q479 4QDescDavid

Larson-Schiffman, "479. 4QText Mentioning Descendants of David," DJD 22. 297-99 (+ pl. XXVII).

4Q480 4QNarrF

Larson-Schiffman, "480. 4QNarrative F," DJD 22. 301-2 (+ pl. XXVII).

4Q481 4QMixedKinds

Larson-Schiffman, "481. 4QText Mentioning Mixed Kinds," DJD 22. 303-4 (+ pl. XXVII): Two frgs. difficult to interpret.

4Q481a 4QapocrElisha

Trebolle Barrera, J., "481a. 4QApocryphe d'Élisée," DJD 22. 305-9 (+ pl. XXX): Three frgs. tell of Elisha in a manner similar to 2 Kgs 2:14-16.

4Q481b 4QNarrG

Larson-Schiffman, "481b. 4QNarrative G," DJD 22. 311-12 (+ pl. XXVIII).

4Q481c 4QPrMercy

Larson-Schiffman, "481c. 4QPrayer for Mercy," DJD 22. 313-14 (+ pl. XXVIII).

4Q481d 4QFrgRedInk

Larson-Schiffman, "481d. 4QFragments with Red Ink," DJD 22. 315-19 (+ pl. XXIX): Eight frgs. (seven transcribed), some of which have words written in red ink.

4Q481e 4QNarrH

Larson-Schiffman, "481e. 4QNarrative H," DJD 22. 321-22 (+ pl. XXIX).

4Q482 4QpapJub[i]

Baillet, M., "482. Livre des Jubilés (?)," *Qumrân Grotte 4: III (4Q482-4Q520)* (DJD 7; ed. M. Baillet; Oxford: Clarendon, 1982) 1-2 (+ pl. I): *Jub.* 13:29; 36:9? The first frg. is rather a quotation of Gen 14:22-24, and the other is not of *Jubilees,* according to J. C. VanderKam, "The Jubilees Fragments from Qumran Cave 4" (cited above under 4Q216), 642 n. 27.

4Q483 4QpapGen[o] (olim 4QpapJub[j])

Baillet, "483. Genèse ou Livre des Jubilés (?)," DJD 7. 2 (+ pl. I): *Jub.* 2:14? (more likely Gen 1:28).

4Q484 4QpapTJud

Baillet, "484. Testament de Juda (?)," DJD 7. 3 (+ pl. I): *T. Judah* 25:1-2 (7).

4Q485 4QpapProph

Baillet, "485. Texte prophétique ou sapientiel," DJD 7. 4 (+ pl. II): Five tiny papyrus frgs.; for the reading of frg. 1, see now J. Baumgarten, *JJS* 43 (1992) 98 n. 8.

4Q486 4QpapSap[a]

Baillet, "486. Ouvrage sapientiel (?)," DJD 7. 4-5 (+ pl. I).

4Q487 4QpapSap[b]

Baillet, "487. Ouvrage sapientiel (?)," DJD 7. 5-10 (+ pl. III-IV).

4Q488 4QpapApocr ar

Baillet, "488. Un apocryphe en araméen," DJD 7. 10 (+ pl. II).

4Q489 4QpapApoc ar

Baillet, "489. Un apocalyptique en araméen," DJD 7. 10-11 (+ pl. II).

4Q490 4QpapFrgs ar

Baillet, "490. Groupe de fragments à rapprocher du précédent (?)," DJD 7. 11 (+ pl. II).

4Q491 4QM[a]

Baillet, "491. La règle de la guerre (premier exemplaire: M[a])," DJD 7. 12-44 (+ pls. V-VI): Parallel to 1QM 2:1-6; 5:16-17; 7:3-7, 10-12; 9:17-18; 12:1; 14:4-18; 16:3-14; 17:10-15.

4Q491c 4QSelfGH[b]

Frgs. 11-12 of 4QM[a] (4Q491); see 4Q471b above.

4Q492 4QM[b]

Baillet, "492. La règle de la guerre (deuxième exemplaire: M[b])," DJD 7. 45-49 (+ pl. VII): Parallel to 1QM 19:1-8; 1Q33 2.

4Q493 4QM[c]

Baillet, "493. La règle de la guerre (troisième exemplaire: M[c])," DJD 7. 49-53 (+ pl. VIII): No parallel to 1QM.

4Q494 4QM[d]

Baillet, "494. La règle de la guerre (quatrième exemplaire: M[d])," DJD 7. 53-54 (+ pl. VIII): Parallel to 1QM 2:1-3.

4Q495 4QM[e]

Baillet, "495. La règle de la guerre (cinquième exemplaire: M[e])," DJD 7. 54-56 (+ pl. VIII): Parallel to 1QM 10:9-10; 13:9-12.

4Q496 4QpapM[f]

Baillet, "496. La règle de la guerre (sixième exemplaire: M[f])," DJD 7. 56-68 (+ pls. X, XII, XIV, XVI, XVIII, XXIV): Parallel to 1QM 1:4-9, 11-17; 2:5-6, 9-12, 13-14, 17; 3:1-2?, 6-7?, 9-11, 13-15; 4:1-2 (= Verso of 4Q505 and 4Q509).

4Q497 4QpapM-likeA (olim 4QpapM[g])

Baillet, "497. Texte ayant quelque rapport avec la règle de la guerre (?)," DJD 7. 69-72 (+ pl. XXVI): A text found on the verso of 4Q499.

4Q498 4QpapHymSap

Baillet, "498. Fragments hymniques ou sapientiels (?)," DJD 7. 73-74 (+ pl. XXVII): 15 tiny frgs.

4Q499 4QpapHymPr

Baillet, "499. Hymnes ou prières," DJD 7. 74-77 (+ pl. XXV): The text is found on the recto of 4Q497.

4Q500 4QpapBened

Baillet, "500. Bénédiction," DJD 7. 78-79 (+ pl. XXVII).

4Q501 4QapocrLam[b]

Baillet, "501. Lamentation," DJD 7. 79-80 (+ pl. XXVIII).

4Q502 4QpapRitMar

Baillet, "502. Rituel de mariage," DJD 7. 81-105 (+ pl. XXIX-XXXIV): Part of the text seems to be dependent on the Book of Tobit.

4Q503 4QpapPrQuot

Baillet, "503. Prières quotidiennes," DJD 7. 105-36 (+ pls. XXXV, XXXVII, XXXIX, XLI, XLIII, XLV, XLVII): The times for the daily prayers are indicated by rising and setting of the sun, and the calendar involved seems to be that of *1 Enoch* 73-75, 78-79 (= Recto of 4Q512).

4Q504 4QDibHam[a]

Baillet, "504. Paroles des luminaires (premier exemplaire: DibHam[a])," DJD 7. 137-68 (+ pls. XLIX-LIII): A liturgical text that distinguishes the days of the week (e.g., Wednesday as the Covenant Day, Saturday as the Day of Praise). The title of the text is given on the verso of frg. 8: *dibrê hammĕʾōrôt,* "words of the luminaries."

4Q505 4QDibHam[b]

Baillet, "505. Paroles des luminaires (deuxième exemplaire: DibHam[b])," DJD 7. 168-70 (+ pl. XXIII).

4Q506 4QDibHam[c]

Baillet, "506. Paroles des luminaires (troisième exemplaire: DibHam[c])," DJD 7. 170-75 (+ pls. XVIII, XX, XXIV).

4Q507 4QPrFêtes[a]

Baillet, "507. Prières pour les fêtes (premier exemplaire: PrFêtes[a])," DJD 7. 175-77 (+ pl. XXVIII): Feast-day prayers that resemble the prayers of 1Q34, 1Q34bis.

4Q508 4QPrFêtes[b]

Baillet, "508. Prières pour les fêtes (deuxième exemplaire: PrFêtes[b])," DJD 7. 177-84 (+ pl. LIV).

4Q509 4QpapPrFêtes[c]

Baillet, "509. Prières pour les fêtes (troisième exemplaire: PrFêtes[c])," DJD 7. 184-215 (+ pls. IX, XI, XIII, XV, XVII, XIX, XXI, XXII). May be the same as 1Q34 (= Recto of 4Q496 and 4Q506).

4Q510 4QShir[a]

Baillet, "510. Cantiques du Sage (premier exemplaire: Shir[a])," DJD 7. 215-19 (+ pl. LV): A set of canticles composed by a *maśkîl,* "sage, instructor," in order to praise God and be delivered from the influence of evil spirits. Angels and demons are mentioned in this text.

4Q511 4QShir[b]

Baillet, "511. Cantiques du Sage (deuxième exemplaire: Shir[b])," DJD 7. 219-62 (+ pls. LVI-LXXI).

4Q512 4QpapRitPur

Baillet, "512. Rituel de purification," DJD 7. 262-86 (+ pl. XXXVI, XXXVIII, XL, XLII, XLIV, XLVI, XLVIII): A text that is difficult to interpret; it seems to mention sexual impurities (= Verso of 4Q503).

4Q513 4QOrd[b]

Baillet, "513. Ordonnances (deuxième exemplaire: Ord[b])," DJD 7. 287-95 (+ pls. LXXII-LXXIII): A text that sets out regulations for tithes, eating kinds of food, defilement by oil, and the year of release. It is related to 4Q159.

4Q514 4QOrd[c]

Baillet, "514. Ordonnances (troisième exemplaire: Ord[c]) (?)," DJD 7. 295-98 (+ pl. LXXIV).

4Q515 4QpapUnc[c]

Baillet, "515. Groupe en petite écriture," DJD 7. 299-300 (+ pl. LXXV). Some frgs. may be part of 4QpIsa[c] (4Q163).

4Q516 4QpapUnid[a]

Baillet, "516. Fragments divers," DJD 7. 300 (+ pl. LXXV).

4Q517 4QpapUnc[d]

Baillet, "517. Fragments non classés inscrits sur une face," DJD 7. 301-4 (+ pls. LXXVI-LXXVII).

4Q518 4QpapUnc[e]

Baillet, "518. Fragments non classés inscrits sur les deux faces. Recto," DJD 7. 304-6 (+ pl. LXXVIII).

4Q519 4QpapUnc[f]

Baillet, "519. Fragments non classés inscrits sur les deux faces. Verso," DJD 7. 307-9 (+ pl. LXXIX).

4Q520 4QpapUnc[g]

Baillet, "520. Fragments non classés inscrits seulement au Verso," DJD 7. 309-12 (+ pl. LXXX).

4Q521 4QApocMess

Puech, E., "521. 4QApocalypse messianique," *Qumrân Grotte 4: XVIII, Textes hébreux (4Q521-4Q528, 4Q576-4Q579)* (DJD 25; ed. E. Puech; Oxford: Clarendon, 1998) 1-38 (+ pl. I-III): There is nothing apocalyptic about this text, which is rather an exhortation that mentions the eschatological benefits accompanying the coming of God's Messiah *(Měšîḥô).*

4Q522 4QprophJosh[c]

Puech, "522. 4QProphétie de Josué (4QapocrJosué[c]?)," DJD 25. 39-74 (+ pls. IV-V): The content of this text is debated. It seems to record memoirs of Joshua, but it also mentions Jesse, David, and his son, along with the tabernacle and Temple of Jerusalem. Frgs. 22-25 quote a form of Ps 122:1-9, a psalm that hails Jerusalem as the goal of pilgrims. See Skehan-Ulrich-Flint, "522. Psalm 122 in '4QProphecy of Joshua,'" DJD 16. 169-70 (+ pl. IV in DJD 25).

4Q523 4QJonathan

Puech, "523. 4QJonathan," DJD 25. 75-83 (+ pl. VI): Frgs. 1-2 mention *Yěhônātan,* who is probably the son of Mattathias, founder of the Maccabees and the Hasmonean dynasty, and who reigned as High Priest (160-43 B.C.; see 1 Macc 9:23–12:53).

4Q524 4QTemple[b]

Puech, "524. 4QRouleau du Temple," DJD 25. 85-114 (+ pls. VII-VIII; fig. 1-2): Perhaps the oldest copy of the Temple text published by Yadin, 11QT[a]. Parallels to 11QT[a] (11Q19): 35:7; 50:17-21; 54:4(5); 55:11-13; 58:10-13; 59:17–60:6; 64:6-11; 66:8-17; 69:6-7?; + 16 frgs. without parallels.

4Q525 4QBeat

Puech, "525. 4QBéatitudes," DJD 25. 115-78 (+ pls. IX-XIII): A sapiential text of 50 frgs. that contains in frg. 2 ii 1-13 a collection of beatitudes, whence the title; but other frgs. are quite different. The collection can be compared to Sir 14:20 and Matt 5:3-10. Puech believes that the collection numbered originally 8 + 1 beatitudes, but that is far from certain. Cf. E. Tigchelaar, *RevQ* 21 (2003-4) 477-85.

4Q526 4QTestament[a]

Puech, "526. 4QTestament (?)," DJD 25. 179-81 (+ pl. XIV).

4Q527 4QLitWD

Puech, "527. 4QOuvrage liturgique (?) D," DJD 25. 183-85 (+ pl. XIV).

4Q528 4QHymSapB

Puech, "528. 4QOuvrage hymnique ou sapientiel B," DJD 25. 187-90 (+ pl. XIV).

4Q529 4QWordsMich ar

Puech, E., "529. 4QParoles de Michel ar," *Qumrân Grotte 4: XXII, Textes araméens, première partie: 4Q529-549* (DJD 31; ed. E. Puech; Oxford: Clarendon, 2001) 1-8 (+ pl. I): The text recounts a vision of Enoch transported to the seventh heaven, where he hears what the archangel Michael says to other angels. The words tell of phases of human history, division of the earth, building of a city in the name of God, divine mercy, etc.

4Q530 4QEnGiants[b] ar

Puech, "530. 4QLivre des Géants[b] ar," DJD 31. 9-47 (+ pls. I-II): This and the following three texts are related to 4QEnGiants[a] (4Q203). See "530-533, 203 1. 4QLivre des Géants[b-e] ar: Introduction," ibid., 9-16.

4Q531 4QEnGiants[c] ar

Puech, "531. 4QLivre des Géants[c] ar," DJD 31. 49-94 (+ pls. III-V).

4Q532 4QEnGiants[d] ar

Puech, "532. 4QLivre des Géants[d] ar," DJD 31. 95-104 (+ pl. VI).

4Q533 4QEnGiants[e] ar

Puech, "533. 4QLivre des Géants[e] ar," DJD 31. 105-15 (+ pl. VI): Sometimes wrongly called 4QpsEnoch ar or 4Q556.

4Q534 4QBirthNoah[a] ar (olim 4QMess ar; 4QElectofGod)

Puech, "534. 4QNaissance de Noé[a] ar," DJD 31. 129-52 (+ pls. VII-IX): This text has had a history of different identifications, because of the piece-meal mode of publication and the tendency to read it as a Christian messianic text. It is still not easy to interpret. See "534-536. 4QNaissance de Noé[a-c] ar: Introduction," ibid., 117-27.

4Q535 4QBirthNoah[b] ar (olim 4QAramaicN)

Puech, "535. 4QNaissance de Noé[b] ar," DJD 31. 153-59 (+ pl. X).

4Q536 4QBirthNoah[c] ar (olim 4QAramaicC)

Puech, "536. 4QNaissance de Noé[c] ar," DJD 31. 161-70 (+ pl. X).

4Q537 4QTJacob ar (olim 4QAJa, 4QTJa)

Puech, "537. 4QTestament de Jacob? ar (4QTJa? ar)," DJD 31. 171-90 (+ pl. XI): The text describes Jacob's dream at Bethel and his decision to build an altar there, as well as other visions, revelations, and exhortations.

4Q538 4QTJudah ar (olim 4QAJu)

Puech, "538. 4QTestament de Juda ar," DJD 31. 191-99 (+ pl. XII): The text recounts the second journey of the sons of Jacob to Egypt (as in Gen 44:1–45:10; *Jub.* 42:25–43:18), when Joseph becomes known to them, especially the role that Judah played (Gen 44:18). The text is also related to the *T. Judah* (20:1; 25:1-2) in the *Testaments of the Twelve Patriarchs.* Cf. 3Q7 (3QTJudah).

4Q539 4QTJoseph ar (olim 4QAJo)

Puech, "539. 4QTestament de Joseph ar," DJD 31. 201-11 (+ pl. XII): This text was used by the author of the Greek *T. Joseph* (14-17) of the *Testaments of the Twelve Patriarchs.*

4Q540 4QapocrLevi[a] ar (olim 4QAhAbis)

Puech, "540. 4QApocryphe de Lévi[a]? ar," DJD 31. 217-23 (+ pl. XII): The text seems to describe the distress that is to come upon the tribe of Levi and the sanctuary; a "little one" will be especially affected for 52 weeks/years(?). See "4Q540-541. 4QApocryphe de Lévi[a-b]? ar: Introduction," ibid., 213-16.

4Q541 4QapocrLevi[b] ar (olim 4QAhA)

Puech, "541. 4QApocryphe de Lévi[b]? ar," DJD 31. 225-56 (+ pls. XIII-XIV). This text seems to have some relationship to 4QLevi[a-f] (4Q213-4Q214b).

4Q542 4QTQahat ar

Puech, "542. 4QTestament de Qahat ar," DJD 31. 257-82 (+ pl. XV): This text contains the farewell address of Kohath to his son ʿAmram and his progeny and describes especially the lot of the godless in a mode similar to Dan 12:2; *1 Enoch* 22.

4Q543 4QVisAmram[a] ar

Puech, "543. 4QVisions de ʿAmram[a] ar," DJD 31. 289-318 (+ pls. XVI-XVII): The title of this text is preserved in the overlaps of several frgs. of the various copies: "Copy of the book of the words of visions of Amram, son of Kohath, son of Levi. . . ." The whole is a sort of Testament or Farewell Address that is at once didactic and hortatory. See further "4Q543-4Q549. 4QVisions de ʿAmram[a-g] ar: Introduction," ibid., 283-88.

4Q544 4QVisAmram[b] ar

Puech, "544. 4QVisions de ʿAmram[b] ar," DJD 31. 319-29 (+ pl. XVIII).

4Q545 4QVisAmram[c] ar

Puech, "545. 4QVisions de ʿAmram[c] ar," DJD 31. 331-49 (+ pl. XIX).

4Q546 4QVisAmram[d] ar

Puech, "546. 4QVisions de ʿAmram[d] ar," DJD 31. 351-74 (+ pl. XX).

4Q547 4QVisAmram[e] ar

Puech, "547. 4QVisions de ʿAmram[e] ar," DJD 31. 375-90 (+ pl. XXI).

4Q548 4QVisAmram[f] ar

Puech, "548. 4QVisions de ʿAmram[f] ar," DJD 31. 391-98 (+ pl. XXII).

4Q549 4QVisAmram[g] ar

Puech, "549. 4QVisions de ʿAmram[g] (?) ar," DJD 31. 399-405 (+ pl. XXII).

4Q550-575; 4Q580-582

Texts 4Q550-4Q575 and 4Q580-4Q582 have not yet been published by E. Puech in the DJD series; they are to appear in the forthcoming volume 37. The numbers and names have been revealed in DJD 39. 73-75, where one can find also the relevant numbers of PAM photographs. In lieu of the awaited DJD page numbers, references are given below to places where one can find some of the texts and translations; but a quick comparison shows how different these tentative publications sometimes are.

4Q550 4QProtoEsth[a] ar
Puech, DJD 37; cf. *DSSSE,* 1096-97; *DSSR,* 6. 6-7.

4Q550a 4QProtoEsth[b] ar
Puech, DJD 37; *DSSSE,* 1098-99; *DSSR,* 6. 8-9.

4Q550b 4QProtoEsth[c] ar
Puech, DJD 37; *DSSSE,* 1098-99; *DSSR,* 6. 8-9.

4Q550c 4QProtoEsth[d] ar
Puech, DJD 37; *DSSSE,* 1098-1101; *DSSR,* 6. 8-11.

4Q550d 4QProtoEsth[e] ar
Puech, DJD 37; *DSSSE,* 1100-1101; *DSSR,* 6. 10-11.

4Q550e 4QProtoEsth[f] ar
Puech, DJD 37; *DSSSE,* 1102-3; *DSSR,* 6. 12-13.

4Q551 4QDanSuz ar
Puech, DJD 37; *DSSSE,* 1102-3; *DSSR,* 6. 334-35.

4Q552 4QFourKgdms[a] ar
Puech, DJD 37; *DSSSE,* 1102-5; *DSSR,* 6. 76-79.

4Q553 4QFourKgdms[b] ar
Puech, DJD 37; *DSSSE,* 1104-7; *DSSR,* 6. 78-81.

4Q554 4QNJ[a] ar
Puech, DJD 37; *DSSSE,* 1106-11; *DSSR,* 6. 44-51.

4Q554a 4QNJ[b] ar
DSSSE, 1110-13; *DSSR*, 6. 50-51.

4Q555 4QNJ[c] ar
Puech, DJD 37; *DSSSE*, 1112-13; *DSSR*, 6. 50-53.

4Q556 4QVision[a] ar
Puech, DJD 37; *DSSR*, 6. 136-41. N.B. The number 4Q556 has been used at times for 4QEnGiants[e] ar (*DSSSE*, 1112-13; Stuckenbruck, *The Book of Giants from Qumran*, 185-91), but that text is now 4Q533 (see Puech in DJD 31. 105).

4Q557 4QVision[c] ar
Puech, DJD 37; *DSSSE*, 1112-13; *DSSR*, 6. 140-43.

4Q558 4QpapVision[b]
Puech, DJD 37; *DSSSE*, 1114-15; *DSSR*, 6. 142-53.

4Q559 4QpapBibChron ar
Puech, DJD 37; *DSSSE*, 1114-15; *DSSR*, 2. 136-39.

4Q560 4QExorcism ar
Puech, DJD 37; *DSSSE*, 1116-17; *DSSR*, 6. 226-27.

4Q561 4QPhysHor ar
Puech, DJD 37; *DSSSE*, 1116-19; *DSSR*, 6. 228-31. See S. Holst and J. Høgenhaven, "Physiognomy and Eschatology: Some More Fragments of 4Q561," *JJS* 57 (2006) 26-43. Tentatively = frgs. 9-11.

4Q562 4QUnidA ar
Puech, DJD 37; *DSSSE*, 1118-19.

4Q563 4QUnidB ar
Puech, DJD 37.

4Q564 4QUnidC ar
Puech, DJD 37; *DSSSE*, 1118-19.

4Q565 4QUnidD ar
Puech, DJD 37.

4Q566 4QUnidE ar
Puech, DJD 37; *DSSSE*, 1118-21.

4Q567 4QUnidF ar
Puech, DJD 37; *DSSSE*, 1120-21.

4Q568 4QUnidG ar
Puech, DJD 37; *DSSSE*, 1120-21.

4Q569 4QProv ar
Puech, DJD 37; *DSSSE*, 1120-21; *DSSR*, 6. 334-37; cf. Puech, "Morceaux de sagesse populaire en araméen: *4QProverbes araméens (= 4Q569)*," *RevQ* 21 (2003-4) 379-86.

4Q570 4QUnidH ar
Puech, DJD 37.

4Q571 4QUnidI ar
Puech, DJD 37; *DSSSE*, 1122-23.

4Q572 4QUnidJ ar
Puech, DJD 37; *DSSSE*, 1122-23.

4Q573 4QUnidK ar
Puech, DJD 37; *DSSSE*, 1122-23.

4Q574 4QUnidL ar
Puech, DJD 37.

4Q575 4QUnidM ar
Puech, DJD 37.

4Q576 4QGen^{n} (olim part of 4Q524)
Puech, "576. 4QGenèse^{n}," DJD 25. 191-93 (+ pl. XV): Gen 34:7-10; 50:3. Cf. Puech, *RevQ* 16 (1993-95) 637-40.

4Q577 4QDeluge
Puech, "577. 4QTexte mentionnant le Déluge," DJD 25. 195-203 (+ pl. XV); *DSSSE*, 1124-25; *DSSR*, 3. 578-81.

4Q578 4QHistText B
Puech, "578. 4QComposition historique B," DJD 25. 205-8 (+ pl. XV): A tiny frg. mentioning *ptlmys*, each time partly restored: "Ptolemy" or "Ptolemais"; *DSSSE*, 1124-25; *DSSR*, 6. 336-37.

4Q579 4QHymW

Puech, "579. 4QOuvrage hymnique (?)," DJD 25. 209-11 (+ pl. XV); *DSSSE*, 1126-27; *DSSR*, 6. 336-37.

4Q580 4QUnidN ar

Puech, DJD 37.

4Q581 4QTestament[b] ar

Puech, DJD 37; *DSSR*, 6. 336-39.

4Q582 4QUnidO ar

Puech, DJD 37.

Qumran Cave 4 Unidentified Fragments

A stout volume in the DJD series finally publishes the thousands of tiny frgs. that belong to many of the texts fitted together in the giant jigsaw puzzle that the frgs. of Cave 4 created. See D. M. Pike and A. C. Skinner et al., *Qumran Cave 4: XXIII, Unidentified Fragments* (DJD 33; Oxford: Clarendon, 2001). Although many unidentified and unclassified frgs. have been published already in their proper places, when it was certain that they belonged to various 4Q texts, the frgs. in this volume from Cave 4 are published now for the first time. Here there are not only the plates (I-XLI) that picture the frgs., but also a discussion of them (pp. 11-317). They are ordered according to the plates that preserve them with the PAM number (i.e., the Palestine Archaeological Museum, where they are housed and were first photographed [today the Rockefeller Museum]). For instance, the first is "PAM 43.660," discussed on pp. 11-12 (with pl. I). No detailed listing of these frgs. is made here.

Attempts are being made to identify some of them, however:

Tigchelaar, E., "On the Unidentified Fragments of *DJD* XXXIII and PAM 43.680: A New Manuscript of *4QNarrative and Poetic Composition*, and Fragments of *4Q13*, *4Q269*, *4Q525* and *4QSb* (?)," *RevQ* 21 (2003-4) 477-85.

e. Caves 5-10

5Q1-25, 6Q1-31, 7Q1-19, 8Q1-5, 9Q1 (pap), 10Q1 (ostr)

Baillet, M., J. T. Milik, and R. de Vaux, *Les 'Petites Grottes' de Qumrân: Exploration de la falaise, Les grottes 2Q, 3Q, 5Q, 6Q, 7Q à 10Q; Le rouleau de cuivre* (DJD 3; Oxford: Clarendon, 1962). Two parts: 1. Textes; 2. Planches.

Detailed Listing of 5Q1-25 in DJD 3

5Q1 5QDeut
Milik, J. T., "1. Deutéronome," 169-71 (+ pl. XXXVI): Deut 7:15-24; 8:5–9:2.

5Q2 5QKgs
Milik, "2. I Rois," 171-72 (+ pl. XXXVI): 1 Kgs 1:1, 16-17, 27-37.

5Q3 5QIsa
Milik, "3. Isaïe," 173 (+ pl. XXXVI): Isa 40:16, 18-19.

5Q4 5QAmos
Milik, "4. Amos," 173-74 (+ pl. XXXVI): Amos 1:3-5; 1:2-3; + seven frgs.

5Q5 5QPs
Milik, "5. Psaume 119," 174 (+ pl. XXXVII): Ps 119:99-101, 104, 113-20, 138-42.

5Q6 5QLam^{a}
Milik, "6. Lamentations (premier exemplaire)," 174-77 (+ pls. XXXVII-XXXVIII): Lam 4:5-8, 11-15, 15-16, 19-20, 20-22; 5:1-3, 4-12, 12-13, 16-17; + 11? frgs.

5Q7 5QLam^{b}
Milik, "7. Lamentations (second exemplaire)," 177-78 (+ pl. XXXVIII): Lam 4:17-20.

5Q8 5Qphyl
Milik, "8. Phylactère," 178 (+ pl. XXXVIII): Phylactery in its unopened case.

5Q9 5QToponyms
Milik, "9. Ouvrage avec toponymes," 179-80 (+ pl. XXXVIII): Seven frgs. with names of places.

5Q10 5QapocrMal
Milik, "10. Écrits avec citations de Malachie," 180 (+ pl. XXXVIII): Apocryphon of Malachi (?); cites Mal 1:13-14. Cf. J. Carmignac, "Vestiges d'un pesher de Malachie," *RevQ* 4 (1963-64) 97-100.

5Q11 5QS
Milik, "11. Règle de la communauté," 180-81 (+ pl. XXXVIII): *Serek hay-Yaḥad* (= 1QS 2:4-7, 12-14?).

5Q12 5QD

Milik, "12. Document de Damas," 181 (+ pl. XXXVIII): Damascus Document (= CD 9:7-10).

5Q13 5QRègle

Milik, "13. Une règle de la secte," 181-83 (+ pls. XXXIX-XL): Frgs. related to 1QS, but not identical with it or with CD. Compare frg. 4 with 1QS 3:4-5; 2:19.

5Q14 5QCurses

Milik, "14. Écrit contenant des malédictions," 183-84 (+ pl. XL): Liturgical composition with curses.

5Q15 5QNJ ar

Milik, "15. Description de la Jérusalem nouvelle," 184-93 (+ pls. XL-XLI): Description of the New Jerusalem (includes readings from 4QNJ and 11QNJ). Cf. J. Licht, "An Ideal Town Plan from Qumran — The Description of the New Jerusalem," *IEJ* 29 (1979) 45-59; Milik, *BE*, 198; *ATTM*, 214-22.

5Q16-24 5QUnid

Milik, "16-24. Groupes non caractérisés," 193-96 (+ pls. XLI-XLII): Tiny, unidentified frgs.; cf. *ATTM*, 271-72 (on 5Q24 ar).

5Q25 5QUnc

Milik, "25. Fragments non classifiés," 196-97 (+ pl. XLII).

Detailed Listing of 6Q1-31 in DJD 3

6Q1 6QpaleoGen

Baillet, M., "1. Genèse en écriture paléo-hébraïque," 105-6 (+ pl. XX): Gen 6:13-21.

6Q2 6QpaleoLev

Baillet, "2. Lévitique en écriture paléo-hébraïque," 106 (+ pl. XX): Lev 8:12-13.

6Q3 pap6QDeut

Baillet, "3. Deutéronome (?)," 106-7 (+ pl. XX): Possibly Deut 26:19.

6Q4 pap6QKgs

Baillet, "4. Livre des Rois," 107-12 (+ pls. XX-XXII): 1 Kgs 3:12-14; 12:28-31; 22:28-31; 2 Kgs 5:26; 6:32; 7:8-10, 20; 8:1-5; 9:1-2; 10:19-21; + 77 isolated frgs.

6Q5 pap6QPs

Baillet, "5. Psaume 78 (?)," 112 (+ pl. XXIII): Ps 78:36-37 (?).

6Q6 6QCant

Baillet, "6. Cantique des cantiques," 112-14 (+ pl. XXIII): Cant 1:1-6, 6-7.

6Q7 pap6QDan

Baillet, "7. Daniel," 114-16 (+ pl. XXIII): Dan 8:20-21?; 10:8-16; 11:33-36, 38; 8:16-17?; + four? frgs.

6Q8 pap6QEnGiants ar (olim pap6QapGen)

Baillet, "8. Un apocryphe de la Genèse," 116-19 (+ pl. XXIV): Frg. 1 is now part of the Enochic "Book of Giants" on papyrus; see Milik, *BE*, 300-301, 309. See the re-edition of 33 frgs. by L. Stuckenbruck, "8. 6QpapGiants ar (Re-edition)," DJD 36. 76-94 (with the same pl. as above). Cf. *ATTM*, 258-68.

6Q9 pap6QapocrSam/Kgs

Baillet, "9. Un apocryphe de Samuel-Rois," 119-23 (+ pls. XXIV-XXV): 72 tiny frgs. of a Samuel-Kings Apocryphon written on papyrus.

6Q10 pap6QProph

Baillet, "10. Une prophétie," 123-25 (+ pl. XXVI): 26 Hebrew frgs. of a prophetic text on papyrus.

6Q11 6QAllegory

Baillet, "11. Allégorie de la vigne," 125-26 (+ pl. XXVI): A Hebrew frg. with an allegory mentioning a vine.

6Q12 6QapProph

Baillet, "12. Une prophétie apocryphe," 126 (+ pl. XXVI): Prophetic apocryphon.

6Q13 6QPriestProph

Baillet, "13. Prophétie sacerdotale (?)," 126-27 (+ pl. XXVI): Possibly a priestly prophecy (text may be related to Ezra-Nehemiah).

6Q14 6QApoc ar

Baillet, "14. Texte apocalyptique," 127-28 (+ pl. XXVI): Two Aramaic frgs. with an apocalyptic text; cf. *ATTM*, 268.

6Q15 6QD

Baillet, "15. Document de Damas," 128-31 (+ pl. XXVI): Damascus Document (= CD 4:19-21; 5:13-14, 18-21; 6:1-2, 20-21; 7:1; + a passage not found in CD); cf. *RB* 63 (1956) 513-23 (+ pl. II).

6Q16 pap6QBen

Baillet, "16. Bénédictions," 131-32 (+ pl. XXVII): Blessings related to 1QSb (1Q28b).

6Q17 6QCalDoc

Baillet, "17. Fragment de calendrier," 132-33 (+ pl. XXVII): Calendaric frg.; cf. Milik, *BE,* 61 n. 1.

6Q18 pap6QHymn

Baillet, "18. Composition hymnique," 133-36 (+ pl. XXVII): 27 frgs. of a hymnic composition possibly related to 1QM.

6Q19 6QGen(?) ar

Baillet, "19. Texte en rapport avec la Genèse," 136 (+ pl. XXVIII): Aramaic text possibly related to Gen 10:6, 20. Cf. *ATTM,* 271-72.

6Q20 6QDeut(?)

Baillet, "20. Texte en rapport avec le Deutéronome (?)," 136-37 (+ pl. XXVIII): Text possibly related to Deut 11:10.

6Q21 6QfrgProph

Baillet, "21. Fragment prophétique (?)," 137 (+ pl. XXVIII): Some sort of prophetic fragment.

6Q22 pap6QUnidA

Baillet, "22. Texte hébreu," 137 (+ pl. XXVIII): Hebrew text on papyrus.

6Q23 pap6QUnidA ar

Baillet, "23. Texte araméen," 138 (+ pl. XXVIII): Milik (*BE,* 91) relates it to the "Words of the Book of Michael" (see 4QWordsMich ar [4Q529]). Cf. *ATTM,* 271.

6Q24-31 6QUnidB

Baillet, "Groupes et fragments divers," 138-41 (+ pls. XXVIII-XXIX). Frgs. 26, 31 are Aramaic. Cf. *ATTM,* 271-72.

6Q30 6QpapProv

Eshel, H., "6Q30, a Cursive *šîn*, and Proverbs 11," *JBL* 122 (2003) 544-46: A new reading of the tiny six-line frg. with parts of Prov 11:4b-7a, 10b.

Detailed Listing of 7Q1-19 in DJD 3

7Q1 pap7QLXXExod gr

Baillet, "1. Exode," 142-43 (+ pl. XXX): Exod 28:4-7.

7Q2 pap7QLXXEpJer gr

Baillet, "2. Lettre de Jérémie," 143 (+ pl. XXX): Vss. 43-44.

7Q3-5 pap7QUnid[a] gr

Baillet, "3-5. Textes bibliques (?)," 143-44 (+ pl. XXX); see section X. 11 below.

7Q6-18 pap7QUnid[b] gr

Baillet, "6-18. Fragments divers," 145 (+ pl. XXX): Very tiny papyrus frgs.; see section X. 11 below.

7Q19 pap7QUnid[c]

Baillet, "19. Empreintes de papyrus," 145-46 (+ pl. XXX): Imprint of papyrus with writing on plaster frgs.

Detailed Listing of 8Q1-5 in DJD 3

8Q1 8QGen

Baillet, "1. Genèse," 147-48 (+ pl. XXXI): Gen 17:12-19; 18:20-25. For new frg. 1a, see E. and H. Eshel, "New Fragments from Qumran: 4QGen[f], 4QIsa[b], 4Q226, 8QGen, and XQpapEnoch," *DSD* 12 (2005) 134-57, esp. 144-46.

8Q2 8QPs

Baillet, "2. Psautier," 148-49 (+ pl. XXXI): Ps 17:5-9, 14; 18:6-9 (= 2 Sam 22:6-9); 18:10-13 (= 2 Sam 22:10-13).

8Q3 8Qphyl

Baillet, "3. Phylactère," 149-57 (+ pls. XXXII-XXXIII): Phylactery (contains Exod 13:1-10, 11-16; Deut 6:4-9; 11:13; 6:1-3; 10:20-22, 12-19; Exod 12:43-51; Deut 5:1-14; Exod 20:11; Deut 10:13?; 11:2-5; 10:21-22; 11:1, 6-12; + 18 frgs.).

8Q4 8Qmez

Baillet, "4. Mezouza," 158-61 (+ pl. XXXIV): Mezuzah (Deut 10:12-22; 11:1-21; + three frgs.).

8Q5 8QHymn

Baillet, "5. Passage hymnique," 161-62 (+ pl. XXXV): Hymnic composition.

9Q–10Q

N.B. From Cave 9 has come only one papyrus frg. (unidentified [see DJD 3. 163 + pl. XXXV]); and from Cave 10 only one piece of inscribed pottery (ostracon? [DJD 3. 164 + pl. XXXV]).

f. Cave 11

11Q1 11QpaleoLev[a]

Freedman, D. N. and K. A. Mathews (with contributions by R. S. Hanson), *The Paleo-Hebrew Leviticus Scroll (11QpaleoLev)* (Philadelphia, PA: American Schools of Oriental Research, 1985 [distributed by Eisenbrauns, Winona Lake, IN]) 25-49 (+ pls. 1-20). Contains Lev 4:24-26, 31, 55; 10:4-7; 11:27-32; 13:3-9, 39-43; 14:16-21, 52-55, 57; 15:2-5; 16:2-4, 34, 1-6; 17:1-5; 18:27-30; 19:1-4; 20:1-6; 21:6-11, 7-12; 22:20-27; 23:22-29; 24:9-14; 25:28-36; 26:17-26; 27:11-19. Cf. D. N. Freedman, "Variant Readings in the Leviticus Scroll from Qumran Cave 11," *CBQ* 36 (1974) 525-34 (+ photo of Lev 14:53–15:5); gives variants in Lev 15:3; 17:2-4; 18:27–19:3; 20:2-3; 21:6-9; 22:21-25; 24:9-10; 25:29-35; 26:20-24; 27:13-17. See especially the corrective article of E. Puech, "Notes en marge de 11Qpaléo-Lévitique: Le fragment L, des fragments inédits et une jarre de la grotte 11," *RB* 96 (1989) 161-83 (+ pls I-III): additional frgs. found on PAM 44.006; 44.114.

11Q2 11QLev[b]

García Martínez, F., E. J. C. Tigchelaar, and A. S. van der Woude, "2. 11QLeviticus[b]," *Qumran Cave 11: II, 11Q2-18, 11Q20-31* (DJD 23; ed. F. García Martínez et al.; Oxford: Clarendon, 1998) 1-9 (+ pl. I): Lev 7:34-35; 8:8(or 9); 9:23-24; 10:1-2; 13:58-59; 14:16-17; 15:18-19; 25:31-33; + two frgs.

11Q3 11QDeut

García Martínez-Tigchelaar-van der Woude, "3. 11QDeuteronomy," DJD 23. 11-14 (+ pl. II): Deut 1:4-5; 2:28-30; + one frg.

11Q4 11QEzekiel

Herbert, E. D., "4. 11QEzekiel," DJD 23. 15-28 (+ pls. II, LIV): Ezek 1:8-10; 4:3-5, 6, 9-10; 5:11-17; 7:9-12; + two frgs.

11Q5 11QPs[a]

Sanders, J. A., *The Psalms Scroll of Qumrân Cave 11 (11QPs[a])* (DJD 4; Oxford:

Clarendon, 1965) 19-93 (+ pls. I-XVII). Pages 51-93 discuss the Apocryphal Compositions of this scroll. See also J. A. Sanders, *The Dead Sea Psalms Scroll* (Ithaca, NY: Cornell University Press, 1967), esp. 155-65 ("Postscriptum"). See Y. Yadin, "Another Fragment (E) of the Psalms Scroll from Qumran Cave 11 (11QPs[a])," *Textus* 5 (1966) 1-10 (+ pls. I-V). Cf. now García Martínez-Tigchelaar-van der Woude, "5. 11QPsalms[a]. Fragments E, F," DJD 23. 29-36 (+ pls. IV-V): a new study of frg. E and its contents. F contains Ps 147:3. Also J. A. Sanders, "The Qumran Psalms Scroll [11QPs[a]] Reviewed," *On Language, Culture, and Religion: In Honor of Eugene A. Nida* [eds. M. Black and W. A. Smalley; The Hague: Mouton, 1974] 79-99; A. S. van der Woude, "Die fünf syrischen Psalmen," *Poetische Schriften* [JSHRZ 4/1; Gütersloh: Mohn, 1974] 29-47; P. W. Flint, *The Dead Sea Psalms Scroll and the Book of Psalms* (STDJ 17; Leiden: Brill, 1997).

Contents of the scroll:

Frgs. A, B, C i	Ps 101:1-8; 102:1-2 (see DJD 4. 19 [+ pl. III]).
Frg. C ii	Ps 102:18-29; 103:1 (or 104:1) (DJD 4. 20 [+ pl. III]).
Frg. D	Ps 109:21-31 (DJD 4. 21 [+ pl. III]).
Frg. E i	Ps 118:25-29; 104:1-6 (*DSPS*, 160-61 [pl. opposite p. 156]; DJD 23. 31-33 [+ pl. V]).
Frg. E ii	Ps 104:22-35; 147:1-2 (*DSPS*, 162-63 [pl. opp. p. 156]; DJD 23. 33-34 [+ pl. IV]).
Frg. E iii	Ps 147:18-20; 105:1-11 (*DSPS*, 164-65 [pl. opp. p. 156]; DJD 23. 34-36 [+ pl. IV]).
Frg. F	Ps 147:3-? (DJD 23. 36 [+ pl. IV]).
Col. i	Ps 105:25-45 (DJD 4. 22 [+ pl. IV]).
Col. ii	Ps 146:9-?-10; 148:1-12 (DJD 4. 23 [+ pl. IV]).
Col. iii	Ps 121:1-8; 122:1-9; 123:1-2 (DJD 4. 24 [+ pl. IV]).
Col. iv	Ps 124:7-8; 125:1-5; 126:1-6; 127:1 (DJD 4. 25 [+ pl. V]).
Col. v	Ps 128:4-6; 129:1-8; 130:1-8; 131:1? (DJD 4. 26 [+ pl. V]).
Col. vi	Ps 132:8-18; 119:1-6 (DJD 4. 27 [+ pl. VI]).
Col. vii	Ps 119:15-28 (DJD 4. 28 [+ pl. VI]).
Col. viii	Ps 119:37-49 (DJD 4. 29 [+ pl. VII]).
Col. ix	Ps 119:59-73 (DJD 4. 30 [+ pl. VII]).
Col. x	Ps 119:82-96 (DJD 4. 31 [+ pl. VIII]).

Col. xi	Ps 119:105-20 (DJD 4. 32 [+ pl. VIII]).
Col. xii	Ps 119:128-42 (DJD 4. 33 [+ pl. IX]).
Col. xiii	Ps 119:150-64 (DJD 4. 34 [+ pl. IX]).
Col. xiv	Ps 119:171-76; 135:1-9 (DJD 4. 35 [+ pl. X]).
Col. xv	Ps 135:17-21; 136:1-16 (DJD 4. 36 [+ pl. X]).
Col. xvi	Ps 136:26b(?); 118:1(?), 15, 16, 8, 9, ?, 29(?); 145:1-7 (DJD 4. 37 [+ pl. XI]).
Col. xvii	Ps 145:13-21+? (DJD 4. 38 [+ pl. XI]).
Col. xviii	Syriac Ps II:3-19 (in Hebrew) [= Psalm 154] (DJD 4. 39 [+ pl. XII]).
Col. xix	Plea for Deliverance (lines 1-18) (DJD 4. 40 [+ pl. XII]).
Col. xx	Ps 139:8-24; 137:1 (DJD 4. 41 [+ pl. XIII]).
Col. xxi	Ps 137:9; 138:1-8; Sir 51:13-20b (DJD 4. 42 [+ pl. XIII]).
Col. xxii	Sir 51:30; Apostrophe to Zion (lines 1b-15); Ps 93:1-3 (DJD 4. 43 [+ pl. XIV]).
Col. xxiii	Ps 141:5-10; 133:1-3; 144:1-7 (DJD 4. 44 [+ pls. II, XIV]).
Col. xxiv	Ps 144:15; Syriac Ps III:1-18 (in Hebrew) [= Psalm 155] (DJD 4. 45 [+ pl. XV]).
Col. xxv	Ps 142:4-8; 143:1-8 (DJD 4. 46 [+ pl. XV]).
Col. xxvi	Ps 149:7-9; 150:1-6; Hymn to the Creator (lines 9-15) (DJD 4. 47 [+ pl. XVI]).
Col. xxvii	2 Sam 23:7 (line 1); David's Compositions (2-11); Ps 140:1-5 (DJD 4. 48 [+ pl. XVI]).
Col. xxviii	Ps 134:1-3; 151 A (Syriac Ps I) (lines 3-12), B (lines 13-14) in Hebrew; (DJD 4. 49 [+ pl. XVII]).

11Q6 11QPs^{b}

García Martínez-Tigchelaar-van der Woude, "6. 11QPsalms^{b}," DJD 23. 37-47 (+ pl. III): Ps 77:18-21; 78:1; 119:163-65; 118:1, 15-16; Plea for Deliverance (overlaps 11QPs^{a} 19:1-16); Apostrophe to Zion (overlaps 11QPs^{a} 22:4-5); Ps 141:10; 133:1-3; 144:1-2; 109:3-4 (or 11QPs^{a} 18:14?); + one frg.

11Q7 11QPs^{c}

García Martínez-Tigchelaar-van der Woude, "7. 11QPsalms^{c}," DJD 23. 49-61 (+ pl. VI): Ps 2:1-8; 9:3-7; 12:5-9; 13:1-6; 14:1-6; 17:9-15; 18:1-12, 15-17?; 19:4-8; 25:2-7.

11Q8 11QPs[d] (olim Mas 1g)

García Martínez-Tigchelaar-van der Woude, "8. 11QPsalms[d]," DJD 23. 63-76 (+ pls. VII-VIII): Ps 6:2-4; 9:3-6; 18:26-29, 39-42; 36:13; 37:1-4; 39:13-14; 40:1; 43:1-3; 45:6-8; 59:5-8; 68:1-5, 14-18; 78:5-12; 81:4-9; 86:11-14; 115:16-18; 116:1; (78:36-37?; 60:9?).

11Q9 11QPs[e]

García Martínez-Tigchelaar-van der Woude, "9. 11QPsalms[e]?," DJD 23. 77-78 (+ pl. VIII): Ps 50:3-7. It seems to be the sole remnant of a fifth Psalms scroll of 11Q.

11Q10 11QtgJob

García Martínez-Tigchelaar-van der Woude, "10. 11QtargumJob," DJD 23. 79-180 (+ pls. IX-XXI): This edition of the targum now supersedes what had been the *editio princeps,* J. P. M. van der Ploeg and A. S. van der Woude, *Le targum de Job de la grotte XI de Qumrân, édité et traduit, avec la collaboration de B. Jongeling* (Koninklijke Nederlandse Akademie van Wetenschappen; Leiden: Brill, 1971). Contains a fragmentary Aramaic translation of Job 17:14–8:4; 19:11-19, 29; 20:1-6; 21:2-10, 20-27; 22:3-9, 16-22; 23:1-8; 24:12-17, 24-25; 25:1-6; 26:1-2, 10-14; 27:1-4, 11-20; 28:4-13, 20-28; 29:7-16, 24-25; 30:1-4, 13-20, 25?-31; 31:1, 8-16, 26-32, 40; 32:1-3, 10-17; 33:6-16, 24-32; 34:6-17, 24-34; 35:6-15; 36:7-16, 23-33; 37:10-19; 38:3-13, 23-34; 39:1-11, 20-29; 40:5-14, 23-31; 41:7-17, 25-26; 42:1-2; 40:5; 42:4-6, 9-12; + frgs. A1-19, G, N, O, P. See E. Puech and F. García Martínez, "Remarques sur la colonne XXXVIII de 11 Q tg Job," *RevQ* 9 (1977-78) 401-7. Cf. M. Sokoloff, *The Targum to Job from Qumran Cave XI* (Bar-Ilan Studies in Near Eastern Languages and Culture; Ramat-Gan: Bar-Ilan University, 1974); B. Zuckerman and S. A. Reed, "A Fragment of an Unstudied Column of 11QtgJob: A Preliminary Report," *NCAL* 10 (1993) 1-7 [about col. viia, frg. 6a, with Job 23:1-8]. Cf. *ATTM,* 280-98; *ATTME,* 133.

11Q11 11QapocrPs

García Martínez-Tigchelaar-van der Woude, "11. 11Qapocryphal Psalms," DJD 23. 181-205 (+ pls. XXII-XXV, LIII): The frgs. contain remnants of three songs against demons, and the last is a paraphrase of canonical Psalm 91. They mention Solomon, the exorcising of demons, the fury of Yhwh, and the curse of Abaddon. They seem to belong to incantations. Cf. 11QPs[a] 27:9-10.

11Q12 11QJub

García Martínez-Tigchelaar-van der Woude, "12. 11QJubilees," DJD 23. 207-20 (+ pl. XXVI): Contains a Hebrew form of what is known from the Ethiopic text of *Jub.* 4:6-11, 13-14, 16-17 (or 11-12), 17-18?, 29-30, 31; 5:1-2; 12:15-17, 28-29; + four frgs. unidentified. See S. Talmon, XQTextA (XQ5a) below, which = 11QJub frg. 7a.

11Q13 11QMelch

García Martínez-Tigchelaar-van der Woude, "13. 11QMelchizedek," DJD 23. 221-41 (+ pl. XXVII): This is a text that comments on or alludes to Leviticus 25, Deuteronomy 15; Isa 52:7; 61:1-3; Ps 7:8-9; 82:1-2 and portrays Melchizedek as a heavenly figure atoning for the sons of light at the end of the tenth jubilee.

11Q14 11QSefM (olim 11QBer)

García Martínez-Tigchelaar-van der Woude, "14. 11QSefer ha-Milḥamah," DJD 23. 243-51 (+ pl. XXVIII). This text is related to 4Q285 (4QSefM), and more remotely to the War Scroll from Caves 1 and 4 (1QM, 4QM).

11Q15 11QHymns[a]

García Martínez-Tigchelaar-van der Woude, "15. 11QHymns[a]," DJD 23. 253-56 (+ pl. XXIX): These hymns resemble the *Hodayot* of Caves 1 and 4, and also 4QBer (4Q286-287).

11Q16 11QHymns[b]

García Martínez-Tigchelaar-van der Woude, "16. 11QHymns[b]," DJD 23. 257-58 (+ pl. XXIX). See Talmon, XQTextB (XQ5b) below, which = 11QHymns[b] frg. 2.

11Q17 11QShirShabb

García Martínez-Tigchelaar-van der Woude, "17. 11QShirot ʿOlat ha-Shabbat," DJD 23. 259-304 (+ pls. XXX-XXXIV, LIII). The Hebrew text of these frgs. has many overlaps with 4Q403, 4Q404, 4Q405 (4QShirShabb).

11Q18 11QNJ ar

García Martínez-Tigchelaar-van der Woude, "18. 11QNew Jerusalem ar," DJD 23. 305-55 (+ pl. XXXV-XL, LIII). This Aramaic text has overlaps with 2QJN (2Q24) and is related to other JN texts (e.g., 1Q32, 4Q554, 4Q555, 5Q15).

11Q19 11QTemple[a]

Yadin, Y., מגילת־המקדש (3 vols., with a Supplement; Jerusalem: Israel Exploration Society, Archaeological Institute of the Hebrew University, Shrine of the Book, 1977). The scroll was published also in an updated English version, *The Temple Scroll* (3 vols., with a Supplement; Jerusalem: Israel Exploration Society, 1983). The scroll has 67 fragmentary cols., some lines of which have been reconstructed on the basis of 11QTemple[b]. Plates 16-82 have the photographs of the 67 cols.; there are also other photographs in the Supplement. See section IX. 5 below.

11Q20 11QTemple[b]

García Martínez-Tigchelaar-van der Woude, "20. 11QTemple[b]," DJD 23. 357-409 (+ pls. XLI-XLVII; see also Yadin, *The Temple Scroll*, Supplement, pls. 35*-40*): 42 (joined) frgs. make up this copy of the Temple Scroll.

11Q21 11QTemple[c]

García Martínez-Tigchelaar-van der Woude, "21. 11QTemple[c]?," DJD 23. 411-14 (+ pl. XLVIII): Three frgs. possibly of a third copy of the Temple Scroll, the first of which seems to parallel 11Q19 3:14-17 in part.

11Q22 11QpaleoUnid

García Martínez-Tigchelaar-van der Woude, "22. 11QpaleoUnidentified Text," DJD 23. 415-18 (+ pl. XLVIII).

11Q23 11QcryptAUnid

García Martínez-Tigchelaar-van der Woude, "23. 11QcryptA Unidentified Text," DJD 23. 419-20 (+ pl. XLVIII).

11Q24 11QUnid ar

García Martínez-Tigchelaar-van der Woude, "24. 11QUnidentified Text ar," DJD 23. 421-22 (+ pl. XLIX).

11Q25 11QUnidA

García Martínez-Tigchelaar-van der Woude, "25. 11QUnidentified Text A," DJD 23. 423-26 (+ pl. XLIX).

11Q26 11QUnidB

García Martínez-Tigchelaar-van der Woude, "26. 11QUnidentified Text B," DJD 23. 427-28 (+ pl. XLIX).

11Q27 11QUnidC

García Martínez-Tigchelaar-van der Woude, "27. 11QUnidentified Text C," DJD 23. 429-30 (+ pl. XLIX).

11Q28 11QpapUnidD

García Martínez-Tigchelaar-van der Woude, "28. 11QpapUnidentified Text D," DJD 23. 431 (+ pl. L).

11Q29 11QS-like

García Martínez-Tigchelaar-van der Woude, "29. 11QFragment Related to Serekh ha-Yaḥad," DJD 23. 433-34 (+ pl. L).

11Q30 11QUnc

García Martínez-Tigchelaar-van der Woude, "30. 11QUnclassified Fragments," DJD 23. 435-44 (+ pls. L-LI). See H. Jacobson, "*11Q30*, Fgs 8-10," *RevQ* 18 (1997-98) 595: He thinks frg. 8 may = Judg 11:6 or 8; and frg. 9, part of the punishment of the Amorites in Judges 11.

11Q31 11QUnidWads

García Martínez-Tigchelaar-van der Woude, "31. 11QUnidentified Wads," DJD 23. 445-46 (+ pl. LII).

g. Unknown Qumran Cave

XQ1-4 XQphyl 1-4

Yadin, Y., תפילין־של־ראש מקומראן: *Tefillin from Qumran (X Q Phyl 1-4)* (Jerusalem: Israel Exploration Society and the Shrine of the Book, 1969). Text in Modern Hebrew and English; the former is found also in the *W. F. Albright Volume* (ErIsr 9; Jerusalem: Israel Exploration Society, 1969) 60-85.

XQ5a XQTextA

Talmon, S., "5a. XQText A (= 11QJub frg. 7a)," DJD 36. 485-86 (+ pl. XXXII): Contains Hebrew text of *Jub.* 7:4-5. See J. C. VanderKam, "The Jubilees Fragments" (quoted above under 4Q216), 642 n. 27.

XQ5b XQTextB

Talmon, "5b. XQText B (= 11QHymns^{b} frg. 2)," DJD 36. 487-89 (+ pl. XXXII).

XQ6 XQOffering ar

Lemaire, A., "6. XQOffering ar," DJD 36. 490-91 (+ pl. XXXII): Small skin frg., which has the Aramaic word לקורבנא.

XQ7 XQUnid

Lange, A., "7. XQUnidentified Text," DJD 36. 492-93 (+ pl. XXXII): Small Hebrew frg.

XQ8 XQpapEn

Eshel, E. and H., "New Fragments from Qumran: 4QGen^{f}, 4QIsa^{b}, 4Q226,

8QGen, and XQpapEnoch," *DSD* 12 (2005) 134-57, esp. 146-57: The five-lined frg. corresponds to *1 Enoch* 8:4–9:3 and is related to 4QEn[a] and 4QEn[b] (4Q201-202).

h. Khirbet Qumran Texts

KhQ1 KhQOstr 1

Cross, F. M. and E. Eshel, "1. Khirbet Qumran Ostracon," DJD 36. 497-507 (+ pl. XXXIII): Written in Hebrew in Late Herodian script, this text is a draft of a deed of gift of an estate that is being given away, apparently by someone entering the Qumran community.

KhQ2 KhQOstr 2

Cross-Eshel, "2. Khirbet Qumran Ostracon," DJD 36. 508 (+ pl. XXXIV): A text that seems to mention "Joseph, son of Nathan."

KhQ3 KhQOstr 3

Eshel, E., "3. Khirbet Qumran Ostracon," DJD 36. 509-12 (+ pl. XXXIV): An abecedary discovered by R. de Vaux in 1953; it may be a writing exercise.

i. Alleged Qumran Texts

The following 20 texts bear 4Q numbers, but there are serious reasons to think that they did not really come from Qumran Cave 4. "It is believed that they were purchased from Bedouin who attributed them to cave 4" (A. Yardeni, "Introduction to the 'Qumran Cave 4' Documentary Texts," *Aramaic, Hebrew and Greek Documentary Texts from Naḥal Ḥever and Other Sites, with an Appendix Containing Alleged Qumran Texts (The Seiyâl Collection II)* (DJD 27; ed. H. M. Cotton and A. Yardeni; Oxford: Clarendon, 1997) 283-84.

4Q342 4QLetter ar

Yardeni, "342. 4QLetter? ar," DJD 27. 285 (+ fig. 28, pl. LIV): A small frg., apparently of a letter written in Aramaic.

4Q343 4QLetter nab (olim 4Q235)

Yardeni, "343. 4QLetter nab," DJD 27. 286-88 (+ fig. 28, pl. LV): An unclear frg. of a Nabatean letter inscribed on both recto and verso; + two frgs.

4Q344 4QDebtAck ar

Yardeni, "344. 4QDebt Acknowledgement ar," DJD 27. 289-91 (+ fig. 29, pl.

LVI): Remnant of an Aramaic promissory note, written by Eleazar bar Yehoseph.

4Q345 4QDeedA

Yardeni, "345. 4QDeed A ar or heb," DJD 27. 292-95 (+ fig. 29, pl. LVI): A very fragmentary text of what seems to be a double document with an upper and lower version (of apparently the same text of a deed); two signatures are preserved.

4Q346 4QDeedSale ar

Yardeni, "346. 4QDeed of Sale ar," DJD 27. 296-98 (+ fig. 30, pl. LVII).

4Q346a 4QUnidFrgA

Yardeni, "346a. 4QUnidentified Fragment A," DJD 27. 299 (+ fig. 30, pl. LVII).

4Q347 See XḤev/Se32.

4Q348 4QDeedB

Yardeni, "348. 4QDeed B heb?," DJD 27. 300-303 (+ fig. 29, pl. LVIII): Fragment of a double document with an upper and lower version. Despite Aramaic *bar*, "son of," the language of the text seems to be Hebrew, but so little of it is left that one cannot tell in which language it has been composed.

4Q351 4QAccCerealA

Yardeni, "351. 4QAccount of Cereal A ar," DJD 27. 304 (+ fig. 30, pl. LIX): A tiny frg. with a few Aramaic words.

4Q352 4QpapAccCerealB

Yardeni, "352. 4QpapAccount of Cereal B ar or heb," DJD 27. 305-6 (+ fig. 31, pl. LIX): Three practically unintelligible frgs.

4Q352a 4QpapAccA

Yardeni, "352a. 4QpapAccount A ar or heb," DJD 27. 307-8 (+ fig. 31, pl. LIX): Five practically unintelligible frgs.

4Q353 4QpapAccCerLiq

Yardeni, "353. 4QpapAccount of Cereal or Liquid ar or heb," DJD 27. 309 (+ fig. 30, pl. LX).

4Q354 4QAccB

Yardeni, "354. 4QAccount B ar or heb," DJD 27. 310 (+ fig. 30, pl. LX).

4Q356 4QAccD

Yardeni, "356. 4QAccount D ar or heb," DJD 27. 311 (+ fig. 30, pl. LX).

4Q357 4QAccE

Yardeni, "357. 4QAccount E ar or heb," DJD 27. 312 (+ fig. 30, pl. LX).

4Q358 4QpapAccF

Yardeni, "358. 4QpapAccount F? ar or heb," DJD 27. 313 (+ fig. 30, pl. LX).

4Q359 4QpapDeedC

Yardeni, "359. 4QpapDeed C? ar or heb," DJD 27. 314 (+ fig. 30, pl. LX). May be from XḤev/Se; see below.

4Q360a 4QpapUnidB ar

Yardeni, "360a. 4QpapUnidentified Fragments B ar," DJD 27. 315-17 (+ fig. 31, pl. LXI).

4Q360b 4QUnidFrgC

Yardeni, "360b. 4QUnidentified Fragment C," DJD 27. 322 (+ pl. LXI): No transcription.

4Q361 4QpapUnid gr

Yardeni, "361. 4QpapUnidentified Fragment gr," DJD 27. 322 (+ pl. LXI): No transcription.

2. *Naḥal Ḥever (Wadi Ḫabra)*

Naḥal Ḥever is a wadi or torrent-bed on the west side of the Dead Sea between Ein-Gedi and Masada. Ten caves in it were used by Jews who took part in the Second Revolt against Rome in the time of Simon ben Kosiba (Bar Kokhba), A.D. 132-135. Two of them yielded important written material, Cave 5/6 (Cave of Letters) on the northern side, and Cave 8 (Cave of Horror) on the southern side. In 5/6Ḥev (Cave of Letters), which was excavated by Y. Yadin in 1960 and 1961, two biblical texts were recovered and many documentary texts from about A.D. 90-135, of which the most important were the Babatha Family-Archive (5/6Ḥev 2-35), leases and subleases of the Bar Kokhba administration in Ein-Gedi (5/6Ḥev 42-47b), and the Letters of Bar

Kokhba (5/6Ḥev 49-63). In 8Ḥev (Cave of Horror), which was excavated by Y. Aharoni in 1960, frgs. of the Greek Minor Prophets scroll (8Ḥev 1), of a prayer (8Ḥev 2), and of a Greek letter (8Ḥev 4) were found.

In addition, there are texts that were discovered by Bedouins and brought to the Palestine Archaeological Museum in East Jerusalem in 1952 and 1953, which were said by them to have come from a cave in Wadi Seiyal (Naḥal Ṣe'elim). For this reason they are often referred to as the original Seiyal Collection, which has been published by E. Tov (1990) and by H. Cotton and A. Yardeni (1997). But the frgs. of the Greek Minor Prophets discovered by Aharoni are part of the text published by Tov and show that that text really came from Cave 8Ḥev, and not from Wadi Seiyal.

Other documents, written in Aramaic, Greek, or Hebrew, said to have come from a cave in Wadi Seiyal, are most likely related to the documents found in Cave 5/6Ḥev; but since the evidence for these texts is not the same as that for the Greek Minor Prophets, they are designated today by the siglum XḤev/Se. This siglum should be used also for two alleged 4Q texts (4Q347 and 4Q359). These and other texts were apparently part of the original Seiyal Collection. So the reader or student of texts said to have been part of that collection must always be aware of the problem of identification. See further H. M. Cotton, "Ḥever, Naḥal: Written Material," *EDSS*, 359-61; also H. M. Cotton and A. Yardeni, "General Introduction," *Aramaic, Hebrew and Greek Documentary Texts from Naḥal Ḥever and Other Sites, with an Appendix Containing Alleged Qumran Texts (The Seiyâl Collection II)* (DJD 27; Oxford: Clarendon, 1997) 1-6.

a. Cave of Letters

5/6Ḥev1 5/6ḤevDebenture nab

Yadin, Y., J. C. Greenfield, A. Yardeni, and B. A. Levine, "P.Yadin 1 (= 5/6Ḥev 1): A Debenture in Nabatean-Aramaic," *The Documents from the Bar Kokhba Period in the Cave of Letters: Hebrew, Aramaic and Nabatean-Aramaic Papyri* (JDS 3; Jerusalem: Israel Exploration Society/Institute of Archaeology, Hebrew University/Shrine of the Book, Israel Museum, 2002) 170-204 (+ pls. 16-20). N. B. The plates were reprinted in a separate companion volume in 2002, but it was a reproduction of the plates "prepared by Yigael Yadin and printed under his supervision in 1963 at Colswold Collotype Co., Ltd., Gloucestershire, England." Hence in the following entries, "pl.," when used with *Documents* (JDS 3), is a reference to this companion volume. Also important in JDS 3 (2002) is the list of "The Yadin Collection" on pp. xvi-xvii, which records the 64 texts often labelled as "P.Yadin" (some subdivided as a, b) and identified according to genre and language (ar, gr, heb, nab).

5/6Ḥev1a 5/6ḤevNum[a] (olim 5/6Ḥev 41)

Flint, P., "1a. 5/6ḤevNumbers[a]," *Miscellaneous Texts from the Judaean Desert* (DJD 38; ed. J. Charlesworth et al.; Oxford: Clarendon, 2000) 137-40 (+ pl. XXIV): Num 19:2-4; 20:7-8; + one unidentified frg. N.B. XḤev/Se1 (XḤev/SeNum[a]) belongs to this text.

5/6Ḥev1b 5/6ḤevPs (olim 5/6Ḥev 40)

Flint, "1b. 5/6ḤevPsalms," DJD 38. 141-66 (+ pls. XXV-XXVII): Ps 7:13–8:1, 4-10; 9:12–10:6, 8-10, 18; 11:1-5a; 12:6–13:3; 14:2-4; 15:1–16:1; 18:6-13a, 17-43; 22:4-9, 15-21; 23:2-6; 24:1-2; 25:4-6; 29:1-2; 30:3; 31:3-22; + one unidentified frg. N.B. XḤev/Se4 (XḤev/SePs) belongs to this text.

5/6Ḥev2-3 5/6ḤevSaleContA nab

Yadin-Greenfield-Yardeni-Levine, "P.Yadin 2 and 3 (= 5/6Ḥev 2 and 3): Two dated sale contracts in Nabatean-Aramaic," *Documents* (JDS 3), 201-44 (+ pls. 21-24).

5/6Ḥev4 5/6ḤevGuarantee nab

Yadin-Greenfield-Yardeni-Levine, "P.Yadin 4 (= 5/6Ḥev 4): A possible guarantor's agreement in Nabatean-Aramaic," *Documents* (JDS 3), 245-56 (+ pls. 25-26).

5/6Ḥev5 5/6ḤevDepositA gr

Lewis, N., "5. Deposit," *The Documents from the Bar Kokhba Period in the Cave of Letters: Greek Papyri.* Yadin, Y. and J. C. Greenfield, *Aramaic and Nabatean Signatures and Subscriptions* (JDS 2; Israel Exploration Society/Hebrew University of Jerusalem/Shrine of the Book, 1989) 35-40.

5/6Ḥev6 5/6ḤevTenancy nab

Yadin-Greenfield-Yardeni-Levine, "P.Yadin 6 (= 5/6Ḥev 6): A Tenancy Agreement in Nabatean (119 CE)," *Documents* (JDS 3), 257-67 (+ pl. 55).

5/6Ḥev7 5/6ḤevDeedGiftA ar

Yadin-Greenfield-Yardeni-Levine, "P.Yadin 7 (= 5/6Ḥev 7): A Deed of Gift," *Documents* (JDS 3), 73-108 (+ pls. 29-30).

5/6Ḥev8 5/6ḤevPurchaseCont ar

Yadin-Greenfield-Yardeni-Levine, "P.Yadin 8 (= 5/6Ḥev 8): A Purchase Contract in Aramaic," *Documents* (JDS 3), 109-17 (+ pl. 33).

5/6Ḥev9 5/6ḤevWaiver nab
Yadin-Greenfield-Yardeni-Levine, "P.Yadin 9 (= 5/6Ḥev 9): A Waiver (?) in Nabatean Aramaic," *Documents* (JDS 3), 268-76 (+ pl. 56).

5/6Ḥev10 5/6ḤevMarrContA ar
Yadin-Greenfield-Yardeni-Levine, "P.Yadin 10 (= 5/6Ḥev 10): Babatha's *Ketubba*," *Documents* (JDS 3), 118-41 (+ pls. 31-32).

5/6Ḥev11 5/6ḤevHypothec-Loan gr
Lewis, "11. Loan on Hypothec," *Documents from the Bar Kokhba Period* (JDS 2), 41-46 (+ pls. 3-4).

5/6Ḥev12 5/6ḤevExtract gr
Lewis, "12. Extract from Council Minutes," *Documents from the Bar Kokhba Period* (JDS 2), 47-50 (+ pls. 5-6). See "12-15. The Orphan Jesus," ibid., 47.

5/6Ḥev13 5/6ḤevPetitionA gr
Lewis, "13. Petition to the Governor," *Documents from the Bar Kokhba Period* (JDS 2), 51-53 (+ pl. 7).

5/6Ḥev14 5/6ḤevSummonsA gr
Lewis, "14. Summons," *Documents from the Bar Kokhba Period* (JDS 2), 54-57 (+ pls. 8-9).

5/6Ḥev15 5/6ḤevDepositionA gr
Lewis, "15. Deposition," *Documents from the Bar Kokhba Period* (JDS 2), 58-64 (+ pls. 10-12); Yadin-Greenfield, *Subscriptions*, 139-40.

5/6Ḥev16 5/6ḤevLand-Registration gr
Lewis, "16. Registration of Land," *Documents from the Bar Kokhba Period* (JDS 2), 65-70 (+ pls. 13-14).

5/6Ḥev17 5/6ḤevDepositB
Lewis, "17. Deposit," *Documents from the Bar Kokhba Period* (JDS 2), 71-75 (+ pls. 15-16); Yadin-Greenfield, *Subscriptions*, 141.

5/6Ḥev18 5/6ḤevMarrContB gr
Lewis, "18. Marriage Contract," *Documents from the Bar Kokhba Period* (JDS 2), 76-82 (+ pls. 17-19); Yadin-Greenfield, *Subscriptions*, 142-43.

5/6Ḥev19 5/6ḤevDeedGiftB gr

Lewis, "19. Deed of Gift," *Documents from the Bar Kokhba Period* (JDS 2), 83-87 (+ pls. 20-21); Yadin-Greenfield, *Subscriptions,* 144.

5/6Ḥev20 5/6ḤevRights gr

Lewis, "20. Concession of Rights," *Documents from the Bar Kokhba Period* (JDS 2), 88-93 (+ pls. 22-24); Yadin-Greenfield, *Subscriptions,* 145. See "20-26. Disputes over Inheritances," ibid., 88.

5/6Ḥev21 5/6ḤevDateCrop gr

Lewis, "21. Purchase of a Date Crop," *Documents from the Bar Kokhba Period* (JDS 2), 94-97 (+ pls. 25-26); Yadin-Greenfield, *Subscriptions,* 146. See "21-22. Transactions Regarding a Date Crop," ibid., 94.

5/6Ḥev22 5/6ḤevDateCropSale gr

Lewis, "22. Sale of a Date Crop," *Documents from the Bar Kokhba Period* (JDS 2), 98-101 (+ pls. 27-28); Yadin-Greenfield, *Subscriptions,* 147.

5/6Ḥev23 5/6ḤevSummonsB gr

Lewis, "23. Summons," *Documents from the Bar Kokhba Period* (JDS 2), 102-4 (+ pls. 29-31). See "23-26. Claims and Counterclaims," ibid., 102.

5/6Ḥev24 5/6ḤevDepositionB gr

Lewis, "24. Deposition," *Documents from the Bar Kokhba Period* (JDS 2), 105-7. See "23-26. Claims and Counterclaims," ibid., 102.

5/6Ḥev25 5/6ḤevSummonsC gr

Lewis, "25. Summons and Countersummons," *Documents from the Bar Kokhba Period* (JDS 2), 108-12 (+ pls. 32-33). See "23-26. Claims and Counterclaims," ibid., 102.

5/6Ḥev26 5/6ḤevSummonsD gr

Lewis, "26. Summons and Reply," *Documents from the Bar Kokhba Period* (JDS 2), 113-15 (+ pls. 34-35). See "23-26. Claims and Counterclaims," ibid., 102.

5/6Ḥev27 5/6ḤevReceiptA gr

Lewis, "27. Receipt," *Documents from the Bar Kokhba Period* (JDS 2), 116-17 (+ pl. 36); Yadin-Greenfield, *Subscriptions,* 148-49.

5/6Ḥev28-30 5/6ḤevJudicRule gr

Lewis, "28-30. Judiciary Rule," *Documents from the Bar Kokhba Period* (JDS 2), 118-20 (+ pls. 37-38).

5/6Ḥev31 5/6ḤevContA gr

Lewis, "31. Contract(?)," *Documents from the Bar Kokhba Period* (JDS 2), 121-22. No plate.

5/6Ḥev32 5/6ḤevContB gr

Lewis, "32. Contract(?)," *Documents from the Bar Kokhba Period* (JDS 2), 123. No plate.

5/6Ḥev32a 5/6ḤevContC gr

Lewis, "32a. Contract(?)," *Documents from the Bar Kokhba Period* (JDS 2), 124. No plate.

5/6Ḥev33 5/6ḤevPetitionB gr

Lewis, "33. Petition," *Documents from the Bar Kokhba Period* (JDS 2), 125-26 (+ pl. 39).

5/6Ḥev34 5/6ḤevPetitionC gr

Lewis, "34. Petition," *Documents from the Bar Kokhba Period* (JDS 2), 127-28. No plate.

5/6Ḥev35 5/6ḤevSummonsE gr

Lewis, "35. Summons(?)," *Documents from the Bar Kokhba Period* (JDS 2), 129. No plate.

5/6Ḥev36 5/6ḤevRedemption nab

Yadin-Greenfield-Yardeni-Levine, *Documents* (JDS 3), 271 (P.Yadin 36a, 36b) [facsimile, no discussion; see J. Starcky, "Un contrat nabatéen sur papyrus," *RB* 61 (1954) 161-81 (+ pls. I-III): Redemption of a Writ of Seizure]. Sometimes called XḤev/SeNab1.

5/6Ḥev37 5/6ḤevMarrContC gr

Lewis, "37. Marriage Contract," *Documents from the Bar Kokhba Period* (JDS 2), 130-33 (+ pl. 40). See XḤev/Se65 (DJD 39. 111).

5/6Ḥev38 5/6ḤevUncText nab

Yadin-Greenfield-Yardeni-Levine, *Documents* (JDS 3), xvii (mentioned as P.Yadin 38 [No plate or facsimile]).

5/6Ḥev39 5/6ḤevUncFrg nab

Yadin-Greenfield-Yardeni-Levine, *Documents* (JDS 3), xvii (mentioned as P.Yadin 39 [No plate or facsimile]).

5/6Ḥev40

Cancelled; see now 5/6Ḥev1b.

5/6Ḥev41

Cancelled; see now 5/6Ḥev1a.

5/6Ḥev42 5/6ḤevLease ar

Yadin-Greenfield-Yardeni-Levine, "P.Yadin 42 (= 5/6Ḥev 42): A Lease Agreement in Aramaic," *Documents* (JDS 3), 142-49 (+ pl. 75).

5/6Ḥev43 5/6ḤevReceiptB ar

Yadin-Greenfield-Yardeni-Levine, "P.Yadin 43 (= 5/6Ḥev 43): A Receipt in Aramaic," *Documents* (JDS 3), 150-55 (+ pl. 75).

5/6Ḥev44-46 5/6ḤevLegalPap

Yadin-Greenfield-Yardeni-Levine, "P.Yadin 44, 45, and 46 (= 5/6Ḥev 45-46): Three Hebrew Legal Papyri," *Documents* (JDS 3), 39-70 (+ pls. 76-78).

5/6Ḥev47 5/6ḤevSaleContB ar

Yadin-Greenfield-Yardeni-Levine, "P.Yadin 47 (= 5/6Ḥev 47): A Sale Contract in Aramaic," *Documents* (JDS 3), 157-68 (+ pls. 79-82).

5/6Ḥev48 5/6Ḥev?

P.Yadin 48: Uninscribed skin frg. (*Documents* [JDS 3], xvii).

5/6Ḥev49 5/6ḤevBarKLettA

Yadin-Greenfield-Yardeni-Levine, "P.Yadin 49 (= 5/6Ḥev 49): A Hebrew Letter from Shimʿon, Son of Kosibaʾ," *Documents* (JDS 3), 279-86 (+ pl. 83): Sent to men of Ein-Gedi, Mesabalaʾ, and Yehonathan, son of Baʿyan.

5/6Ḥev50 5/6ḤevBarKLettB ar

Yadin-Greenfield-Yardeni-Levine, "P.Yadin 50 (= 5/6Ḥev 50): An Aramaic Letter from Shimʿon, Son of Kośibah," *Documents* (JDS 3), 287-92 (+ pl. 83): Sent to Yehonathan and Mesabalaʾ.

5/6Ḥev51 5/6ḤevBarKLettC

Yadin-Greenfield-Yardeni-Levine, "P.Yadin 51 (= 5/6Ḥev 51): A Hebrew Letter from Shimʿon," *Documents* (JDS 3), 293-99 (+ pl. 84): Sent to Yehonathan and the rest of the Eingedites.

5/6Ḥev52 5/6ḤevBarKLettD gr

Cotton, H. M., "P. Yadin 52: Letter from Soumaios to Yonathes and Masabala in Ein Gedi," *Documents* (JDS 3), 351-62 (+ pl. 90). Cotton now says that the site where this document was found is "unknown (between Ein Gedi and Bar Kokhba's camp at the time)." Cf. Lifshitz, B., "Papyrus grecs du Désert de Juda," *Aegyptus* 42 (1962) 240-56 (+ 2 pls.).

5/6Ḥev53 5/6ḤevBarKLettE ar

Yadin-Greenfield-Yardeni-Levine, "P.Yadin 53 (5/6Ḥev 53): An Aramaic Letter from Shimʿon, son of Kosibah," *Documents* (JDS 3), 300-304 (+ pl. 85).

5/6Ḥev54 5/6ḤevBarKLettF ar

Yadin-Greenfield-Yardeni-Levine, "P.Yadin 54 (= 5/6Ḥev 54): An Aramaic Letter from Shimʿon, son of Kosibah," *Documents* (JDS 3), 305-11 (+ pl. 86).

5/6Ḥev55 5/6ḤevBarKLettG ar

Yadin-Greenfield-Yardeni-Levine, "P.Yadin 55 (= 5/6Ḥev 55): An Aramaic Letter from Shimʿon, son of Kośibah," *Documents* (JDS 3), 312-16 (+ pl. 87).

5/6Ḥev56 5/6ḤevBarKLettH ar

Yadin-Greenfield-Yardeni-Levine, "P.Yadin 56 (= 5/6Ḥev 56): An Aramaic Letter from Shimʿon, son of Kosibah," *Documents* (JDS 3), 317-21 (+ pl. 88).

5/6Ḥev57 5/6ḤevBarKLettI ar

Yadin-Greenfield-Yardeni-Levine, "P.Yadin 57 (= 5/6Ḥev 57): An Aramaic Letter from Shimʿon," *Documents* (JDS 3), 322-28 (+ pl. 89).

5/6Ḥev58 5/6ḤevBarKLettJ ar

Yadin-Greenfield-Yardeni-Levine, "P.Yadin 58 (= 5/6Ḥev 58): An Aramaic Letter from Shimʿon," *Documents* (JDS 3), 329-32 (+ pl. 89).

5/6Ḥev59 5/6ḤevBarKLettK gr

Cotton, "P. Yadin 59: Letter in Greek from Annanos to Yonathes in Ein Gedi," *Documents* (JDS 3), 363-66. Site of discovery really unknown.

5/6Ḥev60-61 5/6ḤevBarKLettL-M

Yadin-Greenfield-Yardeni-Levine, "P.Yadin 60 and 61 (= 5/6Ḥev 60 and 61): Two Fragmentary Hebrew Letters from Shimʿon, son of Kosiba," *Documents* (JDS 3), 333-40 (+ pl. 91).

5/6Ḥev62 5/6Ḥev? ar

Yadin-Greenfield-Yardeni-Levine, "P.Yadin 62 (= 5/6Ḥev 62): A Fragmentary Papyrus (Aramaic?)," *Documents* (JDS 3), 341-43 (+ pl. 91).

5/6Ḥev63 5/6ḤevBarKLettN ar

Yadin-Greenfield-Yardeni-Levine, "P.Yadin 63 (= 5/6Ḥev 63): An Aramaic Letter from Shimʿon, son of Kosiba'," *Documents* (JDS 3), 344-48 (+ pl. 92).

5/6Ḥev64 5/6Ḥev? gr

Publication unknown.

b. Cave of Horror

8Ḥev1 8ḤevXII gr

Tov, E. (in collaboration with R. A. Kraft and P. J. Parsons), *The Greek Minor Prophets Scroll from Naḥal Ḥever (8ḤevXIIgr) (The Seiyal Collection I)* (DJD 8; Oxford: Clarendon, 1990; repr. with corrections 1995) 27-78 (+ pls. I-XX): Contains parts of 31 columns:

Col.	ii	Jonah 1:14-16; 2:1-7
	iii	Jonah 3:2-5, 7-10; 4:1-2, 5
	iv	Mic 1:1-7a
	v	Mic 1:7b-8
	vi	Mic 2:7-8; 3:5-6
	vii	Mic 4:3-5
	viii	Mic 4:6-10; 5:1-4(5)
	ix	Mic 5:4(5)-6(7)
	xiii	Nah 1:13-14
	xiv	Nah 2:5-10, 14; 3:3
	xv	Nah 3:6-17
	xvi	Hab 1:5-11
	xvii	Hab 1:14-17; 2:1-8
	xviii	Hab 2:13-20
	xix	Hab 3:9-15
	xx	Zeph 1:1-6
	xxi	Zeph 1:13-18
	xxii	Zeph 2:9-10
	xxiii	Zeph 3:6-7
	xxviii	Zech 1:1-4
	xxix	Zech 1:12-14

xxx	Zech 2:2-4, 7-12
xxxi	Zech 2:16-17; 3:1-2, 4-7
B1	Zech 8:19-21, 23a
B2	Zech 8:23b; 9:1-5

There are also six unidentified frgs., about which see E. Puech, "Les fragments non identifiès de 8KhXIIgr et le manuscrit grec des Douze Petits Prophètes," *RB* 98 (1991) 161-69; "Notes en marge de 8KhXIIgr," *RevQ* 15 (1991-92) 583-93.

8Ḥev2 8ḤevPrayer

Morgenstern, M., "2. 8ḤevPrayer," DJD 38. 167-69 (+ pl. XXVIII): a very fragmentary Hebrew(?) text.

8Ḥev3 8ḤevpapFrgs

Aharoni, Y., "Expedition B — The Cave of Horror," *IEJ* 12 (1962) 186-99 (pl. 30E).

8Ḥev4 8ḤevpapUnid gr

Cotton, H. M., "4. 8Ḥev papUnidentified Text gr," DJD 38. 171-72 (+ pl. XXVIII).

8Ḥev5 8ḤevostrA

Aharoni, "Expedition B," *IEJ* 12 (1962) 196 (+ pl. 29A).

8Ḥev6 8ḤevostrB

Aharoni, "Expedition B," *IEJ* 12 (1962) 196-97 (+ pl. 29B).

8Ḥev7 8Ḥevostrfrgs

Aharoni, "Expedition B," *IEJ* 12 (1962), pl. 31A-D.

c. Unknown Ḥever/Ṣe'lim Cave

XḤev/Se1 XḤev/SeNum[a]

Cancelled; now part of 5/6Ḥev1a (5/6ḤevNum[a]).

XḤev/Se2 XḤev/SeNum[b]

Flint, "2. XḤev/SeNumbers[b]," DJD 38. 173-77 (+ pl. XXIX): Num 27:2-13; 28:11-12; + one unidentified frg. See "Biblical Scrolls from Naḥal Ḥever and 'Wadi Seiyal': Introduction," ibid., 133-35.

XḤev/Se3 XḤev/SeDeut

Flint, "3. XḤev/SeDeuteronomy," DJD 38. 179-82 (+ pl. XXIX): Deut 9:4-7, 21-23.

XḤev/Se4 XḤev/SePs

Cancelled; now part of 5/6Ḥev1b (5/6ḤevPs).

XḤev/Se5 XḤev/Sephyl

Morgenstern, M. and M. Segal, "5. XḤev/SePhylactery," DJD 38. 183-91 (+ pl. XXX): Contains Exod 13:1-16; Deut 6:4-9; 11:13-17; Deut 11:17-21. See A. Yardeni, "Introduction to the Aramaic and Hebrew Documentary Texts," DJD 27. 9-17.

XḤev/Se6 XḤev/SeEschHymn

Morgenstern, "6. XḤev/SeEschatological Hymn," DJD 38. 193-200 (+ pl. XXXI): The text seems to be a song of thanksgiving to God for blessings, which uses many biblical phrases.

XḤev/Se7 XḤev/SeSaleDeedA ar

Yardeni, A., "7. XḤev/Se Deed of Sale A ar (134 or 135 CE)," DJD 27. 19-25 (+ pl. 1, fig. 1): An Aramaic double deed, with upper and lower texts.

XḤev/Se8 XḤev/SeSaleDeedB ar

Yardeni, "8. XḤev/Se papDeed of Sale B ar and heb (135 CE)," DJD 27. 26-33 (+ pl. II, figs. 2-3): Deed for the sale of a house in Kefar Baru in the days of Bar Kokhba.

XḤev/Se8a XḤev/SeSaleDeedC ar

Yardeni, "8a. XḤev/Se papDeed of Sale C ar (134 or 135 CE)," DJD 27. 34-37 (+ pl. III, figs. 4-5): Sale of a house by Ḥadad to ʾElʿazar; its boundaries south, east, north, and west.

XḤev/Se9 XḤev/SeSaleDeedD ar

Yardeni, "9. XḤev/Se papDeed of Sale D ar," DJD 27. 38-51 (+ pls. IV-V, figs. 6-8): A double document recording the sale of property.

XḤev/Se9a XḤev/SeUncFrgA ar

Yardeni, "9a. XḤev/Se papUnclassified Fragment A ar," DJD 27. 52-53 (+ pl. VI, fig. 9).

XḤev/Se10 XḤev/SeReceiptA ar

Yardeni, "10. XḤev/Se papReceipt for Payment of Fine? ar," DJD 27. 54-56 (+ pl. VII, fig. 9): Document of uncertain nature.

XḤev/Se11 XḤev/SeMarrCont ar

Yardeni, "11. XḤev/Se papMarriage Contract? ar," DJD 27. 57-59 (+ pl. VII, fig. 9).

XḤev/Se12 XḤev/SeReceiptB ar

Yardeni, "12. XḤev/Se papReceipt for Dates ar (131 CE)," DJD 27. 60-64 (+ pls. VIII-IX, fig. 10).

XḤev/Se13 XḤev/SeWaiver ar

Yardeni, "13. XḤev/Se papWaiver of Claims? ar (134 or 135 CE)," DJD 27. 65-70 (+ pls. VIII-IX, fig. 11): This text is neither a writ of divorce nor a marriage contract, as has been claimed at times; it is a divorce quittance, an acknowledgement by a divorced woman that her former husband is no longer indebted to her. See J. A. Fitzmyer, "The So-Called Aramaic Divorce Text from Wadi Seiyal," *Frank Moore Cross Volume* (ErIsr 26; Jerusalem: Israel Exploration Society, 1999) 16*-22*.

XḤev/Se14 XḤev/SeFrgDeed ar

Yardeni, "14. XḤev/Se papFragment of a Deed ar?," DJD 27. 71 (+ pl. X, fig. 12).

XḤev/Se15 XḤev/SeUncFrgB

Yardeni, "15. XḤev/Se papUnclassified Fragments B," DJD 27. 72 (+ pl. X, fig. 12).

XḤev/Se16-17 XḤev/SeUncFrgC-D

Yardeni, "16-17. XḤev/Se papUnclassified Fragments C-D," DJD 27. 73 (+ pl. X, fig. 12).

XḤev/Se18 XḤev/SeUncFrgE

Yardeni, "18. XḤev/Se papUnclassified Fragment E," DJD 27. 74 (+ pl. X, fig. 12).

XḤev/Se19 XḤev/SeUncFrgF

Yardeni, "19. XḤev/Se papUnclassified Fragment F," DJD 27. 75 (+ pl. X, fig. 12).

XḤev/Se20
Cancelled.

XḤev/Se21 XḤev/SeSaleDeedE ar
Yardeni, "21. XḤev/Se papDeed of Sale E ar," DJD 27. 76-83 (+ pls. XI-XII, fig. 12-13): The buyer is Yehoseph, and the sale is one of "places."

XḤev/Se22 XḤev/SeSaleDeedF ar
Yardeni, "22. XḤev/Se papDeed of Sale F? ar," DJD 27. 84-86 (+ pl. XIII, fig. 14): Very fragmentary double document.

XḤev/Se23 XḤev/SeSaleDeedG ar
Yardeni, "23. XḤev/Se papDeed of Sale G ar," DJD 27. 87-88 (+ pl. XIV, fig. 15).

XḤev/Se24 XḤev/SepapDeedA ar
Yardeni, "24. XḤev/Se papDeed A ar," DJD 27. 89-90 (+ pl. XV, fig. 15).

XḤev/Se24a XḤev/SepapDeedB ar
Yardeni, "24a. XḤev/Se papDeed B ar," DJD 27. 91-92 (+ pl. XVI, fig. 15).

XḤev/Se25 XḤev/SepapDeedC ar
Yardeni, "25. XḤev/Se papDeed C ar," DJD 27. 93-94 (+ pl. XVII, fig. 16).

XḤev/Se26 XḤev/SeDepositBarley ar
Yardeni, "26. XḤev/Se papText Dealing with Deposits and Barley ar," DJD 27. 95-96 (+ pl. XVII, fig. 16).

XḤev/Se27 XḤev/SepapDeedD ar
Yardeni, "27. XḤev/Se papDeed D ar," DJD 27. 97-98 (+ pl. XVIII, fig. 16).

XḤev/Se28 XḤev/SeUncFrgG ar
Yardeni, "28. XḤev/Se papUnclassified Fragment G ar," DJD 27. 99 (+ pl. XIX, fig. 17).

XḤev/Se29 XḤev/SeUncFrgH
Yardeni, "29. XḤev/Se papUnclassified Fragments H," DJD 27. 100-102 (+ pl. XIX, fig. 17).

XḤev/Se30 XḤev/SeBarKLett
Yardeni, "30. XḤev/Se papLetter to Shimʿon ben Kosibah," DJD 27. 103-4 (+ pl. XX, fig. 18). Letter from Shimʿon ben MTNYM/H.

XḤev/Se31 XḤev/SepapDeedE ar
Yardeni, "31. XḤev/Se papDeed E ar," DJD 27. 105 (+ pl. XXI, fig. 19).

XḤev/Se32 XḤev/SepapDeedF ar
Yardeni, "XḤev/Se 32 + 4Q347. papDeed F ar," DJD 27. 106-77 (+ pl. XXI, fig. 19): 4Q347 apparently belongs with this XḤev/Se frg.

XḤev/Se33 XḤev/SeUncFrgI ar
Yardeni, "33. XḤev/Se papUnclassified Fragment I ar," DJD 27. 108 (+ pl. XXII, fig. 19).

XḤev/Se34 XḤev/SepapDeedG ar
Yardeni, "34. XḤev/Se papDeed G ar," DJD 27. 109-10 (+ pl. XXII, fig. 19).

XḤev/Se35 XḤev/SeUncFrgJ ar
Yardeni, "35. XḤev/Se papUnclassified Fragment J ar," DJD 27. 111 (+ pl. XXII, fig. 19).

XḤev/Se36 XḤev/SeUncFrgK ar
Yardeni, "36. XḤev/Se papUnclassified Fragment K," DJD 27. 112 (+ pl. XXII, fig. 19).

XḤev/Se37 XḤev/SepapDeedH ar
Yardeni, "37. XḤev/Se papDeed H ar?," DJD 27. 113-16 (+ pls. XXIII-XXIV, fig. 20).

XḤev/Se38-47h XḤev/SeUncFrgL-BB
Yardeni, "38-47h. XḤev/Se papUnclassified Fragments L-BB," DJD 27. 117-20 (+ pls. XXV-XXVI, figs. 20-21).

XḤev/Se48
Cancelled.

XḤev/Se49 XḤev/SePromNoteA
Yardeni, "49. XḤev/Se Promissory Note (133 CE)," DJD 27. 121-22 (+ pl. XXVII, figs. 22-23): A Hebrew text, written on hide, related to time of Bar Kokhba.

XḤev/Se50 XḤev/SeSaleDeedH ar
Yardeni, "XḤev/Se 50 + Mur 26. papDeed of Sale H ar," DJD 27. 123-29 (+ pls. XXVIII-XXX, figs. 24-26): See P. Benoit et al., DJD 2. 137-38 (Mur 26).

XḤev/Se51 XḤev/SepapDeedI ar

Yardeni, "Naḥal Ṣe'elim 51: Papyrus Fragments of a Deed," *Textbook of Aramaic, Hebrew and Nabataean Documentary Texts from the Judaean Desert and Related Material* (2 vols.; Jerusalem: Hebrew University/Ben-Zion Dinur Center, 2000), 2. 39 (+ pl. 85).

XḤev/Se52 XḤev/SePromNoteB ar

Yardeni, "Naḥal Ṣe'elim 52: Papyrus Fragments of a Promissory Note?," *Textbook,* 2. 39 (+ pl. 85).

XḤev/Se53-59

Missing texts (see DJD 39. 110).

XḤev/Se60 XḤev/SeTaxReceipt gr

Cotton, H. M., "60. XḤev/Se papTax (or Rent) Receipt from Maḥoza gr," DJD 27. 166-73 (+ pls. XXXI-XXXII, fig. 27). Dated A.D. 125. See Cotton, "Introduction to the Greek Documentary Texts," ibid., 133-57; "Introduction to the Archive of Salome Komaïse, Daughter of Levi," ibid., 158-65.

XḤev/Se61 XḤev/SeConclusion gr (olim XḤev/Se 62; SHR 3001)

Cotton, "61. XḤev/Se papConclusion to a Land Declaration gr," DJD 27. 174-80 (+ pls. XXXI, XXXIII): Two frgs., written in Greek, are from Rabbath Moab, Arabia, dated 25 April 127 and are related to XḤev/Se62 and P.Yadin 16.

XḤev/Se62 XḤev/SeDeclaration gr (olim XḤev/Se Gr 7)

Cotton, "62. XḤev/Se papLand Declaration gr," DJD 27. 181-94 (+ pls. XXXIV-XXXVII). Dated A.D. 127.

XḤev/Se63 XḤev/SeRenunciation gr

Cotton, "63. XḤev/Se papDeed of Renunciation of Claims gr," DJD 27. 195-202 (+ pls. XXXI, XXXVIII). Dated A.D. 127.

XḤev/Se64 XḤev/SeGiftDeed gr

Cotton, "64. XḤev/Se papDeed of Gift gr," DJD 27. 203-23 (+ pls. XXXIX-XL, fig. 27). Dated A.D. 129.

XḤev/Se65 XḤev/SeMarrCont gr

Cotton, "65. XḤev/Se papMarriage Contract gr," DJD 27. 224-37 (+ pl. XLI). Inner text of a double document published by Lewis as 5/6Ḥev37, which Cotton now says is P.Yadin 37, part of the Babatha Archive in Greek, although Lewis did not identify it as such. Dated A.D. 131.

XḤev/Se66 XḤev/SeLoan gr

Cotton, "66. XḤev/Se papLoan with Hypothec gr," DJD 27. 238-43 (+ pl. XLII). Dated A.D. 99 or 109.

XḤev/Se67 XḤev/SeTimber gr

Cotton, "67. XḤev/Se papText Mentioning Timber gr," DJD 27. 244-47 (+ pls. XXXI and XLIII). Before A.D. 127 or 128.

XḤev/Se68 XḤev/SeGuardian gr

Cotton, "68. XḤev/Se papText Mentioning a Guardian gr," DJD 27. 248-49 (+ pls. XXXI and XLIV).

XḤev/Se69 XḤev/SeCancMarr gr

Cotton, "69. XḤev/Se papCancelled Marriage Contract gr," DJD 27. 250-74 (+ pls. XLV-XLVI). Dated A.D. 130.

XḤev/Se70 XḤev/SeUnidFrgA gr

Cotton, "70. XḤev/Se papUnidentified Fragment A gr," DJD 27. 275 (+ pls. XXXI and XLVII).

XḤev/Se71 XḤev/SeUnidFrgB gr

Cotton, "71. XḤev/Se papUnidentified Fragment B gr," DJD 27. 276 (+ pls. XXXI and XLVII).

XḤev/Se72 XḤev/SeUnidFrgC gr

Cotton, "72. XḤev/Se papUnidentified Fragment C gr," DJD 27. 277 (+ pls. XXXI and XLVII).

XḤev/Se73 XḤev/SeEndDoc gr

Cotton, "73. XḤev/Se papEnd of a Document gr," DJD 27. 278-79 (+ pl. XLVII). Dated A.D. 106/7 or 109.

XḤev/Se74-169 XḤev/SeUnidFrgs gr

Cotton, DJD 27, pls. XLVIII-XLIX (no transcription).

XḤev/Se?1-12 XḤev/SeUnid

Cotton, DJD 27, pl. L.

XḤev/Se?13-23 XḤev/SeUnid

Cotton, DJD 27, pl. LI.

XḤev/Se?24-35 XḤev/SeUnid
Cotton, DJD 27, pl. LII.

XḤev/Se?36-57 XḤev/SeUnid
Cotton, DJD 27, pl. LIII.

XḤev/SeNab1
See 5/6Ḥev 36.

XḤev/SeNab2-6 XḤev/SeUnid
Tov, E., "List of the Texts from the Judaean Desert," DJD 39. 111.

3. *Naḥal Ṣe'elim (Wadi Seiyal)*

Cave 34 of this wadi, sometimes called "Cave of the Scrolls," yielded written material (see H. Eshel and H. M. Cotton, "Ṣe'elim, Naḥal," *EDSS*, 859-61).

34Se1 34Sephyl
Aharoni, Y., "Expedition B," *IEJ* 11 (1961) 11-24, esp. 22-23 (+ pl. 11); cf. *Yedi'ot* 25 (1961) 19-33; *ILN*, 20 February 1960, p. 230 (photograph).

34Se2 34SeNum
Morgenstern, M., "2. 34Se Numbers," DJD 38. 209 (+ pl. XXXIII): Two tiny frgs., of which one is inscribed with the tops of letters that may be from Num 18:21 and Num 19:11.

34Se3 34Se papDeed ar
Morgenstern, "3. 34Se papDeed ar," DJD 38. 211-14 (+ pl. XXXIV): 12 tiny frgs., of which only frg. 2 has partially legible lines.

34Se4 34SeCensus gr
Cotton, "34Ṣe papCensus List from Judaea or Arabia gr," DJD 38. 217-25 (+ pls. XXXIV-XXXV): Six frgs. with names, patronymics, and ages, perhaps of refugees associated with the Bar Kokhba revolt.

34Se5 34SeAcc gr
Cotton, "34Ṣe papAccount gr," DJD 38. 227-28 (+ pl. XXXV).

4. *Wadi Murabbaʿat*

Five caves were discovered in this wadi, but only three yielded written material: 1Mur, texts 2, 78; 2Mur, texts 3-77, 79-87, 89-173; 5Mur, text 88 (see DJD 2. 50). These texts, however, are not distinguished by cave; they are simply designated by Mur and numbered consecutively according to genre and language. All 173 texts are grouped conveniently in one volume: P. Benoit, J. T. Milik, and R. de Vaux, *Les grottes de Murabbaʿât* (DJD 2; Oxford: Clarendon, 1961; in two parts: 1. Texte; 2. Planches). Mur 1-16, 88-107 are inscribed on skin; Mur 17-71 on papyrus; Mur 72-87 on ostraca (in either Aramaic, Hebrew, or Nabatean). The Greek texts Mur 89-107, 164 are inscribed on skin; Mur 108-57 on papyrus; and Mur 165-68 on ostraca. Latin texts on Mur 158-63 are written on papyrus; and the Arabic texts Mur 169-73 (of much later date) are written on paper. For the site and the history of the discovery, see R. de Vaux, "Archéologie," 1-63; cf. E. Stern and H. Eshel, "Murabbaʿat, Wadi," *EDSS*, 581-86.

Detailed Listing of Mur 1-173 in DJD 2

See J. T. Milik, "Textes Hébreux et Araméens," ibid., 65-74.

Mur 1 MurGen-Exod-Num

"1. Genèse, Exode, Nombres," DJD 2. 75-78 (+ pls. XIX-XXI): Gen 32:4-5, 30, 33; 33:1; 34:5-7, 30-31; 35:1, 4-7; Exod 4:28-31; 5:3; 6:5-11; Num 34:10; 36:7-11.

Mur 2 MurDeut

"2. Deutéronome," DJD 2. 78-79 (+ pl. XXI): Deut 10:1-3; 11:2-3; 12:25-26; 14:29–15:1 or 2.

Mur 3 MurIsa

"3. Isaïe," DJD 2. 79-80 (+ pl. XXII): Isa 1:4-14.

Mur 4 Murphyl

"4. Phylactère," DJD 2. 80-85 (+ pls. XXII-XXIV): Exod 13:1-10, 11-16; Deut 11:13-21; 6:4-9.

Mur 5 MurMez

"5. Mezouza(?)," DJD 2. 85-86 (+ pl. XXIV): Illegible.

Mur 6 MurNon-bib

"6. Texte littéraire non biblique," DJD 2. 86 (+ pl. XXV).

Mur 7 MurCont

"7. Contrat(?), en Hébreu," DJD 2. 86-87 (+ pl. XXV).

Mur 8 MurAccCereal ar

"8. Compte de céréales et légumineuses, en araméen," DJD 2. 87-89 (+ pl. XXV): Cereals and vegetables.

Mur 9 MurAccA

"9. Compte," DJD 2. 89-90 (+ pl. XXVI): List (with numerical ciphers).

Mur 10 MurPalimpsestA

"10. Palimpseste: Compte, Abécédaires," DJD 2. 90-92 (+ pl. XXVI): A list of names with accounts, and an abecedary.

Mur 11 MurAbecedary

"11. Abécédaire," DJD 2. 92 (+ pl. XXVII).

Mur 12-16 MurUncfrgs

"12-16. Fragments non caractérisés," DJD 2. 92 (+ pl. XXVII).

Mur 17 MurPalimpsestB

"17. Palimpseste: Lettre, Liste de personnes (viiie siècle avant J.-C.)," DJD 2. 93-100 (+ pl. XXVIII): Palimpsest letter of 8th cent. B.C.; list of persons of 2d cent. A.D.

Mur 18 MurIOU ar

"18. Reconnaissance de dette, en araméen (55/56 ap. J.-C.)," DJD 2. 100-104 (+ pl. XXIX). Dated in 2d year of Nero Caesar.

Mur 19 MurDivorce ar

"19. Acte de répudiation, en araméen (111 ap. J.-C.)," DJD 2. 104-9 (+ pls. XXX-XXXI): Writ of divorce, dated A.D. 111.

Mur 20 MurMarrContA ar

"20. Contrat de mariage, en araméen (117 ap. J.-C.)," DJD 2. 109-14 (+ pls. XXX-XXXI): Marriage contract, dated A.D. 117.

Mur 21 MurMarrContB ar

"21. Contrat de mariage, en araméen," DJD 2. 114-17 (+ pls. XXXII-XXXIII). Date missing; perhaps earlier than Mur 20.

Mur 22 MurSaleDeedA
"22. Acte de vente de terrain, en hébreu (131 ap. J.-C.)," DJD 2. 118-21 (+ pls. XXXIII-XXXIV): Deed of sale of land, dated A.D. 131.

Mur 23 MurSaleDeedB ar
"23. Acte de vente(?), en araméen (132 ap. J.-C.?)," DJD 2. 121-22 (+ pl. XXXIV): Perhaps a deed of sale, dated A.D. 132.

Mur 24 MurFarmCont
"24. Contrats de fermage, en hébreu (an 133)," DJD 2. 122-34 (+ pls. XXXV-XXXVII): 12 διαστρώματα (farming contracts), dated A.D. 133; texts A-F: more or less complete; texts G-L: quite fragmentary.

Mur 25 MurSaleDeedC ar
"25. Acte de vente de terrain, en araméen (133 ap. J.-C.)," DJD 2. 134-37 (+ pl. XXXVIII): Deed of sale of land, dated A.D. 133.

Mur 26 MurSaleDeedD ar
"26. Acte de vente, en araméen," DJD 2. 137-38 (+ pl. XXXIX): Deed of sale.

Mur 27 MurSaleDeedE ar
"27. Acte de vente, en araméen," DJD 2. 138-39 (+ pl. XXXIX): Deed of sale.

Mur 28 MurPropDeed ar
"28. Acte concernant une propriété, en araméen," DJD 2. 139-40 (+ pls. XL-XL bis): Property deed.

Mur 29 MurSaleDeedF
"29. Acte de vente, en hébreu (133 ap. J.-C.)," DJD 2. 140-44, 205 (+ pls. XLI-XLI bis): Deed of sale, dated A.D. 133.

Mur 30 MurSaleDeedG
"30. Acte de vente d'un terrain, en hébreu (134 ap. J.-C.)," DJD 2. 144-48, 205 (+ pls. XLI bis-XLII bis): Deed of sale of land, dated A.D. 134.

Mur 31 MurDeedFrgs ar
"31. Fragments d'actes de vente," DJD 2. 148-49 (+ pl. XLII bis).

Mur 32 MurMoneyDeedA ar
"32. Acte concernant de l'argent, en araméen," DJD 2. 149-50 (+ pl. XLIII).

Mur 33 MurMoneyDeedB ar

"33. Acte concernant de l'argent, en araméen," DJD 2. 150-51 (+ pl. XLIII).

Mur 34-35 MurContFrgs ar

"34-35. Fragments de contrats araméens," DJD 2. 151 (+ pl. XLIII).

Mur 36 MurFrgCont

"36. Fragment d'un contrat hébreu," DJD 2. 152 (+ pl. XLIII).

Mur 37-40 MurScraps

"37-40. Restes de contrats et de signatures," DJD 2. 152-54 (+ pls. XLIII-XLIV).

Mur 41 MurListPersA

"41. Liste de personnes," DJD 2. 154-55 (+ pl. XLIV).

Mur 42 MurLettBeth-Mašiko

"42. Lettre des administrateurs de Bet-Mašiko à Yešuaʿ fils de Galgula," DJD 2. 155-59 (+ pl. XLV): Letter of the administrators of Beth-Mashiko to Yeshuaʿ ben Galgula' [with *aleph*].

Mur 43 MurLettBarKA

"43. Lettre de Šimʿon fils de Kosba à Yešuaʿ fils de Galgula," DJD 2. 159-61 (+ pl. XLVI): Letter of Shimʿon ben Kosibah to Yeshuaʿ ben Galgulah [with *hē*].

Mur 44 MurLettBarKB

"44. Lettre de Šimʿon (fils de Kosba) à Yešuaʿ fils de Galgula," DJD 2. 161-63 (+ pl. XLVI): Letter of Shimʿon to Yeshuaʿ ben Galgulah.

Mur 45 MurLettFrgA

"45. Lettre," DJD 2. 163-64 (+ pl. XLVII): Fragmentary letter mentioning *Mĕṣad Ḥasîdîn* (line 6), which Milik identifies with Khirbet Qumran.

Mur 46 MurLettEinG

"46. Lettre envoyée d'Engaddi," DJD 2. 164-66 (+ pl. XLVII): Letter of Jonathan ben X to Joseph [ben . . .], sent from ʿEin-Gedi.

Mur 47 MurLettFrgB

"47. Lettre," DJD 2. 166-67 (+ pl. XLVIII).

Mur 48 MurLettFrgC
"48. Lettre," DJD 2. 167-68 (+ pl. XLVIII).

Mur 49-52 MurLettFrgs
"49-52. Lettres(?)," DJD 2. 168-69 (+ pl. XLVIII).

Mur 53-70 MurUncFrgsA
"53-70. Fragments non caractérisés," DJD 2. 169-71 (+ pls. XLIX-LI).

Mur 71 MurFrg nab
"71. Fragment d'un texte en écriture nabatéenne," DJD 2. 171 (+ pl. LI): No transcription; only photograph.

Mur 72 MurNarrostr ar
"72. Texte narratif en araméen," DJD 2. 172-74 (+ pl. LII): This and the following 15 texts (Mur 73-87) are inscribed on ostraca, but it is almost impossible to determine the genre of the writing.

Mur 73 MurAbecedary
"73. Abécédaire et noms de personnes," DJD 2. 175 (+ pl. LII).

Mur 74 MurListPers B
"74. Liste de personnes," DJD 2. 175-77 (+ pl. LIII).

Mur 75-77 MurNamesPers
"75-77. Noms de personnes," DJD 2. 177-78 (+ pls. LIII-LIV): Each ostracon bears the name of one man.

Mur 78-80 MurAbecedaries
"78-80. Abécédaires," DJD 2. 178-79 (+ pls. LIV-LV).

Mur 81-86 MurUncFrgsB
"81-86. Fragments non caractérisés," DJD 2. 179 (+ pl. LV).

Mur 87 MurName
"87. Nom de personne," DJD 2. 179-80 (+ pl. LV).

Mur 88 MurXIIProph
"88. Rouleau des Douze Prophètes," DJD 2. 181-205 (+ pls. LVI-LXXIII): 20 fragmentary columns contain parts of Joel 2:20, 26; 3:1-5; 4:1-16; Amos 1:5-15;

2:1; 7:3-16; 8:1-7, 11-14; 9:1-14; Obad 1-21; Jonah 1:1-16; 2:1-11; 3:2-10; 4:1-11; Mic 1:1-16; 2:1-13; 3:1-12; 4:1-14; 5:1-14; 6:1-14; 7:1-18; Nah 1:14; 2:1-14; 3:1-19; Hab 1:3-15; 2:1-11, 18-19; 3:1-19; Zeph 1:1, 11-18; 2:1-15; 3:1-6, 8-20; Hag 1:1-11, 12-15; 2:1-10, 12-23; Zech 1:1-4; + unidentified frgs. on pl. LXXIII. This text comes from MurCave 5 (see DJD 2. 50).

Greek and Latin Texts (Mur 89-168)

See P. Benoit, "III. Textes Grecs et Latins: Introduction," DJD 2. 207-15.

Mur 89 MurAccMoney gr
"89. Compte d'argent," DJD 2. 216-17 (+ pl. LXXIV).

Mur 90 MurAccCerealA gr
"90. Compte de céréales et légumineuses," DJD 2. 217-20 (+ pl. LXXV): Account of cereals and vegetables.

Mur 91 MurAccCerealB gr
"91. Compte de céréales et légumineuses," DJD 2. 220-22 (+ pl. LXXVI): Account of cereals and vegetables.

Mur 92 MurAccCerealC gr
"92. Compte de céréales," DJD 2. 222-23 (+ pl. LXXVI): Account of cereals.

Mur 93 MurAccB gr
"93. Compte," DJD 2. 223-24 (+ pl. LXXVI).

Mur 94 MurRecap gr
"94. Relevé récapitulatif de comptes," DJD 2. 224-27 (+ pl. LXXVII): Recapitulation of accounts.

Mur 95 MurListNames gr
"95. Liste de noms," DJD 2. 227-28 (+ pl. LXXVIII).

Mur 96 MurAccCerealD gr
"96. Compte de céréales et légumineuses," DJD 2. 228-29 (+ pl. LXXVIII): Account of cereals and vegetables.

Mur 97 MurAccCerealE gr
"97. Compte de céréales," DJD 2. 229-30 (+ pl. LXXVIII): Account of cereals.

Mur 98-102 MurFrgAcc gr
"98-102. Fragments de Comptes (?)," DJD 2. 230-31 (+ pl. LXXIX): Fragmentary accounts.

Mur 103-7 MurCorners gr
"103-7. Coins de feuilles et onglets," DJD 2. 231-33 (+ pl. LXXX).

Mur 108 MurpapPhilos gr
"108. Fragments d'un texte philosophique (?)," DJD 2. 234-36 (+ pl. LXXXI): Fragmentary philosophical text (on papyrus).

Mur 109-11 MurFrgsLitTexts gr
"109-11. Fragments de textes littéraires," DJD 2. 236-38 (+ pl. LXXXII).

Mur 112 MurFrgLitText gr
"112. Fragments d'un texte littéraire," DJD 2. 238 (+ pl. LXXXIII).

Mur 113 MurLawsuit gr
"113. Actes d'un procès (?)," DJD 2. 239-40 (+ pl. LXXXIV): Proceedings of a lawsuit.

Mur 114 MurIOU gr
"114. Reconnaissance de dette (171 ap. J.-C.)," DJD 2. 240-43 (+ pl. LXXXV): Greek bond, dated A.D. 171 (?).

Mur 115 MurpapRemarr gr
"115. Contrat de remariage (124 ap. J.-C.)," DJD 2. 243-54 (+ pls. LXXXVI-LXXXVIII): Contract of remarriage, double document on papyrus, dated A.D. 124.

Mur 116 MurMarrCont gr
"116. Contrat de mariage," DJD 2. 254-56 (+ pl. LXXXIX).

Mur 117 MurOrd gr
"117. Extraits d'ordonnances officielles (fin du IIe siècle ap. J.-C.)," DJD 2. 256-58 (+ pl. XC): Extracts of official ordinances (end of 2d cent.).

Mur 118 MurAccC gr
"118. Compte," DJD 2. 258-59 (+ pl. XCI): Frg. of an account.

Mur 119 MurAccD gr

"119. Compte(?)," DJD 2. 259 (+ pl. XCI).

Mur 120 MurAccE gr

"120. Compte(?)," DJD 2. 259-60 (+ pl. XCII).

Mur 121 MurAccF gr

"121. Compte," DJD 2. 260 (+ pl. XCIII).

Mur 122 MurExer gr

"122. Compte ou exercice scolaire (?)," DJD 2. 261 (+ pl. XCIII).

Mur 123-25 MurFrgsA gr

"123-25. Compte," DJD 2. 261-62 (+ pls. XCIII-XCIV).

Mur 126-32 MurFrgsB gr

"126-32. Fragments avec écriture littéraire ou notariale," DJD 2. 262-63 (+ pl. XCV): Greek frgs. in literary or notarial script.

Mur 133-54 MurCursiveFrgs

"133-44, 145-9, 150-4. Fragments avec écriture cursive," DJD 2. 263-66 (+ pls. XCVI-XCVIII).

Mur 155 MurFrgsC gr

"155. Fragments d'un document," DJD 2. 267 (+ pl. XCIX).

Mur 156 MurChrisLit gr

"156. Fragment liturgique chrétien (XIe siècle ap. J.-C. ?)," DJD 2. 267-68 (+ pl. C): Prayer of St. Basil, recited at Nones in the Greek liturgy of the hours.

Mur 157 MurMagic gr

"157. Fragment de texte magique (Xe siècle ap. J.-C.)," DJD 2. 269 (+ pl. C): A magical text (10th cent.).

Mur 158-59 lat

"158-9," DJD 2. 270-72 (+ pl. CI): Fragmentary texts of official nature.

Mur 160-63 lat

"160-3," DJD 2. 272-74 (+ pl. CII): Latin frgs., on papyrus.

Mur 164 gr

"164. Document en tachygraphie grecque," DJD 2. 275-79 (+ pls. CIII-CIV): Document in Greek shorthand (as yet undeciphered).

Mur 165-68

"165-8," DJD 2. 280 (+ pl. CV): Fragmentary ostraca texts in Greek or Latin.

Arabic Texts from the 9th-10th Cent. (Mur 169-73)

See Ad. Grohmann, "IV Textes Arabes: Introduction," DJD 2. 283.

Mur 169 MurReceipt arab

"169. Reçu," DJD 2. 284 (+ pl. CVI).

Mur 170 MurCont arab

"170. Fragment d'un contrat d'achat," DJD 2. 284-85 (+ pl. CVI).

Mur 171 MurMagic arab

"171. Fragment de texte magique," DJD 2. 285-86 (+ pl. CVI).

Mur 172 MurRelMag arab

"172. Texte religieux ou magique," DJD 2. 286 (+ pl. CVI).

Mur 173 MurAmulet arab

"173. Amulette," DJD 2. 286-90 (+ pl. CVII).

Select Bibliography on Murabbaʿat Problems

Cotton, H. M., "The Bar Kokhba Revolt and the Documents from the Judaean Desert: Nabataean Participation in the Revolt (*P. Yadin* 52)," *The Bar Kokhba War Reconsidered: New Perspectives on the Second Jewish Revolt against Rome* (TSAJ 100; ed. P. Schäfer; Tübingen: Mohr Siebeck, 2003) 133-52.

———, "Die Papyrusdokumente aus der jüdischen Wüste und ihre Beitrag zur Erforschung der jüdischen Geschichte des 1. und 2. Jh.s n. Chr.," *ZDPV* 115 (1999) 228-47.

Eck, W., "Hadrian, the Bar Kokhba Revolt, and the Epigraphic Transmission," *The Bar Kokhba War Reconsidered* (see above), 153-70.

Fitzmyer, J. A., "The Bar Cochba Period," *ESBNT* or *SBNT*, 305-54.

Koffmahn, E., *Die Doppelurkunden aus der Wüste Juda: Recht und Praxis der jüdischen Papyri des 1. und 2. Jahrhunderts n. Chr. samt Übertragung der Texte und deutscher Übersetzung* (STDJ 5; Leiden: Brill, 1968).

Yadin, Y., *Bar-Kokhba* (London: Weidenfeld and Nicolson, 1971).

5. *Ketef Jericho*

Ketef Jericho (in the Wadi el-Mafjar) is the name of a ridge that rises about 200 m above the oasis and is about one km west of Jericho. For the site, its caves, artifacts, and frgs. found in them, see H. Eshel and B. Zissu, "Jericho: Archaeological Introduction," DJD 38. 3-20 (+ pls. I-V, figs. 1-15); also H. Eshel, "Mafjar, Wadi el-," *EDSS*, 500-501.

Jer 1 JerLoansList ar

Eshel, H. and H. Misgav, "1. Jericho papList of Loans ar," DJD 38. 21-30 (+ pls. VI-VII, figs. 16-17).

Jer 2 JerSaleDeedA ar

Eshel, H. and E. Eshel, "2. Jericho papDeed of Sale or Lease ar," DJD 38. 31-36 (+ pl. VII, fig. 18).

Jer 3 JerSaleDeedB ar

Eshel-Eshel, "3. Jericho papDeed of Sale ar," DJD 38. 37-41 (+ pl. VIII, fig. 18).

Jer 4 JerSaleDeed gr

Cohen, N., "4. Jericho papDeed of Sale or Lease? gr (P.Jericho 4 gr)," DJD 38. 45-47 (+ pl. IX). See "4-5e. Jericho pap gr (P.Jericho 4-5e gr)," ibid., 43.

Jer 5a-d JerUnidTexts gr

Cohen, "5a-d. Jericho papUnidentified Text(s) gr (P.Jericho 5a-d gr)," DJD 38. 49-50 (+ pl. X).

Jer 5e JerSeeds gr

Cohen, "5e. Jericho papTransaction Concerning Seeds gr (P.Jericho 5e gr)," DJD 38. 51-52 (+ pl. X).

Jer 6 JerUnidTexts ar

Eshel, E., "6. Jericho papUnidentified Texts ar," DJD 38. 53-54 (+ pl. XI).

Jer 7 JerDateCrop ar

Eshel, E., H. Eshel, and H. Misgav, "7. Jericho papSale of Date Crop ar," DJD 38. 55-61 (+ pls. XI-XII, figs. 19-20).

Jer 8 JerpapDeedA ar

Yardeni, A. "8. Jericho papDeed A ar (1st Century CE)," DJD 38. 63-65 (+ pl. XIII, fig. 21).

Jer 9 JerpapDeedA

Yardeni, "9. Jericho papDeed A heb? (1st Century CE)," DJD 38. 67-69 (+ pls. XIII-XIV, figs. 21-22).

Jer 10 JerpapDeedB

Yardeni, "10. Jericho papDeed B heb? (1st Century CE)," DJD 38. 71-72 (+ pl. XIV, fig. 22).

Jer 11 JerDeed/Lett

Yardeni, "11. Jericho papDeed or Letter (1st Century CE)," DJD 38. 73-75 (+ pl. XV, fig. 23).

Jer 12 JerpapDeedB ar

Yardeni, "12. Jericho papDeed B ar (1st Century CE)," DJD 38. 77-78 (+ pl. XV, fig. 23).

Jer 13 JerUncText ar

Yardeni, "13. Jericho papUnclassified Text ar (116 CE?)," DJD 38. 79-80 (+ pl. XV, fig. 23).

Jer 14 JerUncText

Yardeni, "14. Jericho papUnclassified Text heb? (1st Century CE)," DJD 38. 81-82 (+ pl. XVI, fig. 24).

Jer 15 JerUncText ar/heb

Yardeni, "15. Jericho papUnclassified Fragments ar/heb (1st or 2nd Century CE)," DJD 38. 83-91 (+ pls. XVI-XVII, figs. 24-25).

Jer 16 JerHadrian gr

Cotton, H. M., "16. Jericho papText Mentioning the Emperor Hadrian gr," DJD 38. 93-95 (+ pl. XVIII).

Jer 17 JerpapDeed gr

Cotton, "17. Jericho papDeed? gr (P.Jericho 17 gr)," DJD 38. 97 (+ pl. XIX).

Jer 18 JerFiscAck gr

Cotton, "18. Jericho papFiscal Acknowledgement gr (P.Jericho 18 gr)," DJD 38. 99-100 (+ pl. XIX).

Jer 19 JerpapOrder gr

Cohen, "19. Jericho papWritten Order? gr," DJD 38. 103-5 (+ pls. XX-XXI). See Cohen, "19-19h. Jericho pap gr (P.Jericho 19-19h)," ibid., 101.

Jer 19a JerUnidTextA ar

Cohen, "19a. Jericho papUnidentified Text A gr (P.Jericho 19a)," DJD 38. 107 (+ pls. XX-XXI).

Jer 19b JerWitnessList gr

Cohen, "19b. Jericho papList of Witnesses? gr (P.Jericho 19b)," DJD 38. 109 (+ pls. XX-XXI).

Jer 19c-h JerUnidTextB

Cohen, "19c-h. Jericho papUnidentified Texts B gr (P.Jericho 19c-h)," DJD 38. 111-13 (+ pls. XX-XXI).

6. Wadi Sdeir

Wadi Sdeir is also called Naḥal David, containing various burial caves and the "Cave of the Pool," in which Bedouins apparently found written documents in 1952. See H. Eshel, "Sdeir, Wadi," *EDSS*, 851-52.

Sdeir 1 SdeirGen

Murphy, C., "1. SdeirGenesis," DJD 38. 117-24 (+ pl. XXII): Gen 35:6-10, 26-29; 36:1-2, 5-17. Also Y. Baruchi and H. Eshel, "Another Fragment of SdeirGenesis," *JJS* 57 (2006) 136-38: Contains Gen 36:3-5. Cf. C. Burchard, "Gen 35 6-10 und 36 5-12 MT aus der Wüste Juda," *ZAW* 78 (1966) 71-75.

Sdeir 2 SdeirPromNote ar

Yardeni, "2. Sdeir papPromissory Note? ar," DJD 38. 125-29 (+ pl. XXIII). Dated A.D. 135.

Sdeir 3 SdeirUnidTextA gr
DJD 38, pl. XXIII (photograph only; no transcription).

Sdeir 4 SdeirUnidTextB gr
DJD 38, pl. XXIV (photograph only; no transcription).

7. Naḥal Mishmar (Wadi Mahras)

In the so-called Cave of the Treasure fragmentary documents and ostraca were found. See H. Eshel, "Mishmar, Naḥal: Roman Period," *EDSS*, 568-69; P. Bar Adon, "Expedition C," *IEJ* 11 (1961) 25-35; *BJES* 25 (1961) 34-48; and especially P. Bar Adon, *The Cave of the Treasure: The Finds from the Caves in Naḥal Mishmar* (Jerusalem: Israel Exploration Society, 1980) 205-8, 217. Most of the finds in this cave date from the Chalcolithic period, but a few come from the Bar Kokhba period.

1Mish 1 MishUnid
Bar Adon, *Cave of the Treasure*, 205-6. One Hebrew word (ניתנו, "they were given"?).

1Mish 2 MishpapNames gr
Cotton, "2. 1Mish papList of Names and Account gr," DJD 38. 203-4 (+ pl. XXXII); Bar Adon, *Cave of the Treasure*, 205-6. Cf. B. Lifshitz, "The Greek Documents from Naḥal Ṣeelim and Naḥal Mishmar," *IEJ* 11 (1961) 53-62 (+ pls. 13E and 23I), esp. 59-60.

1Mish 3 MishpapSignatures ar, gr
Bar Adon, *Cave of the Treasure*, 205-7.

1Mish 4-7 MishUncOstr
Bar Adon, *Cave of the Treasure*, 207-8.

1Mish 8 MishUncOstr gr
Bar Adon, *Cave of the Treasure*, 208.

8. Masada

On the discovery of fragments at Masada, see S. Talmon, "Hebrew Fragments from Masada," in S. Talmon and Y. Yadin, *Masada VI: Yigael Yadin Excava-*

tions 1963-1965, Final Reports (Masada Reports; Jerusalem: Israel Exploration Society and the Hebrew University of Jerusalem, 1999) 1-29.

Mas 1 MasGen (olim Mas 1 i Jub)
Talmon, *Masada VI,* 31-35 (+ Ill. 2): Gen 46:7-11.

Mas 1a MasLev[a]
Talmon, *Masada VI,* 36-39 (+ Ill. 3): Lev 4:3-9.

Mas 1b MasLev[b]
Talmon, *Masada VI,* 40-50 (+ Ill. 4): Lev 8:31–11:40.

Mas 1c MasDeut
Talmon, *Masada VI,* 51-58 (+ Ill. 6): Deut 33:17–34:6.

Mas 1d MasEzek
Talmon, *Masada VI,* 59-75 (+ Ill. 8): Ezek 35:11–38:14.

Mas 1e MasPs[a]
Talmon, *Masada VI,* 76-90 (+ Ill. 9): Ps 81:2–85:6a.

Mas 1f MasPs[b]
Talmon, *Masada VI,* 91-97 (+ Ill. 10): Ps 150:1-6.

Mas 1g
Cancelled; now = 11QPs[d] (11Q8).

Mas 1h MasSir
Yadin, Y., "The Ben Sira Scroll from Masada: Introduction, Emendations and Commentary," *Masada VI,* 151-252 (+ pls. 1-8 [on pp. 197-211]): A revised edition of his book, *The Ben Sira Scroll from Masada* (Jerusalem: Israel Exploration Society and the Shrine of the Book, 1965). The revision contains "Notes on the Reading," by E. Qimron, pp. 227-31; and "Ben Sira: A Bibliography of Studies, 1965-1997," by F. García Martínez, on pp. 233-52.

Mas 1j MasJub
Talmon, *Masada VI,* 117-19 (+ Ill. 14): The frg. may be related to *Jubilees,* or may be like *Pseudo-Jubilees,* because it has phrases similar to 4Q225 (4QpsJub[a]).

Mas 1k MasShirShabb

Newsom, C., "1k. MasShirot ʿOlat HaShabbat," DJD 11. 239-52 (+ pl. XIX): Contains extensive overlaps with 4QShirShabb[d] (4Q403) 1 i 1-11. A slightly different translation and discussion by C. Newsom and Y. Yadin are found in "The Masada Fragment of the Qumran Songs of the Sabbath Sacrifice," *Masada VI,* 120-32 (+ Ill. 15).

Mas 1l MasapocrJosh

Talmon, *Masada VI,* 105-16 (+ Ill. 13): A paraphrase of Josh 21:45 and 23:14. Talmon's siglum is MasapocrJosh.

Mas 1m MasapocrGen

Talmon, *Masada VI,* 98-104 (+ Ill. 12): These frgs. are in Hebrew and resemble the paraphrase of Genesis one finds in *Jubilees;* they have nothing to do with the Aramaic text of 1QapGen (1Q20). Talmon's siglum in MasapocrGen.

Mas 1n MasUnid

Talmon, *Masada VI,* 133-35 (+ Ill. 16): A Qumran-like Hebrew text.

Mas 1o MasSamFrg

Talmon, *Masada VI,* 138-49 (+ Ill. 18): A papyrus fragment inscribed on both recto and verso in paleo-Hebrew script with a text of Samaritan origin.

Mas 1p MasUncFrg

Talmon, *Masada VI,* 136-37 (+ Ill. 17): Contains a few lines; on line 2 occurs a word (אלכן) not found in biblical Hebrew. Talmon thinks it is "apparently Aramaic," which would be unusual because all the other Masada texts are in Hebrew.

Mas 1-553 MasostrA

Yadin, Y. and J. Naveh, "The Aramaic and Hebrew Ostraca and Jar Inscriptions from Masada," *Masada I: The Yigael Yadin Excavations 1963-1965, Final Reports* (Masada Reports; Jerusalem: Israel Exploration Society and the Hebrew University of Jerusalem, 1989) 1-48 (+ pls. 1-44). This volume also contains a section on "The Coins of Masada," by Y. Meshorer, pp. 69-132 (+ pls. 61-81).

Mas 554-56 MasostrLett

Yadin-Naveh, *Masada I,* 49-51 (+ pl. 45).

Mas 557-720 MasostrB

Yadin-Naveh, *Masada I,* 52-68 (+ pls. 46-59).

Mas 721-38 Maspap lat

Cotton, H. M. and J. Geiger, "The Latin and Greek Documents," *Masada II: The Yigael Yadin Excavations 1963-1965, Final Reports* (Masada Reports; Jerusalem: Israel Exploration Society and the Hebrew University of Jerusalem, 1989) 27-79 (+ pls. 1-7): Contains Virgil, *Aeneid* 4.9 and many other Latin frgs. See also "Introduction," pp. 1-24.

Mas 739 MaspapLitText gr

Cotton-Geiger, *Masada II,* 81-82 (+ pl. 8): A one-line (literary ?) text on papyrus.

Mas 740 MaspapDoc gr

Cotton-Geiger, *Masada II,* 82-85 (+ pl. 8): Contains documents of some sort written on papyrus about A.D. 25-35.

Mas 741 MaspapLettA gr

Cotton-Geiger, *Masada II,* 85-88 (+ pl. 8): A papyrus letter of Abaskantos to Judas.

Mas 742 MaspapByzDoc

Cotton-Geiger, *Masada II,* 89-90 (+ pl. 9): A papyrus document from Byzantine times.

Mas 743 MasWoodTab gr

Cotton-Geiger, *Masada II,* 90 (+ pl. 9): Contains three Greek letters.

Mas 744 MaspapNames gr

Cotton-Geiger, *Masada II,* 90-91 (+ pl. 9).

Mas 745 MaspapLettB gr

Cotton-Geiger, *Masada II,* 91-92 (+ pl. 9).

Mas 746 MaspapLettC gr

Cotton-Geiger, *Masada II,* 92-93 (+ pl. 9).

Mas 747 MaspapUnidFrg gr

Cotton-Geiger, *Masada II,* 93 (+ pl. 9).

Mas 748 MasBilNames

Cotton-Geiger, *Masada II*, 95-98 (+ pl. 10): Contains bilingual (Greek and Latin) list of names.

Mas 749 MaspapFrgs

Cotton-Geiger, *Masada II*, 98-100 (+ pl. 10): Miscellaneous papyrus frgs. with Greek and Latin words.

Mas 750-927 MasostrC gr

Cotton-Geiger, *Masada II*, 103-203 (+ pls. 11-41): Contain many Latin and Greek words or names.

Mas 928-45 MasGraffiti

Cotton-Geiger, *Masada II*, 207-15 (+ pls. 42-47): Greek or Latin graffiti found in various buildings.

Mas 946-51 MasAmphora

Cotton-Geiger, *Masada II*, 217-21 (+ pl. 48): Various Latin stamps found on imported amphorae (see pp. 4, 8).

9. *Cairo Genizah*

Though not discovered in the vicinity of the Dead Sea, these texts are medieval copies of some of the documents that have been discovered in the Qumran caves or at Masada and are thus related to them. These texts were found at the end of the 19th century in a genizah of the Ezra Synagogue in Old Cairo.

CSir

Schechter, S. and C. Taylor, *The Wisdom of Ben Sira: Portions of the Book Ecclesiasticus from Hebrew Manuscripts in the Cairo Genizah Collection Presented to the University of Cambridge by the Editors* (Cambridge, UK: Cambridge University Press, 1899).

Schechter, S., *Facsimiles of the Fragments Hitherto Recovered of the Book of Ecclesiasticus in Hebrew* (Oxford: Oxford University Press, 1901).

Levi, I., *The Hebrew Text of the Book of Ecclesiasticus: Edited with Brief Notes and a Selected Glossary* (Semitic Study Series 3; Leiden: Brill, 1904).

Segal, M. Z., ספר בן סירא השלם (Jerusalem: Bialik Institute, 1958).

Vattioni, F., *Ecclesiastico: Testo ebraico con apparato critico e versioni greca, latina e siriaca* (Pubblicazioni del Seminario di Semitistica, Testi 1; Naples: Istituto Orientale di Napoli, 1968).

CWis

Berger, K., *Die Weisheitsschrift aus der Kairoer Geniza: Erstedition, Kommentar und Übersetzung* (Texte und Arbeiten zum neutestamentlichen Zeitalter 1; Tübingen: Francke V., 1989) 11-46. The text seems to be related to 1QS 3-4; cf. K. Berger, "Die Bedeutung der wiederentdeckten Weisheitsschrift aus der Kairoer Geniza für das Neue Testament," *NTS* 36 (1990) 415-30.

CD

Schechter, S., *Documents of Jewish Sectaries: Volume 1: Fragments of a Zadokite Work* (2 vols.; Cambridge, UK: Cambridge University Press, 1910), 1. 1-20 (+ two plates); introduction (ix-xxix); translation (xxxi-lvi). Reprinted in one volume with a prolegomenon by J. A. Fitzmyer (New York: Ktav, 1970), a bibliography up to that date, pp. 25-34. This edition has photographs of only two columns of the Hebrew text. The photographs of the entire text were published eventually by S. Zeitlin, *The Zadokite Fragments: Facsimile of the Manuscripts in the Cairo Genizah Collection in the Possession of the University Library, Cambridge, England* (JQR Monograph Series 1; Philadelphia: Dropsie College, 1952). See now M. Broshi, *The Damascus Document Reconsidered* (Jerusalem: Israel Exploration Society, Shrine of the Book, Israel Museum, 1992): Contains good photographs of all columns, transcription of the text, and two essays: one by J. M. Baumgarten, "The Laws of the Damascus Document in Current Research" (pp. 51-62); the other by F. García Martínez, "Damascus Document: A Bibliography of Studies 1970-1989" (pp. 63-83).

CTLevi ar

Known to exist in two sources: (a) Cambridge University Genizah Frg. T-S 16.94; (b) Bodleian Library Genizah Frg., Ms Heb c 27 f 56. See H. L. Pass and J. Arendzen, "Fragment of an Aramaic Text of the Testament of Levi," *JQR* 12 (1899-1900) 651-61 (= Cambridge frg.; no photograph); R. H. Charles and A. Cowley, "An Early Source of the Testaments of the Patriarchs," *JQR* 19 (1906-7) 566-83 (= Bodleian frg. with photograph + text of Cambridge frg. [without photograph]); cf. J. C. Greenfield and M. E. Stone, "Remarks on the Aramaic Testament of Levi from the Geniza," *RB* 86 (1979) 214-30 (+ pls. XIII-XIV [photograph of Cambridge frg.1). Cf. P. Grelot, "Le Testament araméen de Levi, est-il traduit de l'hébreu? A propos du fragment de Cambridge, col. c 10 à d 1," *REJ* 114 (1955) 91-99; also J. T. Milik, *RB* 62 (1955) 398-406. Cf. 1Q21.

10. Wadi en-Nar (Naḥal Qidron)

See DJD 39. 97.

Nar 1 NarpapUnidA gr
Not published.

Nar 2 NarpapUnid sem
Not published.

Nar 3 NarUnidB gr
Not published.

Nar 4 NarpapUncFrgs
Not published.

Nar 5 NarFrgsLinen, Hide
Not published.

11. Wadi Ghweir (Naḥal David)

See DJD 39. 97.

Ghweir? 1 GhweirpapCursiveFrg gr
Not published.

Ghweir? 2 GhweirpaperFrg sem
Not published.

12. Wadi ed-Daliyeh

The texts found in Wadi ed-Daliyeh have all been published in part of one volume of the series: D. M. Gropp, *Wadi Daliyeh II: The Samaria Papyri from Wadi Daliyeh* (DJD 28; Oxford: Clarendon, 2001) 1-116 (+ pls. I-XXXIX). Related to these papyrus texts are the artifacts discovered in the wadi, which can be found in M. J. Winn Leith, *Wadi Daliyeh I: The Wadi Daliyeh Seal Impressions* (DJD 24; Oxford: Clarendon, 1997); another such volume has been promised. For an account of the discovery and excavation of the site, see

P. Lapp and N. Lapp, *Discoveries in the Wâdi ed-Dâliyeh* (AASOR 41; Cambridge, MA: American Schools of Oriental Research, 1974). In col. 2 below, prefix all the sigla with WDSP.

WDSP 1 DeedSSaleA ar

Gropp, "1. WDSP papDeed of Slave Sale A ar," DJD 28. 33-44 (+ pl. I). See "The Samaria Papyri from Wadi Daliyeh: Introduction," ibid., 3-32.

WDSP 2 DeedSSaleB ar

Gropp, "2. WDSP papDeed of Slave Sale B ar," DJD 28. 45-55 (+ pl. II).

WDSP 3 DeedSSaleC ar

Gropp, "3. WDSP papDeed of Slave Sale C ar," DJD 28. 57-64 (+ pl. III).

WDSP 4 DeedSSaleD ar

Gropp, "4. WDSP papDeed of Slave Sale D ar," DJD 28. 65-68 (+ pl. IV).

WDSP 5 DeedSSaleE ar

Gropp, "5. WDSP papDeed of Slave Sale E ar," DJD 28. 69-73 (+ pl. V).

WDSP 6 DeedSSaleF ar

Gropp, "6. WDSP papDeed of Slave Sale F ar," DJD 28. 75-78 (+ pl. VI).

WDSP 7 DeedSSaleG ar

Gropp, "7. WDSP papDeed of Slave Sale G ar," DJD 28. 79-86 (+ pl. VII).

WDSP 8 DeedSSaleH ar

Gropp, "8. WDSP papDeed of Slave Sale H ar," DJD 28. 87-91 (+ pl. VIII).

WDSP 9 DeedSSaleI ar

Gropp, "9. WDSP papDeed of Slave Sale I ar," DJD 28. 93-96 (+ pl. IX).

WDSP 10 DeedPledgeA ar

Gropp, "10. WDSP papDeed of Pledge of Slave A ar," DJD 28. 97-101 (+ pl. X).

WDSP 11r DeedSSaleJ? ar

Gropp, "11r. WDSP papDeed of Slave Sale J? ar," DJD 28, pl. XI (photograph only; no discussion).

WDSP 11v DeedCession? ar

Gropp, "11v. WDSP papDeed of Cession? ar," DJD 28, pl. XII (photograph only; no discussion).

WDSP 12 DeedPledgeB ar

Gropp, "12. WDSP papDeed of Pledge of Slave B ar," DJD 28, pl. XIII (photograph only; no discussion).

WDSP 13r DeedPledgeC ar

Gropp, "13r. WDSP papDeed of Pledge of Slave C ar," DJD 28, pl. XIV (photograph only; no discussion).

WDSP 13v Release ar

Gropp, "13v. WDSP papRelease of Pledged Slave? ar," DJD 28, pl. XV (photograph only; no discussion).

WDSP 14 DeedConsignment ar

Gropp, "14. WDSP papDeed of Consignment of Public Rooms ar," DJD 28, pl. XVI (photograph only; no discussion).

WDSP 15 DeedHouseSale ar

Gropp, "15. WDSP papDeed of House Sale ar," DJD 28. 103-12 (+ pl. XVI).

WDSP 16 DeedVineyard? ar

Gropp, "16. WDSP papDeed of Pledge of Vineyard? ar," DJD 28, pl. XVII (photograph only; no discussion).

WDSP 17 ReceiptPayment ar

Gropp, "17. WDSP papReceipt of Payment in Relation to Pledge ar," DJD 28, pl. XVIII (photograph only; no discussion).

WDSP 18 DeedSSaleK ar

Gropp, "18. WDSP papDeed of Slave Sale K ar," DJD 28. 113-16 (+ pl. XIX).

WDSP 19 DeedSSaleL ar

Gropp, "19. WDSP papDeed of Slave Sale L ar," DJD 28, pl. XX (photograph only; no discussion).

WDSP 20 DeedSSaleM ar

Gropp, "20. WDSP papDeed of Slave Sale M ar," DJD 28, pl. XX (photograph only; no discussion).

WDSP 21 DeedSaleA ar

Gropp, "21. WDSP papDeed of Sale A ar," DJD 28, pl. XXI (photograph only; no discussion).

WDSP 22 DeedSSaleN ar

Gropp, "22. WDSP papDeed of Slave Sale N ar," DJD 28, pl. XXI (photograph only; no discussion).

WDSP 23r DeedA? ar

Gropp, "23r. WDSP papDeed A? ar," DJD 28, pl. XXII (photograph only; no discussion).

WDSP 23v DeedB? ar

Gropp, "23v. WDSP papDeed B? ar," DJD 28, pl. XXIII (photograph only; no discussion).

WDSP 24 DeedSaleB ar

Gropp, "24. WDSP papDeed of Sale B ar," DJD 28, pl. XXIV (photograph only; no discussion).

WDSP 25 DeedSaleC ar

Gropp, "25. WDSP papDeed of Sale C ar," DJD 28, pl. XXIV (photograph only; no discussion).

WDSP 26 DeedSSaleO ar

Gropp, "26. WDSP papDeed of Slave Sale O ar," DJD 28, pl. XXIV (photograph only; no discussion).

WDSP 27 DeedPledgeSD ar

Gropp, "27. WDSP papDeed of Pledge of Slave D? ar," DJD 28, pl. XXV (photograph only; no discussion).

WDSP 28-37 MiscFrgsA-N ar

Gropp, "28. WDSP papMiscellaneous Fragments A-N ar," DJD 28, pls. XXVI-XXXVIII (photographs only; no discussion).

WDSP 38 MiscFrgs gr

Gropp, "38. WDSP papMiscellaneous Fragments gr," DJD 28, pl. XXXIX (photograph only; no discussion).

13. Ḫirbet Mird

Ḫirbet (or Khirbet) Mird is the site of the remains of a 5th-6th century Greek monastery on a hill in the Judean Desert about 200 m. above the Buqeia. El-Mird is the Arabic form of a Syriac word *mardā'*, "fortress," which was the translation of Greek Καστέλλιον, "fort," derived from Latin *castellum.* The monastery was built on the remains of the fort at the site that was earlier called Hyrcania (see Josephus, *Ant.* 13.16.3 §417: Ὑρκανία), one of the three forts that Queen Salome Alexandra (76-67 B.C.) had built in the Judean Desert. The site has not yet been fully excavated, but it was often explored. After the discovery of Qumran caves, the monastery remains were investigated by a Belgian team led by R. de Langhe in the spring of 1953. They found papyri and hide fragments inscribed in Arabic, Greek, and Christian Palestinian Aramaic. The site was investigated further in 1960 by G. R. H. Wright (see his article, "The Archaeological Remains at El Mird in the Wilderness of Judaea," *Bib* 42 [1961] 1-21 [+ figs.]), and other examinations were carried out later by Israeli scholars (see J. Patrich, "Mird, Khirbet," *EDSS,* 563-66).

The Arabic texts are preserved on 31 plates in the Palestine Archaeological Museum (now renamed Rockefeller Museum) in East Jerusalem and on 36 plates of the Belgian Archaeological Mission; in all 100 texts (papMird 1-100 arab), which have the official siglum APHM, derived from the title of the following publication: A. Grohmann, *Arabic Papyri from Ḫirbet el-Mird* (Bibliothèque du Muséon 53; Louvain: Publications Universitaires, 1963). They date from the first two centuries of the Hegira. The following list briefly indicates the contents of these Arabic papyri:

APHM 1-7
Various types of protocols

APHM 8-9
Ends of legal texts

APHM 10-32
Official letters

APHM 33-41
Administrative or economic texts

APHM 42-70
Private letters

APHM 71-73
Literary texts

APHM 74-99
Frgs. of varied types of texts

APHM 100
Frg. of a drawing

Of the Christian Palestinian Aramaic papyri, only the following have been published:

Mird 657r-v MirdActs cpa
Perrot, C., "Un fragment christo-palestinien découvert à Khirbet Mird (Actes des Apôtres, X, 28-29; 32-41)," *RB* 70 (1963) 506-55 (+ pls. XVIII-XIX); see also Müller-Kessler and Sokoloff, *The Christian Palestinian Aramaic New Testament Version from the Early Period: Acts of the Apostles and Epistles* (Corpus of Christian Palestinian Aramaic IIB; Groningen: STYX, 1998), 15-16.

Mird 1237r-v MirdJosh cpa
Müller-Kessler, C. and M. Sokoloff, *The Christian Palestinian Aramaic Old Testament and Apocrypha Version from the Early Period* (Corpus of Christian Palestinian Aramaic I; Groningen: STYX, 1997) 84-85. May contain Josh 22:6-7, 9-10.

Mird 1238 IIr-v MirdMatt cpa
Müller-Kessler and Sokoloff, *The Christian Palestinian Aramaic New Testament Version from the Early Period: Gospels* (Corpus of Christian Palestinian Aramaic IIA; Groningen: STYX, 1998) 73-74. A photograph of the text is found in R. H. Eisenman and J. M. Robinson, *A Facsimile Edition of the Dead Sea Scrolls Prepared with an Introduction and Index* (2 vols.; Washington, DC: Biblical Archaeology Society, 1991), pls. 1676-77. Contains Matt 21:30-32, 32-34.

Mird 1238 IIIr-v MirdLuke cpa
Müller-Kessler and Sokoloff, *CPA New Testament* IIA, 166 (no photograph). Contains Luke 3:1, 3-4.

Mird 1238 IV MirdCol cpa
Müller-Kessler and Sokoloff, *CPA New Testament* IIB, 154. A photograph is

found in Eisenman-Robinson, *Facsimile Edition,* pls. 1680-81. Contains Col 1:16-18, 20-21.

Mird A MirdpapLett cpa

Milik, J. T., "Une inscription et une lettre en araméen christo-palestinien," *RB* 60 (1953) 526-39; "The Monastery of Kastellion," *Bib* 42 (1961) 21-27. The letter was written by a 7th-century monk named Gabriel to the superior of the nearby Monastery of Mar Saba.

Mird ? MirdAmul cpa

Baillet, M., "Un livret magique en christo-palestinien à l'Université de Louvain," *Muséon* 76 (1963) 375-401: An amulet.

Of the Greek texts, five have been published: J. van Haelst, "Cinq textes provenant de Khirbet Mird," *Ancient Society* 22 (1991) 297-317.

Mird 1 MirdLettMon gr

Van Haelst, *AncSoc* 22 (1991) 302-5 (+ pl. 1).

Mird 2 MirdLettEccles gr

Van Haelst, *AncSoc* 22 (1991) 305-6 (+ pl. 2).

Mird 3 MirdTropologion A-C gr

Van Haelst, *AncSoc* 22 (1991) 306-15 (+ pls. 3-5).

Mird 4 Doxastica gr

Van Haelst, *AncSoc* 22 (1991) 315-16 (+ pl. 6).

Mird 5 Alphabet + G3a gr

Van Haelst, *AncSoc* 22 (1991) 316 (+ pl. 7).

Mird 6 Alphabet + G4b gr

Van Haelst, *AncSoc* 22 (1991) 316 (+ pl. 7).

In addition, there are many Greek papyrus frgs. (old sigla: G3b-G31b), which are still unpublished; see the list in DJD 39. 96-97. Some Greek texts are known to be part of the Belgian Archaeological Commission's collection and are housed somewhere in Leuven, but they have not yet been published. The old sigla used for them, however, may indicate that they are part of the same group (G3b-G31b):

(now) (olim)
(said to contain)

Aland p83 16gr
Matt 20:23-25

Aland p83 16Bgr
Matt 20:30-31?

Aland p83 29gr

Aland p83 29Bgr

Aland p84 26gr
Mark 2:3-5; John 17:3

Aland p84 26Bgr
Mark 2:8-9; John 17:7-8

Aland p84 27gr
Mark 6:30-31, 33-34

Aland p84 27Bgr
Mark 6:36-37, 39-41

Aland p84 4gr

Aland p84 4Bgr

Aland p84 11gr

Aland p84 11Bgr

Uncial 0244 8gr
Acts 11:29–12:1

Uncial 0244 8Bgr
Acts 12:2-5

14. Naḥal ʿArugot

Naḥal ʿArugot is a 31-kilometer torrent-bed that runs southeast from Tekoa to the Dead Sea near Ein-Gedi. See G. Hadas, "Arugot, Naḥal," *DSSE,* 67-68. In 2004, some inscribed fragments were found in a cave by Bedouins, which turned out to be a biblical text.

Arug 1 ArugLev

Eshel, H., Y. Baruchi, and R. Porat, "Fragments of a Leviticus Scroll (ArugLev) Found in the Judean Desert in 2004," *DSD* 13 (2006) 55-60: Lev 23:38-44; 24:16-19.

15. Unknown Provenience

X1 XJosh

Charlesworth, J., "1. XJoshua," DJD 38. 231-39 (+ pl. XXXVI): Two skin frgs. containing Josh 1:9-12; 2:4-5. Charlesworth compares it with 4QJosh[b] (4Q48).

X2 XReceipt ar/gr

Misgav, H., "2. XReceipt ar and gr," DJD 28. 223-24 (+ pl. LXIII).

X3 UnidText 1

Misgav, "3. XUnidentified Text 1," DJD 28. 225 (+ pl. LXIII); see now 4Q401 frg. 3A (published by H. Eshel [2003]).

X4 XBibText

Misgav, "4. XBiblical Text?," DJD 28. 227 (+ pl. LXIII).

X5 UnidText 2

Misgav, "5. XUnidentified Text 2," DJD 28. 229 (+ pl. LXIII).

X6 XJudg

Charlesworth, "6. XJudges," DJD 28. 231-33 (+ pl. LXIII): Judg 4:5-6.

X7 XGen

Puech, E., "Fragment d'un rouleau de la Genèse provenant du Désert de Juda (*Gen.* 33, 18-34, 3)," *RevQ* 10 (1979-81) 163-66. The frg. of skin may belong to a Murabbaʿat text.

III

Bibliographies of the Dead Sea Scrolls

General

Burchard, C., *Bibliographie zu den Handschriften vom Toten Meer* (BZAW 76; Berlin: Töpelmann, 1957). Alphabetical arrangement by authors.

———, *Bibliographie zu den Handschriften vom Toten Meer, II: Nr. 1557-4459* (BZAW 89; Berlin: Töpelmann, 1965). Continuation of the preceding; up to end of 1962.

García Martínez, F. and D. W. Parry, *A Bibliography of the Finds in the Desert of Judah 1970-95: Arranged by Author with Citation and Subject Indexes* (STDJ 19; Leiden: Brill, 1996).

García Martínez, F. and E. J. C. Tigchelaar, "Bibliography of the Dead Sea Scrolls," *RevQ* 18 (1997-98) 459-90, 605-39. This ongoing bibliography is being continued by the following items from the Orion Center of the Hebrew University of Jerusalem:

Pinnick, A., "Orion Center Bibliography of the Dead Sea Scrolls (May 1998–January 1999)," *RevQ* 19 (1999-2000) 153-68; "(February–September 1999)," ibid., 291-329; "(October 1999–May 2000)," ibid., 467-95; "(May-October 2000)," *RevQ* 20 (2001-2) 139-63.

———, *The Orion Center Bibliography of the Dead Sea Scrolls (1995-2000)* (STDJ 41; Leiden: Brill, 2001).

Emanuel, D., "Orion Center Bibliography of the Dead Sea Scrolls (November 2000–September 2001)," *RevQ* 20 (2001-2) 323-55; "(November 2001–May 2002)," ibid., 495-508; "(May 2002–November 2002)," ibid., 599-623.

Clements, R. and S. Zilberfarb-Eshkoli, "Orion Center Bibliography of the Dead Sea Scrolls (December 2002–February 2003)," *RevQ* 21 (2003-4)

137-61; "(March 2003–July 2003)," ibid., 331-61; "(August-December 2003)," ibid., 505-25; "(January-June 2004)," ibid., 659-73.

Clements, R. and N. Sharon, "The Orion Center Bibliography of the Dead Sea Scrolls (July 2004–December 2004)," *RevQ* 22 (2005-6) 141-62; "(January-June 2005)," ibid., 301-23.

Habermann, A. M., "**ביבליוגרפיה לחקר מגילות מדבר יהודה ושאר הממצאים שנמצאו שם**," [title varies in different installments], *Beth Mikra* (Jerusalem) 1 (1956) 116-21; 2 (1957) 92-97; 3 (1958) 103-11; 4 (1959) 91-95; 5 (1960) 89-93; 6 (1961) 87-91; 13 (1962) 126-33; 16 (1963) 147-51; 18-19 (1964) 215-19; 23-24 (1965) 125-33; 27 (1966) 162-67; 32 (1967) 134-36; 35 (1968) 134-40; 41 (1969-70) 208-16. Alphabetical arrangement of authors' names.

Jongeling, B., *A Classified Bibliography of the Finds in the Desert of Judah 1958-1969* (STDJ 7; Leiden: Brill, 1971). Sequel to LaSor's *Bibliography;* topical arrangement.

Kapera, Z. J., "Current Bibliography on the Dead Sea Scrolls 1992," *QC* 2 (1993) 129-31, 198-99; "Current . . . 1992-1993 (Part III)," *QC* 3 (1993) 175-207; "Current . . . 1994 (Part I)," *QC* 4 (1994) 114-24; "Current . . . 1994 (Part II)," ibid., 225-48; "Current . . . 1994 (Part III)," *QC* 5 (1995) 181-92; "Current . . . 1995," ibid., 281-94; "Current . . . 1996," *QC* 6 (1996) 211-46; "Current . . . 1997 (Part I)," *QC* 7 (1997) 127-44; "Current . . . 1997 (Part II)," ibid., 263-87; "Current . . . 1998 (Part I)," *QC* 8 (1998) 133-58.

LaSor, W. S., *Bibliography of the Dead Sea Scrolls 1948-1957* (Fuller Library Bulletin 31; Pasadena: Fuller Theological Seminary Library, 1958). Topical arrangement.

Nober, P., "Elenchus bibliographicus," *Biblica,* each year up to 1967, section IV/c, "Qumranica et praemishnica." Since 1968, the "Elenchus" has been published separately as *Elenchus bibliographicus biblicus* (Rome: Biblical Institute), see chapter IV/3 (until 60 [1979], when R. North took over *EBB*). Since 61 (1980) "Qumran Surveys" appears in section K3. *EBB* changed its name after 65 (1984); it is now called *Elenchus of Biblica* with the year added, 1985 etc. (Elenchus of Biblical Bibliography 1; Rome: Biblical Institute, 1988-). It is being continued by R. Althann. Alphabetical arrangement of authors' names.

Yizhar, M., *Bibliography of Hebrew Publications on the Dead Sea Scrolls 1948-1964* (HTS 23; Cambridge, MA: Harvard University Press, 1967). Topical arrangement.

(Various Authors), "Bibliographie," *RevQ* 1 (1958-59) 149-60 (J. Carmignac), 309-20 (J.C.), 461-79 (C. Burchard), 547-626 (C.B.); 2 (1959-60) 117-51 (C.B.), 299-312 (J.C.), 459-72 (W. S. LaSor), 587-601 (W.S.L.); 3 (1961-62) 149-60 (W.S.L.), 313-20 (W.S.L.), 467-80 (W.S.L.), 593-602 (W.S.L.); 4 (1963-64)

139-59 (W.S.L.), 311-20 (W.S.L.), 467-80 (W.S.L.), 597-606 (J.C.); 5 (1964-66) 149-60 (W.S.L.), 293-320 (W.S.L.), 463-79 (J.C.), 597-607 (J.C.); 6 (1967-69) 301-20 (J.C.), 457-79 (J.C.); 7 (1969-71) 131-59 (J.C.), 305-19 (J.C.), 463-80 (J.C.); 8 (1972-75) 131-59 (J.C.), 299-319 (J.C.), 459-79 (J.C.); 9 (1977-78) 139-60 (J.C.), 293-319 (J.C.), 463-79; 10 (1979-81) 129-59 (J.C.), 455-79 (J.C.); 11 (1982-84) 119-59 (F. García Martínez), 295-320 (F.G.M.), 461-78 (F.G.M.); 12 (1985-87) 129-60 (F.G.M.), 293-315 (F.G.M.), 455-80 (F.G.M.). Neither alphabetical nor topical arrangement; listed by periodicals from which the entries were culled, but the indices of each volume can be consulted for authors' names. This "Bibliographie" is continued in the book by García Martínez and Parry (STDJ 19) listed above near the beginning of this section.

(Various Authors), "Dokumentation über Neuveröffentlichungen aus den Qumranfunden" or "Bibliographische Dokumentation: Qumran" or "Dokumentation neuer Texte" (title changes), *ZAH* 3 (1990) 232-34; 4 (1991) 210-12; 5 (1992) 115 (H. Lichtenberger); 7 (1994) 102-21, 268-82 (E. Eshel et al.); 8 (1995) 104-19 (A. Lange and K. F. D. Römheld); 8 (1995) 326-38; 9 (1996) 96-107 (J. Kamlah et al.); 9 (1996) 223-32; 10 (1997) 116-22 (B. Ego et al.); 10 (1997) 227-36; 11 (1998) 116-24 (D. Betz et al.); 11 (1998) 230-31 (B. Ego et al.); 13 (2000) 121-31 (M. Hoffmann et al.); 14 (2001) 99-115, 207-19 (S. Ahrnke et al.); 15/16 (2002-3) 195-211 (B. Embry et al.).

Specific

Cloward, R. A., *The Old Testament Apocrypha and Pseudepigrapha and The Dead Sea Scrolls: A Selected Bibliography of Text Editions and English Translations* (Provo, UT: F.A.R.M.S., 1988).

Fröhlich, I., "Bibliographie des recherches hongroises sur les manuscrits de la Mer Morte," *FO* 25 (1988) 79-83.

García Martínez, F., "A Bibliography of MMT," *Reading 4QMMT: New Perspectives on Qumran Law and History* (SBLSS 2; ed. J. Kampen and M. J. Bernstein; Atlanta, GA: Scholars Press, 1996) 145-56.

———, "A Classified Bibliography" [on the Temple Scroll], in E. Qimron, *The Temple Scroll: A Critical Edition with Extensive Reconstructions* (JDS; Beer Sheba: Ben-Gurion University of the Negev; Jerusalem: Israel Exploration Society, 1996) 95-121.

———, "Damascus Document: Bibliography of Studies 1970-1989," *The Damascus Document Reconsidered* (ed. M. Broshi; Jerusalem: Israel Exploration Society and the Shrine of the Book, 1992) 63-83.

———, "Nouveaux livres sur les manuscrits de la Mer Morte," *JSJ* 27 (1996) 46-74.
———, "Nuevos textos no bíblicos procedentes de Qumrán (I)," *EstBíb* 49 (1991) 97-134.
———, "El rollo del templo *(11QTemple):* Bibliografía sistemática," *RevQ* 12 (1985-87) 425-40.
———, "The Temple Scroll: A Systematic Bibliography 1985-1991," *The Madrid Qumran Congress: Proceedings of the International Congress on the Dead Sea Scrolls, Madrid 18-21 March 1991* (STDJ 11/1-2; ed. J. Trebolle Barrera and L. Vegas Montaner; Leiden: Brill, 1992), 2. 393-403.
——— and E. J. C. Tigchelaar, "*1 Enoch* and the Figure of Enoch: A Bibliography of Studies 1970-1988," *RevQ* 14 (1989-90) 149-74.
Glessmer, U., "Liste der biblischen Texte aus Qumran," *RevQ* 16 (1993-95) 153-92.
Kapera, Z. J., "A Bibliography of J. D. Amussin Concerning the Dead Sea Scrolls," *RevQ* 14 (1989-90) 121-26.
———, "Bibliography of Norman Golb's Hypothesis of the Jerusalem Origin of the Dead Sea Scrolls," *FO* 27 (1990) 217-21.
———, "Bibliography of the Unauthorized Edition of the Dead Sea Scrolls," *QC* 2 (1992) 66-67.
———, "Selected Polish Subject Bibliography of the Dead Sea Discoveries," *FO* 23 (1985-86) 269-338.
Koester, C., "A Qumran Bibliography: 1974-1984," *BTB* 15 (1985) 110-20.
Mędala, S., "Recherches sur le problématique des documents de Qumran en Pologne," *FO* 23 (1985-86) 257-68.
Muchowski, P., "Bibliography of the Copper Scroll (3Q15)," *FO* 26 (1989) 65-70.
Nebe, G. W., "Qumranica I: Zu unveröffentlichten Handschriften aus Höhle 4 von Qumran," *ZAW* 106 (1994) 307-22.
———, "Qumranica II: Zu unveröffentlichten Handschriften aus Höhle 4 von Qumran," *ZAH* 10 (1997) 134-38.
———, "Qumranica III: Zu unveröffentlichten Handschriften vom Toten Meer: Vertrag über den Kauf eines Eselsfohlen aus dem Jahr 122 nach Chr. (5/6Ḥev 8)," *ZAH* 11 (1998) 205-9.
———, "Qumranica IV: Die jüngst in Khirbet Qumran gefundene hebräische Schenkungsurkunde auf einer Tonscherbe," *ZAH* 12 (1999) 96-103.
Rosso Ubigli, L., "Gli apocrifi (o pseudepigrafi) dell'Antico Testamento: Bibliografia 1979-1989," *Henoch* 12 (1990) 259-321.

IV

Survey Reports of the Discovery of the Scrolls and Their Contents

Books

1. *Early Reports That Are Still of Value*

Milik, J. T., *Dix ans de découvertes dans le Désert de Juda* (Paris: Éditions du Cerf, 1957). Translated as *Ten Years of Discovery in the Wilderness of Judaea* (SBT 26; London: SCM; Naperville, IL: Allenson, 1959).

Cross, F. M., *The Ancient Library of Qumran and Modern Biblical Studies* (Garden City, NY: Doubleday, 1958). Revised edition: Anchor Books A 272; Garden City, NY: Doubleday, 1961; repr., Grand Rapids, MI: Baker, 1980. Third edition: Minneapolis, MN: Fortress; Sheffield, UK: Sheffield Academic Press, 1995. Translated as *Die antike Bibliothek von Qumran und die moderne biblische Wissenschaft: Ein zusammenfassender Überblick über die Handschriften vom Toten Meer und ihre einstigen Besitzer* (Neukirchener Studienbücher 5; Neukirchen/Vluyn: Neukirchener Verlag, 1967).

Avigad, N. et al., *The Expedition to the Judean Desert, 1961* (= *IEJ* 12/3-4; Jerusalem: Israel Exploration Society, 1962).

Aviram, J. et al., *The Judean Desert Caves Archaeological Survey, 1961* (= *Yediʿot* 26/3-4; Jerusalem: Hebrew University and Department of Antiquities, 1963) [in modern Hebrew].

Driver, G. R., *The Judaean Scrolls: The Problem and a Solution* (Oxford: Blackwell, 1965) (to be used with discretion, see R. de Vaux, *NTS* 13 [1966-67] 89-104).

Soggin, J. A., *I manoscritti del Mar Morto* (Civiltà scomparse 22; Rome: Newton Compton Editori, 1978).

2. *More Recent Surveys*

Berger, K., *Qumran: Funde — Texte — Geschichte* (Universal-Bibliothek 9668; Stuttgart: Reclam, 1998).

Campbell, J., *The Dead Sea Scrolls: The Complete Story* (Berkeley, CA: Ulysses, 1998).

Davies, P. R., G. J. Brooke, and P. R. Callaway, *The Complete World of the Dead Sea Scrolls* (London: Thames & Hudson, 2002).

Delcor, M. and F. García Martínez, *Introducción a la literatura esenia de Qumrán* (Academia cristiana 20; Madrid: Cristiandad, 1982).

Fitzmyer, J. A., *Responses to 101 Questions on the Dead Sea Scrolls* (New York/ Mahwah, NJ: Paulist Press, 1992).

Fujita, N. S., *A Crack in the Jar: What Ancient Jewish Documents Tell Us about the New Testament* (Mahwah, NJ/New York: Paulist, 1986). The subtitle is misleading; the book treats of more than the influence of the Scrolls on the NT.

Golb, N., *Who Wrote the Dead Sea Scrolls? The Search for the Secret of Qumran* (New York/London: Scribner, 1995).

Grözinger, K. E. et al., *Qumran* (WF 410; Darmstadt: Wissenschaftliche Buchgesellschaft, 1981).

Hodge, S., *The Dead Sea Scrolls Rediscovered* (Berkeley, CA: Seastone, 2003).

Nickelsburg, G. W. E., *Jewish Literature between the Bible and the Mishnah: A Historical and Literary Introduction* (Philadelphia: Fortress, 1981) 122-42, 231-41, 263-65.

Paul, A., *Les manuscrits de la Mer Morte: La voix des Esséniens retrouvés* (Paris: Bayard/Centurion, 1997).

Pearlman, M., *The Dead Sea Scrolls in the Shrine of the Book* (Jerusalem: Israel Museum, 1988).

Price, R., *Secrets of the Dead Sea Scrolls* (Eugene, OR: Harvest House Publishers, 1996).

Schiffman, L. H., *Reclaiming the Dead Sea Scrolls: The History of Judaism, the Background of Christianity, the Lost Library of Qumran* (Philadelphia, PA: Jewish Publication Society, 1994; repr. New York: Doubleday, 1995).

Schürer, E., *The History of the Jewish People in the Age of Jesus Christ (175 B.C.–A.D. 135)* (3 vols.; rev. ed., G. Vermes et al.; Edinburgh: Clark) III/1 (1986) passim.

Silberman, N. A., *The Hidden Scrolls, Christianity, Judaism & the War for the Dead Sea Scrolls* (New York: Putnam's Sons, 1994).

VanderKam, J. C., *The Dead Sea Scrolls Today* (Grand Rapids, MI: London: SPCK, 1994).

——— and P. Flint, *The Meaning of the Dead Sea Scrolls: Their Significance for*

Understanding the Bible, Judaism, Jesus, and Christianity (San Francisco, CA: HarperSanFrancisco, 2004).
Vermes, G., *The Dead Sea Scrolls: Qumran in Perspective* (rev. ed.; London: Collins, 1977; Philadelphia: Fortress, 1981).
———, *The Dead Sea Scrolls Forty Years On* (Oxford: Oxford Centre for Postgraduate Studies, 1987).
Wilson, E., *The Dead Sea Scrolls 1947-1969* (New York: Oxford University Press, 1969).
Yadin, Y., *Bar-Kokhba: The Rediscovery of the Legendary Hero of the Second Jewish Revolt against Rome* (London: Weidenfeld and Nicolson, 1971) 124-253.

Articles

1. Of Earlier Vintage

Starcky, J. and J. Milik, "L'État actuel du déchiffrement des manuscrits du Désert de Juda et le plan de leur publication," *CRAIBL*, 1954, 403-9.
Benoit, P. et al., "Le travail d'édition des fragments manuscrits de Qumrân," *RB* 63 (1956) 49-67 (Report on 2-6Q); translated as "Editing the Manuscript Fragments from Qumran," *BA* 19 (1956) 75-96.
Milik, J. T., "Le travail d'édition des manuscrits du Désert de Juda," *Volume du Congrès, Strasbourg 1956* (VTSup 4; Leiden: Brill, 1957) 17-26 (Report on Murabbaʿat, Ḥever, Minor Caves, 4Q texts).
Sanders, J. A., "The Dead Sea Scrolls — A Quarter Century of Study," *BA* 36 (1973) 110-48.
Vermes, G., "The Impact of the Dead Sea Scrolls on Jewish Studies during the Last Twenty-Five Years," *JJS* 26 (1975) 1-14; repr. in *Approaches to Ancient Judaism* (BJS 1; ed. W. S. Green; Missoula, MT: Scholars, 1978) 201-14.

2. More Recent Surveys

Brooke, G. J., "The Dead Sea Scrolls: A Review of the Last Decade's Publications and Activities," *Epworth Review* 26/3 (1999) 87-97.
García Martínez, F., "Estudios Qumránicos 1975-1985: Panorama crítico (I)," *EstBíb* 45 (1987) 125-206; (II), ibid., 361-402; (III), *EstBíb* 46 (1988) 325-74; (IV), ibid., 527-48; (V), *EstBíb* 47 (1989) 93-118; (VI), ibid., 225-67.
Lémonon, J.-P., "Qumran: Où en est-on?," *Études* 397 (2002) 499-511.
Ruderman, A., "The Dead Sea Scrolls — 40 Years Later," *JBQ* 21 (1993) 256-58.

Schuller, E., "The Dead Sea Scrolls at Fifty Years," *TBT* 35 (1997) 365-71.

Tov, E., "Five Decades of Discoveries, Editions, and Research," *The Dead Sea Scrolls: Fifty Years after Their Discovery: Proceedings of the Jerusalem Congress, July 20-25, 1997* (ed. L. H. Schiffman et al.; Jerusalem: Israel Exploration Society and the Shrine of the Book, Israel Museum, 2000) 951-60.

Wise, M. O., "Dead Sea Scrolls," *The Oxford Encyclopedia of Archaeology in the Near East* (5 vols.; ed. E. M. Meyers; New York: Oxford University Press, 1997), 2. 118-27.

Woude, A. S. van der, "Fifty Years of Qumran Research," *Dead Sea Scrolls after Fifty Years: A Comprehensive Assessment* (2 vols.; ed. P. W. Flint and J. C. VanderKam; Leiden: Brill, 1998-99), 1. 1-45.

———, "Fünfzehn Jahre Qumranforschung (1974-1988)," *TRu* 54 (1989) 221-61; (Fortsetzung) 55 (1990) 245-307; 57 (1992) 1-57, 225-53.

V

Lists of the Dead Sea Scrolls and Fragments

The lists mentioned below are similar to that of section II above, but they are usually less complete; some, however, include notice of texts known to exist but not yet published. Each list has its advantages and disadvantages, and the mode of listing in one reveals aspects of the study not found in others. The lists are arranged no longer according to the date of publication, because of the almost complete publication of the scrolls and fragments in DJD, which has been presented in section II above; they are now given in alphabetical order according to the author.

Burchard, C., *Bibliographie II* (see section III above), 313-59: "Register: Ausgaben und Übersetzungen der neugefundenen Texte, Antike Essenerberichte."

Fitzmyer, J. A., *The Dead Sea Scrolls: Major Publications and Tools for Study* (SBLSBS 8; Missoula, MT: Scholars, 1975; with an Addendum, 1977; rev. ed., Atlanta, GA: Scholars, 1990). These were earlier forms of the present work.

Flint, P. W., "The Psalms Scrolls from the Judaean Desert: Relationships and Textual Affiliations," *New Qumran Texts and Studies: Proceedings of the First Meeting of the International Organization for Qumran Studies, Paris 1992* (STDJ 15; ed. G. J. Brooke; Leiden: Brill, 1994) 31-51. Appendix I lists the Psalms scrolls and frgs. from Qumran, Ḥever, Seiyal, and Masada; Appendix II lists the Psalms texts.

García Martínez, F., "Lista de MSS procedentes de Qumrán," *Henoch* 11 (1989) 149-232. (This list mentions many fragmentary texts of 4Q known to exist but not yet published up to the time of writing.)

———, "Texts from Qumran Cave 11," *The Dead Sea Scrolls: Forty Years of Research* (STDJ 10; ed. D. Dimant and U. Rappaport; Leiden: Brill, 1992) 18-26.

Glessmer, U., "Liste der biblischen Texte aus Qumran," *RevQ* 16 (1993-95) 153-92. (This list includes many deuterocanonical and apocryphal writings.)

Müller, K., "Die Handschriften und Editionen der ausserbiblischen Qumranliteratur," *Einführung in die Methoden der biblischen Exegese* (ed. J. Schreiner; Würzburg: Echter Verlag, 1971) 303-10.

Rosso Ubigli, L., "Indice italiano-inglese dei testi di Qumran: Italian-English Index of Qumran Texts," *Henoch* 11 (1989) 233-70.

Sanders, J. A., "Palestinian Manuscripts 1947-67," *JBL* 86 (1967) 431-40.

———, "Pre-Masoretic Psalter Texts," *CBQ* 27 (1965) 114-23.

Stegemann, H., "Anhang," *ZDPV* 83 (1967) 95-100 (a supplement to Burchard's list mentioned above).

Tov, E., "The Unpublished Qumran Texts from Caves 4 and 11," *JJS* 43 (1992) 101-36; updated form in *BA* 55 (1992) 94-104; see also "The Unpublished Texts from the Judean Desert," *New Qumran Texts and Studies* (see above), 81-88.

Ulrich, E., "The Biblical Scrolls from Qumran Cave 4: An Overview and a Progress Report on Their Publication," *RevQ* 14 (1989-90) 207-28 (with two charts listing biblical texts).

———, "An Index of the Passages in the Biblical Manuscripts from the Judean Desert (Genesis-Kings)," *DSD* 1 (1994) 113-29.

VI

Concordances, Dictionaries, Grammars, etc. for the Study of the Dead Sea Scrolls

These books are intended for use in the study of the original texts (in Aramaic, Hebrew, or Greek). The list presupposes the use of ordinary concordances, dictionaries, and grammars in the study of these biblical languages. Concordances to the Qumran texts are found in many of the volumes of the DJD series, most of them the work of S. J. Pfann. Concordances appear also in the publications of such Qumran texts as Y. Yadin, *The Temple Scroll* (1983), E. M. Schuller, *Non-Canonical Psalms from Qumran* (1986), or C. Newsom, *Songs for the Sabbath Sacrifice* (1985).

Abegg, Jr., M. G., "Concordance of Proper Nouns in the Non-biblical Texts from Qumran," DJD 39. 229-64.

———, J. E. Bowley, and E. M. Cook, *The Dead Sea Scrolls Concordance: Volume One, The Non-Biblical Texts from Qumran, Parts One and Two* (Leiden/Boston: Brill, 2003). This work was prepared in consultation with E. Tov. Part I has a general introduction, key to the sigla, and the Hebrew concordance (Aleph-Mem); part II continues the Hebrew concordance (Nun-Tav) and has the Aramaic concordance, Greek concordance, and two appendices (I: Concordance of signs for numbers; II: Typographical and transcriptional errors in the text editions). This is the most important concordance of Qumran non-biblical texts. At least another volume is projected.

Beyer, K., *Die aramäischen Texte vom Toten Meer, samt den Inschriften aus Palästina, dem Testament Levis aus der Kairoer Genisa, der Fastenrolle und den alten talmudischen Zitaten: Aramaistische Einleitung, Text, Übersetzung, Deutung: Grammatik/Worterbuch, Deutsch-aramäische Wortliste, Register* (Göttingen: Vandenhoeck & Ruprecht, 1984). (Contains the Aramaic texts of 1QapGen, 4QVisJac, 4QTJud, 4QTJos, 1QTLevi, 4QTLevi, CTLevi,

4QTQahat, 4QAmram, 1QNJ, 2QNJ, 4QNJ, 5QNJ, 11QNJ, 4QprNab, 4QpsDan, 1QNoah, 4QEnastr, 4QEnGiants, 4QEn, 4QMess, 4QMilMik, 4QtgLev, 4QtgJob, 11QtgJob, 4QTob, 4QJer [10:11], 1QDan; Mur 18-21, 23, 25-28, 31-33, 38, 43-44, 72; 5/6ḤevBA, pap?ḤevB, C.) Texts in *ATTM* are accompanied by a German translation and bibliographies. The differences in readings that Beyer often proposes have to be checked always against the photographs in the *editiones principes.* An *Ergänzungsband* (*ATTME,* 1994) is a supplement that provides additions to the texts mentioned in *ATTM,* along with many other writings from Murabbaʿat and Ḥever; Hasmonean and Galilean inscriptions; Samaritan and Christian Palestinian Aramaic texts. The first chapter of *ATTM* has been translated into English by J. F. Healey, *The Aramaic Language: Its Distribution and Subdivisions* (Göttingen: Vandenhoeck & Ruprecht, 1986).

Carmignac, J., "Concordance de la 'Regle de la Guerre,'" *RevQ* 1 (1958-59) 7-49.

Charlesworth, J. H. et al., *Graphic Concordance to the Dead Sea Scrolls* (PTSDSSP 5; Louisville, KY: Westminster/John Knox; Tübingen: Mohr [Siebeck], 1991). This concordance is called "graphic" because it books the words alphabetically in their attested Hebrew and Aramaic forms, and not analyzed according to their root consonants or separately according to their languages; but with the prefixed prepositions, conjunctions, and preformatives [such as *m-* noun forms]. It is also of the KWIC-type of concordance, i.e., keyword-in-context, so that the attested form is seen in its context.

Clines, D. J. A. (ed.), *The Dictionary of Classical Hebrew* (5 vols. to date [up to מ-נ]; Sheffield: Sheffield Academic Press, 1993-). The sources analyzed for this dictionary are the Hebrew Scriptures, Ben Sira, Qumran and related nonbiblical texts, and inscriptions. Given this coverage, it is the best dictionary to use for the Hebrew texts treated in this book.

Dahmen, U., "Nachträge zur Qumran-Konkordanz," *ZAH* 4 (1991) 213-35; 8 (1995) 340-54; 9 (1996) 109-28. These concordances, covering many of the texts that had been published in 1980s-1990s, are meant to be a supplement to Kuhn et al., *Konkordanz* (see below).

Habermann, A. M., מגילות מדבר יהודה: *The Scrolls from the Judean Desert, Edited with Vocalization, Introduction, Notes and Concordance* (Tel Aviv: Machbaroth Lesifruth, 1959) [1]-[175]. This concordance is limited to CD, 1QH[a], 1QM, 1QS, 1QSb, 1QpHab, 1QpMic, 1QpPs, 1QMyst, 1QLitA, 1Q29, 1Q34bis, 4QpIsa[a], 4QpNah, 4QpPs[a], 4QFlor, 4QCommGen A. Moreover, one cannot always trust the readings or the numbering of fragments or lines; they must always be checked against other editions.

Kuhn, K. G. et al., *Konkordanz zu den Qumrantexten* (Göttingen: Vandenhoeck & Ruprecht, 1960). (All nonbiblical texts of 1Q; 4QpIsa[a-d], 4QpHos[a-b],

4QpNah, 4QpPs^a, 4QPBless [now 4Q252, frg. 6], 4QFlor, 4QTestim, 4QM^a, 6QD, CD.)

———, "Nachträge zur 'Konkordanz zu den Qumrantexten,'" *RevQ* 4 (1963-64) 163-234. (Adds 4QpNah, 4QpPs^a, 4QFlor, 4QShirShabb, 4QDibHam, 4QOrd^a to preceding entry.)

———, *Rückläufiges hebräisches Wörterbuch* (Göttingen: Vandenhoeck & Ruprecht, 1958). A reverse-index of Hebrew words in biblical and Qumran writings; it lists the words spelled backwards as an aid to the restoration of lacunae in texts.

Kutscher, E. Y., *The Language and Linguistic Background of the Isaiah Scroll (1QIsa^a)* (STDJ 6; Leiden: Brill, 1974; new edition revised by E. Qimron [STDJ 6A], 1979).

Lignée, H., "Concordance de 'I Q Genesis Apocryphon,'" *RevQ* 1 (1958-59) 163-86.

Martone, C., "A Concordance to the Newly Published Qumran Texts," *Henoch* 15 (1993) 155-206. The texts analyzed are: 4Q216, 219, 221, 222, 252, 256, 258, 265-271, 285, 320-321, 364-365, 371-374, 385b, 389a, 390, 409, 434, 448, 462, 464, 471, 471a, 521-522; 11Q20.

Muraoka, T. and J. F. Elwolde (eds.), *The Hebrew of the Dead Sea Scrolls and Ben Sira: Proceedings of a Symposium Held at Leiden University 11-14 December 1995* (STDJ 26; Leiden: Brill, 1997).

Qimron, E., *The Hebrew of the Dead Sea Scrolls* (HSS 29; Atlanta, GA: Scholars, 1986).

Richter, H.-P., "Konkordanz zu XIQMelkîsédeq (éd. E. Puech)," *RevQ* 12 (1985-87) 515-18.

———, *A Preliminary Concordance to the Hebrew and Aramaic Fragments from Qumran Caves II-X, Including Especially the Unpublished Material from Cave IV* (5 vols.; Göttingen: Private Publication, 1988). This concordance of Cave 4 non-biblical texts was begun in the PAM 1957-58 by J. A. Fitzmyer and was continued subsequently by R. E. Brown (1958-59) and W. G. Oxtoby (1959-60); texts from Caves 2-3, 5-10 were added later by J. Teixidor. The cards were photographed in the 1980s, and the printed photographs were bound in five vols. As such, the concordance was limited in distribution to the team of Cave 4 researchers and a few others, but no copy of it was made available to those who originally compiled the concordance on cards! It is called "Preliminary Concordance," because the texts analyzed in it were based on the *tentative transcriptions* of texts made (in 1950s-60s) by members of the team to whom the Cave 4 non-biblical texts were entrusted for publication. This concordance was used by B. Z. Wacholder and M. G. Abegg to reconstruct texts in *A Preliminary Edition of the Unpublished Dead*

Sea Scrolls: The Hebrew and Aramaic Texts from Cave Four (4 fascicles; Washington, DC: Biblical Archaeology Society, 1991, 1992, 1995, 1996).

Schattner-Rieser, U., *L'Araméen des manuscrits de la mer Morte: I. Grammaire* (Instruments pour l'étude des langues de l'Orient Ancien 5; Lausanne: Editions du Zèbre, 2004).

Schiffman. L. H. and J. C. VanderKam (eds.), *Encyclopedia of the Dead Sea Scrolls* (2 vols.; Oxford/New York: Oxford University Press, 2000). This is the basic publication for general and specific information about the Dead Sea Scrolls.

Sokoloff, M., *A Dictionary of Judean Aramaic* (Ramat-Gan: Bar Ilan University Press, 2003). This work collects "the vocabulary of the texts written in Judean Aramaic . . . composed by Jews in the period between the Maccabean Period and the Tannaitic (ca. 165 BCE–200 CE)." This means the documentary texts of Ḥever, Ketef Jericho, Masada, Murabbaʿat, and Seiyal, but not of Qumran. For the latter we must still await another volume.

VII

Secondary Collections of Qumran Texts

Listed here are manuals that have brought together various Qumran texts in convenient form. Sometimes they are accompanied by translations into a modern language; sometimes they are vocalized.

Bardtke, H., *Hebräische Konsonantentexte aus biblischem und ausserbiblischem Schrifttum für Übungszwecke ausgewählt* (Leipzig: Harrassowitz, 1954). (Parts of 1QIsa^a, 1QS, 1QpHab, 1QH^a, CD, Mur 42, 43.)

Beyer, K., *ATTM, ATTME* (see section VI above).

Boccaccio, P. and C. Berardi (eds. of a series, "Materiale didattico"):

סרך העדה: *Regula congregationis* (Fani, Italy: Seminarium Picenum; Rome: Biblical Institute, 1956) (1QSa).

מלחמת בני אור בבני חושך: *Bellum filiorum lucis contra filios tenebrarum: Fasc. A: Transcriptio e versio latina* (Fani: Seminarium Picenum, 1956) (1QM).

פשר חבקוק: *Interpretatio Habacuc (1QpHab: Transcriptio et versio latina)* (Appendix: *Interpretatio Naḥum [2, 12b-14]*) (Fani: Seminarium Picenum, 1958) (1QpHab). (Second printing also contains *Interpretatio Ps 37.8-11, 19b-26* [Fani: Seminarium Picenum; Rome: Biblical Institute, 1958]) (4QpPs^a).

סרך היחד: *Regula unionis seu manuale disciplinae (1QS): Transcriptio et versio latina* (3d ed.; Fani: Seminarium Picenum; Rome: Biblical Institute, 1958).

Charlesworth, J. H. et al. (eds.), *The Dead Sea Scrolls: Hebrew, Aramaic, and Greek Texts with English Translations: Volume 1, Rule of the Community and Related Documents* (PTSDSSP 1; Louisville, KY: Westminster/John Knox; Tübingen: Mohr [Siebeck], 1994) [1QS; 4QS^{a-j}; 5Q11; 1QSa; 1QSb; 5Q13;

4QOrd^{a-c} (4Q159, 4Q513, 4Q514)]; *Volume 2, Damascus Document, War Scroll, and Related Documents* (PTSDSSP 2; 1995) [CD; 4QD^{a-h}; 5QD; 6QD; 1QM; 4QM^{a-f}; 4Q497; 4Q180-181; 1Q51; 2Q25; 2Q28]; *Volume 3, Damascus Document II, Some Works of the Torah, and Related Documents* (PTSDSSP 3; 2006) [4QD^{a-h}; 4QMMT^{a-f}; 4Q313; 4Q265; 4Q251; 4Q264a; 4Q472a; 4Q284a]; *Volume 4A, Pseudepigraphic and Non-Masoretic Psalms and Prayers* (PTSDSSP 4A; 1997) [4Q380-381; 4Q236; 1Q34-34bis; 4Q507-509; 4Q504-506; 4Q88; 11Q5-6; 11QPs^{a} ; 11QPsAp^{a}; 4QPrQuot]; *Volume 4B, Angelic Liturgy: Songs of the Sabbath Sacrifice* (PTSDSSP 4B; 1999) [4Q400-407; 11Q17; Masık]; *Volume 6B, Pesharim, Other Commentaries, and Related Documents* (PTSDSSP 6B; 2002) [4Q171; 1Q16; 4Q173; 3Q4; 4Q162-163; 4Q161; 4Q165; 4Q164; 4Q166-167; 1Q14; 4Q168-169; 1QpHab; 4Q170; 1Q15; 4Q172; 4QCommGen A-D; 4QCommMal A-B; 4QFlor; 11QMelch; 4Q464; 4Q177; 4QCat^{b}; 4QTestim; 4QTanḥ; 4Q464a-464b; 4Q183; 4Q173a].

Fitzmyer, J. A. and D. J. Harrington, *A Manual of Palestinian Aramaic Texts (Second Century B.C.–Second Century A.D.)* (BibOr 34; Rome: Biblical Institute, 1978) [*MPAT*]. Contains the Aramaic texts of 1QDan, 1QapGen (1Q20), 1QTLevi, 1QJN, 1QEnGiants, 2QJN, 2QEnGiants, 4QJer^{b}, 4QprNab, 4QpsDan; parts of 4QEnastr, 4QEnGiants, and 4QEn; 4QTLevi, 4QAmram, 4QTQahat, 4QMess, 4QVisJac (olim 4QTestuz), unidentified frgs. of 1Q, 3Q, 5Q, 6Q; MasOstr; Mur 8, 19-21, 23, 25-28, 31, 33-35, 72; pap?ḤevB, pap?ḤevC, 5/6Ḥev1, 2, 4, 8, 10, 11, 14, 15, 5/6ḤevBA 1-2, 5/6Ḥev nab. Texts are accompanied by a translation and secondary bibliography.

García Martínez, F. and E. J. C. Tigchelaar (eds.), *The Dead Sea Scrolls Study Edition* (2 vols.; Leiden: Brill, 1997, 1998; in a slightly corrected paperback edition, Leiden: Brill; Grand Rapids, MI: Eerdmans, 2000) [*DSSSE*]. Hebrew and Aramaic non-biblical texts with facing English translation and ordered according to the numbers of the DJD series.

Habermann, A. M., מגילות מדבר יהודה: *The Scrolls* . . . (see section VI above). The texts incorporated here are: CD, 1QH^{a}, 1QM, 1QS, 1QSb, 1QpHab, 1QpMic, 1QpPs, 1QMyst, 1QLitA, 1Q29, 1Q34bis, 4QpIsa^{a}, 4QpNah, 4QpPs^{a}, 4QFlor, 4QCommGen A; they are vocalized with Masoretic pointing.

———, עדה ועדות: *Three Scrolls from the Judaean Desert: The Legacy of a Community, Edited with Vocalization, Introduction, Notes and Indices* (Tel Aviv: Machbaroth Lesifruth, 1952). Contains CD, 1QS, 1QpHab, and a text from the Cairo Genizah, published by I. Levi, *REJ* 65 [1913] 24-31.

Jongeling, B., C. J. Labuschagne, and A. S. van der Woude, *Aramaic Texts from Qumran, with Translations and Annotations* (Semitic Study Series 4; Leiden: Brill, 1976). Contains the Aramaic texts of 11QtgJob, 1QapGen, 4QprNab; the translations have brief notes.

Licht, J., מגילת הסרכים: סרך היחד, סרך לכול עדת ישראל לאחרית הימים, סרך הברכות (Jerusalem: Student Association of Hebrew University, 1961-62) (Annotated unpointed Hebrew text of 1QS, 1QSa, 1QSb).

Lohse, E., *Die Texte aus Qumran: Hebräisch und deutsch, mit masoretischer Punktation, Übersetzung, Einführung und Anmerkungen* (Munich: Kösel; Darmstadt: Wissenschaftliche Buchgesellschaft, 1964; 2d ed., 1971). Contains the pointed Hebrew texts of 1QS, 1QSa, 1QSb, CD, 1QH, 1QM, 1QpHab, 4QPBless, 4QTestim, 4QFlor, 4QpNah, 4QpPs[a] with a German translation and brief notes.

Parry, D. W. and E. Tov (eds.), *The Dead Sea Scrolls Reader* (6 vols.; Leiden: Brill, 2004, 2004, 2005, 2004, 2005, 2005) [*DSSR*]. Hebrew and Aramaic non-biblical texts with facing English translation; the texts are ordered by genres: 1. Texts concerned with religious law; 2. Exegetical texts; 3. Parabiblical texts; 4. Calendrical and sapiential texts; 5. Poetic and liturgical texts; and 6. Additional genres and unclassified texts.

Schattner-Rieser, U., *Textes araméens de la Mer Morte: Édition bilingue, vocalisée et commentée* (Langues et cultures anciennes 5; Brussels: Edition Safran, 2005).

Steudel, A. et al., *Die Texte aus Qumran II: Hebräisch/Aramäisch und Deutsch mit masoretischer Punktation, Übersetzung, Einführung und Anmerkungen* (Darmstadt: Wissenschaftliche Buchgesellschaft, 2001). This is the sequel to the book of E. Lohse mentioned above. It contains the following pointed Hebrew or Aramaic texts: 11QTemple[a-c] (with 4Q254), 4QprNab ar (4Q242), 4QSon of God ar (4Q246), 11QMelch (11Q13), 4QMidrEschat (4Q174, 4Q177), 1QpMic (1Q14), 4QpIsa[b] (4Q164), 4QpHos[a] (4Q166), 4QpHos[b] (4Q167).

Vegas Montaner, L., *Biblia del Mar Muerto: Profetas Menores: Edición crítica según manuscritos hebreos procedentes del Mar Muerto* (Textos y Estudios "Cardenal Cisneros" 29; Madrid: Instituto "Arias Montano," 1980). (This publication brings together the texts of the canonical Minor Prophets as they appear in 1QpHab, 1QpMic, 1QpZeph, 4QpHos, 4QpMic, 4QpNah, 4QpZeph, 4QFlor, 4QTanh, 4QCatena[a], 4QapLam, 4QXII? [Testuz], 5QAmos, 5QpMal [= 5Q10], Mur 88.)

Weiss, R., המקרא בקומראן (Jerusalem: Hebrew University, 1966) (A collection of samples of the biblical texts used at Qumran: e.g., 1QLev [= 1Q31 frgs. 1-7]; 4QExod[a]; 4QExod[m]; 4QSam[a]; samples of biblical quotations in non-biblical writings of Qumran; cols. 1:29-33 of 1QIsa[a]; 1QIsa[b]; 11QPs[a] cols. 16-19, 21-22, 24, 27-28; 1QpHab cols. 1-13; 4QpNah cols. 1-4; 4QpPs[a] [olim 4QpPs37] cols. 1-4; CD 3:13–4:21; 5:12–6:13; 7:9-21; 1QS cols. 1-11; 1QH[a] col. 5).

VIII

Translations of the Dead Sea Scrolls in Collections

Listed here are the books in which one finds translations into a modern language of various Qumran texts published at a given time, as well as more wide-ranging discussions of them, which often have incorporated sizeable portions of the texts in translation. Serious study of texts must take such translations into consideration as well as those in the formal editions, since the latter often bear witness to pioneer attempts to cope with the problems of translating the Dead Sea Scrolls. Translations of single texts, which form part of commentaries on such texts, are not listed here. Certain collections of translations have already been mentioned in the preceding section of this book, when they accompanied secondary publications of the texts: e.g., Beyer, *ATTM, ATTME;* García Martínez, *DSSSE;* Lohse, *Die Texte aus Qumran;* Parry-Tov, *DSSR;* Steudel, *Die Texte aus Qumran II.*

Abegg, M., Jr., P. Flint, and E. Ulrich, The Dead Sea Scrolls Bible (San Francisco: HarperSan Francisco, CA, 1999). English transl. of 220 biblical scrolls in canonical order.

Allegro, J. M., *The Dead Sea Scrolls* (Pelican A376; Baltimore: Penguin, 1956; 2d ed., 1964): partial transl. of 4QSam^{a}, 4QDeut^{a}, 1QS, IQH, Mur 42-43.

Amussin, J. D., *Nakhodki u Mertvogo moria* (Moscow: Akademia Nauk, 1964).

———, *Teksty Kumrana* (Moscow: Akademia Nauk, 1971): Russian transl. of 1QpHab, 4QpNah, 4QpHos^{b,a}, 1QpMic, 4QpPs37, 4QFlor, 4QPBless, 11QMelch, 4QTestim, 1QMyst, 4QPrNab.

Bardtke, H., *Die Handschriftenfunde am Toten Meer: Die Sekte von Qumran* (2d ed.; Berlin: Evangelische Haupt-Bibelgesellschaft, 1961): German transl. of 1QIsa^{a}, 1QS, 1QM, 1QH, CD, 1QapGen, 1QSa, 1QSb, 1Q34, 1QDM, 1QMyst, 1QpHab, 1QpMic, 1QpZeph, 1QpPs, 4QPrNab, 4QpNah, 4QFlor, 4QTestim.

Burrows, M., *The Dead Sea Scrolls* (New York: Viking, 1955): First English transl. of CD, 1QpHab, 1QS, 1QM (selections), 1QH[a] (selections).

———, *More Light on the Dead Sea Scrolls: New Scrolls and New Interpretations with Translations of Important Recent Discoveries* (New York: Viking, 1958): Transl. of 1QapGen, 1QSa, 1QSb, 1QMyst, 1QLitPr, 4QPrNab, 4QTestim, 4QFlor, 4QpPs37, 4QPBless, 4QpIsa[a], 1QpMic, 4QpNah.

Campbell, J. G., *The Exegetical Texts* (Companion to the Qumran Scrolls 4; New York/London: T&T Clark, 2004).

Carmignac, J., P. Guilbert, and E. Cothenet, *Les textes de Qumran traduits et annotés* (2 vols.; Paris: Letouzey et Ane, 1961, 1963): Annotated French transl. of 1QS, 1QM, 1QH, 1QSa, 1QSb, 3QpIsa, 4QpIsa[b], 4QpIsa[a-d], 4QpHos[a-b], 1QpMic, 4QpNah, 1QpHab, 1QpZeph, 4QpPs37, CD, 1QapGen, 1QDM, 1QMyst, 1QLitPr, 4QTestim, 4QFlor, 4QPBless, 4QPrNab, 4QDibHam, 4QShirShabb.

Dupont-Sommer, A., *Les écrits esséniens découverts près de la Mer Morte* (Bibliothèque historique; Paris: Payot, 1959; 3d ed., 1964): French transl. of 1QS, 1QSa, 1QSb, CD, 1QM, 1QH, 1QpHab, 4QpNah, 4QpPs37, 4QpIsa[a], 4QpHos[b], 1QpMic, 1QpZeph, 1QapGen, 1QDM, 4QFlor, 4QPBless, 4QTestim, 4QpsDan, 4QPrNab, 1QMyst, 1QJN, 1QLitPr. — English version in *The Essene Writings from Qumran* (tr. G. Vermes; Oxford: Blackwell, 1961; repr., Cleveland: World, 1962; Magnolia, MA: Peter Smith, 1971).

——— and M. Philonenko (eds.), *La Bible: Écrits intertestamentaires* (Bibliothèque de la Pléiade; Paris: Gallimard, 1987): Transl. of 1QS, 11QTemple[a], CD, 1QM, 1QH, 11QPsa, 1QpHab, 4QpNah, 4QpPs37, 1QapGen, 4QFlor, 4QTestim, 11QMelch, 4QShirShabb, 4QWiles, 1QMyst; *1 Enoch, Jubilees, T. 12 Patr., Ps. Sol., T. Moses, Mart. Isa., Sib. Orac., 3 Apoc. Bar., 2 Enoch, Ps.-Philo, 4 Ezra, 2 Apoc. Bar., Joseph and Aseneth, T. Job, T. Abraham, Apoc. Abraham, Par. Jer., Adam and Eve, Apoc. Elijah.*

Edelkoort, A. H., *De Handschriften van de Dode Zee* (Baarn: Bosch en Keuning, 1952; 2d ed., 1954): Dutch transl. of 1QpHab, 1QS, 1QH[a], 1QM, 1QJub[a].

García Martínez, F., *Textos de Qumrán: Introducción y edición* (Madrid: Editorial Trotta, 1992).

——— (ed.), *The Dead Sea Scrolls Translated: The Qumran Texts in English* (tr. W. G. E. Watson; Leiden: Brill, 1994). This is the best one-volume English translation.

Harrington, H. K., *The Purity Texts* (Companion to the Qumran Scrolls 5; New York/London: T&T Clark, 2004).

Knibb, M. A., *The Qumran Community* (Cambridge, UK; London/New York: Cambridge University Press, 1987): English transl. of CD, 1QS, 1QSa, 1QH, 1QapGen, 4QprNab, 4QpNah, 1QpHab, 4QpPs, 4QFlor, 4QTestim.

Lamadrid, A. C., *Los descubrimientos del Mar Muerto: Balance de veinticinco años de hallazgos y estudio* (BAC 317; Madrid: Editorial Católica, 1971): Partial Spanish transl. of major texts.

Maier, J., *Die Qumran-Essener: Die Texte vom Toten Meer* (Uni-Taschenbücher 1862-63; 2 vols.; Munich/Basel: E. Reinhardt, 1995). Vol. 1 has the translation of texts from Caves 1-3 and 5-11; vol. 2 has the translation of Cave 4. This is an updated version of Qumran texts published earlier as *Die Texte vom Toten Meer: I. Übersetzung; II. Anmerkungen* (2 vols.; Munich/Basel: E. Reinhardt, 1960).

Medico, H. E. del, *L'énigme des manuscrits de la Mer Morte: Étude sur la provenance et le contenu des manuscrits découverts dans la grotte I de Qumrân suivi de la traduction commentée des principaux textes* (Paris: Plon, 1957): French transl. of 1QS, 1QSa, 1QSb, 1QpHab, 1QM, 1QH, 1QapGen, CD. — English version in *The Riddle of the Scrolls* (London: Burke, 1958). To be used with discernment.

Michelini Tocci, F., *I manoscritti del Mar Morto: Introduzione, traduzione e commento* (Bari: Laterza, 1967): Italian transl. of 1QS, 1QSa, 1QSb, CD, 1QM, 1QH, 4QShirShabb, 4QDibHam, 1QLitPr, 11QPsa, 4QpPs37, 4QpHos, 1QpMic, 4QpNah, 1QpHab, 3QpIsa, 4QpIsa^{a}, 1QapGen, 4QPrNab, 1QDM, 4QTestim, 4QFlor, 4QOrd^{a}, 4QPBless, 11QMelch, 1QMyst, 5QJN, 4QMess ar, 4QCryptic, 4QWiles, 3Q15.

Molin, G., *Die Söhne des Lichtes: Zeit und Stellung der Handschriften vom Toten Meer* (Vienna/Munich: Herold, 1954): German transl. of 1QpHab, 1QpMic, 1QS, 1QH^{a}, 1QM, 1QMyst, CD.

Moraldi, L., *I manoscritti di Qumrân* (Classici delle religioni; Turin: Unione Tipografico — Editrice Torinese, 1971): Italian transl. of 1QS, 1QSa, 1QSb, CD, 1QM, 1QH^{a}, 11QPs^{a}, 4QpPs37, 3QpIsa, 4QpIsa^{a-e}, 4QpHos^{a-b}, 4QpMic, 1QpMic, 4QpNah, 1QpHab, 4QPBless, 4QFlor, 11QMelch, 4QVisSam (4Q160), 4QCatena^{a-b}, 4QTanh (4Q176), 4QTestim, 1QDM, 1QapGen, 1QMyst, 1QLitPr, 4QDibHam, 4QOrd^{a}, 4QShirShabb, 4QPrNab, 4QCryptic, 4QMess ar, 4QAgesCreat, 4QLam^{a} (4Q179), 4QWis (4Q185), 4QWiles, 3Q15, 5QJN. This was the most comprehensive collection of translated texts up to the time of its publication.

Sutcliffe, E. F., *The Monks of Qumran* (Westminster, MD: Newman, 1960): English transl. of CD, 1QSa, 1QS, 1QpHab, 1QpMic, 4QpNah, 4QpPs37, 1QH, 1QSb, 1QM.

Tyloch, W., *Rekopisy z Qumran ned Morzem Martwym* (Warsaw: Panstowe Wyd. Naukowe, 1963): Polish transl. of 1QS, 1QSa, 1QM, 1QH, 1QpHab, CD.

Vermes, G., *The Complete Dead Sea Scrolls in English* (New York: Allen Lane, Penguin Press, 1997). This is the most comprehensive, one-volume English translation of the Scrolls to date; unfortunately the lines of the texts are not numbered, and so this translation is not easy to consult. Earlier editions of this book, with the title *The Dead Sea Scrolls in English* (London: Penguin; New York: Viking Penguin), appeared in 1962 [first], 1965, 1975 [2d ed.], 1987 [3d ed.], 1995 [4th ed.]).

Wise, M., M. Abegg, Jr., and E. Cook, *The Dead Sea Scrolls: A New Translation* (San Francisco, CA: HarperSanFrancisco, 1996; rev. ed., 2005).

IX

Outlines of Some Qumran Texts (with Select Bibliography)

In this section, outlines are provided for the Rule of the Community (1QS), the Damascus Document (CD + 4QD), the Genesis Apocryphon (1QapGen), the War Scroll (1QM), the Temple Scroll (11QTemple^{a}), the Thanksgiving Psalms (1QH^{a-b}, 4QH^{a-f}), and the Halakhic Letter (4QMMT), i.e., the longer, mostly sectarian scrolls. No attempt is made to outline the pesharim, since they follow for the most part the biblical texts on which they are commenting and cannot be divided up logically. The list of their contents and that of other scrolls, such as 11QPs^{a}, given in section II, is tantamount to an outline and should be consulted for study. The smaller texts, often because of their fragmentary character, do not lend themselves to outlining. The outlines provided are followed in some instances by bibliographical references; in others by indications where extensive bibliographies can be found.

1. Serek Hay-Yaḥad: The Rule of the Community (1QS)

(I)	1:1-15	Introduction: The Aim and Purpose of the Community
(II)	1:16–3:12	Entrance into the Covenant
(A)	1:16–2:18	Rite for Entrance into the Covenant
(B)	2:19-25a	Ceremony for the Assembly of Members
(C)	2:25b–3:12	Denunciation of Those Who Refuse to Enter
(III)	3:13–4:26	The Tenets of the Community
(A)	3:13–4:1	The Two Spirits
(B)	4:2-14	Activity of the Spirits in Human Life
(C)	4:15-26	Destiny and End of the Spirits

(IV) 5:1–6:23		Purpose and Way of Life in the Community
(A)	5:1-7a	Statement of the Purpose and the Way
(B)	5:7b–6:1a	Fidelity to the Way: Avoidance of Outsiders
(C)	6:1b-8	Rules for Community Life
(D)	6:8-13a	Rules for a Session of the Members
(E)	6:13b-23	Rules for Candidates
(V) 6:24–7:25		Penal Code of the Community
(VI) 8:1–10:8a		The Model, Pioneer Community
(A)	8:1-15a	Constitution and Negative Confession
(B)	8:15b–9:11	Conduct and Study of the Law until Messianic Times
(C)	9:12-26	Guidance for the Instructor of the Pioneer Community
(D)	10:1-8a	The Creator to be Praised in Times of Worship
(VII) 10:8b–11:22		The Hymn of the Community
(A)	10:8b–11:2a	Hymn of Praise and Service
(B)	11:2b-15a	Hymn to God's Righteousness
(C)	11:15b-22	Hymn of Blessing and Thanksgiving

Principal Studies and/or Translations of 1QS (beyond those listed in section VIII):

Alexander, P. S., "The Redaction-History of *Serekh ha-Yaḥad:* A Proposal," *RevQ* 17 (1996-97) 437-56.

Bardtke, H., "Literaturbericht über Qumrān VII. Teil: Die Sektenrolle, 1QS," *TRu* 38 (1973-74) 257-91.

Bockmuehl, M., "1QS and Salvation at Qumran," *Justification and Variegated Nomism: 1. The Complexities of Second Temple Judaism* (ed. D. A. Carson et al.; Tübingen: Mohr Siebeck; Grand Rapids, MI: Baker Academic, 2001) 381-414.

———, "Redaction and Ideology in the *Rule of the Community* (1QS/4QS)," *RevQ* 18 (1997-98) 541-60.

Brownlee, W. H., *The Dead Sea Manual of Discipline: Translation and Notes* (BASORSup 10-12; New Haven: American Schools of Oriental Research, 1951). The pioneer translation.

Charlesworth, J. H. (ed.), *The Dead Sea Scrolls: Rule of the Community, Photographic Multi-Language Edition* (Philadelphia, PA: American Interfaith Institute/World Alliance, 1996): English (Charlesworth), Modern Hebrew

(Qimron), French (Duhaime), Italian (Sacchi), German (Lichtenberger), Spanish (García Martínez).

Conway, C. M., "Toward a Well-Formed Subject: The Function of Purity Language in the Serek ha-Yaḥad," *JSP* 21 (2000) 103-20.

Daise, M. A., "'The Days of Sukkot of the Month of Kislev': The Festival of Dedication and the Delay of Feasts in 1QS 1:13-15," *Enoch and Qumran Origins: New Light on a Forgotten Connection* (ed. G. Boccaccini et al.; Grand Rapids, MI: Eerdmans, 2005) 119-28.

Denis, A. M., "Évolution de structures dans le secte de Qumrân," *Aux origines de l'Église* (RechBib 7; ed. J. Giblet; Bruges: Desclée de Brouwer, 1965) 23-49.

Destro, A. and M. Pesce, "The Gospel of John and the Community Rule of Qumran: A Comparison of Systems," *Judaism in Late Antiquity, Part 5: The Judaism of Qumran: A Systemic Reading of the Dead Sea Scrolls* (Handbook of Oriental Studies: Part 1, The Near and Middle East; 2 vols.; ed. A. J. Avery-Peck et al.; Leiden: Brill, 2001), 2. 201-29.

Duhaime, J. L., "Cohérence structurelle et tensions internes dans l'Instruction des Deux Esprits (1QS iii 13-iv 26)," *Wisdom and Apocalypticism in the Dead Sea Scrolls and in the Biblical Tradition* (BETL 168; ed. F. García Martínez; Louvain: Leuven University Press/Peeters, 2003) 103-31.

———, "L'Instruction sur les deux esprits et les interpolations dualistes à Qumrân (1QS iii, 13-iv, 26)," *RB* 84 (1977) 566-94.

———, "Les voies des deux esprits (*1QS* iv 2-14): Une analyse structurelle," *RevQ* 19 (1999-2000) 349-67.

García Martínez, F., "Sektarische composities: de Regel van de gemeenschap (Serek ha-Jahad)," *Schrift* 191 (2000) 151-54.

Goedhart, H., *De slothymne van het Manual of Discipline: A theological-exegetical Study of 1QS x,9–xi,22* (Rotterdam: Bronder-Offset, 1965).

Gramaglia, P. A., "1QS xi,21-22," *Henoch* 19 (1997) 143-47.

Guilbert, P., "La règle de la Communauté," *Les textes de Qumran traduits et annotés* (2 vols.; ed. J. Carmignac et al.; Paris: Letouzey et Ané, 1961-63) 1.9-80.

———, "Le plan de la 'Règle de la Communauté,'" *RevQ* 1 (1958-59) 323-44.

Hempel, C., "The Community and Its Rivals according to the *Community Rule* from Caves 1 and 4," *RevQ* 21 (2003-4) 47-81.

———, "Interpretative Authority in the Community Rule Tradition," *DSD* 10 (2003) 59-80.

———, "The Penal Code Reconsidered," *Legal Texts and Legal Issues: Proceedings of the Second Meeting of the International Organization for Qumran Studies, Cambridge 1995: Published in Honour of Joseph M. Baumgarten* (STDJ 23; ed. M. Bernstein et al.; Leiden: Brill, 1997) 337-48.

Himmelfarb, M., "Impurity and Sin in 4QD, 1QS, and 4Q512," *DSD* 8 (2001) 9-37.

Klinghardt, M., "The Manual of Discipline in the Light of Statutes of Hellenistic Associations," *Methods of Investigation of the Dead Sea Scrolls and the Khirbet Qumran Site: Present Realities and Future Prospects* (Annals of the New York Academy of Sciences 722; ed. M. O. Wise et al.; New York: New York Academy of Sciences, 1994) 251-67.

Kottsieper, I., "Zur Syntax von *1QS* ii 24f. und seiner Bedeutung in *1QS* ii 19–iii 12," *RevQ* 21 (2003-4) 285-95.

Krašovec, J., "Sources of Confession of Sin in 1QS 1:24-26 and CD 29:28-30," *The Dead Sea Scrolls Fifty Years after Their Discovery: Proceedings of the Jerusalem Congress, July 20-25, 1997* (ed. L. H. Schiffman et al.: Jerusalem: Israel Exploration Society and Shrine of the Book, Israel Museum, 2000) 306-21.

Kruse, C. G., "Community Functionaries in the Rule of the Community and the Damascus Document: A Test of Chronological Relationships," *RevQ* 10 (1979-81) 543-51.

Kugler, R., "A Note on 1QS 9:4: The Sons of Righteousness or the Sons of Zadok?" *DSD* 3 (1996) 315-20.

Lawrence, L. J., "'Men of Perfect Holiness' (1QS 7.20): Social-Scientific Thoughts on Group Identity, Asceticism and Ethical Development in the *Rule of the Community*," *New Directions in Qumran Studies: Proceedings of the Bristol Colloquium on the Dead Sea Scrolls, 8-10th September 2003* (Library of Second Temple Studies 52; ed. J. G. Campbell et al.; London/New York: T&T Clark, 2005) 83-100.

Leahy, T., "Studies in the Syntax of 1QS," *Bib* 41 (1960) 135-57.

Leaney, A. R. C., *The Rule of Qumran and Its Meaning: Introduction, Translation and Commentary* (New Testament Library; London: SCM; Philadelphia: Westminster, 1966).

Licht, J., מגילת הסרכים: *The Rule Scroll: A Scroll from the Wilderness of Judaea: 1QS, 1QSa, 1QSb: Text, Introduction and Commentary* (Jerusalem: Bialik, 1965).

Mantovani, P. A., "La stratificazione literaria della Regola della Comunità: A proposito di uno studio recente," *Henoch* 5 (1983) 69-91.

Martone, C., *La 'Regola della Comunità': Edizione critica* (Quaderni di Henoch 8; Turin: Silvio Zamorani Editore, 1995).

———, "Nuovi testimoni qumranici della Regola della Comunità," *Henoch* 16 (1994) 173-87.

Metso, S., "Biblical Quotations in the Community Rule," *The Bible as Book: The Hebrew Bible and the Judaean Desert Discoveries* (ed. E. D. Herbert and E. Tov; London: The British Library & Oak Knoll Press, 2002) 81-92.

———, "Constitutional Rules at Qumran," *The Dead Sea Scrolls after Fifty Years:*

A Comprehensive Assessment (2 vols.; ed. P. W. Flint and J. C. VanderKam; Leiden: Brill, 1998-99), 1. 186-210.

———, "The Redaction of the Community Rule," *The Dead Sea Scrolls Fifty Years after Their Discovery* (see above) 377-84.

———, "The Relationship between the Damascus Document and the Community Rule," *The Damascus Document: A Centennial of Discovery. Proceedings of the Third International Symposium of the Orion Center . . .* (STDJ 34; ed. J. M. Baumgarten et al.; Leiden: Brill, 2000) 85-93.

———, *The Textual Development of the Qumran Community Rule* (STDJ 21; Leiden: Brill, 1997).

Muraoka, T., "The Community Rule (1QS), Column 4," *Emanuel: Studies in Hebrew Bible, Septuagint, and Dead Sea Scrolls in Honor of Emanuel Tov* (VTSup 94; ed. S. M. Paul et al.; Leiden: Brill, 2003) 335-46.

———, "Notae qumranicae philologicae (1)," *RevQ* 17 (1996-97) 573-83.

Murphy-O'Connor, J., "Community, Rule of the (1QS)," *ABD* 1. 1110-12.

———, "La genèse littéraire de la Règle de la Communauté," *RB* 76 (1969) 528-49.

Pouilly, J., *La règle de la communauté de Qumrân: Son évolution littéraire* (Cahiers de la *RB* 17; Paris: Gabalda, 1976).

Qimron, E. and J. H. Charlesworth, "Rule of the Community (1QS; cf. 4QMSS A-J, 5Q11)," PTSDSSP, 1. 1-51.

Raurell, F., *Regla de la Comunitat de Qumran: Introduciô, text revisat, traducciô i notes* (Barcelona: Institut Cambô — Editorial Alpha, 2004).

Rogland, M., "המתנדבים," *ANES (AbrN)* 35 (1998) 65-73.

Schmidt, F., "Élection et tirage au sort (1QS vi,13-23 et Ac 1,15-26)," *RHPR* 80 (2000) 105-17.

Shemesh, A., "Expulsion and Exclusion in the Community Rule and the Damascus Document," *DSD* 9 (2002) 44-74.

Tigchelaar, E. J. C., "In Search of the Scribe of 1QS," *Emanuel: Studies in Hebrew Bible* (see above), 439-52.

Toews, C., "Moral Purification in 1QS," *BBR* 13 (2003) 71-96.

Werline, R. A., "The Curses of the Covenant Renewal Ceremony in 1QS 1.16–2.19 and the Prayers of the Condemned," *For a Later Generation: The Transformation of Tradition in Israel, Early Judaism, and Early Christianity* (ed. R. A. Argall et al.; Harrisburg, PA: Trinity Press International, 2000) 280-88.

Wernberg-Møller, P., *The Manual of Discipline* (STDJ 1; Leiden: Brill, 1957).

Zurli, E., "La giustificazione 'solo per grazia' in *1QS* x,9–xi e *1QH*[a]," *RevQ* 20 (2001-2) 445-77.

2. The Damascus Document (CD and 4QD)

This outline utilizes mainly the Cairo Genizah ms A and the frgs. from Qumran Caves 4, 5, 6 and is arranged according to the indications given by J. T. Milik, *Ten Years of Discovery in the Wilderness of Judaea* (SBT 26; London: SCM; Naperville, IL: Allenson, 1959) 151-52. These indications are derived mainly from the copies of 4QD[b,e].

- (I) 4Q Columns [missing in CD] + CD 1:1–8:21 (= 19:1–20:34 [ms B]) Admonition: Exhortation about God's Saving Plan in History
  - (A) Introductory Columns in 4Q Texts (4Q266, 4Q267, 4Q268)
  - (B) Meditation on the Lessons of History (CD 1:1–2:1)
  - (C) Predestination of the Upright and the Wicked (2:2-13)
  - (D) Second Meditation on Lessons of History (2:14–4:12a)
  - (E) The Three Nets of Belial (4:12b–6:2a [6Q15 1:1-3 = CD 4:19-21; 6Q15 2:1-2 = CD 5:13-14; 6Q15 3:1-5a = CD 5:18–6:2a])
  - (F) The Community of the New Covenant (6:2b–7:9a [6Q15 3:5 = CD 6:2b; 6Q15 4:1-4 = CD 6:20–7:1. CD 19:1-5a (ms B) = 7:5b-9a])
  - (G) Diverse Fates of Those Who Are Faithful to the Covenant and of Those Who are Apostates (7:9b–8:21 [= (ms B) 19:5b-34])
  - (H) Conclusion (ms B: 19:35–20:34)
- (II) 4Q Columns [missing in CD] Prescriptions
  - (A) Cultic Purity of Priests and Sacrifices
  - (B) The Law of Diseases (cf. Lev 13:29ff.)
  - (C) The Fluxes of Men and Women (Leviticus 15)
  - (D) Laws of Marriage
  - (E) Prescriptions Relating to Agricultural Life, Payment of Tithes, Relations with Pagans, Relations between the Sexes; Prohibition of Magic
- (III) CD 15:1–16:20; 9:1–14:22 Constitution: Laws in the New Covenant [+ 4Q texts]
  - (A) Rules for Entrance into the Covenant and for Oaths (15:1–16:16)
    - (1) The Oath by Which One Is to Swear (15:1-5a)
    - (2) Admission into the Community (15:5b-19 [15:15-17 can be restored as in 4QD[a]]; see Milik, *Ten Years,* 114)
    - (3) Oath on Entering the Covenant (16:1-6a)
    - (4) The Validity of Oaths (16:6b-12)
    - (5) Voluntary Gifts (16:13-16)
  - (B) Laws within the Community (9:1–10:10a)

(1) Fraternal Correction (9:1-6; 4QD 10 iii ?-20; 9:7-8a [= 5Q12 1:21])
(2) Judicial Oaths (9:8b-16a [5Q12 1:3-5 = CD 9:8b-101])
(3) Witnesses (9:16b–10:3)
(4) Judges (10:4-10a)

(C) Rites to be Observed in the Community (10:10b–12:18)
(1) Purification with Water (10:10b-13)
(2) Sabbath Regulations (10:14–11:18a)
(3) Sundry Regulations (11:18b–12:11a)
(a) Sacrificial Offerings through an Unclean Intermediary (11:18b-21a)
(b) Entrance into Temple in a State of Uncleanness (11:21b-23)
(c) Defilement of the Sanctuary (12:1-3 [cf. 6Q15 5:1-5: belongs here?])
(d) Profanation of the Sabbath (12:3b-6a)
(e) Killing or Robbing Pagans (12:6b-8a)
(f) Commerce with Outsiders (12:8b-11a)
(4) Ritual Purity Laws (12:11b-18)

(D) The Organization of the Community (12:19–14:19)
(1) Preamble (12:19–13:2a)
(2) Local Communities (13:2b-7a)
(3) The Overseer of the Camp (13:7b–14:2)
(4) Functionaries in the Community (14:3-12a)
(5) The Works of the Community (14:12b-19)

(E) The Penal Code (14:20-22)

(F) Liturgy for the Feast of the Renewal of the Covenant [4Q columns]

(IV) [4Q columns] Conclusion (see Milik, *RB* 63 [1956] 61)

N.B. Two mss of CD came from the Cairo Genizah: Ms A (10th cent.) contains eight sheets with cols. 1-16; ms B (12th cent.) contains one sheet with cols. 19-20. The latter columns coincide roughly with cols. 7 and 8 of ms A, but the last part of col. 20 corresponds to nothing in ms A. The frgs. of 4D now make it clear that cols. 15-16 of CD have to precede col. 9. For an extensive older bibliography on CD, see S. Schechter, *Documents of Jewish Sectaries* (with a prolegomenon by J. A. Fitzmyer; 2 vols. in one; New York: Ktav, 1970) 25-34.

Bardtke, H., "Literaturbericht über Qumran VIII. Teil: Die Damaskusschrift CD," *TRu* 39 (1974-75) 189-221.

Baumgarten, A. I., "The Perception of the Past in the Damascus Document," *The Damascus Document: A Centennial of Discovery. Proceedings of the Third International Symposium of the Orion Center . . .* (STDJ 34; ed. J. M. Baumgarten et al.; Leiden: Brill, 2000) 1-15.

Baumgarten, J. M., "Damascus Document," *EDSS*, 166-70.

———, "The Damascus Document Reconsidered," *The Dead Sea Scrolls at Fifty: Proceedings of the 1997 Society of Biblical Literature Qumran Section Meetings* (SBLEJL 15; ed. R. A. Kugler and E. M. Schuller; Atlanta, GA: Scholars, 1999) 149-50; cf. 199-201.

———, "The Laws of the Damascus Document — Between Bible and Mishnah," *The Damascus Document: A Centennial of Discovery* (see above), 17-26.

———, "The Laws of the *Damascus Document* in Current Research," in Broshi, *The Damascus Document Reconsidered* (see below), 51-62.

———, "The Qumran Cave 4 Fragments of the Damascus Document," *Biblical Archaeology Today, 1990: Proceedings of the Second International Congress on Biblical Archaeology, Jerusalem, June-July 1990* (Jerusalem: Israel Exploration Society, 1993) 391-97.

———, "A 'Scriptural' Citation in 4Q Fragments of the Damascus Document," *JJS* 43 (1992) 95-98.

——— et al., "Damascus Document (CD)" and "Cave IV, V, VI Fragments," PTSDSSP, 2. 4-57, 59-79.

Broshi, M. (ed.), *The Damascus Document Reconsidered* (Jerusalem: Israel Exploration Society and the Shrine of the Book, Israel Museum, 1991).

Campbell, J. G., *The Use of Scripture in the Damascus Document 1-8, 19-20* (BZAW 228; Berlin/New York: de Gruyter, 1995).

Coulot, C., "La nouvelle alliance au pays de Damas," *Typologie biblique: De quelques figures vives* (ed. R. Kuntzmann; Paris: Editions du Cerf, 2002) 103-18.

Davies, P. R., *The Damascus Covenant: An Interpretation of the "Damascus Document"* (JSOTSup 25; Sheffield, UK: JSOT, 1983).

———, "The 'Damascus' Sect and Judaism," *Pursuing the Text: Studies in Honor of Ben Zion Wacholder . . .* (JSOTSup 184; ed. J. C. Reeves and J. Kampen; Sheffield, UK: Academic Press, 1994) 70-84.

———, "The Ideology of the Temple in the Damascus Document," *JJS* 33 (1982) 287-301; repr. in *Essays in Honour of Yigael Yadin* (ed. G. Vermes and J. Neusner; Totowa, NJ: Allanheld, Osmun & Co., 1983) 287-301.

———, "The Judaism(s) of the Damascus Document," *The Damascus Document: A Centennial of Discovery* (see above), 27-43.

———, "The Teacher of Righteousness and the 'End of Days,'" *RevQ* 13 (1988) 313-17.

———, "Who Can Join the 'Damascus Covenant'?" *JJS* 46 (1995) 134-42.

Dimant, D., "Two 'Scientific' Fictions: The So-called *Book of Noah* and the Alleged Quotation of *Jubilees* in CD 16:3-4," *Studies in the Hebrew Bible, Qumran, and the Septuagint Presented to Eugene Ulrich* (VTSup 101; ed. P. W. Flint et al.; Leiden: Brill, 2006) 230-49.

Dion, P. E., "The Hebrew Particle את in the Paraenetic Part of the 'Damascus Document,'" *RevQ* 9 (1977-78) 197-212.

Elwolde, J. F., "Distinguishing the Linguistic and the Exegetical: The Biblical Book of Numbers in the Damascus Document," *DSD* 7 (2000) 1-25.

———, "*RWQMH* in the *Damascus Document* and Ps 139:15," *Diggers at the Well: Proceedings of a Third International Symposium on the Hebrew of the Dead Sea Scrolls and Ben Sira* (STDJ 36; ed. T. Muraoka and J. F. Elwolde; Leiden: Brill, 2000) 65-83.

Eshel, H., "CD 12:15-17 and the Stone Vessels Found at Qumran," *The Damascus Document: A Centennial of Discovery* (see above), 45-52.

Fassberg, S. E., "The Linguistic Study of the Damascus Document: A Historical Perspective," *The Damascus Document: A Centennial of Discovery* (see above), 53-67.

Fitzmyer, J. A., "The Gathering in of the Community's Teacher," *Let Your Colleagues Praise You: Studies in Memory of Stanley Gevirtz* (= *Maarav* 8/2 [1992]) 223-28.

García Martínez, F., "Damascus Document: A Bibliography of Studies 1970-1989," in Broshi, *The Damascus Document Reconsidered* (see above), 63-83.

Greenfield, J. C., "The Words of Levi Son of Jacob in Damascus Document iv, 15-19," *RevQ* 13 (1988) 319-22.

Grossman, M. L., "Reading for Gender in the Damascus Document," *DSD* 11 (2004) 212-39.

———, *Reading for History in the Damascus Document: A Methodological Study* (STDJ 45; Leiden: Brill, 2002).

Heger, P., "Sabbath Offerings according to the Damascus Document: Scholarly Opinions and a New Hypothesis," *ZAW* 118 (2006) 62-81.

Hempel, C., *The Damascus Texts* (Companion to the Qumran Scrolls 1; Sheffield, UK: Sheffield Academic, 2000).

———, "4QOrd[a] (4Q159) and the Laws of the Damascus Document," *The Dead Sea Scrolls Fifty Years after Their Discovery: Proceedings of the Jerusalem Congress, July 20-25, 1997* (ed. L. H. Schiffman et al.; Jerusalem: Israel Exploration Society and the Shrine of the Book, Israel Museum, 2000) 372-76.

———, "The Laws of the Damascus Document and 4QMMT," *The Damascus Document: A Centennial of Discovery* (see above), 69-84.

———, *The Laws of the Damascus Document: Sources, Tradition and Redaction* (STDJ 29; Leiden: Brill, 1998).

Himmelfarb, M., "Impurity and Sin in 4QD, 1QS, and 4Q512," *DSD* 8 (2001) 9-37.

———, "The Purity Laws of 4QD: Exegesis and Sectarianism," *Things Revealed: Studies in Early Jewish and Christian Literature in Honor of Michael E. Stone* (JSJSup 89; ed. E. G. Chazon et al.; Leiden: Brill, 2004) 155-69.

Hultgren, S., "A New Literary Analysis of *CD* xix-xx, Part I: *CD* xix:1-32a (with *CD* vii:4b–viii:18b). The Midrashim and the 'Princes of Judah,'" *RevQ* 21 (2003-4) 549-78; "Part II: *CD* xix:32b–xx:34. The Punctuation of *CD* xix:33b–xx:1a and the Identity of the 'New Covenant,'" *RevQ* 22 (2005-6) 7-32.

Huppenbauer, H. W., "Zur Eschatologie der Damaskusschrift," *RevQ* 4 (1963-64) 567-73.

Hurowitz, V. A., "רוקמה in Damascus Document 4QD[e] (4Q270) 7 i 14," *DSD* 9 (2002) 34-37.

Kampen, J., "The Significance of the Temple in the Manuscripts of the Damascus Document," *The Dead Sea Scrolls at Fifty* (see above), 185-97.

Kesterson, J. C., "Cohortative and Short Imperfect Forms in *Serakim* and *Dam. Doc.,*" *RevQ* 12 (1985-87) 369-82.

Kister, M., "Demons, Theology and Abraham's Covenant (CD 16:4-6 and Related Texts)," *The Dead Sea Scrolls at Fifty* (see above), 167-84.

Knibb, M. A., "Community Organization in the Damascus Document," *EDSS,* 136-38.

———, "Exile in the Damascus Document," *JSOT* 25 (1983) 99-117.

Krašovec, J., "Sources of Confession of Sin in 1QS 1:24-26 and CD 20:28-30," *The Dead Sea Scrolls Fifty Years after Their Discovery* (see above), 306-21.

Laato, A., "The Chronology in the *Damascus Document* of Qumran," *RevQ* 15 (1991-92) 605-7.

Levine, B. A., "Damascus Document ix, 17-22: A New Translation and Comments," *RevQ* 8 (1972-75) 195-96.

Levy, R., "First 'Dead Sea Scroll' Found in Egypt Fifty Years before Qumran Discoveries," *BARev* 8/5 (1982) 38-53.

Lied, L. I., "Another Look at the Land of Damascus: The Spaces of the *Damascus Document* in the Light of Edward W. Soja's Thirdspace Approach," *New Directions in Qumran Studies: Proceedings of the Bristol Colloquium on the Dead Sea Scrolls, 8-10 September 2003* (Library of Second Temple Studies 52; ed. J. G. Campbell et al.; London: T&T Clark, 2005) 101-25.

Martone, C. "La *Regola di Damasco:* Una regola qumranica *sui generis*," *Henoch* 17 (1995) 103-15.

Metso, S., "The Relationship between the Damascus Document and the Community Rule," *The Damascus Document: A Centennial of Discovery* (see above), 85-93.

Milik, J. T., "Fragment d'une source du Psautier (4QPs89) et fragments des Jubilés, du Document de Damas, d'un phylactère dans la grotte 4 de Qumran," *RB* 73 (1966) 94-106 (= 4QD 1 xvii 1-16 [corresponding to nothing in CD]).

Milikowsky, C., "Again: *Damascus* in Damascus Document and in Rabbinic Literature," *RevQ* 11 (1982-84) 97-106.

Murphy-O'Connor, J., "The Critique of the Princes of Judah (CD viii, 3-19)," *RB* 79 (1972) 200-16.

———, "The Damascus Document Revisited," *RB* 92 (1985) 223-46.

———, "An Essene Missionary Document? CD ii,14–vi,1," *RB* 77 (1970) 201-29.

———, "A Literary Analysis of Damascus Document vi,2–viii,3," *RB* 78 (1971) 210-32.

———, "A Literary Analysis of Damascus Document xix,33–xx,34," *RB* 79 (1972) 544-64.

———, "The Translation of Damascus Document vi, 11-14," *RevQ* 7 (1969-71) 553-56.

Nebe, G. W., "Der Gebrauch der sogenannten 'Nota Accusativi' את in Damaskusschrift xv, 5. 9 und 12," *RevQ* 8 (1972-75) 257-63.

———, "Nocheinmal zu Text and Übersetzung von *CD* vi, 11-14," *RevQ* 16 (1993-95) 285-87.

———, "Das Sprachvermögen des Mebaqqer in *Damaskusschrift* xiv, 10," *RevQ* 16 (1993-95) 289-91.

Neusner, J., "By the Testimony of Two Witnesses' in the Damascus Document ix, 17-22 and in Pharisaic-Rabbinic Law," *RevQ* 8 (1972-75) 197-217.

Osten-Sacken, P. von der, "Die Bücher der Tora als Hütte der Gemeinde: Amos 5:26f. in der Damaskusschrift," *ZAW* 91 (1979) 423-35.

Qimron, E., "Further Observations on the Laws of Oaths in the Damascus Document 15," *JQR* 85 (1994-95) 251-57.

———, לפתרון חידה התיבות החסרות שבמגילת ברית דמשק ("The Riddle of the Missing Text in the Damascus Document"), יובל לחקר מגילות ים המלח: *Fifty Years of Dead Sea Scrolls Research* (ed. G. Brin and B. Nitzan; Jerusalem: Isaac ben Zvi, 2001) 244-50.

Rabin, C., *The Zadokite Documents: I. The Admonition; II. The Laws, Edited with a Translation* (Oxford: Clarendon, 1954; 2d ed., 1958).

Regev, E., "Yose ben Yoezer and the Qumran Sectarians on Purity Laws: Agreement and Controversy," *The Damascus Document: A Centennial of Discovery* (see above), 95-107.

Reif, S. C., "The Damascus Document from the Cairo Genizah: Its Discovery, Early Study and Historical Significance," *The Damascus Document: A Centennial of Discovery* (see above), 109-31.

Rofé, A., "'No *Ephod* or *Teraphim*'? — *oude hierateias oude dēlōn:* Hosea 3:4 in the LXX and in the Paraphrases of Chronicles and the *Damascus Document*," *Sefer Moshe: The Moshe Weinfeld Jubilee Volume: Studies in the Bible and the Ancient Near East, Qumran, and Post-Biblical Judaism* (ed. C. Cohen et al.; Winona Lake, IN: Eisenbrauns, 2004) 135-49.

Rosso-Ubigli, L., "Il *Documento di Damasco* e la halakah settaria (Rassegna di studi)," *RevQ* 9 (1977-78) 357-99.

———, "Il *Documento di Damasco* e l'etica coniugale: A proposito di un nuovo passo Qumranico," *Henoch* 14 (1992) 3-10.

Schiffman, L. H., "Legislation Concerning Relations with Non-Jews in the *Zadokite Fragments* and in Tannaitic Literature," *RevQ* 11 (1982-84) 379-89.

———, "The Relationship of the Zadokite Fragments to the Temple Scroll," *The Damascus Document: A Centennial of Discovery* (see above), 133-45.

Schremer, A., "Qumran Polemic on Marital Law: CD 4:20–5:11 and Its Social Background," *The Damascus Document: A Centennial of Discovery* (see above), 147-60.

Shemesh, A., "Expulsion and Exclusion in the Community Rule and the Damascus Document," *DSD* 9 (2002) 44-74.

———, "Scriptural Interpretations in the Damascus Document and Their Parallels in Rabbinic Midrash," *The Damascus Document: A Centennial of Discovery* (see above), 161-75.

Stegemann, H., "Towards Physical Reconstructions of the Qumran Damascus Document Scrolls," *The Damascus Document: A Centennial of Discovery* (see above), 177-200.

Stowasser, M., "Am 5,25-27; 9,11 f. in der Qumranüberlieferung und in der Apostelgeschichte: Text- und traditionsgeschichtliche Überlegungen zu 4Q174 (Florilegium) III 12/CD VII 16/Apg 7,42b-43; 15,16-18," *ZNW* 92 (2001) 47-63.

Strickert, F. M., "Damascus Document vii, 10-20 and Qumran Messianic Expectation," *RevQ* 12 (1985-87) 327-49.

Thorion-Vardi, T., "The Use of the Tenses in the Zadokite Documents," *RevQ* 12 (1985-87) 65-88.

Tigchelaar, E., "The Cave 4 Damascus Document Manuscripts and the Text of the Bible," *The Bible as Book: The Hebrew Bible and the Judaean Desert Discov-*

eries (ed. E. D. Herbert and E. Tov; New Castle, Del.: Oak Knoll Press; London: British Library, 2002) 93-111.

VanderKam, J. C., "Zadok and the spr htwrh hḥtwm in Dam. Doc. v, 2-5," *RevQ* 11 (1982-84) 561-70.

Vázquez Allegue, J., "Jurar por Dios en Qumrán (CD 15, 1-2)," *Salmanticensis* 48 (2001) 123-48.

Vermes, G., "Sectarian Matrimonial Halakah in the Damascus Rule," *JJS* 25 (1974) 197-202.

Wacholder, B. Z., "Does Qumran Record the Death of the *Moreh?:* The Meaning of *he'aseph* in *Damascus Covenant* xix, 35, xx, 14," *RevQ* 13 (1988) 323-30.

———, *The New Damascus Document: The Midrash on the Eschatological Torah of the Dead Sea Scrolls. Reconstruction, Translation, and Commentary* (STDJ 56; Leiden: Brill, 2007).

———, "The 'Sealed' Torah versus the 'Revealed' Torah: An Exegesis of Damascus Covenant v, 1-6 and Jeremiah 32, 10-14," *RevQ* 12 (1985-87) 351-68.

Wassen, C., *Women in the Damascus Document* (Academia Biblica 21; Leiden: Brill, 2005).

Werman, C., "CD xi:17: Apart from Your Sabbaths," *The Damascus Document: A Centennial of Discovery* (see above), 201-12.

White, S. A., "A Comparison of the 'A' and 'B' Manuscripts of the Damascus Document," *RevQ* 12 (1985-87) 537-53.

Zahavy, T., "The Sabbath Code of Damascus Document x, 14-xi, 18: Form Analytical and Redaction Critical Observations," *RevQ* 10 (1979-81) 589-91.

3. The Genesis Apocryphon (1QapGen [1Q20])
(The beginning of the text is lost)

(I) The Story of Noah (1QapGen 0:?–17:?)
  (A) Depravity of Humanity and the Birth of Noah (0–1:28)
  (B) Lamech's Anxiety about the Conception of His Son Noah (2:1–5:?)
  (C) Noah and the Flood (6:?–10:-?)
  (D) God's Covenant with Noah (11:?–15:?)
  (E) Noah Divides the Earth among His Sons (16:?–17:?)
(II) The Story of Abram (18:?–22:34)
  (A) Abram in Ur and Haran (18:?-?)
  (B) Abram in Canaan (18:?–19:10a)
    (a) Abram's Journey to Bethel (19:?-6)

- (b) Abram's Journey from the Altar Built at Bethel to Hebron (19:7-10a)

(C) Abram in Egypt (19:10b–20:33a)

- (a) Abram's Descent to Egypt because of the Famine in the Land of Canaan (19:10b-13)
- (b) Abram's Dream on Entering Egypt: The Cedar and the Date-Palm (19:14-23a)
- (c) Three Egyptian Courtiers Visit and Dine with Abram (19:23b-27)
- (d) Sarai's Beauty Described by the Courtiers to Pharaoh Zoan (20:2-8a)
- (e) Sarai Is Carried off to Pharaoh Zoan: Abram's Grief (20:8b-11)
- (f) Abram's Prayer That Sarai May Not Be Defiled (20:12-16a)
- (g) In Answer to Abram's Prayer, a Plague Strikes Pharaoh and His Household (20:16b-21a)
- (h) Pharaoh Is Cured by the Prayer and Exorcism of Abram (20:21b-31a)
- (i) Pharaoh Sends Sarai and Abram from Egypt with Gifts and an Escort (20:31b-33a)

(D) Abram in the Promised Land (20:33b–21:22)

- (a) Abram Returns with Lot to Bethel (20:33b–21:4)
- (b) Lot Departs from Abram and Settles in the Region of Sodom (21:5-7)
- (c) Abram's Dream: God's Promise of the Land to Him and His Descendants (21:8-14)
- (d) Abram Explores the Extent of the Land Promised to Him (21:15-22)

(E) Abram's Defeat of the Four Eastern Kings (21:23–22:26)

- (a) War of Four Eastern Kings against Five Canaanite Kings (21:23-34a)
- (b) Lot Is Taken Captive (21:34b–22:1a)
- (c) Abram Learns of Lot's Capture and Goes in Pursuit of the Kings (22:1b-12a)
- (d) Kings of Sodom and Salem Come out to Meet Abram Returning from Defeat of the Kings (22:12b-17)
- (e) Abram's Refusal to Retain Any of the Booty Belonging to the King of Sodom (22:18-26)

(F) Abram's Vision: God Promises Him an Heir to Be Born (22:27-?)

(a) Eliezer, His Household Slave, Will Not Inherit Him (22:27-34)
(b) [lost]

For an extensive older bibliography on 1QapGen (1Q20), see J. A. Fitzmyer, *The Genesis Apocryphon of Qumran Cave 1: A Commentary* (BibOr 18A; Rome: Biblical Institute, 1971) 42-45.

Archer, Jr., G. L., "The Aramaic of the 'Genesis Apocryphon' Compared with the Aramaic of Daniel," *New Perspectives on the Old Testament* (ed. J. B. Payne; Waco, TX: Word Books, 1970 [appeared 1971]) 160-69.

Bardtke, H., "Literaturbericht über Qumran VI. Teil: II. Das Genesis Apocryphon 1 QGenAp," *TRu* 37 (1972) 193-219, esp. 193-204.

Batto, B. F., "The Reed Sea: *Requiescat in Pace*," *JBL* 102 (1983) 27-35.

Bernstein, M. J., "From the Watchers to the Flood: Story and Exegesis in the Early Columns of the *Genesis Apocryphon*," *Reworking the Bible: Apocryphal and Related Texts at Qumran: Proceedings of a Joint Symposium by the Orion Center . . .* (STDJ 58; ed. E. G. Chazon et al.: Leiden: Brill, 2005) 39-63.

———, "Noah and the Flood at Qumran," *The Provo International Conference on the Dead Sea Scrolls: Technological Innovations, New Texts, and Reformulated Issues* (STDJ 30; ed. D. W. Parry and E. Ulrich; Leiden: Brill, 1999) 199-231.

———, "Re-arrangement, Anticipation and Harmonization as Exegetical Features in the Genesis Apocryphon," *DSD* 3 (1996) 37-57.

Bloch, A. A., "The Cedar and the Palm Tree: A Paired Male/Female Symbol in Hebrew and Aramaic," *Solving Riddles and Untying Knots: Biblical, Epigraphic, and Semitic Studies in Honor of Jonas C. Greenfield* (ed. Z. Zevit et al.; Winona Lake, IN: Eisenbrauns, 1995) 13-17.

Caquot, A., "Le livre des Jubilés, Melkisedeq et les dimes," *JJS* 33 (1982) 257-64.

———, "Suppléments Qoumrâniens à la Genèse," *RHPR* 80 (2000) 339-58.

Carmignac, J., "Le complément d'agent après un verbe passif dans l'hébreu et l'araméen de Qumrân," *RevQ* 9 (1977-78) 409-27.

Cook, E. M., "The Aramaic of the Dead Sea Scrolls," *The Dead Sea Scrolls after Fifty Years: A Comprehensive Assessment* (2 vols.; ed. P. W. Flint and J. C. VanderKam; Leiden: Brill, 1998-99), 1. 359-78.

Cowling, G., "Notes, Mainly Orthographical, on the Galilaean Targum and 1Q Genesis Apocryphon," *AJBA* 2 (1972) 35-49.

Coxon, P. W., "The Nunation Variant in the Perfect of the Aramaic Verb," *JNES* 36 (1977) 297-98.

———, "The Problem of Nasalization in Biblical Aramaic in the Light of 1 Q GA and 11 Q tg Job," *RevQ* 9 (1977-78) 253-58.

Dehandschutter, B., "Le rêve dans l'Apocryphe de la Genèse," *La littérature juive entre Tenach et Mischna: Quelques problèmes* (RechBib 9; Leiden: Brill, 1974) 48-55.

Delcor, M., "Qumran et découvertes au Désert de Juda: J. L'Apocryphe de la Genèse," *DBSup* 9 (1979) 931-44.

Eichler, B. L., "אמרי־נא אחותי את: הערכה חדשה בשמושלוחות נוזי להארת המקרא ('Please Say That You Are My Sister': Nuzi and Biblical Studies)," *Shnaton* 3 (1978-79) 108-15.

Eshel, E., "Isaiah 11:15: A New Interpretation Based on the *Genesis Apocryphon,*" *DSD* 13 (2006) 38-45.

Evans, C. A., "The Genesis Apocryphon and the Rewritten Bible," *RevQ* 13 (1988) 153-65.

Fitzmyer, J. A., "Genesis Apocryphon," *EDSS,* 302-4.

———, *The Genesis Apocryphon of Qumran Cave 1 (1Q20): A Commentary, Third Edition* (BibOr 18B; Rome: Editrice Pontificio Istituto Biblico, 2004).

——— and D. J. Harrington, *MPAT,* 100-127 (§29B).

Freedman, D. N. and A. Ritterspach, "The Use of Aleph as a Vowel Letter in the Genesis Apocryphon," *RevQ* 6 (1967-69) 293-300.

Garbini, G., "L''Apocrifo della Genesi' nella letteratura giudaica," *AION* 37 (1977) 1-18.

Gevirtz, M. L., "Abram's Dream in the Genesis Apocryphon: Its Motifs and Their Function," *Maarav* 8 (1992) 229-43.

Gordon, R. P., "Exorcism in a Dead Sea Scroll (1 Q GenApoc)," *The Harvester* 59 (1979) 2-3.

Greenfield, J. C., "Early Aramaic Poetry," *JANES* 11 (1979) 45-51, esp. 49-51.

———, "The Genesis Apocryphon — Observations on Some Words and Phrases," *Studies in Hebrew and Semitic Languages* (ed. G. B. Sarfatti et al.; Ramat-Gan: Bar-Ilan University, 1980) xxxii-xxxix; repr. in *'Al Kanfei Yonah: Collected Studies of Jonas C. Greenfield on Semitic Philology* (2 vols.; ed. S. M. Paul et al.; Leiden: Brill, 2001), 2. 610-17.

——— and M. Sokoloff, "The Contribution of Qumran Aramaic to the Aramaic Vocabulary," *Studies in Qumran Aramaic* (Abr-NSup 3; ed. T. Muraoka; Louvain: Peeters, 1992) 78-98.

Grelot, P., "De l'*Apocryphe de la Genèse* aux *Targoums:* Sur Genèse 14, 18-20," *Intertestamental Essays in Honour of Józef Tadeusz Milik* (Qumranica mogilanensia 6; ed. Z. J. Kapera; Cracow: Enigma Press, 1992) 77-90.

———, "Un nom égyptien dans l'Apocryphe de la Genèse," *RevQ* 7 (1969-71) 557-66.

Jongeling, B., "A propos de 1 Q GenAp XX, 28," *RevQ* 10 (1979-81) 301-3.
——— et al. (eds.), *Aramaic Texts from Qumran with Translations and Annotations, vol. 1* (Semitic Study Series 4; Leiden: Brill, 1976) 75-119.
Kee, H. C., *The Sources of Christianity: Sources and Documents* (Englewood Cliffs, NJ: Prentice Hall, 1973) 147-49 ("Non-Rabbinic Midrash").
Kennedy, J. M., "The Root G'R in the Light of Semantic Analysis," *JBL* 106 (1987) 47-64.
Lange, A., "1Q Gen Ap xix 10–xx 32 and the Wisdom Didactic Narrative," *QC* 3 (1993) 49-54.
Liverani, M. "Un'ipotesi sul nome di Abramo," *Henoch* 1 (1979) 9-18.
Lukaszewski, A. L., "'This' or 'That': The Far Demonstrative Pronoun in 1QapGen ii 6," *RevQ* 20 (2001-2) 589-92.
Luria, B. Z., "מלכי צדק מלך שלם כהן לאל עליון (Melchizedek, King of Salem, Priest of El Elyon)," *Beth Mikra* 32 (1986-87) 1-3 [in Modern Hebrew].
Margalith, O., "The Riddle of Genesis 14 and Melchizedek," *ZAW* 112 (2000) 501-8.
Meehan, C., "Some Semantic and Morpho-Syntactic Observations on Genesis Apocryphon 22:30-32," *Hamlet on a Hill: Semitic and Greek Studies Presented to Professor T. Muraoka . . .* (Orientalia Lovaniensia Analecta 118; ed. M. F. J. Baasten and W. T. van Peursen; Louvain: Peeters, 2003) 341-47.
Miller, P. D., Jr., "El, the Creator of Earth," *BASOR* 239 (1980) 43-46.
Morgenstern, M., "A New Clue to the Original Length of the Genesis Apocryphon," *JJS* 47 (1996) 345-47.
Muraoka, T., "Further Notes on the Aramaic of the *Genesis Apocryphon*," *RevQ* 16 (1993-95) 39-48.
———, "Notes on the Aramaic of the *Genesis Apocryphon*," *RevQ* 8 (1972-75) 7-51.
———, "Segholate Nouns in Biblical and Other Aramaic Dialects," *JAOS* 96 (1976) 226-35, esp. 231-32.
Nickelsburg, G. W. E., "Patriarchs Who Worry about Their Wives: A Haggadic Tendency in the Genesis Apocryphon," *Biblical Perspectives: Early Use and Interpretation of the Bible in the Light of the Dead Sea Scrolls: Proceedings of the First International Symposium of the Orion Center . . .* (STDJ 28; ed. M. Stone and E. G. Chazon; Leiden: Brill, 1998) 137-58.
Peter, M., "Wer sprach den Segen nach Genesis 14, 19 über Abraham aus?" *Collectanea theologica* 47 (1977) 127-37.
Qimron, E., "Towards a New Edition of the Genesis Apocryphon," *JSP* 10 (1992) 11-18; revised in *Qumran Questions* (Biblical Seminar 36; ed. J. H. Charlesworth; Sheffield, UK: Sheffield Academic Press, 1995) 20-27; and in *The Provo International Conference on the Dead Sea Scrolls* (see above), 106-9.

Reeves, J. C., "What Does Noah Offer in 1 QapGen X, 15?" *RevQ* 12 (1985-87) 415-19.

Reif, S. C., "A Note on *g'r*," *VT* 21 (1971) 241-44.

Schattner-Rieser, U., "À propos de l'araméen à Qoumrân," *Qoumran et les manuscrits de la Mer Morte: Un cinquantenaire* (ed. E.-M. Laperrousaz; Paris: Editions du Cerf, 1997) 175-204, esp. 199-203.

Schuller, E., "Response to 'Patriarchs Who Worry about Their Wives: A Haggadic Tendency in the Genesis Apocryphon,'" *George W. E. Nickelsburg in Perspective: An Ongoing Dialogue of Learning* (JSJSup 80; 2 vols.; ed. J. Neusner and A. J. Avery-Peck; Leiden: Brill, 2003), 1. 200-212.

Steiner, R. C., "The Heading of the *Book of the Words of Noah* on a Fragment of the Genesis Apocryphon: New Light on a 'Lost' Work," *DSD* 2 (1995) 66-71.

———, "The Mountains of Ararat, Mount Lubar and הר הקדם," *JJS* 42 (1991) 247-49.

Stone, M. E., "The Book(s) Attributed to Noah," *DSD* 13 (2006) 4-23.

VanderKam, J. C., "The Birth of Noah," *Intertestamental Essays in Honour of Jósef Tadeusz Milik* (see above), 1. 213-31.

———, "The Granddaughters and Grandsons of Noah," *RevQ* 16 (1993-95) 457-61.

———, "The Poetry of 1 Q Ap Gen, XX, 2-8a," *RevQ* 10 (1979-81) 57-66.

———, "The Textual Affinities of the Biblical Citations in the Genesis Apocryphon," *JBL* 97 (1978) 45-55.

Vasholz, R. I., "A Further Note on the Problem of Nasalization in Biblical Aramaic, 11 Q tg Job and 1 Q Genesis Apocryphon," *RevQ* 10 (1979-81) 95-96.

Vattioni, F., "Aspetti del culto del signore dei cieli," *Augustinianum* 12 (1972) 479-515.

Weinfeld, M., "Sarah and Abimelech (Genesis 20) against the Background of an Assyrian Law and the Genesis Apocryphon," *Mélanges bibliques et orientaux en l'honneur de M. Matthias Delcor* (AOAT 214; ed. A. Caquot et al.; Neukirchen-Vluyn: Neukirchener-V.; Kevelaer: Butzon & Bercker, 1985) 431-36.

White, R. T., "Genesis Apocryphon," *ABD*, 2. 932-33.

Widengren, C., "Aramaica et syriaca," *Hommages à André Dupont-Sommer* (Paris: Maisonneuve, 1971) 221-31.

Wise, M. O., "Accidents and Accidence: A Scribal View of Linguistic Dating of the Aramaic Scrolls from Qumran," *Studies in Qumran Aramaic* (see above), 124-67; repr. in *Thunder in Gemini and Other Essays on the History, Language and Literature of Second Temple Palestine* (JSPSup 15; Sheffield, UK: JSOT, 1994) 103-51.

———, "Genesis Apocryphon," *The Oxford Encyclopedia of Archaeology in the*

Near East (5 vols.; ed. E. M. Meyers; New York: Oxford University Press, 1997), 2. 390-91.

Zuckerman, B., "'For Your Sake . . .': A Case Study in Aramaic Semantics," *JANES* 15 (1983) 119-29.

4. The War Scroll (1QM)

(I) Introduction (1:1-?)
- (A) The Rule of the War to Come (1:1-7)
- (B) The Time Appointed for the Final Carnage (1:8-15)
- (C) The Annihilation of the Sons of Darkness (1:16-?)

(II) Preparation for the Final War (1:?–2:14)
- (A) Reorganization of Worship to be Carried on during the Struggle (1:?–2:6a)
- (B) Gathering for the War (2:6b-9a)
- (C) Thirty-Five Years of Battle and Its Operations (2:9b-14)

(III) Rules concerning Trumpets, Standards, and Shields in the Struggle (2:15–5:2)
- (A) Rule for the Trumpets (2:15–3:11)
  - (a) Sounding of the Trumpets (2:15–3:2a)
  - (b) Inscriptions on the Trumpets (3:2b-11)
- (B) Rule for the Standards (3:13–4:17+)
  - (a) Inscriptions on the Standards of the Entire Congregation (3:13-17+)
  - (b) Inscriptions on the Standards of the Clan of Merari (4:1-5)
  - (c) Changes on the Standards of the Levites (4:6-8)
  - (d) Changes on the Standards of the Congregation (4:9-14)
  - (e) Dimensions of the Standards (4:15-17+)
- (C) Rule for the Shields (4:?–5:2)
  - (a) ? (4:?-?)
  - (b) Inscriptions on the Shields (4:?–5:2)

(IV) Battle-Array and Weapons of the Infantry (5:3–6:6)
- (A) Rule for the Arming and Drawing Up of the Troops (5:3-14)
- (B) The Battle Array (5:16–6:6)

(V) Array of the Cavalry (6:8-17+)

(VI) Recruitment and Age of Soldiers (6:?–7:7)

(VII) Role of Priests and Levites in the Camp (7:9–9:9)

(VIII) Rule for Changes in Battle-Array for an Attack (9:10-18+)

(IX) High Priest's Exhortation in the Battle-Liturgy (9:?–12:18+)

- (A) Discourse of the High Priest (9:?–10:8a)
- (B) Prayer of the High Priest (10:8b–12:18+)
  - (a) Praise of God's Power Shown in His Deeds (10:8b–11:12)
  - (b) God's Power Will Accomplish New Things (11:13–12:5)
  - (c) The Call for Divine Intervention (12:7-18+)

(X) Blessing Uttered by All Community Leaders at Victory (12:?–14:1)
- (A) God Be Blest (12:?–13:3)
- (B) Belial Be Cursed (13:4-6)
- (C) Victory for the Sons of Light Comes from God (13:7-16)
- (D) ? (13:17–14:1)

(XI) Ceremony of Thanksgiving (14:2-18+)
- (A) Blest Be God (14:2-15)
- (B) Call for Aid (14:16-18+)

(XII) The Last Battle against the Kittim (14:?–19:13)
- (A) Beginning of the Last Battle (14:?–16:9)
  - (a) Arrival of Troops (14:?–15:3)
  - (b) Exhortation Addressed to the First Troop (15:4–16:1)
  - (c) Combat Engagement of the First Troop (16:3-9)
- (B) The Second Troop (16:11–17:17+)
  - (a) Coming Forth of the Second Troop (16:11-14)
  - (b) Exhortation Addressed to the Second Troop (16:15–17:3)
  - (c) Exhortation to Bravery (17:4-9)
  - (d) Combat Engagement of the Second Troop (17:10-17+)
- (C) The Third to the Seventh Troops (17:?–18:3a)
- (D) Destruction of the Kittim (18:3b-6a)
- (E) Prayer of Thanksgiving (18:6b–19:8)
- (F) Ceremony after the Battle (19:9-13)

Principal Studies or Translations of 1QM (beyond those listed in section VIII above)

Bardtke, H., "Literaturbericht über Qumran VI. Teil I. Die Kriegsrolle 1 QM," *TRu* 37 (1972) 97-120.

Batsch, C., *La guerre et les rites de guerre dans le judaïsme du deuxième Temple* (JSJSup 93; Leiden: Brill, 2005).

Bolotnikov, A., "The Theme of Apocalyptic War in the Dead Sea Scrolls," *Andrews University Seminary Studies* 43 (2005) 261-66.

Carmignac, J., "Les citations de l'Ancien Testament dans 'La guerre des fils de lumière contre les fils de ténèbres,'" *RB* 63 (1956) 234-60, 375-90.

———, "Concordance de la 'Règle de la guerre,'" *RevQ* 1 (1958-59) 7-49.

———, "La règle de la guerre," *Les textes de Qumran traduits et annotés* (2 vols.; ed. J. Carmignac et al.; Paris: Letouzey et Ané, 1961, 1963), 1. 81-125.

———, *La règle de la guerre des fils de lumière contre les fils de ténèbres: Texte restauré, traduit, commenté* (Paris: Letouzey et Ané, 1958).

Collins, J. J., "Dualism and Eschatology in 1 QM: A Reply to P. R. Davies," *VT* 29 (1979) 212-15.

———, "The Mythology of the Holy War in Daniel and the Qumran War Scroll: A Point of Transition in Jewish Apocalyptic," *VT* 25 (1975) 596-612.

Davies, P. R., "Dualism and Eschatology in 1QM: A Rejoinder," *VT* 30 (1980) 93-97.

———, "Dualism and Eschatology in the Qumran War Scroll," *VT* 28 (1978) 28-36.

———, *1QM, the War Scroll from Qumran: Its Structure and History* (BibOr 32; Rome: Biblical Institute, 1977).

———, "War Rule (1QM)," *ABD*, 6. 875-76.

Duhaime, J., "Dualistic Reworking in the Scrolls from Qumran," *CBQ* 49 (1987) 32-56.

———, "La rédaction de *1 QM* xiii et l'évolution du dualisme à Qumrân," *RB* 84 (1977) 210-38.

———, "'Le temps des guerres de tes mains': Étude intertextuelle de 1QM xi 1-12," *En ce temps-là . . . Conceptions et expériences bibliques du temps* (Sciences bibliques 10; ed. M. Gourgues et M. Talbot; Montreal: Mediaspaul, 2002) 67-87.

———, *The War Scroll from Qumran and Greco-Roman Military Manuals* (SBLSP 1986).

———, "The *War Scroll* from Qumran and the Greco-Roman Tactical Treatises," *RevQ* 13 (1988-89) 133-51.

———, *The War Texts: 1QM and Related Manuscripts* (London/New York: T&T Clark, 2004).

Dupont-Sommer, A., "Règlement de la guerre des fils de lumière: Traduction et notes," *RHR* 148 (1955) 25-43, 141-80.

Eshel, E. and H. Eshel, "Recensions of the War Scroll," *The Dead Sea Scrolls Fifty Years after Their Discovery: Proceedings of the Jerusalem Congress, July 20-25, 1997* (ed. L. H. Schiffman et al.; Jerusalem: Israel Exploration Society and the Shrine of the Book, Israel Museum, 2000) 351-63.

Eshel, H., "The Kittim in the *War Scroll* and in the Pesharim," *Historical Perspectives: From the Hasmoneans to Bar Kokhba in Light of the Dead Sea Scrolls: Proceedings of the Fourth International Symposium of the Orion Center . . .* (STDJ 37; ed. D. Goodblatt et al.; Leiden: Brill, 2001) 29-44.

Gmirkin, R., "Historical Allusions in the War Scroll," *DSD* 5 (1998) 172-214.
———, "The War Scroll and Roman Weaponry Reconsidered," *DSD* 3 (1996) 89-129.
———, "The War Scroll, the Hasidim, and the Maccabean Conflict," *The Dead Sea Scrolls Fifty Years after Their Discovery* (see above) 486-96.
Hunzinger, C.-H., "Fragmente einer älteren Fassung des Buches Milḥamah aus Höhle 4 von Qumran," *ZAW* 68 (1957) 131-51. (Cave 4 frgs. = 4QM[a-f] [4Q491-496].)
Ibba, G., "Alcune considerazioni sul tempo escatologico di 1QM I," *Henoch* 19 (1997) 283-94.
———, "Gli angeli del 'Rotolo della Guerra' (1QM)," *Henoch* 19 (1997) 149-59.
———, *Le ideologie del Rotolo della Guerra (1QM): Studio sulla genesi e la datazione dell'opera* (AISG Testi e Studi 17: Florence: Giuntina, 2005).
———, "Le lacune di 1QM i,3-5," *Henoch* 18 (1996) 251-58.
———, *Il "Rotolo della guerra": Edizione critica* (Quaderni di Henoch 10; Turin: Zamorani, 1998).
Jongeling, B., *Le rouleau de la guerre des manuscrits de Qumrân* (Studia semitica neerlandica 4; Assen: Van Gorcum, 1962).
Ploeg, J. van der, *Le rouleau de la guerre: Traduit et annoté avec une introduction* (STDJ 2; Leiden: Brill, 1959).
Rothstein, D., "More on the Book of Proverbs and Legal Exegesis at Qumran," *BN* 128 (2006) 31-42 (on 1QM 7:3-7).
Shatzman, I., "על הצבא במגילת מלחמת בני אור בבני חושך (The Army of the Sons of Light in the War Scroll [1QM])," היהודים בעולם ההלניסטי והרומי: *The Jews in the Hellenistic-Roman World: Studies in Memory of Menahem Stern* (ed. I. M. Gafni et al.; Jerusalem: Zalman Shazar Center for Jewish History, 1996) 105-36.
Wenthe, D. O., "The Use of the Hebrew Scriptures in 1QM," *DSD* 5 (1998) 290-319.
Yadin, Y., מגילת מלחמת בני אור ובני חשך (Jerusalem: Bialik Institute, 1955); *The Scroll of the War of the Sons of Light against the Sons of Darkness* (tr. C. Rabin; Oxford: Oxford University Press, 1962).
Zhu-en Wee, J., "A Model for the Composition and Purpose of Columns xv-xix of the *War Scroll (1QM)*," *RevQ* 21 (2003-4) 263-83.

5. The Temple Scroll (11QTemple[a] [11Q19])

(I) Introduction: Renewal of the Sinaitic Covenant (1:?–2:15)
(II) The Jerusalem Temple: Its Cult and Feasts (3:1–47:18)
  (A) The Temple and the Altar (3:1–13:7)

(a) Materials for the Temple and Altar (3:1-17)
(b) Walls, Porches, Terraces of the Temple (4:1-15)
(c) Gates of the Temple (5:1-14)
(d) Furnishings of the Temple (6:?–7:13)
(e) The Table of Shewbread (8:3-14)
(f) The Menorah (9:3-14)
(g) The Veil (10:8-12)
(h) The Altar for Burnt Offerings (11:10–13:7)

(B) The Feasts and Their Sacrifices (13:8–29:10)
(a) The Tamid-Offering (13:10-17)
(b) Offerings at the Beginning of the Months (14:1-18)
(c) Offering for the Consecration (15:1–17:5)
(d) Passover and Unleavened Bread (17:6-16)
(e) Feast of Sheafwaving (18:3-10)
(f) Feast of Weeks: First Fruits of Grain (18:10–19:9)
(g) First Fruits of Wine (19:11–21:11)
(h) First Fruits of Oil (21:12–23:?)
(i) Burnt Offerings of the Tribes (23:10–25:9)
(j) The Day of Atonement (25:10–27:10)
(k) The Feast of Tabernacles (27:10–29:10)

(C) The Construction of the Temple Court (30:4–45:7)
(a) The Buildings of the Outer Area (30:4–36:4)
(b) The Inner Court of the Priests (36:5–38:11)
(c) The Inner Court of Men (38:12–40:5)
(d) The Outer Court of the Israelites (40:5–45:7)

(D) The Sanctity of the Temple and the City (45:7–47:18)
(a) Various Persons Who are Excluded (45:7–46:18)
(b) Exclusion of Things That Defile (47:1-18)

(III) General Laws: Halakhot of Different Sorts (48:1–66:17)

(A) Purity Laws (48:1–51:10)
(a) Clean and Unclean Animals (48:1-7)
(b) Prohibition of Pagan Mourning Practices (48:8-14)
(c) Places outside the City for Lepers, etc. (48:14-17)
(d) Purification from Leprosy (48:17–49:4)
(e) Defilement from a Dead Person (49:5–50:9)
(f) Defilement from the Stillborn (50:10-19)
(g) Defilement from Impure Small Animals (50:19–51:10)

(B) Judicial Regulations I (51:11-18)

(C) Cultic Regulations (51:19–54:7)
(a) Pagan Practices Forbidden (51:19–52:3)

(b) Unsuitable Sacrifices (52:4-12)
(c) Use of Domestic Animals (52:12-13)
(d) Slaughter and Eating of Unclean Animals (52:13–53:8)
(e) About Vows and Oaths of Men and Women (53:9–54:7)

(D) On Idolatry (54:8–55:20)
(E) Judicial Regulations II (56:1-11)
(F) The Statutes of the King (56:12–59:21)

(a) Setting up a King in Israel (56:12-21)
(b) The King's Soldiers (57:1-11)
(c) The King's Council (57:12-15)
(d) The King's Wife: No Polygamy, No Divorce (57:15-19)
(e) The King's Obligation to Justice (57:19–58:2)
(f) Warfare, Mobilization, Booty (58:3-17)
(g) The High Priest's Role in the King's War (58:18-21)
(h) Curses and Blessings (59:1-21)

(G) Priestly and Levitical Perquisites (60:1-15)
(H) Divination and Prophecy, False Prophecy, False Testimony (60:16–61:12)
(I) Military Regulations (61:13–62:16)
(J) Protection of the Land from Blood Guilt (63:2-9)
(K) Family Regulations (63:10–64:6)
(L) Penalties for Capital Crimes (64:7-13)
(M) Laws to Safeguard Israelites (64:13–66:11)
(N) Laws about Incest (66:11-17)

Extensive older bibliography on 11QTemple[a] can be found in F. García Martínez, "El rollo del Templo *(11 Q Temple):* Bibliografía sistemática," *RevQ* 12 (1985-87) 425-40 [up to December 1985]; see also Z. Kapera, "A Review of East European Studies on the Temple Scroll," *Temple Scroll Studies* (JSPSup 7; ed. G. J. Brooke; Sheffield, UK: JSOT, 1989) 275-86.

Baumgarten, J. M., "The Calendars of the Book of Jubilees and the Temple Scroll," *VT* 37 (1987) 71-78.

———, "The First and Second Tithes in the *Temple Scroll,*" *Biblical and Related Studies Presented to Samuel Iwry* (ed. A. Kort and S. Morschauser; Winona Lake, IN: Eisenbrauns, 1985) 5-15.

———, "The Pharisaic-Sadducean Controversies about Purity and the Qumran Texts," *JJS* 31 (1980) 157-70.

Betz, O., "The Temple Scroll (11 Q Miqd 64,7-13) and the Trial of Jesus," *QC* 1 (1990-91) 21-24; cf. *Southwestern Journal of Theology* 30 (1987-88) 5-8.

Brin, G., "Concerning Some of the Uses of the Bible in the Temple Scroll," *RevQ* 12 (1986-87) 519-28.

Brooke, G. J., "The Temple Scroll and the Archaeology of Qumran, 'Ain Feshkha and Masada," *RevQ* 13 (1988) 225-37.

——— (ed.), *Temple Scroll Studies: Papers Presented at the International Symposium on the Temple Scroll, Manchester, December 1987* (JSPSup 7; Sheffield, UK: JSOT, 1989).

Callaway, P., "Exegetische Erwägungen zur Tempelrolle xxix, 7-10," *RevQ* 12 (1985-87) 95-104.

———, "Source Criticism of the Temple Scroll: The Purity Laws," *RevQ* 12 (1985-87) 213-22.

———, "The Temple Scroll and the Canonization of Jewish Law," *RevQ* 13 (1988) 239-50.

Caquot, A., "Le rouleau du Temple de Qoumrân," *ETR* 53 (1978) 443-500.

———, "La secte de Qoumrân et le Temple: Essai de synthèse," *RHPR* 72 (1992) 3-14.

Castelli, S., "Josephan *Halakhah* and the *Temple Scroll:* Questions of Sources and Exegetic Traditions in the Laws of Purity," *Henoch* 24 (2002) 331-41.

Charlesworth, J. H., "The *Temple Scroll*[a] [11Q19, 11QT[a]], Columns 16 and 17: More Consonants Revealed," *Emanuel: Studies in Hebrew Bible, Septuagint, and Dead Sea Scrolls in Honor of Emanuel Tov* (VTSup 94; ed. S. M. Paul et al.; Leiden: Brill, 2003) 71-83.

Delcor, M., "Réflexions sur la fête de la xylophorie dans le rouleau du Temple et les textes parallèles," *RevQ* 12 (1985-87) 561-69.

———, "Réflexions sur l'investiture sacerdotale sans onction à la fête du Nouvel An d'après *le Rouleau du Temple* de Qumrân (XIV, 15-17)," *Hellenica et Judaica: Hommage à Valentin Nikiprowetzky* ז״ל (ed. A. Caquot; Louvain: Peeters, 1986) 155-64.

———, "Le statut du roi d'après le Rouleau du Temple," *Henoch* 3 (1981) 47-68.

Dion, P. E., "Early Evidence for the Ritual Significance of the 'Base of the Altar' around Deut 12:27 LXX," *JBL* 106 (1987) 487-90.

Elgvin, T., "The Qumran Covenant Festival and the Temple Scroll," *JJS* 36 (1985) 103-6.

Emerton, J. A., "A Consideration of Two Recent Theories about Bethso in Josephus' Description of Jerusalem and a Passage in the Temple Scroll," *Text and Context: Old Testament and Semitic Studies for F. C. Fensham* (JSOTSup 48; ed. W. Claasen; Sheffield, UK: JSOT, 1988) 93-104.

Fabry, H.-J., "Der Begriff 'Tora' in der *Tempelrolle*," *RevQ* 18 (1997-98) 63-72.

Fraade, S. D., "The 'Torah of the King' (Deut 17:14-20) in the Temple Scroll and Early Rabbinic Law," *The Dead Sea Scrolls as Background to Postbiblical Ju-*

daism and Early Christianity: Papers from an International Conference at St. Andrews in 2001 (STDJ 46; ed. J. R. Davila; Leiden: Brill, 2003) 25-60.

García Martínez, F., "Multiple Literary Editions of the Temple Scroll?" *The Dead Sea Scrolls Fifty Years after Their Discovery: Proceedings of the Jerusalem Congress, July 20-25, 1997* (ed. L. H. Schiffman et al.; Jerusalem: Israel Exploration Society and the Shrine of the Book, Israel Museum, 2000) 364-71.

———, "El Rollo del Tempio," *EstBíb* 36 (1977) 247-92.

———, "Temple Scroll," *EDSS*, 927-33.

———, "The Temple Scroll and the New Jerusalem," *The Dead Sea Scrolls after Fifty Years: A Comprehensive Assessment* (2 vols.; ed. P. W. Flint and J. C. VanderKam; Leiden: Brill, 1998-99), 2. 431-60.

———, "The Temple Scrolls," *NEA* 63 (2000) 172-74.

Hengel, M., J. H. Charlesworth, and D. Mendels, "The Polemical Character of 'On Kingship' in the Temple Scroll: An Attempt at Dating 11QTemple," *JJS* 37 (1986) 28-38.

Jacobs, S. L., *The Biblical Masorah and the Temple Scroll: An Orthographic Inquiry* (Lanham, MD: University Press of America, 2002).

Kaufman, A. S., "The Courts of the First Temple and of the Temple in the Temple Scroll," *The Dead Sea Scrolls Fifty Years after Their Discovery* (see above), 684-90.

———, "The Temple Scroll and Higher Criticism," *HUCA* 53 (1982) 29-43.

Körting, C., "Theology of Atonement in the Feast Calendar of the Temple Scroll: Some Observations," *SJOT* 18 (2004) 232-47.

Lemaire, A., "Nouveaux fragments du *Rouleau du Temple* de Qumrân," *RevQ* 17 (1996-97) 271-74.

Levine, B., "The Temple Scroll: Aspects of Its Historical Provenance and Literary Character," *BASOR* 232 (1978) 5-23.

Levinson, B. M. and M. M. Zahn, "Revelation Regained: The Hermeneutics of כי and אם in the Temple Scroll," *DSD* 9 (2002) 295-346.

Lyons, W. J., "'An Unauthorized Version': The *Temple Scroll* in Narratological Perspective," *New Directions in Qumran Studies: Proceedings of the Bristol Colloquium on the Dead Sea Scrolls, 8-10 September 2003* (Library of Second Temple Studies 52; ed. J. G. Campbell et al.; London/New York: T&T Clark International, 2005) 126-48.

McCready, W. O., "A Second Torah at Qumran?" *SR* 14 (1985) 5-15.

Maier, J., *Die Tempelrolle vom Toten Meer übersetzt und erläutert* (Uni-Taschenbücher 829; Munich/Basel: E. Reinhardt, 1978). English version: *The Temple Scroll: An Introduction, Translation & Commentary* (tr. R. T. White; JSOTSup 34; Sheffield, UK: JSOT, 1985).

Milgrom, J., "The City of the Temple: A Response to Lawrence H. Schiffman," *JQR* 85 (1994-95) 125-28.

———, "Deviations from Scripture in the Purity Laws of the *Temple Scroll*," *Jewish Civilization in the Hellenistic-Roman Period* (ed. S. Talmon; Philadelphia, PA; Trinity Press International, 1991) 159-67.

———, "Further Studies in the Temple Scroll," *JQR* 71 (1980-81) 1-17, 89-106.

———, "The Paradox of the Red Cow (Num. xix)," *VT* 31 (1981) 62-72.

———, "Studies in the Temple Scroll," *JBL* 97 (1978) 501-23.

Mink, H.-A., "Tempel und Hofanlagen in der Tempelrolle," *RevQ* 13 (1988) 273-85.

———, "The Use of Scripture in the Temple Scroll and the Status of the Scroll as Law," *SJOT* 1 (1987) 20-50.

Økland, J., "The Language of Gates and Entering: On Sacred Space in the *Temple Scroll*," *New Directions in Qumran Studies* (see above), 149-65.

Patrich, J., "The *Mesibbah* of the Temple according to the Tractate *Middot*," *IEJ* 36 (1986) 215-33 (+ pl. 27A).

Puech, E., "Notes sur *11Q19* lxiv 6-13 et 4Q524 14,2-4: À propos de la crucifixion dans le *Rouleau du Temple* et dans le judaïsme ancien," *RevQ* 18 (1997-98) 109-24.

Qimron, E., "Column 14 of the Temple Scroll," *IEJ* 38 (1988) 44-46.

———, "Further New Readings in the Temple Scroll," *IEJ* 37 (1987) 31-35.

———, *The Temple Scroll: A Critical Edition with Extensive Reconstructions* and F. García Martínez, *Bibliography* (JDS; Beer Sheva: Ben-Gurion University of the Negev Press; Jerusalem: Israel Exploration Society, 1996). The classified bibliography on pp. 95-121 includes earlier installments of 1985 and 1992.

Reeves, J. C., "The Meaning of *Moreh Ṣedeq* in the Light of 11QTorah," *RevQ* 13 (1988) 287-98.

Riska, M., *The Temple Scroll and the Biblical Text Traditions: A Study of the Columns 2–13:9* (Publications of the Finnish Exegetical Society 81; Helsinki: Finnish Exegetical Society, 2001).

Rofé, A., "Qumranic Paraphrases, the Greek Deuteronomy and the Late History of the Biblical *nśy'*," *Textus* 14 (1988) 163-74.

Rosen, D. and A. Salvesen, "A Note on the Qumran Temple Scroll 56:15-18 and Psalm of Solomon 17:33," *JJS* 38 (1987) 99-101.

Rothstein, D., "More on the Book of Proverbs and Legal Exegesis at Qumran," *BN* 128 (2006) 31-42.

Schiffman, L. H., "The Architectural Vocabulary of the Copper Scroll and the Temple Scroll," *Copper Scroll Studies* (JSPSup 40; ed. G. J. Brooke and P. R. Davies; London: Sheffield Academic, 2002) 180-95.

———, "The Construction of the Temple according to the *Temple Scroll*," *RevQ* 17 (1996-97) 555-71.

———, "Descriptions of the Jerusalem Temple in Josephus and the *Temple Scroll*," *Historical Perspectives: From the Hasmoneans to Bar Kokhba in Light of the Dead Sea Scrolls: Proceedings of the Fourth International Symposium of the Orion Center . . .* (STDJ 37; ed. D. Goodblatt et al.; Leiden: Brill, 2001) 69-82.

———, "Exclusion from the Sanctuary and the City of the Sanctuary in the Temple Scroll," *Biblical and Other Studies in Memory of Shelomo D. Goitein* (Hebrew Annual Review 9; ed. R. Ahroni; Columbus, OH: Ohio State University, 1986) 301-20.

———, "The Laws of War in the Temple Scroll," *RevQ* 13 (1988) 299-311.

———, "The Relationship of the Zadokite Fragments to the Temple Scroll," *The Damascus Document: A Centennial of Discovery: Proceedings of the Third International Symposium of the Orion Center . . .* (STDJ 34; ed. J. M. Baumgarten et al.; Leiden: Brill, 2000) 133-45.

———, "*Shelamim* Sacrifices in the *Temple Scroll*," *Yigael Yadin Memorial Volume* (ErIsr 20; Jerusalem: Israel Exploration Society, 1989) 176*-83*.

———, "The Temple Scroll and the Systems of Jewish Law of the Second Temple Period," *Temple Scroll Studies: Papers Presented at the International Symposium on the Temple Scroll, Manchester, December 1987)* (JSPSup 7; ed. G. J. Brooke; Sheffield, UK: JSOT, 1989) 239-55.

———, "The Theology of the Temple Scroll," *JQR* 85 (1994-95) 109-23.

Shanks, H., "Intrigue and the Scroll — Behind the Scenes of Israel's Acquisition of the Temple Scroll," *BARev* 13/6 (1987) 23-27.

Shemesh, A., "The Holiness According to the *Temple Scroll*," *RevQ* 19 (1999-2000) 369-82.

———, "'Three-Days' Journey from the Temple': The Use of This Expression in the Temple Scroll," *DSD* 6 (1999) 126-38.

Stegemann, H., "Is the Temple Scroll a Sixth Book of the Torah — Lost for 2,500 Years?" *BARev* 13/6 (1987) 28-35.

———, "The Origins of the Temple Scroll," *Congress Volume, Jerusalem 1986* (VTSup 40; ed. J. A. Emerton; Leiden: Brill, 1988) 235-56.

Swanson, D. D., *The Temple Scroll and the Bible: The Methodology of 11 QT* (STDJ 14; Leiden: Brill, 1995).

Sweeney, M. A., "Midrashic Perspective in the Torat Ham-Melek of the Temple Scroll," *Hebrew Studies* 28 (1987) 51-66.

Thiering, B., "The Temple Scroll Courts Governed by Precise Times," *DSD* 11 (2004) 336-58.

Tyloch, W., "La provenance et la date du Rouleau du Temple," *FO* 25 (1988) 33-39.

VanderKam, J. C., "The Theology of the Temple Scroll: A Response to Lawrence H. Schiffman," *JQR* 85 (1994-95) 129-35.

Vivian, A., *Rotolo del Tempio* (Testi del vicino oriente antico 6, Letteratura giudaica 1; Brescia: Paideia, 1990).

Wacholder, B. Z., *The Dawn of Qumran: The Sectarian Torah and the Teacher of Righteousness* (MHUC 8; Cincinnati, OH: Hebrew Union College, 1983).

Weinfeld, M., "God versus Moses in the Temple Scroll, 'I Do not Speak on My Own but on God's Authority' (*Sifrei Deut.* sec. 5; *John* 12, 48f)," *RevQ* 15 (1991-92) 175-80.

———, "High Treason in the Temple Scroll and in the Ancient Near Eastern Sources," *Emanuel* (see above), 827-31.

White Crawford, S., "The Meaning of the Phrase עיר המקדש in the Temple Scroll," *DSD* 8 (2001) 242-54.

———, *The Temple Scroll and Related Texts* (Companion to the Qumran Scrolls 2; Sheffield, UK: Sheffield Academic, 2000).

Wilk, R., "יוחנן הורקנוס הראשון ומגילת המקדש (John Hyrcanus I and the Temple Scroll)," *Shnaton* 9 (1987) 221-30.

Wilson, A. M. and L. Wills, "Literary Sources of the Temple Scroll," *HTR* 75 (1982) 275-88.

Wise, M. O., *A Critical Study of the Temple Scroll from Qumran Cave 11* (Studies in Ancient Oriental Civilization 49; Chicago, IL: Oriental Institute of the University of Chicago, 1990).

———, "A New Manuscript Join in the 'Festival of Wood Offering' (Temple Scroll xxiii)," *JNES* 47 (1988) 113-21.

———, "The Teacher of Righteousness and the Temple Scroll," *QC* 1 (1990) 59-60.

Yadin, Y., *The Temple Scroll: The Hidden Law of the Dead Sea Sect* (New York: Random House, 1985).

Zahn, M. M., "New Voices, Ancient Words: The *Temple Scroll*'s Reuse of the Bible," *Temple and Worship in Biblical Israel* (Library of Hebrew Bible/Old Testament Studies 422; ed. J. Day; London/New York: T&T Clark, 2005) 435-58.

6. The Thanksgiving Psalms/הודיות (1QH^{a-b}, 4QH^{a-f})

It is not possible to outline the texts of these writings, but the list of contents already given above in section II under 1QH^{a} helps to understand the buildup of the reconstructed columns. Here the lines will indicate where one finds twenty-some different psalms that have a distinctive incipit:

Hymn	*Reconstructed Columns and Lines*
1	4:9-15
2	4:17-25
3	4:26–6:7
4	6:8-22
5	6:23–7:12
6	7:12–8:28
7	9:1–10:19
8	10:20-30
9	10:31-39
10	11:1?-18
11	11:19-36
12	11:37–12:4
13	12:5–13:4
14	13:5-19
15	13:20–15:5
16	14:1?–15:5
17	15:6-25
18	15:26-33
19	15:34–16:3
20	16:4–17:36
21	17:38–18:12
22	18:14-36 (+ frg. 10); 19:1-2
23	19:3-14
24	19:15–20:3
25	20:4-39
26	21:1?-18
27	22:1?-14 (+ frg. 4)
28	22:15-20 (+ frg. 47)
29	23:1-16 (+ frg. 2 i?)
30	24:5-15 (+ frgs. 45, 2 ii, 6)

Cf. H. Stegemann, "The Number of Psalms in *1QHodayot*[a] and Some of Their Sections," *Liturgical Perspectives: Prayer and Poetry in Light of the Dead Sea Scrolls: Proceedings of the Fifth International Symposium of the Orion Center . . .* (STDJ 48; ed. E. G. Chazon; Leiden: Brill, 2003) 191-234. His line-numbering differs at times from that used above. Some scholars try to distinguish two kinds of psalms: (a) Psalms of the Teacher, which are often hymns of revelation or personal release; and (b) Psalms of the Community, which are mainly soteriological confessions. The unity of style and vocabulary in both, however, is striking, and the use of the first-person singular is not really a sufficient criterion to designate the Psalms of the Teacher, because the "I" can also be understood as the voice of the community. These Thanksgiving Psalms are good instances of the hymns that Philo mentions as composed by the Essenes or Therapeutae (see *De vita contemplativa* 3 §29; 10 §80; 11 §84).

Stegemann, E., E. Schuller, and C. Newsom, *Qumran Cave 1: III, 1QHodayot a, with Incorporation of 4QHodayot a-f and 1QHodayot b* (DJD 40; Oxford: Clarendon, 2008). Pp. 410 + XXVI pls. Reconstructed text translated with commentary.

An extensive classified bibliography on 1QH[a], 1QH[b] (1Q35), and 4QH[a-f] (4Q427-4Q432) can be found in E. M. Schuller and L. Di Tommaso, "A Bibliography of the Hodayot, 1948-1996," *DSD* 1 (1997) 55-101. Note especially the following:

Caquot, A., "Retour à la mère du Messie 1QH 3 (Sukenik), 6-18," *RHPR* 80 (2000) 5-12.

Carmignac, J., "Compléments au texte des Hymnes de Qumran," *RevQ* 2 (1959-60) 267-76, 549-58.

———, "Localisation des fragments 15, 18 et 22 des Hymnes," *RevQ* 1 (1958-59) 425-30.

———, "Remarques sur le texte des Hymnes de Qumran," *Bib* 39 (1958) 139-55.

Castaño Fonseca, A. M., "Algunos rasgos característicos del Maestro de Justicia en los Himnos de Qumrán: Un ejemplo en 1QH 5,5-19," *Qol* (Tlalpan, Mexico) 39 (2005) 41-59.

Charlesworth, J. H., "Autumnal Rain (המורה) for the Faithful Followers of the Moreh (מורה): Joel and the Hodayot," *Der Mensch vor Gott: Forschungen zum Menschenbild in Bibel, antiken Judentum und Koran: Festschrift für Hermann Lichtenberger . . .* (ed. U. Mittmann-Richert et al.; Neukirchen-Vluyn: Neukirchener-V., 2003) 193-210.

Daise, M. A., "Biblical Creation Motifs in the Qumran Hodayot," *The Dead Sea Scrolls Fifty Years after Their Discovery: Proceedings of the Jerusalem Conference, July 20-25, 1997* (ed. L. H. Schiffman et al.; Jerusalem: Israel Exploration Society and the Shrine of the Book, Israel Museum, 2000) 293-305.

Delcor, M., *Les hymnes de Qumran (Hodayot): Texte hébreu, introduction, traduction, commentaire* (Paris: Letouzey et Ané, 1962).

Douglas, M. C., "The Teacher Hymn Hypothesis Revisited: New Data for an Old Crux," *DSD* 6 (1999) 239-66.

Dupont-Sommer, A., "Les Livre des Hymnes découvert près de la Mer Morte (1QH): Traduction intégrale avec introduction et notes," *Sem* 7 (1957) 3-120.

Elwolde, J. F., "Interrogatives in the Hodayot: Some Preliminary Observations," *Hamlet on a Hill: Semitic and Greek Studies Presented to Professor T. Muraoka . . .* (Orientalia Lovaniensia Analecta 118; ed. M. F. J. Baasten and W. T. van Peursen; Louvain: Peeters, 2003) 129-51.

Frechette, C. G., "Chiasm, Reversal and Biblical Reference in 1QH 11.3-18 (= Sukenik Column 3): A Structural Proposal," *JSP* 21 (2000) 71-102.

Goff, M. J., "Reading Wisdom at Qumran: 4QInstruction and the Hodayot," *DSD* 11 (2004) 263-88.

Harkins, A. K., "Observations on the Editorial Shaping of the So-Called Community Hymns from 1QH[a] and 4QH[a] (4Q427)," *DSD* 12 (2005) 233-56.

Holm-Nielsen, S., *Hodayot: Psalms from Qumran* (Acta theologica Danica 2; Aarhus: Universitetsforlaget, 1960).

Hughes, J. A., *Scriptural Allusions and Exegesis in the Hodayot* (STDJ 59; Leiden: Brill, 2006).

Jeremias, G., *Der Lehrer der Gerechtigkeit* (SUNT 2; Göttingen: Vandenhoeck & Ruprecht, 1963).

Kittel, B. P., *The Hymns of Qumran: Translation and Commentary* (SBLDS 50; Chico, CA: Scholars Press, 1981).

Klęczar, A., "Do the *Hodayot* Psalms Display a Consistent Theology?" *QC* 11 (2003) 79-90.

Licht, J., מגילת ההודיות ממגילות מדבר יהודה: *The Thanksgiving Scroll: A Scroll from the Wilderness of Judaea: Text, Introduction, Commentary and Glossary* (Jerusalem: Bialik Institute, 1957).

Mansoor, M., *The Thanksgiving Hymns Translated and Annotated with an Introduction* (STDJ 3; Leiden: Brill, 1961).

Morawe, G., *Aufbau und Abgrenzung der Loblieder von Qumran: Studien zur gattungsgeschichtlichen Einordnung der Hodajôth* (Theologische Arbeiten 16; Berlin: Evangelische Verlagsanstalt, 1961).

Newsom, C. A., "Apocalyptic Subjects: Social Construction of the Self in the Qumran Hodayot," *JSP* 12 (2001) 3-35.

Puech, E., "Hodayot," *EDSS*, 365-69.

———, "Un hymne essénien en partie retrouvé et les Béatitudes: *1QH* v 12–vi 18 (= col. xiii-xiv 7) et *4QBéat.*," *RevQ* 13 (1988) 59-88.

———, "Quelques aspects de la restauration du Rouleau des Hymnes (1QH)," *JJS* 39 (1988) 38-55.

———, "Restauration d'un texte hymnique à partir de trois manuscrits fragmentaires: 1QH[(a)] xv 37–xvi 4 (vii 34–viii 3), 1Q35 (H[b]) 1, 9-14, 4Q428 (H[b]) 7," *RevQ* 16 (1993-95) 543-58.

Rand, M., "Metathesis as a Poetic Technique in Hodayot Poetry and Its Relevance in the Development of Hebrew Rhyme," *DSD* 8 (2001) 51-66.

Ringgren, H., "Two Biblical Words in the Qumran Hymns," *Yigael Yadin Memorial Volume* (ErIsr 20; Jerusalem: Israel Exploration Society, 1989) 174*-75*.

Schuller, E. M., "The Cave 4 Hodayot Manuscripts: A Preliminary Description," *JQR* 85 (1994-95) 137-50.

———, "The Classification *Hodayot* and *Hodayot*-like (with Particular Attention to 4Q433, 4Q433a and 4Q440)," *Sapiential, Liturgical and Poetical Texts from Qumran: Proceedings of the Third Meeting of the International Organization for Qumran Studies, Oslo 1998: Published in Memory of Maurice Baillet* (STDJ 35; ed. D. K. Falk et al.; Leiden: Brill, 2000) 182-93.

———, "Some Contributions of the Cave Four Manuscripts (4Q427-432) to the Study of the Hodayot," *DSD* 8 (2001) 278-87.

———, "Some Reflections on the Function and Use of Poetical Texts among the Dead Sea Scrolls," *Liturgical Perspectives* (see above), 173-89.

Selms, A. van, *De rol der Lofprijzingen: Een der Dode Zee-Rollen vertaald en toegelicht* (Baarn: Bosch & Keuning, 1957).

Stegemann, H., "The Material Reconstruction of 1QHodayot," *The Dead Sea Scrolls Fifty Years after Their Discovery* (see above), 272-84.

———, "Methods for the Reconstruction of Scrolls from Scattered Fragments," *Archaeology and History in the Dead Sea Scrolls: The New York University Conference in Memory of Yigael Yadin* (JSPSup 8; ed. L. H. Schiffman; Sheffield, UK: Sheffield Academic Press, 1990) 189-220.

Strugnell, J. and E. Schuller, "Further *Hodayot* Manuscripts from Qumran?" *Antikes Judentum und frühes Christentum: Festschrift für Hartmut Stegemann . . .* (BZNW 97; ed. B. Kollmann et al.; Berlin: de Gruyter, 1999) 51-72 (+ 3 plates).

Wise, M. O., "מי כמוני באלים: A Study of 4Q491c, 4Q471b, 4Q427 7 and 1QH[a] 23:25–26:10," *DSD* 7 (2000) 173-219.

Zurli, E., "La giustificazione 'solo per grazia' in *1QS* x, 9-xi e *1QH[a]*," *RevQ* 20 (2001-2) 445-77.

7. Halakhic Letter or "Some Deeds of the Law" (4QMMT[a-f])

The "deeds" (**המעשים**, *hammaʿăśîm*) are those required to be done by the Torah; hence the translation often used, "Some Precepts of the Torah." The deeds are set forth in a letter written by some sectarians who speak merely as "we" (**אנחנו**, B 2, 29; C 26). It is sent to an individual in authority among Jews in Jerusalem (B 29, 60-61), who is addressed mainly as "you" (singular, **אליכה**,

C 10, 26; לך, C27, 31), and through him to "your people" (ולעמך, C 27); and sometimes as "you" (plural, אתם, B 68; C 7). The text of the letter is found on six fragmentary copies (4Q394-4Q399), but a composite text of 135 lines has been reconstructed from them. Three parts of the composite texts are designated by A, B, C.

Prefixed to the letter is a calendaric prologue, the beginning of which has been lost. What is preserved is the end of a writing that lists Sabbaths, special feasts (of New Wine, New Oil, and Wood Offering), and the added days to make up the four 91-day cycles of the 364 days of the year. Whether the remnant of this calendaric prologue (A 1-21) is really part of the Halakhic Letter is a matter of debate. Likewise debatable is the identity of the "we" in the text. Schiffman, Baumgarten, et al. claim that the halakhot in the text resemble the tenets of the Sadducees in well-known controversies between them and the Pharisees recorded in the Mishnah of later date. Others, however, insist that the halakhot are Essene (O. Betz, Fitzmyer).

The letter itself has two parts: a list of halakhot (B 1-82), and an epilogue (C 1-32), which states reasons why the sect has seceded and exhorts those addressed to adopt its halakhot. The composite text can be outlined thus:

A. Calendaric Prologue (1-21): From the 16th day of the second month to the end of the year of the 364 days.

B. Sectarian Halakhot (1-82):

1. Some of our rulings about purity (1-3a)
2. Gentile grain is not to be eaten or brought into the Temple (3b-5)
3. Concerning the cooking of offerings (6)
4. Concerning sacrificial meats (7-8a)
5. Concerning sacrifices from Gentiles (8b-9a)
6. Cereal offerings are not to be left overnight (9b-13a)
7. Purity rulings for those preparing the red cow for slaughter (13b-16)
8. Concerning the sons of Aaron and the purity of hides (17-20)
9. Concerning hides and bones of clean and unclean animals (21-23)
10. Conduct of priests in all these practices (24-27a)
11. The place where sheep and goats are to be slaughtered and offered (27b-28)
12. Purity of the sanctuary and of Jerusalem (29-32a)
13. God's choice of Jerusalem as the place of worship (32b-33)
14. Slaughter of pregnant animals is forbidden (35-38)
15. Concerning Ammonites, Moabites, bastards, and eunuchs (39)
16. Various sexual unions forbidden to those who enter the sanctuary (40-49a)

17. The blind and the dead are to have no access to sacred food (49b-54)
18. Ruling about the purity of liquid flowing from one vessel to another (55-57)
19. Dogs not allowed in "the holy camp," i.e., Jerusalem (58-59)
20. The holiness of Jerusalem (60-62a)
21. First fruits belong to Temple priests, also the tithe of herd and flock (62b-64a)
22. Ritual of purification for lepers (64b-72a)
23. The bones of dead human beings cause impurity (72b-74)
24. Forbidden marriages and matings with another species (76-78)
25. Certain marriages forbidden for the sons of Aaron (79-82)

C. Epilogue (1-32)
   1. A ruling about women (1-7a)
   2. The sectarians have seceded from the masses so that no treachery, deceit, or evil may be found among them (7b-9)
   3. We write to you (sing.) to urge you to study the books of Moses, the Prophets, and David and not to stray from the path of the Torah (10-12)
   4. Recall the curses and blessings of the end of days mentioned by those writers (13-19)
   5. Some of them have already been fulfilled; so beware (20-22)
   6. Think about the kings of Israel and imitate them (23-25a)
   7. Recall David, a man of righteous deeds (25b-26a)
   8. We write to you now "some of the deeds of the Law," which we consider good for your welfare and that of your people (26b-27)
   9. God will deliver you from the plotting of Belial (28-29)
   10. When you find that some of our words are right, it will be reckoned to you as righteousness (לצדקה) (30-32)

For the *editio princeps* of 4QMMT[a-f] (4Q394-4Q399), see p. 80 above. Important secondary literature follows:

Adamczewski, B., "The Hasmonean Temple and Its Water-Supply System in 4QMMT," *QC* 13 (2006) 101-12.

Atkinson, K., "4QMMT and Psalm of Solomon 8: Two Anti-Sadducean Documents," *QC* 11 (2003) 57-77.

Baumgarten, J. M., "The 'Halakha' in *Miqṣat Maʿaśe ha-Torah (MMT)*," *JAOS* 116 (1996) 512-16.

———, "The Pharisaic-Sadducean Controversies about Purity and the Qumran Texts," *JJS* 31 (1980) 157-70.

———, "The Red Cow Purification Rites in Qumran Texts," *JJS* 46 (1995) 112-19.

Bernard, J., "Pour lire 4QMMT: Quelques-unes des mises en pratique de la Torah," *Le judaïsme à l'aube de l'ère chrétienne* (Lectio divina 186; ed. P. Abadie and J.-P. Lémonon; Paris: Cerf, 2001) 63-94.

Betz, O., "The Qumran Halakhah Text *Miqṣat Maʿasê ha-Tôrāh* (4QMMT) and Sadducean, Essene, and Early Pharisaic Tradition," *The Aramaic Bible: Targums in Their Historical Context* (JSOTSup 166; ed. D. R. G. Beattie and M. J. McNamara; Sheffield, UK: Sheffield Academic, 1994) 176-202.

Birenboym, H., "דין קרבן במגילת מקצת מעשה התורה (The Law of the Well-Being Sacrifice in the *Miqṣat maʿaśeh ha-Torah* Scroll)," *Tarbiz* 67 (1997-98) 241-44.

Brooke, G. J., "The Explicit Presentation of Scripture in 4QMMT," *Legal Texts and Legal Issues: Proceedings of the Second Meeting of the International Organization for Qumran Studies, Cambridge 1995: Published in Honour of Joseph M. Baumgarten* (STDJ 23; ed. M. Bernstein et al.; Leiden: Brill, 1997) 67-88.

Burgmann, H., "4 Q MMT: Versuch einer historisch-begründbaren Datierung," *FO* 27 (1990) 43-62.

Callaway, P. R., "4QMMT and Recent Hypotheses on the Origin of the Qumran Community," *Mogilany 1993: Papers on the Dead Sea Scrolls Offered in Memory of Hans Burgmann* (Qumranica mogilanensia 13; ed. Z. Kapera; Cracow: Enigma, 1996) 15-29.

Campbell, J. G., "4QMMT[d] and the Tripartite Canon," *JJS* 51 (2000) 181-90.

Caquot, A., "Un exposé polémique de pratiques sectaires (4Q MMT)," *RHPR* 76 (1996) 257-76.

Dombrowski, B. W. W., *An Annotated Translation of Miqṣāt Maʿaśēh ha-Tôrâ (4QMMT)* (Weenzen: Private publication, 1993); also in the Appendix of *QC* 2 (1992-93).

———, "4QMMT after DJD X Qumran Cave 4 Part V," *QC* 5 (1995) 151-70.

———, "*Miqṣat Maʿaśēh Hattôrâ* (4QMMT) in English," *QC* 4 (1994) 28-36.

Dunn, J. D. G., "Noch einmal 'Works of the Law': The Dialogue Continues," *Fair Play: Diversity and Conflicts in Early Christianity: Essays in Honour of Heikki Räisänen* (NovTSup 103; ed. I. Dunderberg et al.; Leiden: Brill, 2002) 273-90.

Eisenman, R., "MMT as a Jamesian Letter to 'The Great King of the Peoples beyond the Euphrates,'" *JHC* 11 (2005) 55-68.

Elman, Y., "MMT B 3-5 and Its Ritual Context," *DSD* 6 (1999) 148-56.

———, "Some Remarks on 4QMMT and the Rabbinic Tradition: Or, When Is a Parallel Not a Parallel," *Reading 4QMMT* (see Kampen below), 99-128.

Eshel, E., "4QLev[d]: A Possible Source for the Temple Scroll and *Miqṣat Maʿaśe ha-Torah*." *DSD* 2 (1995) 1-13.

———, "4QMMT and the History of the Hasmonean Period," *Reading 4QMMT* (see Kampen below), 53-65.

Fink, A. S., "Why Did *'yrh'* Play the Dog? Dogs in RS 24.258 (= KTU 1/114) and 4QMMT," *Aula orientalis* 21 (2003) 35-61.

Flusser, D., "מקצת מעשי התורה וברכת המינים, Some of the Precepts of the Torah from Qumran (4QMMT) and the Benediction against the Heretics," *Tarbiz* 61 (1991-92) 333-74.

Fraade, S. D., "Rhetoric and Hermeneutics in Miqṣat Maʿaśe ha-Torah (4QMMT): The Case of the Blessings and Curses," *DSD* 10 (2003) 150-61.

———, "To Whom It May Concern: *4QMMT* and Its Addressee(s)," *RevQ* 19 (1999-2000) 507-26.

García Martínez, F., "Discoveries in the Judaean Desert: Textes légaux (I)," *JSJ* 32 (2001) 71-89.

———, "Dos notas sobre *4QMMT*," *RevQ* 16 (1993-95) 293-97.

———, "4QMMT in a Qumran Context," *Reading 4QMMT* (see Kampen below), 15-27.

———, "Literatura jurídico-religiosa de Qumrán," *Paganos, judíos y cristianos en los textos de Qumrán* (Biblioteca de ciencias bíblicas y orientales 5; ed. J. Trebolle Barrera; Madrid: Trotta, 1999) 155-79.

Grabbe, L. L., "4QMMT and Second Temple Jewish Society," *Legal Texts and Legal Issues* (see above), 89-108.

Grossman, M. L., "Reading *4QMMT:* Genre and History," *RevQ* 20 (2001-2) 3-22.

Harrington, H. K., "Holiness in the Laws of 4QMMT," *Legal Texts and Legal Issues* (see above), 109-28.

Hempel, C., "The Laws of the Damascus Document and 4QMMT," *The Damascus Document: A Centennial of Discovery: Proceedings of the Third International Symposium of the Orion Center . . .* (STDJ 34; ed. J. M. Baumgarten et al.: Leiden: Brill, 2000) 69-84.

Henshke, D., "קדושת ירושלים במקצת מעשי התורה: עיון חוזר (The Sanctity of Jerusalem in *Miqṣat maʿaśe ha-Torah:* A Reconsideration)," *Tarbiz* 69 (1999-2000) 145-50.

Høgenhaven, J., "Rhetorical Devices in 4QMMT," *DSD* 10 (2003) 187-204.

Kampen, J. and M. J. Bernstein (eds.), *Reading 4QMMT: New Perspectives on Qumran Law and History* (SBLSS 2; Atlanta, GA: Scholars Press, 1996).

Kapera, Z. J., "A Preliminary Subject Bibliography of 4QMMT: 1956-1991," *QC* 1 (1990-91) 75-80.

Kirtchuk, P.-I., "Some Cognitive and Typological Semantic Remarks on the Language of 4QMMT[a]," *Diggers at the Well: Proceedings of a Third International Symposium on the Hebrew of the Dead Sea Scrolls and Ben Sira* (STDJ 36; ed. T. Muraoka and J. F. Elwolde; Leiden: Brill, 2000) 131-36.

Knohl, I., "New Light on the Copper Scroll and 4QMMT," *Copper Scroll Studies* (JSPSup 40; ed. G. J. Brooke and P. R. Davies; London: Sheffield Academic, 2002) 233-56.

———, "Re-considering the Dating and Recipient of *Miqṣat Maʿaśe ha-Torah,*" *Hebrew Studies* 37 (1996) 119-25.

Męedala, S., "The Character and Historical Setting of 4QMMT," *QC* 4 (1994) 1-27.

———, "Some Remarks on the Official Publication of MMT," *QC* 4 (1994) 193-202.

Morag, S., "**האם כתב 'המורה הצדקי איגרת זאת? סגנון ולשון במגילת מקצת מעשי התורה** — (Language and Style in *Miqṣat maʿaśe ha-Torah* — Did *Moreh ha-Ṣedeq* Write This Document?)," *Tarbiz* 65 (1995-96) 209-23.

Pérez Fernández, M., "4QMMT: La carta halákica," *Paganos, judíos y cristianos* (see above), 213-27.

———, "*4QMMT:* Redactional Study," *RevQ* 18 (1997-98) 191-205.

Qimron, E., "The Nature of the Reconstructed Composite Text of 4QMMT," *Reading 4QMMT* (see above), 9-13.

——— and J. Strugnell, "An Unpublished Halakhic Letter from Qumran," *Biblical Archaeology Today: Proceedings of the International Congress on Biblical Archaeology, Jerusalem, April 1984* (ed. J. Amitai; Jerusalem: Israel Exploration Society, 1985) 400-407, 429-31; in a shorter form, in *Israel Museum Journal* 4 (1985) 9-12.

Regev, E., "Abominated Temple and a Holy Community: The Formation of the Notions of Purity and Impurity in Qumran," *DSD* 10 (2003) 243-78.

Schiffman, L. H., "*Miqṣat Maʿaśeh ha-Torah* and the *Temple Scroll,*" *RevQ* 14 (1989-90) 435-57.

———, "Miqtsat Maʿasei ha-Torah," *EDSS,* 558-60.

———, "The New Halakhic Letter *(4QMMT)* and the Origins of the Dead Sea Sect," *BA* 53 (1990) 64-73; also in *Mogilany 1989: Papers on the Dead Sea Scrolls Offered in Memory of Jean Carmignac* (Qumranica moglanensia 2; ed. Z. J. Kapera; Cracow: Enigma, 1993), 1. 59-70.

———, "New Halakhic Texts from Qumran," *Hebrew Studies* 34 (1993) 21-33.

———, "The Place of 4QMMT in the Corpus of Qumran Manuscripts," *Reading 4QMMT* (see above), 81-98.

———, "The Temple Scroll and the Systems of Jewish Law of the Second Temple Period," *Temple Scroll Studies: Papers Presented at the International Sympo-*

sium on the Temple Scroll, Manchester, December 1987 (JSPSup 7; ed. G. J. Brooke; Sheffield, UK: JSOT, 1989) 239-55.

Schwartz, D. R., "MMT, Josephus and the Pharisees," *Reading 4QMMT* (see above), 67-80.

Sharp, C. J., "Phinehan Zeal and Rhetorical Strategy in *4QMMT*," *RevQ* 18 (1997-98) 207-22.

Smith, M. S., "The *Waw*-Consecutive at Qumran," *ZAH* 4 (1991) 161-64.

Strugnell, J., "MMT: Second Thought on a Forthcoming Edition," *The Community of the Renewed Covenant: The Notre Dame Symposium on the Dead Sea Scrolls* (Christianity and Judaism in Antiquity 10; ed. E. Ulrich and J. C. VanderKam, 1994), 57-73.

Ulrich, E., "The Non-attestation of a Tripartite Canon in 4QMMT," *CBQ* 65 (2003) 202-14.

Weissenberg, H. von, "*4QMMT* — Towards an Understanding of the Epilogue," *RevQ* 21 (2003-4) 29-45.

Yadin, A., "4QMMT, Rabbi Ishmael, and the Origins of Legal Midrash," *DSD* 10 (2003) 130-49.

On 4QMMT and the New Testament:

Abegg, Jr., M. G., "4QMMT C 27, 31 and 'Works Righteousness,'" *DSD* 6 (1999) 139-47.

———, "4QMMT, Paul, and 'Works of the Law,'" *The Bible at Qumran: Text, Shape, and Interpretation* (SDSSRL; ed. P. W. Flint; Grand Rapids, MI: Eerdmans, 2001) 203-16.

Bachmann, M., "4QMMT und Galaterbrief, מעשי התורה und ἔργα νόμου," *ZNW* 89 (1998) 91-113.

Flusser, D., "Die Gesetzeswerke in Qumran und bei Paulus," *Geschichte — Tradition — Reflexion: Festschrift für Martin Hengel* . . . (3 vols.; ed. H. Cancik et al.; Tübingen: Mohr [Siebeck], 1996), 1. 395-403.

Grelot, P., "Les oeuvres de la loi (à propos de 4Q394-398)," *RevQ* 16 (1993-95) 441-48.

Philonenko, M., "'Dehors les chiens' (Apocalypse 22.16 et 4QMMT B 58-62)," *NTS* 43 (1997) 445-50.

Roo, J. C. R. de, "The Concept of 'Works of the Law' in Jewish and Christian Literature," *Christian-Jewish Relations through the Centuries* (JSNTSup 192; ed. S. E. Porter and B. R. Pearson; Sheffield, UK: Sheffield Academic, 2000) 116-47.

On the questionable edition of 4QMMT:

Anon., "An Anonymously Received Pre-publication of the 4QMMT," *QC* 1 (1990-91) Appendix A, 1-9.

Eisenman, R. H. and J. M. Robinson (eds.), *A Facsimile Edition of the Dead Sea Scrolls Prepared with an Introduction and Index* (2 vols; Washington, DC: Biblical Archaeology Society, 1991) xxxi (fig. 8: photocopy of text of 4QMMT published in *QC* 1 [1990-91] Appendix A).

Shanks, H., "The Difference between Scholarly Mistakes and Scholarly Concealment: The Case of MMT," *BARev* 16/5 (1990) 64-65.

———, "Qimron Wins Lawsuit: Paying the Price for Freeing the Scrolls," *BARev* 19/4 (1993) 65-68.

X

Important Bibliography on Some Topics of Dead Sea Scrolls Study

The purpose of this section is to guide the reader to the more important writings on various topics that have become areas of research in the study of the Dead Sea Scrolls. No effort is made here to be exhaustive on any of the topics, since it suffices to list the more important materials, which will of themselves contain references and guides to further literature. In some instances the literature on a topic is more abundant than others; but that is not to be taken as a gauge of the importance of the topic. Sometimes the literature has grown about a topic simply because of an extrinsic reason, e.g., the piecemeal fashion in which some of the texts have been published. Now that most of the texts are available in some form, that reason is gradually becoming less important.

The areas for special bibliographies are the following:

1. Archaeology of the Dead Sea Scrolls
2. Palaeography of the Dead Sea Scrolls
3. The Old Testament at Qumran and Murabbaʿat
4. Old Testament Interpretation in Qumran Literature
5. Qumran Theology
6. Qumran Messianism
7. The Qumran Calendar
8. Qumran Wisdom Literature
9. Qumran Halakhah or Legal Issues
10. History of the Qumran Community
11. The New Testament in Qumran Cave 7?
12. The Qumran Scrolls and the New Testament

1. Archaeology of the Dead Sea Scrolls

The Qumran and ʿAin Feshkha Area

The long-awaited final reports of the excavations at Khirbet Qumran and ʿAin Feshkha are being released in different languages, and the titles vary:

Humbert, J.-B. et A. Chambon (eds.), *Fouilles de Khirbet Qumrân et de Aïn Feshkha: Album de photographies, Repertoire du fonds photographique; Synthèse des notes de chantier du Père Roland de Vaux OP* (NTOA, Series archaeologica 1; Fribourg, Suisse: Éditions Universitaires; Göttingen: Vandenhoeck & Ruprecht, 1994).

Vaux, R. de, *Die Ausgrabungen von Qumran und En Feschcha IA, Die Grabungstagebücher: Deutsche Übersetzung und Informationsaufbereitung durch Ferdinand Rohrhirsch und Bettina Hofmeir* (NTOA, Ser. arch. 1A; Göttingen: Vandenhoeck & Ruprecht; Freiburg, Schweiz: Universitätsverlag, 1996).

Humbert, J.-B. and A. Chambon (eds.), *The Excavations of Khirbet Qumran and Ain Feshkha: Synthesis of Roland de Vaux's Field Notes* (NTOA, Ser. arch. 1B; tr. S. J. Pfann; Fribourg: University Press; Göttingen: Vandenhoeck & Ruprecht, 2003). See J. Magness, *DSD* 13 (2006) 262-66; M. Popović, *JSJ* 37 (2006) 452-56.

Humbert, J.-B. et J. Gunneweg (eds.), *Khirbet Qumrân et ʿAin Feshkha II: Études d'anthropologie, de physique et de chemie; Studies of Anthropology, Physics and Chemistry* (NTOA, Ser. arch. 3; Fribourg: Academic Press; Göttingen: Vandenhoeck & Ruprecht, 2003).

The following five surveys and preliminary reports on Khirbet Qumran and various Qumran caves, though they have been superseded by the final reports now being issued, at times reveal details about stages and the process of excavation, and some of them announce further excavations beyond those of R. de Vaux. These archaeological reports accompany publication of texts in the DJD series, and some repeat details in earlier articles.

Lankester Harding, G., R. de Vaux et al., "The Archaeological Finds," DJD 1. 1-40 (on Khirbet Qumran, Qumran Cave 1).

Vaux, R. de et al., "Archéologie," DJD 2. 1-63 (on Murabbaʿat).

———, "Archéologie," DJD 3. 1-41 (with an appendix by J. T. Milik, "Deux jarres inscrites d'une grotte de Qumrân," 37-41; on the cliffs near Wadi Qumran, and Caves 5-10).

———, "Archéologie," DJD 6.1-29 (on Cave 4).

Tov, E., "Archaeological Data and Identification," DJD 8. 1-2 (on Wadi Seiyal).

The further reports are arranged according to the date of publication:

Vaux, R. de, "Post-scriptum: La cachette des manuscrits hébreux," *RB* 56 (1949) 234-37 (on the excavation of Qumran Cave 1).

———, "La grotte des manuscrits hébreux," *RB* 56 (1949) 586-609.

———, "À propos des manuscrits de la Mer Morte," *RB* 57 (1950) 417-29 (de Vaux's initial dating of the pottery, which proved to be too early).

———, "Chronique archéologique: Khirbet Qumrân," *RB* 61 (1954) 567-68 (third campaign).

———, "Chronique archéologique: Khirbet Qumrân," *RB* 63 (1956) 73-74 (fourth campaign).

———, "Fouilles de Feshkha: Rapport préliminaire," *RB* 66 (1959) 225-55.

———, "Excavations at 'Ain Feshkha," *ADAJ* 4-5 (1960) 7-11.

———, *L'Archéologie et les manuscrits de la Mer Morte* (The Schweich Lectures of the British Academy 1959; London: Oxford University Press, 1961); in a revised translation: *Archaeology and the Dead Sea Scrolls* (London: Oxford University Press, 1973).

Laperrousaz, E.-M., *Qoumrân: L'Etablissement essénien des bords de la Mer Morte: Histoire et archéologie du site* (Paris: Picard, 1976). An interpretation of the archaeology of Qumran that differs from that of de Vaux in some details.

Davies, P. R., *Qumran* (Cities of the Biblical World; Guilford, Surrey, UK: Lutterworth; Grand Rapids, MI: Eerdmans, 1982).

Broshi, M., "The Archeology of Qumran — A Reconsideration," *The Dead Sea Scrolls: Forty Years of Research* (STDJ 10; ed. D. Dimant and U. Rappaport; Leiden: Brill; Jerusalem: Magnes Press, 1992) 103-15.

Patrich, J., "חורבת קומראן לאור המחקר הארכיאולוגי החדש (Khirbet Qumran in Light of New Archaeological Explorations in Qumran Caves)," *Proceedings of the Eleventh World Congress of Jewish Studies, Jerusalem, June 22-29, 1993: Division A* (Jerusalem: World Union of Jewish Studies, 1994) 95-102.

Donceel, R., "Qumran," *The Oxford Encyclopedia of Archaeology in the Near East* (5 vols.; ed. E. M. Meyers; Oxford/New York: Oxford University Press, 1997), 4. 392-96.

Magness, J., "The Archaeology of Qumran: A Review," *QC* 8 (1998) 49-62.

Humbert, J.-B., "Qumrân, Esséniens et architecture," *Antikes Judentum und frühes Christentum: Festschrift für Hartmut Stegemann . . .* (BZNW 97; ed. B. Kollmann et al.; Berlin: de Gruyter, 1999) 183-96 (+ six figs.).

Taylor, J. E., "The Cemeteries of Khirbet Qumran and Women's Presence at the Site," *DSD* 6 (1999) 285-323.

Broshi, M. and H. Eshel, "Residential Caves at Qumran," *DSD* 6 (1999) 328-48.

Magness, J., "A Reassessment of the Excavations of Qumran," *The Dead Sea Scrolls Fifty Years after Their Discovery: Proceedings of the Jerusalem Congress, July 20-25, 1997* (ed. L. H. Schiffman et al.; Jerusalem: Israel Exploration Society and the Shrine of the Book, Israel Museum, 2000), 708-19.

Patrich, J., "Did Extra-Mural Dwelling Quarters Exist at Qumran?" ibid., 720-27.

Reich, R., "*Miqva'ot* at Khirbet Qumran and the Jerusalem Connection," ibid., 728-31.

Zias, J., "Human Skeletal Remains from the Southern Cave at Masada and the Question of Ethnicity," ibid., 732-38.

Yellin, J., M. Broshi, and H. Eshel, "Pottery of Qumran and Ein Ghuweir: The First Chemical Exploration of Provenience," *BASOR* 321 (2001) 65-78.

Eshel, H., "Qumran Studies in Light of Archeological Excavations between 1967 and 1997," *Journal of Religious History* 26 (2002) 179-88.

Magness, J., *The Archaeology of Qumran and the Dead Sea Scrolls* (Grand Rapids, MI: Eerdmans, 2002). An important recent study of the archaeology of Qumran, which basically agrees with de Vaux, but offers some important corrections.

Donceel, R., "Synthèse des observations faites fouillant les tombes des nécropoles de Khirbet Qumrân et des environs," *QC* 10 (2002) 3-114 (+ 20 figs. and one foldout photograph).

Broshi, M. and H. Eshel, "Whose Bones? New Qumran Excavations, New Debates," *BARev* 29/1 (2003) 26-33, 71.

Eshel, H. and M. Broshi, "Excavations at Qumran, Summer of 2001," *IEJ* 53 (2003) 61-73.

Broshi, M. and H. Eshel, "Three Seasons of Excavations at Qumran," *JRA* 17 (2004) 321-32.

Hirschfeld, Y., "Excavations at 'Ein Feshkha, 2001: Final Report," *IEJ* 54 (2004) 37-74.

Broshi, M. and H. Eshel, "Zias' Qumran Cemetery," *RevQ* 21 (2003-4) 487-89.

Schultz, B., "The Qumran Cemetery: 150 Years of Research," *DSD* 13 (2006) 194-228.

Murabbaʿat

Lankester Harding, C., "Khirbet Qumran and Wady Murabbaʿat," *PEQ* 84 (1952) 104-9 (+ pls. XXVIII-XXX).

Milik, J. T. and H. Seyrig, "Trésor monétaire de Murabbaʿat," *Revue numismatique* 6 (1958) 11-26.

Stern, E., "Murabbaʿat, Wadi," *EDSS*, 581-83.

Masada

Yadin, Y., "The Excavation of Masada — 1963/64: Preliminary Report," *IEJ* 15 (1965) 1-120.

———, *Masada: Herod's Fortress and the Zealots' Last Stand* (London: Weidenfeld and Nicolson; New York: Random House, 1966). A popular presentation of the excavation and finds.

Aviram, J. et al. (eds.), *Masada IV: The Yigael Yadin Excavations 1963-1965 Final Reports* (Jerusalem: Israel Exploration Society and the Hebrew University of Jerusalem, 1994).

Geva, H., "The Siege Ramp Laid by the Romans to Conquer the Northern Palace at Masada," *Joseph Aviram Volume* (ErIsr 25; Jerusalem: Israel Exploration Society, 1996) 297-306 (Hebrew).

Magness, J., "Masada 1995: Discoveries at Camp F," *BA* 59 (1996) 181.

———, "Masada," *EDSS*, 515-19.

Various Sites in the Judean Desert

Aharoni, Y., "The Caves of Naḥal Ḥever," *ʿAtiqot* (English) 3 (1961) 148-62.

———, "Expedition B — The Cave of Horror," *IEJ* 12 (1962) 186-99.

Avigad, N. et al., "The Expedition to the Judean Desert, 1961," *IEJ* 12 (1962) 165-262 (+ pls. 15-48).

Aviram, J. et al., "The Expedition to the Judean Desert, 1960," *IEJ* 11 (1961) 3-72.

Bar-Adon, P., "Another Settlement of the Judean Desert Sect at ʿEn el-Ghuweir on the Shores of the Dead Sea," *BASOR* 227 (1977) 1-25; cf. *Zalman Shazar Volume* (ErIsr 10; Jerusalem: Israel Exploration Society, 1971) 72-89; R. de Vaux, *Archaeology*, 88-90.

Eshel, H., "Ḥever, Naḥal," *EDSS*, 357-59.

———, "Ṣe'elim, Naḥal," *EDSS*, 859-60.

——— and Z. Greenhut, "Ḥiam el-Sagha: A Cemetery of the Qumran Type, Judaean Desert," *RB* 100 (1993) 252-59.

Yadin, Y., "Expedition D," *IEJ* 11 (1961) 36-52; "Expedition D — The Cave of Letters," *IEJ* 12 (1962) 227-57.

———, *The Finds from the Bar-Kokhba Period in the Cave of Letters* (JDS 1; Jerusalem: Israel Exploration Society, 1963).

———, *Bar Kokhba: The Rediscovery of the Legendary Hero of the Second Jewish Revolt against Rome* (London: Weidenfeld and Nicolson, 1971).

Other Important Archaeological or Scientific Articles

Burton, D., J. B. Poole, and R. Reed, "A New Approach to the Dating of the Dead Sea Scrolls," *Nature* 184 (No. 4685, 15 August 1959) 533-34.

Donceel, R., "Khirbet Qumrân (Palestine): Le locus 130 et les 'ossements sous jarre': Mise à jour de la documentation," *QC* 13 (2005) 3-70 (+ pls. 1-25)

Duhaime, J. L., "Remarques sur les dépôts d'ossements d'animaux à Qumran," *RevQ* 9 (1977-78) 245-51.

Eshel, H., "A Note on Joshua 15:61-62 and the Identification of the City of Salt," *IEJ* 45 (1995) 37-40. ("City of Salt" = modern Maṣad Gozal, south of 'En-Gedi; whereas Qumran = ancient Secacah.)

Goranson, S., "Further Qumran Archaeology Publications in Progress," *BA* 54 (1991) 110-11.

Haas, N. and H. Nathan, "Anthropological Survey on the Human Skeletal Remains from Qumran," *RevQ* 6 (1967-69) 345-52.

Hachlili, R., "Burial Practices at Qumran," *RevQ* 16 (1993-95) 247-64.

Hidiroglou, P., "Aqueducts, Basins and Cisterns: The Water System at Qumran," *NEA* 63 (2000) 128-39.

Laperrousaz, E.-M., "A propos des dépôts d'ossements d'animaux trouvés a Qumrân," *RevQ* 9 (1977-78) 569-78. (Comments on the article of Duhaime.)

———, "Brèves remarques archéologiques concernant la chronologie des occupations esséniennes de Qoumrân," *RevQ* 12 (1985-87) 199-212.

Lapp, P. W., *Palestinian Ceramic Chronology 200 B.C.–A.D. 70* (New Haven, CT: American Schools of Oriental Research, 1961).

Lemaire, A., "Qoumrân: Sa fonction et ses manuscrits," *Qoumrân et les manuscrits de la Mer Morte: Un cinquantenaire* (ed. E.-M. Laperrousaz; Paris: Editions du Cerf, 1997) 117-49.

Pixner, B., "The History of the 'Essene Gate' Area," *ZDPV* 105 (1989) 96-104.

——— et al., "Mount Zion: The 'Gate of the Essenes' Re-excavated," *ZDPV* 105 (1989) 85-95.

Poole, J. B. and R. Reed, "The 'Tannery' of 'Ain Feshkha," *PEQ* 93 (1961) 114-23.

———, "The Preparation of Leather and Parchment by the Dead Sea Scrolls Community," *Technological Culture* 3 (1962) 1-26.

———, "A Study of Some Dead Sea Scroll and Leather Fragments from Cave 4 at Qumran: Part II, Chemical Examination," *Proceedings of the Leeds Philosophical and Literary Society,* Scientific Section 9/6 (1964) 171-82.

Riesner, R., "Josephus' 'Gate of the Essenes' in Modern Discussion," *ZDPV* 105 (1989) 105-9.

Ruderman, A., "The Qumran Settlement: Scriptorium, Villa or Fortress," *JBQ* 23 (1995) 131-32.

Schulz, S., "Chirbet kumran, ʿĒn Feschcha und die bukēʿa: Zugleich ein archäologischer Beitrag zum Felsenaquädukt und zur Strasse durch das wādi kumrān," *ZDPV* 76 (1960) 50-72.

Sellers, O. R., "Radiocarbon Dating of Cloth from the ʿAin Feshkha Cave," *BASOR* 123 (1951) 24-26.

Strobel, A., "Die Wasseranlagen der Ḫirbet Qumran: Versuch einer Deutung," *ZDPV* 88 (1972) 55-86.

Vaux, R. de, "Une hachette essénienne," *VT* 9 (1959) 399-407.

Zeuner, F. E., "Notes on Qumran," *PEQ* 92 (1960) 27-36.

Zissu, B., "'Qumran Type' Graves in Jerusalem: Archaeological Evidence of an Essene Community?" *DSD* 5 (1998) 158-71.

Controversial Aspects of the Archaeology of Qumran

Bioul, B., *Qumrân et les manuscrits de la mer Morte: Les hypothèses, le débat* (Paris: de Guibert, 2004).

Broshi, M., "Was Qumran, Indeed, a Monastery? The Consensus and Its Challengers, an Archaeologist's View," *Caves of Enlightenment: Proceedings of the American Schools of Oriental Research Dead Sea Scrolls Jubilee Symposium (1947-1997)* (ed. J. H. Charlesworth; North Richland Hills, TX: Bibal Press, 1998) 19-37.

Cansdale, L., *Qumran and the Essenes: A Re-Evaluation of the Evidence* (TSAJ 60; Tübingen: Mohr [Siebeck], 1997).

Davies, P. R., "How Not to Do Archaeology: The Story of Qumran," *BA* 51 (1988) 203-7.

Donceel-Voûte, P. H. E., "'Coenaculum' — La salle à l'étage du *locus* 30 à Khirbet Qumrân sur la Mer Morte," *Banquets d'Orient* (Res Orientales 4; Leuven: Peeters, 1992) 61-84.

Haas, N. and H. Nathan, "Anthropological Survey on the Human Skeletal Remains from Qumran," *RevQ* 6 (1967-69) 345-52.

Hirschfeld, Y., "Early Roman Manor Houses in Judea and the Site of Khirbet Qumran," *JNES* 57 (1998) 161-89. (See the reaction of Magness to Hirschfeld's interpretation of Qumran as a manor house [*Archaeology of Qumran,* 17, 96-99].)

———, "Qumran: Back to the Beginning," *JRA* 16 (2003) 648-52 (review of Magness, *Archaeology of Qumran*).

———, *Qumran in Context: Reassessing the Archaeological Evidence* (Peabody, MA: Hendrickson, 2004).

Reich, R., "A Note on the Function of Room 30 (the 'Scriptorium') at Khirbet Qumran," *JJS* 46 (1995) 157-60.

Shanks, H., "The Qumran Settlement: Monastery, Villa or Fortress?" *BARev* 19/3 (1993) 62-65.

Steckoll, S. H., "Preliminary Excavation Report in the Qumran Cemetery," *RevQ* 6 (1967-69) 323-44. (On this entry, see the comment of de Vaux, *Archaeology,* 47-48.)

Vaux, R. de, "Archaeology and the Dead Sea Scrolls," *Antiquity* 37 (1963) 126-27 (Reaction to J. L. Teicher).

———, "Essenes or Zealots," *NTS* 13 (1966-67) 89-104 (Reaction to G. R. Driver).

———, "Marginal Notes on the Qumran Excavations," *RevQ* 7 (1969-71) 33-44.

Zangenberg, J. and K. Galor, "Qumran Archaeology in Transition," *QC* 11 (2003) 1-6.

Zias, J., "Qumran Archaeology: Skeletons with Multiple Personality Disorders and Other Grave Errors," *RevQ* 21 (2003-4) 83-98.

2. Palaeography of the Dead Sea Scrolls

The three most fundamental studies are:

Avigad, N., "The Palaeography of the Dead Sea Scrolls and Related Documents," *Aspects of the Dead Sea Scrolls* (Scripta hierosolymitana 4; Jerusalem: Magnes, 1958) 56-87.

Cross, F. M., "The Development of the Jewish Scripts," *The Bible and the Ancient Near East: Essays in Honor of William Foxwell Albright* (Anchor Books A431; Garden City, NY: Doubleday, 1965) 170-264.

———, "Palaeography and the Dead Sea Scrolls," *The Dead Sea Scrolls after Fifty Years: A Comprehensive Assessment* (2 vols.; ed. P. W. Flint and J. C. VanderKam; Leiden: Brill, 1998, 1999), 1. 379-402.

See further:

Birnbaum, S. A., *The Qumrân (Dead Sea) Scrolls and Palaeography* (BASOR Supplementary Studies 13-14; New Haven, CT: American Schools of Oriental Research, 1952).

———, *The Hebrew Scripts Part I: The Text* (Leiden: Brill, 1971); *Part II: The Plates* (London: Palaeographica, 1954-57).

Cross, F. M., "The Oldest Manuscripts from Qumran," *JBL* 74 (1955) 147-72.

———, "Epigraphic Notes on Hebrew Documents of the Eighth-Sixth Centuries B.C.: II. The Murabbaʿat Papyrus and the Letter Found near Yabneh-Yam," *BASOR* 165 (1962) 34-46.

——— and E. Eshel, "Ostraca from Khirbet Qumrân," *IEJ* 47 (1997) 17-28.

Eshel, E. and A. Kloner, "An Aramaic Ostracon of an Edomite Marriage Contract from Maresha, Dated 176 B.C.E.," *IEJ* 46 (1996) 1-22.

Hanson, R. S., "Paleo-Hebrew Scripts in the Hasmonean Age," *BASOR* 175 (1964) 26-42.

———, "Jewish Palaeography and Its Bearing on Text Critical Studies," *Magnalia Dei: The Mighty Acts of God: Essays in Memory of G. E. Wright* (ed. F. M. Cross et al.; Garden City, NY: Doubleday, 1976) 561-76.

Tov, E., "Letters of the Cryptic Script A and Paleo-Hebrew Letters Used as Scribal Marks in Some Qumran Scrolls," *DSD* 2 (1995) 330-39.

Radiocarbon Testing and the Palaeographic Dating of Scrolls

Laperrousaz, E.-M. and G. Odent, "La datation d'objets provenant de Qoumran, en particulier par la méthode utilisant les propriétés du carbone 14," *Sem* 27 (1977) 83-98.

Shanks, H., "Carbon-14 Tests Substantiate Scroll Dates," *BARev* 17/6 (1991) 72.

Bonani, G. et al., "Radiocarbon Dating of Fourteen Dead Sea Scrolls," *Radiocarbon* 34/3 (1992) 843-49; also in *ʿAtiqot* 20 (1991) 27-32.

Rodley, G. A., "An Assessment of the Radiocarbon Dating of the Dead Sea Scrolls," *Radiocarbon* 35 (1993) 335-38.

Jull, T. et al., "Radiocarbon Dating of Scrolls and Linen Fragments from the Judean Desert," *Radiocarbon* 37 (1995) 11-19; also in *ʿAtiqot* 28 (1996) 85-91.

Shanks, H., "New Carbon-14 Results Leave Room for Debate," *BARev* 21/4 (1995) 61.

Water, R. van de, "Reconsidering Palaeographic and Radiocarbon Dating of the Dead Sea Scrolls," *RevQ* 19 (1998-2001) 423-39.

Doudna, G., "Dating the Scrolls on the Basis of Radiocarbon Analysis," *The Dead Sea Scrolls after Fifty Years: A Comprehensive Assessment* (2 vols.; ed. P. W. Flint and J. C. VanderKam; Leiden: Brill, 1998-99), 1. 430-71.

Atwill, J. and S. Braunheim, "They Used the Wrong Dating Curve: Wishful Thinking and Over-Stating in Qumran Radiocarbon Dating Analysis," *QC* 11 (2003) 21-35.

——— and R. Eisenman, "Redating the Radiocarbon Dating of the Dead Sea Scrolls," *DSD* 11 (2004) 143-57.

3. The Old Testament at Qumran and Murabba'at

The Hebrew and Aramaic Text

Brooke, G. J., "The Twelve Minor Prophets and the Dead Sea Scrolls," *Congress Volume Leiden 2004* (VTSup 109; ed. A. Lemaire; Leiden: Brill, 2006) 19-43.

Catastini, A., "Da Qumran al testo masoretico dell'Antico Testamento: Spunti metodologici per la valutazione delle varianti," *RevQ* 15 (1991-92) 303-13.

Chiesa, B., "Textual History and Textual Criticism of the Hebrew Old Testament," *The Madrid Qumran Congress: Proceedings of the International Congress on the Dead Sea Scrolls, Madrid 18-21 March 1991* (STDJ 11/1-2; ed. J. Trebolle Barrera and L. Vega Montaner; Leiden: Brill; Madrid: Editorial Complutense, 1992) 257-72.

Cross, F. M., "The Contribution of the Qumran Discoveries to the Study of the Biblical Text," *IEJ* 16 (1966) 81-95.

———, "The Evolution of a Theory of Local Texts," *1971 Proceedings, International Organisation for Septuagint and Cognate Studies* (Septuagint and Cognate Studies 2; Missoula, MT: Society of Biblical Literature, 1972) 108-26.

———, "The History of the Biblical Text in the Light of Discoveries in the Judaean Desert," *HTR* 57 (1964) 282-99.

——— and R. J. Saley, "A Statistical Analysis of the Textual Character of 4QSamuel[a] (4Q51)," *DSD* 13 (2006) 46-54.

——— and S. Talmon (eds.), *Qumran and the History of the Biblical Text* (Cambridge, MA: Harvard University Press, 1975).

Delcor, M., "Zum Psalter von Qumran," *BZ* 10 (1966) 15-29.

Ego, B. et al. (eds.), *Minor Prophets* (Biblia Qumranica 3B; Leiden: Brill, 2005).

Fincke, A., *A Samuel Scroll from Qumran: 4QSam[a] Restored and Compared to the Septuagint and 4QSam[c]* (STDJ 43; Leiden: Brill, 2001).

Glessmer, U., "Liste der biblischen Texte aus Qumran," *RevQ* 16 (1993-95) 153-92.

Goshen-Gottstein, M. H., "The Hebrew Bible in the Light of Qumran Scrolls and the Hebrew University Bible," *Congress Volume, Jerusalem 1986* (VTSup 40; ed. J. A. Emerton; Leiden: Brill, 1988) 42-53.

Greenberg, M., "The Stabilization of the Text of the Hebrew Bible, Reviewed in the Light of the Biblical Materials from the Judean Desert," *JAOS* 76 (1956) 157-67.

Herbert, E. D., *Reconstructing Biblical Dead Sea Scrolls: A New Method Applied to the Reconstruction of 4QSam*[a] (STDJ 22; Leiden: Brill, 1997).

Herbst, A., "Los textos de Qumrán, el Pentateuco Samaritano y la crítica textual de la Biblia hebrea," *RevistBíb* 63 (2001) 129-51.

Howard, G., "Frank Cross and Recensional Critisism [sic]," *VT* 21 (1971) 440-50.

Kutscher, E. Y., *The Language and Linguistic Background of the Isaiah Scroll (1 Q Isa*[a]*)* (STDJ 6; Leiden: Brill, 1974).

Orlinsky, H. M., "Qumran and the Present State of Old Testament Text Studies: The Septuagint Text," *JBL* 78 (1959) 26-33.

———, "The Textual Criticism of the Old Testament," *The Bible and the Ancient Near East: Essays in Honor of William Foxwell Albright* (Anchor Books A431; ed. G. E. Wright; Garden City, NY: Doubleday, 1965) 140-69.

Puech, E., "Qumran et le texte de l'Ancien Testament," *Congress Volume Oslo 1998* (VTSup 80; ed. A. Lemaire and M. Saebø; Leiden: Brill, 2000) 437-64.

Sanders, J. A., "Cave 11 Surprises and the Question of Canon," *McCormick Quarterly* 21 (1968) 1-15.

———, "The Dead Sea Scrolls and Biblical Studies," *"Shaʿarei Talmon": Studies in the Bible, Qumran, and the Ancient Near East Presented to Shemaryahu Talmon* (ed. M. Fishbane and E. Tov; Winona Lake, IN: Eisenbrauns, 1992) 323-36.

———, "Pre-Masoretic Psalter Texts," *CBQ* 27 (1965) 114-23.

———, "The Qumran Psalms Scroll (11QPs[a]) Reviewed," *On Language, Culture, and Religion: In Honor of Eugene A. Nida* (ed. M. Black and W. A. Smalley; The Hague: Mouton, 1974) 79-99.

Skehan, P. W., "Qumran and Old Testament Criticism," *Qumrân: Sa piété, sa théologie et son milieu* (BETL 46; ed. M. Delcor; Gembloux: Duculot; Louvain: Leuven University, 1978) 163-82 (with collation of 4QPs mss that vary from *Biblia Hebraica Stuttgartensia*).

———, "Qumran and the Present State of Old Testament Text Studies: The Masoretic Text," *JBL* 78 (1959) 21-25.

———, "Qumran, IV. Littérature de Qumran — A. Textes bibliques," *DBSup* 9 (1978) 805-28.

Talmon, S., "Aspects of the Textual Transmission of the Bible in the Light of Qumran Manuscripts," *Textus* 4 (1964) 95-132.

———, "The Old Testament Text," *Cambridge History of the Bible* (ed. P. R Ackroyd and C. F. Evans; Cambridge, UK: Cambridge University Press) 1 (1970) 159-99.

Tov, E., "A Categorized List of All the 'Biblical Texts' Found in the Judaean Desert," *DSD* 8 (2001) 67-84.

———, "Hebrew Biblical Manuscripts from the Judaean Desert: Their Contribution to Textual Criticism," *JJS* 39 (1988) 5-37.

———, "A New Understanding of the Samaritan Pentateuch in the Wake of the Discovery of the Qumran Scrolls," *Proceedings of the First International Congress of the Société d'Études Samaritaines, Tel-Aviv, April 11-13, 1988* (ed. A. Tal and M. Florentin; Tel-Aviv: Chaim Rosenberg School for Jewish Studies, Tel-Aviv University, 1991) 293-303.

———, "The Original Shape of the Biblical Text," *Congress Volume Leuven 1989* (VTSup 43; ed. J. A. Emerton; Leiden: Brill, 1991) 345-59.

———, "The Orthography and Language of the Hebrew Scrolls Found at Qumran and the Origin of These Scrolls," *Textus* 13 (1986) 31-57.

———, "Paratextual Elements in the Masoretic Manuscripts of the Bible Compared with the Qumran Evidence," *Antikes Judentum und frühes Christentum: Festschrift für Hartmut Stegemann . . .* (BZNW 97; ed. B. Kollmann et al.; Berlin: de Gruyter, 1999) 73-83.

———, *Scribal Practices and Approaches Reflected in the Texts Found in the Judean Desert* (STDJ 54; Leiden: Brill, 2004).

———, "The Significance of the Texts from the Judean Desert for the History of the Text of the Hebrew Bible: A New Synthesis," *Qumran between the Old and New Testaments* (JSOTSup 290: Copenhagen International Seminar 6; ed. F. H. Cryer and T. L. Thompson; Sheffield, UK: Sheffield Academic, 1998) 277-309.

———, *Textual Criticism of the Hebrew Bible* (Minneapolis, MN: Fortress; Assen: Van Gorcum, 1992; 2nd rev. ed., 2001).

——— and J. Cook, "A Computerized Database for the Qumran Biblical Scrolls with an Appendix on the Samaritan Pentateuch," *JNSL* 12 (1984) 133-37.

Trebolle Barrera, J., "Qumran Evidence for a Biblical Standard Text and for Non-Standard and Parabiblical Texts," *The Dead Sea Scrolls in Their Historical Context* (ed. T. H. Lim et al.: Edinburgh: Clark, 2000) 89-106.

Ulrich, E., "The Bible in the Making: The Scriptures at Qumran," *The Community of the Renewed Covenant: The Notre Dame Symposium on the Dead Sea Scrolls* (Christianity and Judaism in Antiquity 10; ed. E. Ulrich and J. C. VanderKam; Notre Dame, IN: University of Notre Dame, 1994) 77-93.

———. "The Biblical Scrolls from Qumran Cave 4: An Overview and a Progress Report on Their Publication," *RevQ* 14 (1989-90) 207-28.

———. "The Dead Sea Scrolls and the Biblical Text," *The Dead Sea Scrolls after Fifty Years: A Comprehensive Assessment* (2 vols.; ed. P. W. Flint and J. C. VanderKam; Leiden: Brill, 1998, 1999), 1. 79-100.

———, *The Dead Sea Scrolls and the Origins of the Bible* (SDSSRL; Grand Rapids, MI: Eerdmans, 1999).

———, "Horizons of Old Testament Textual Research at the Thirtieth Anniversary of Qumran Cave 4," *CBQ* 46 (1984) 613-36.

———, "An Index of the Passages in the Biblical Manuscripts from the Judean Desert (Genesis–Kings)," *DSD* 1 (1994) 113-29; "(Part 2: Isaiah–Chronicles)," *DSD* 2 (1995) 86-107.

———, "The Qumran Biblical Scrolls — The Scriptures of the Late Second Temple Judaism," *The Dead Sea Scrolls in Their Historical Context* (see above), 67-87.

Vegas Montaner, L., "Nuevos textos bíblicos procedentes de Qumrán: Implicaciones exegéticas," *III Simposio bíblico español (i Luso-Espanhol)* (ed. J. Carreira das Neves et al.; Valencia/Lisbon: Fundación Bíblica Española, 1991) 151-59.

Washburn, D. L., *A Catalog of Biblical Passages in the Dead Sea Scrolls* (SBL Text-Critical Studies 2; Atlanta, GA: Society of Biblical Literature, 2002).

Young, I., "The Stabilization of the Biblical Text in the Light of Qumran and Masada: A Challenge for Conventional Qumran Chronology?" *DSD* 9 (2002) 364-90.

The Septuagint

Barthélemy, D., *Les devanciers d'Aquila: Première publication intégrale du texte des fragments du Dodécaprophéton trouvés dans le Désert de Juda, précédée d'une étude sur les traductions et recensions grecques de la Bible réalisées au premier siècle de notre ère sous l'influence du rabbinat palestinien* (VTSup 10; Leiden: Brill, 1963).

———, "Redécouverte d'un chaînon manquant de l'histoire de la LXX," *RB* 60 (1953) 18-29.

Brooke, G. J. and B. Lindars, *Septuagint, Scrolls and Cognate Writings: Papers Presented to the International Symposium on the Septuagint and Its Relations to the Dead Sea Scrolls and Other Writings (Manchester 1990)* (SBLSCS 33; Atlanta, GA: Scholars, 1992).

Combs, W. W., "The Transmission-History of the Septuagint," *BSac* 146 (1989) 255-69.

Dogniez, C., *Bibliography of the Septuagint/Bibliographie de la Septante (1970-1993)* (VTSup 60; Leiden: Brill, 1995).

Fabry, H.-J., "Die griechischen Handschriften vom Toten Meer," *Im Brennpunkt, Die Septuaginta: Studien zur Entstehung und Bedeutung der griechischen Bibel* (BWANT 153; ed. H.-J. Fabry und U. Offerhaus; Stuttgart: Kohlhammer, 2001) 131-53.

Flint, P. W., "Variant Readings of the Dead Sea Psalms Scrolls against the Massoretic Text and the Septuagint Psalter," *Der Septuaginta-Psalter und seine Tochterübersetzungen: Symposium in Göttingen 1997)* (Mitteilungen des Septuaginta-Unternehmens 24; Göttingen: Vandenhoeck & Ruprecht, 2000) 337-65.

Greenspoon, L. J., "The Dead Sea Scrolls and the Greek Bible," *The Dead Sea Scrolls after Fifty Years: A Comprehensive Assessment* (2 vols.; ed. P. W. Flint and J. C. VanderKam; Leiden: Brill, 1998-99), 1. 101-27.

Janzen, J. G., *Studies in the Text of Jeremiah* (HSM 6; Cambridge, MA: Harvard University Press, 1973).

Jellicoe, S. (ed.), *Studies in the Septuagint: Origins, Recensions, and Interpretations: Selected Essays with a Prolegomenon* (New York: Ktav Publishing House, 1974).

Klein, R. W., *Textual Criticism of the Old Testament: From the Septuagint to Qumran* (Philadelphia, PA: Fortress, 1974).

Leaney, A. R. C., "Greek Manuscripts from the Judaean Desert," *Studies in New Testament Language and Text: Essays in Honour of George D. Kilpatrick . . .* (NovTSup 44; ed. J. K. Elliott; Leiden: Brill, 1976) 283-300.

Maier, J., "Das jüdische Gesetz zwischen Qumran und Septuaginta," *Im Brennpunkt, Die Septuaginta* (see above), 155-65.

Miller, D. R., "The Greek Biblical Fragments from Qumran in Text-Critical Perspective," *BeO* 48 (2001) 235-48.

Olofsson, S., "Qumran and LXX," *Qumran between the Old and New Testaments* (JSOTSup 290; ed. F. H. Cryer and T. L. Thompson; Sheffield, UK: Sheffield Academic, 1998) 232-48.

Tov, E., "The Contribution of the Qumran Scrolls to the Understanding of the LXX," *Septuagint, Scrolls* (see above), 11-47.

———, *The Greek and Hebrew Bible: Collected Essays on the Septuagint* (VTSup 72; Leiden: Brill, 1999).

———, "Greek Texts from the Judean Desert," *QC* 8 (1999) 161-68.

———, "The Nature of the Greek Texts from the Judean Desert," *NovT* 43 (2001) 1-11.

———, "Some Reflections on the Hebrew Texts from Which the Septuagint Was Translated," *JNSL* 19 (1993) 107-22.

———, *The Text-Critical Use of the Septuagint in Biblical Research* (JBS 3; Jerusalem: Simor, 1981).

Trebolle Barrera, J., "La Biblia hebrea y la Biblia griega: Un clásico de oriente y occidente," *Paganos, judíos y cristianos en los textos de Qumrán* (ed. J. Trebolle Barrera: Madrid: Trotta, 1999) 335-55.

Ulrich, E., "The Dead Sea Scrolls and Their Implications for an Edition of the Septuagint Psalter," *Der Septuaginta-Psalter* (see above), 323-36.

Wevers, J. W., "Barthélemy and Proto-Septuagint Studies," *BIOSCS* 21 (1988) 23-34.

4. Old Testament Interpretation in Qumran Literature

Alexander, P. S. "Retelling the Old Testament," *It is Written — Scripture Citing Scripture: Essays in Honour of Barnabas Lindars, SSF* (ed. D. A. Carson and H. G. M. Williamson; Cambridge: Cambridge University Press, 1988) 99-121.

Bernstein, M., "Interpretation of Scriptures," *EDSS*, 376-83.

———, "Introductory Formulas for Citation and Recitaton of Biblical Verses in the Qumran Pesharim: Observations on a Pesher Technique," *DSD* 1 (1994) 30-70.

Berrin, S. L., *The Pesher Nahum Scroll: An Exegetical Study of 4Q169* (STDJ 53; Leiden: Brill, 2004).

Betz, O., *Offenbarung und Schriftforschung in der Qumransekte* (WUNT 6; Tübingen: Mohr [Siebeck], 1960).

Brin, G., "Concerning Some of the Uses of the Bible in the Temple Scroll," *RevQ* 12 (1985-87) 519-28.

Brooke, C. J., "*E pluribus Unum:* Textual Variety and Definitive Interpretation in the Qumran Scrolls," *The Dead Sea Scrolls in Their Historical Context* (ed. T. H. Lim et al.; Edinburgh: Clark, 2000) 107-19.

———, *Exegesis at Qumran: 4QFlorilegium in Its Jewish Context* (JSOTSup 29; Sheffield, UK: JSOT, 1985) (the subtitle is more accurate than the main title).

———, "Qumran Pesher: Towards the Redefinition of a Genre," *RevQ* 10 (1979-81) 483-503.

Brownlee, W. H., "Biblical Interpretation among the Sectaries of the Dead Sea Scrolls," *BA* 14 (1951) 54-76.

Bruce, F. F., *Biblical Exegesis in the Qumran Texts* (Grand Rapids, MI: Eerdmans, 1959).

Campbell, J. G., *The Use of Scripture in the Damascus Document 1-8, 19-20* (BZAW 228; Berlin: de Gruyter, 1995).

Charlesworth, J. H., *The Pesharim and Qumran History: Chaos or Consensus?* (Grand Rapids, MI: Eerdmans, 2002).

Davila, J. R., "The Dead Sea Scrolls and Merkavah Mysticism," *The Dead Sea Scrolls in Their Historical Context* (see above), 249-64.

De Waard, J., *A Comparative Study of the Old Testament Text in the Dead Sea Scrolls and in the New Testament* (STDJ 4; Leiden: Brill, 1965).

Dimant, D., "Pesharim, Qumran," *ABD*, 5. 244-51

Elledge, C. D., "Exegetical Styles at Qumran: A Cumulative Index and Commentary," *RevQ* 21 (2003-4) 165-208.

Falk, D. K. *The Parabiblical Texts: Strategies for Extending the Scriptures among the Dead Sea Scrolls* (Companion to the Qumran Scrolls/Library of Second Temple Studies 8/63; New York: Clark, 2007).

Finkel, A., "The Pesher of Dreams and Scriptures," *RevQ* 4 (1963-64) 357-70.

Fishbane, M., "Use, Authority and Interpretation of Mikra at Qumran," *Mikra: Text, Translation, Reading, and Interpretation of the Hebrew Bible in Ancient Judaism and Early Christianity* (CRINT 2/1; ed. M. J. Mulder; Assen: Van Gorcum; Minneapolis, MN: Fortress, 1988) 339-77.

Fitzmyer, J. A., "The Use of Explicit Old Testament Quotations in Qumran Literature and in the New Testament," *NTS* 7 (1960-61) 297-333; revised form, *ESBNT* or *SBNT*, 3-58.

Friebel, K. G., "Biblical Interpretation in the Pesharim of the Qumran Community," *Hebrew Studies* 22 (1981) 13-24.

Fröhlich, I., "'Narrative Exegesis' in the Dead Sea Scrolls," *Biblical Perspectives: Early Use and Interpretation of the Bible in Light of the Dead Sea Scrolls . . .* (STDJ 28; ed. M. Stone and E. G. Chazon; Leiden: Brill, 1998) 81-99.

García Martínez, F., "Apocryphal, Pesudepigraphal, and Para-Biblical Texts from Qumran," *RevQ* 83 (2004) 365-78.

———, "Interpretación de la Biblia en Qumrán," *Fortunatae* (Canary Islands) 9 (1997) 261-86.

———, "El Pesher: Interpretación profética de la Escritura," *Salmanticensis* 26 (1979) 125-39.

Gottstein, M. H., "Bible Quotations in the Sectarian Dead Sea Scrolls," *VT* 3 (1953) 79-82.

Harris, J. G., "Early Trends in Biblical Commentaries as Reflected in Some Qumran Texts," *EvQ* 32 (1964) 100-105.

Henze, M. (ed.), *Biblical Interpretation at Qumran* (SDSSRL; Grand Rapids, MI: Eerdmans, 2005).

Horgan, M. P., *Pesharim: Qumran Interpretations of Biblical Books* (CBQMS 8; Washington, DC: Catholic Biblical Association of America, 1979).

Instone Brewer, D., *Techniques and Assumptions in Jewish Exegesis before 70 CE* (TSAJ 30; Tübingen: Mohr [Siebeck], 1992) 187-98.

Lim, T. H., *Pesharim* (Companion to the Qumran Scrolls 3; Sheffield, UK: Sheffield Academic, 2002).

Maier, J., "Early Jewish Biblical Interpretation in the Qumran Literature," *Hebrew*

Bible/Old Testament: The History of Its Interpretation, I.1, From the Beginning to the Middle Ages (until 1300): Antiquity (ed. M. Saebø; Göttingen: Vandenhoeck & Ruprecht, 1996) 108-29.

Nickelsburg, G. W. E., "The Bible Rewritten and Expanded," *Jewish Writings of the Second Temple Period: Apocrypha, Pseudepigrapha, Qumran Sectarian Writings, Philo, Josephus* (CRINT 2/II; ed. M. E. Stone; Assen: Van Gorcum; Philadelphia: Fortress, 1984) 89-156.

Osswald, F., "Zur Hermeneutik des Habakuk-Kommentar," *ZAW* 68 (1956) 243-56.

Patte, D., *Early Jewish Hermeneutic in Palestine* (Missoula, MT: Scholars, 1975).

Ploeg, J. van der, "Bijbelverklaring te Qumrân," *Mededelingen der koninklijke Akademie van Wetenschappen,* Afd. Letterkunde, nieuwe reeks, deel 23, No. 8 (1960) 207-29.

Roth, C., "The Subject Matter of Qumran Exegesis," *VT* 10 (1960) 51-65.

Schuller, E. M., "The Use of Biblical Terms as Designations for Non-Biblical Hymnic and Prayer Compositions," *Biblical Perspectives* (see above), 207-22.

Schwarz, O. J. R., *Der erste Teil der Damaskusschrift und das Alte Testament* (Diest: Lichtland, 1965).

Segal, M., "Between Bible and Rewritten Bible," *Biblical Interpretation at Qumran* (see above), 10-28.

Slomovic, E., "Toward an Understanding of the Exegesis in the Dead Sea Scrolls," *RevQ* 7 (1969-71) 3-15.

Swanson, D. D., "How Scriptural Is Re-Written Bible?" *RevQ* 83 (2004) 407-28.

Talmon, S., "DSI[a] as a Witness to Ancient Exegesis of the Book of Isaiah," *ASTI* 1 (1962) 62-72.

Trever, J. C., "The Qumran Covenanters and Their Use of Scripture," *Personalist* 39 (1958) 127-38.

Vermes, G., "A propos des commentaires bibliques découverts à Qumrân," *RHPR* 33 (1955) 95-102.

———, "Bible Interpretation at Qumran," *Yigael Yadin Volume* (ErIsr 20; Jerusalem: Israel Exploration Society, 1989) 184*-91*.

———, "The Qumran Interpretation of Scripture in Its Historical Setting," *ALUOS* 6 (1966-68) 85-97.

———, *Scripture and Tradition in Judaism: Haggadic Studies* (SPB 4; Leiden: Brill, 1961).

Wernberg-Møller, P., "Some Reflections on the Biblical Material in the Manual of Discipline," *ST* 9 (1955) 40-66.

White Crawford, S., *Rewriting Scripture in Second Temple Times* (SDSSRL; Grand Rapids, MI: Eerdmans, 2008).

Wieder, N., "The Dead Sea Scrolls Type of Biblical Exegesis among the Karaites," *Between East and West* (1958) 75-106.

Willitts, J., "The Remnant of Israel in 4QpIsaiah[a] (4Q161) and the Dead Sea Scrolls," *JJS* 57 (2006) 11-25.

5. Qumran Theology

For the almost numberless articles on various aspects of Qumran theology or religion, consult the topical bibliographies of W. S. LaSor and B. Jongeling, and the yearly bibliography of P. Nober, R. North, or R. Althann (noted in section III above); as well as *NTA* (ed. D. J. Harrington; Cambridge, MA: Weston Jesuit School of Theology [3 times a year]) and *OTA* (ed. C. T. Begg; Washington, DC: Catholic Biblical Association of America [3 times a year]). Listed below are merely the more important books on the general topic.

N.B. Fabry, H.-J., "Theologisches Wörterbuch zu den Qumranschriften," *ZAH* 9 (1996) 48-51. This article announces the plan to construct a Theological Dictionary on Qumran writings comparable to *TDNT* and *TDOT.*

Altmann, A. (ed.), *Biblical Motifs: Origins and Transformations* (Philip W. Lown Institute for Advanced Judaic Studies, Brandeis University, Texts and Studies 3; Cambridge, MA: Harvard University Press, 1966).

Betz, O., *Offenbarung und Schriftforschung in der Qumransekte* (WUNT 6; Tübingen: Mohr [Siebeck], 1960).

———, *Der Paraklet: Fürsprecher im häretischen Spätjudentum, im Johannesevangelium und in neu gefundenen gnostischen Schriften* (Leiden: Brill, 1963).

Collins, J. J. and R. A. Kugler (eds.), *Religion in the Dead Sea Scrolls* (SDSSRL; Grand Rapids, MI: Eerdmans, 2000).

Deasley, A. R. G., *The Shape of Qumran Theology* (Carlisle, Cumbria, UK: Paternoster, 2000).

Denis, A.-M., *Les thèmes de connaissance dans le Document de Damas* (Studia hellenistica 15; Louvain: Publications universitaires, 1967).

Elliott, M. A., *The Survivors of Israel: A Reconsideration of the Theology of Pre-Christian Judaism* (Grand Rapids, MI: Eerdmans, 2000).

Garnet, P., *Salvation and Atonement in the Qumran Scrolls* (WUNT 2/3; Tübingen: Mohr [Siebeck], 1977).

Harrington, H., *The Impurity Systems of Qumran and the Rabbis* (SBLDS 143; Atlanta, GA: Society of Biblical Literature, 1993).

Huppenbauer, H. W., *Der Mensch zwischen zwei Welten: Der Dualismus der Texte von Qumran (Höhle I) und der Damaskusfragmente: Ein Beitrag zur Vorgeschichte des Evangeliums* (Zurich: Zwingli, 1959).

Jeremias, J., *Die theologische Bedeutung der Funde am Toten Meer* (Göttingen: Vandenhoeck & Ruprecht, 1962) (translated as "Qumrân et la théologie," *NRT* 85 [1963] 674-90).

Klinzing, G., *Die Umdeutung des Kultus in der Qumrangemeinde und im Neuen Testament* (SUNT 7; Göttingen: Vandenhoeck & Ruprecht, 1971).

Kobelski, P. J., *Melchizedek and Melchireša'* (CBQMS 10; Washington, DC: Catholic Biblical Association of America, 1981).

Kuhn, H.-W., *Enderwartung und gegenwärtiges Heil: Untersuchungen zu den Gemeindeliedern von Qumran, mit einem Anhang über Eschatologie und Gegenwart in der Verkündigung Jesu* (SUNT 4; Göttingen: Vandenhoeck & Ruprecht, 1966).

Lichtenberger, H., *Studien zum Menschenbild in Texten der Qumrangemeinde* (SUNT 15; Göttingen: Vandenhoeck & Ruprecht, 1980).

Mach, M., *Entwicklungsstadien des jüdischen Engelglaubens in vorrabbinischer Zeit* (TSAJ 34; Tübingen: Mohr [Siebeck], 1992).

Merrill, F. H., *Qumran and Predestination: A Theological Study of the Thanksgiving Hymns* (STDJ 8; Leiden: Brill, 1975).

Newton, M., *The Concept of Purity at Qumran and in the Letters of Paul* (SNTSMS 53; Cambridge, UK: Cambridge University Press, 1985).

Nickelsburg, G. W. E., *Resurrection, Immortality and Eternal Life in Intertestamental Judaism* (Cambridge, MA: Harvard University Press; London: Oxford University Press, 1972).

Nötscher, F., *Gotteswege und Menschenwege in der Bibel und in Qumran* (BBB 15; Bonn: Hanstein, 1958).

———, *Zur theologischen Terminologie der Qumran-Texte* (BBB 10; Bonn: Hanstein, 1956).

Osten-Sacken, P. von der, *Gott und Belial: Traditionsgeschichtliche Untersuchungen zum Dualismus in den Texten aus Qumran* (SUNT 6; Göttingen: Vandenhoeck & Ruprecht, 1969).

Puech, E., *La croyance des Esséniens en la vie future: Immortalité, résurrection, vie éternelle? Histoire d'une croyance dans le judaïsme ancien* (EBib 22; 2 vols.; Paris: Gabalda, 1993).

Ringgren, H., *The Faith of Qumran: Theology of the Dead Sea Scrolls* (tr. E. T. Sander; Philadelphia: Fortress, 1963; expanded edition [ed. J. H. Charlesworth], New York: Crossroad, 1995).

Rowley, H. H., *Jewish Apocalyptic and the Dead Sea Scrolls* (London: University of London Athlone Press, 1957).

Schiffman, L. H., *The Halakhah at Qumran* (SJLA 16; Leiden: Brill, 1975).

Schubert, K., *Die Gemeinde vom Toten Meer: Ihre Entstehung und ihre Lehren* (Munich/Basel: E. Reinhardt, 1958).

Sekki, A. E., *The Meaning of Ruaḥ at Qumran* (SBLDS 110; Atlanta, GA: Scholars, 1989).

Strobel, A., *Untersuchungen zum eschatologischen Verzögerungsproblem auf Grund der spätjüdisch-urchristlichen Geschichte von Habakuk 2:2ff.* (NovTSup 2; Leiden: Brill, 1961).

Stuckenbruck, L. T., *Angel Veneration and Christology: A Study in Early Judaism and in the Christology of the Apocalypse of John* (Tübingen: Mohr [Siebeck], 1995).

Widengren, G. et al. (eds.), *Apocalyptique iranienne et dualisme qoumrânien* (Recherches intertestamentaires 2; Paris: A. Maisonneuve, 1995).

6. Qumran Messianism

Abegg Jr., M. G., "The Messiah at Qumran: Are We Still Seeing Double?" *DSD* 2 (1995) 125-44.

———, "Messianic Hope and 4Q285: A Reassessment," *JBL* 113 (1994) 81-91.

——— et al., "Bibliography of Messianism and the Dead Sea Scrolls," *Qumran-Messianism: Studies on the Messianic Expectations in the Dead Sea Scrolls* (ed. J. H. Charlesworth et al.; Tübingen: Mohr Siebeck, 1998) 204-14.

——— and C. A. Evans, "Messianic Passages in the Dead Sea Scrolls," ibid., 191-203.

Ådna, J., "The Servant of Isaiah 53 as Triumphant and Interceding Messiah: The Reception of Isaiah 52:13–53:12 in the Targum of Isaiah with Special Attention to the Concept of the Messiah," *The Suffering Servant: Isaiah 53 in Jewish and Christian Sources* (ed. B. Janowski and P. Stuhlmacher; Grand Rapids, MI: Eerdmans, 2004) 189-224.

Allegro, J. M., "Further Messianic References in Qumran Literature," *JBL* 75 (1956) 174-87.

Atkinson, K., "On the Herodian Origin of Militant Davidic Messianism at Qumran: New Light from *Psalm of Solomon* 17," *JBL* 118 (1999) 435-60.

Aune, D. E., "A Note on Jesus' Messianic Consciousness and 11HQ [sic] Melchizedek," *EvQ* 45 (1973) 161-65.

Bauckham, R., "The Messianic Interpretation of Isa. 10:34 in the Dead Sea Scrolls, 2 Baruch and the Preaching of John the Baptist," *DSD* 2 (1995) 202-16.

Beasley-Murray, G. R., "The Two Messiahs in the Testaments of the Twelve Patriarchs," *JTS* 48 (1947) 1-12.

Becker, M., "*4Q521* und die Gesalbten," *RevQ* 18 (1997-98) 73-96.

Beckwith, R. T., "Daniel 9 and the Date of Messiah's Coming in Essene, Hellenistic, Pharisaic, Zealot and Early Christian Computation," *RevQ* 10 (1979-81) 521-42.

Black, M., "The Messiah in the Testament of Levi xviii," *ExpTim* 60 (1948-49) 321-22; 61 (1949-50) 157-58.

———, "Messianic Doctrine in the Qumran Scrolls," *Studia patristica I* (= TU 63; ed. K. Aland and F. L. Cross; Berlin: Akademie-V., 1957), 1. 441-59.

Blidstein, G. J., "A Rabbinic Reaction to the Messianic Doctrine of the Scrolls," *JBL* 90 (1971) 330-32.

Bockmuehl, M., "A 'Slain Messiah' in 4Q Serekh Milḥamah (4Q285)?" *TynBul* 43 (1992) 155-69.

Brooke, G. J., "The Amos-Numbers Midrash (CD 7,13b–8,1a) and Messianic Expectation," *ZAW* 92 (1980) 397-404.

———, "The Messiah of Aaron in the *Damascus Document*," *RevQ* 15 (1991-92) 215-30.

Brown, R. E., "J. Starcky's Theory of Qumran Messianic Development," *CBQ* 28 (1966) 51-57.

———, "The Messianism of Qumran" *CBQ* 19 (1957) 53-82.

———, "The Teacher of Righteousness and the Messiah(s)," *The Scrolls and Christianity* (SPCK Theological Collections 11; ed. M. Black; London: SPCK, 1969) 37-44, 109-12.

Brownlee, W. H., "Messianic Motifs of Qumran and the New Testament," *NTS* 3 (1956-57) 12-30, 195-210.

Burrows, M., "The Messiahs of Aaron and Israel," *ATR* 34 (1952) 202-6.

Caquot, A., "Ben Sira et le messianisme," *Sem* 16 (1966) 43-68.

———, "Le messianisme qumrânien," *Qumrân: Sa piété, sa théologie et son milieu* (BETL 46; ed. M. Delcor; Gembloux: Duculot; Louvain: Leuven University Press, 1978) 231-47.

Charlesworth, J. H., "Challenging the *Consensus Communis* Regarding Qumran Messianism (1QS, 4QS mss)," *Qumran-Messianism* (see above), 120-34.

——— et al. (eds.), *The Messiah: Developments in Earliest Judaism and Christianity* (Minneapolis, MN: Fortress, 1992).

Collins, J. J., "'He Shall not Judge by What His Eyes See': Messianic Authority in the Dead Sea Scrolls," *DSD* 2 (1995) 145-64.

———, "Messiahs in Context: Method in the Study of Messianism in the Dead Sea Scrolls," *Methods of Investigation of the Dead Sea Scrolls and the Khirbet Qumran Site: Present Realities and Future Prospects* (Annals of the New York Academy of Sciences 722; ed. M. O. Wise et al.; New York: New York Academy of Sciences, 1994) 213-29.

———, *The Scepter and the Star: The Messiahs of the Dead Sea Scrolls and Other Ancient Literature* (ABRL; New York: Doubleday, 1995).

———, "Teacher and Messiah? The One Who Will Teach Righteousness at the End of Days," *The Community of the Renewed Covenant: The Notre Dame Symposium on the Dead Sea Scrolls* (Christianity and Judaism in Antiquity 10; ed. E. Ulrich and J. C. VanderKam; Notre Dame, IN: University of Notre Dame Press, 1994) 193-210.

———, "The Works of the Messiah," *DSD* 1 (1994) 98-112.

Croatto, J. S., "De messianismo qumranico," *VDom* 35 (1957) 279-86, 344-60.

Cross, F. M., "Notes on the Doctrine of the Two Messiahs at Qumran and the Extracanonical *Daniel Apocalypse (4Q246)*," *Current Research and Technological Developments on the Dead Sea Scrolls: Conference on the Texts from the Judean Desert, Jerusalem, 30 April 1995* (STDJ 20; ed. D. W. Parry and S. D. Ricks; Leiden: Brill, 1996) 1-13.

Deichgräber, R., "Zur Messiaserwartung der Damaskusschrift," *ZAW* 78 (1966) 333-43.

Delcor, M., "Un psaume messianique de Qumran," *Mélanges bibliques rédigés en l'honneur de André Robert* (Paris: Bloud et Gay, 1957) 334-40.

———, "Un psaume messianique de Qumran: Traduction et commentaire," *Environnement et tradition de l'Ancien Testament* (AOAT 228; Neukirchen-Vluyn: Neukirchener-V., 1990) 380-86.

Donaldson, T. L., "Levitical Messianology in Late Judaism: Origins, Development and Decline," *JETS* 24 (1981) 193-207.

Dunn, J. D. G., "'Son of God' as 'Son of Man' in the Dead Sea Scrolls? A Response to John Collins on 4Q246," *The Scrolls and the Scriptures: Qumran Fifty Years After* (JSPSup 26; Roehampton Institute London Papers 3; ed. S. E. Porter and C. A. Evans; Sheffield, UK: Sheffield Academic, 1997) 198-210.

Ehrlich, E. L., "Ein Beitrag zur Messiaslehre der Qumransekte," *ZAW* 68 (1956) 234-43.

Eisenman, R. H. and G. Vermes, "More on the Pierced Messiah Text from Eisenman and Vermes," *BARev* 19/1 (1993) 66-67.

Elledge, C. D., "The Prince of the Congregation: Qumran 'Messianism' in the Context of *Milḥāmâ*," *Qumran Studies: New Approaches, New Questions* (ed. M. T. Davis and B. A. Strawn; Grand Rapids, MI: Eerdmans, 2007) 178-207.

Evans, C. A., "Are the 'Son' Texts at Qumran Messianic? Reflections on 4Q369 and Related Scrolls," *Qumran-Messianism* (see above), 135-53.

———, "Jesus and the Messianic Texts from Qumran: A Preliminary Assessment of the Recently Published Materials," *Jesus and His Contemporaries: Comparative Studies* (Leiden: Brill, 1995) 83-154.

———, "The Messiah in the Dead Sea Scrolls," *Israel's Messiah in the Bible and in the Dead Sea Scrolls* (ed. R. S. Hess and M. D. Carroll R.; Grand Rapids, MI: Baker Academic, 2003) 85-101.

———, "Messiahs," *EDSS*, 537-42.

———, "'The Two Sons of Oil': Early Evidence of Messianic Interpretation of Zechariah 4:14 in 4Q254 4,2," *The Provo International Conference on the Dead Sea Scrolls: Technological Innovations, New Texts, and Reformulated Issues* (STDJ 40; ed. D. W. Parry and E. Ulrich; Leiden: Brill, 1999) 566-75.

Fitzmyer, J. A., "The Aramaic 'Elect of God' Text from Qumran Cave 4," *CBQ* 27 (1965) 348-72; slightly revised in *ESBNT* or *SBNT*, 127-60.

———, "The Aramaic 'Son of God' Text from Qumran Cave 4," *Methods of Investigation* (see above), 163-78.

———, "4Q246: The 'Son of God' Document from Qumran," *Bib* 74 (1993) 153-74; repr. in a revised form in *The Dead Sea Scrolls and Christian Origins* (SDSSRL; Grand Rapids, MI: Eerdmans, 2000) 41-72.

———, *He Who Is to Come* (Grand Rapids, MI: Eerdmans, 2007).

———, "Qumran Messianism," *The Dead Sea Scrolls and Christian Origins* (see above), 73-110.

Flusser, D., "Messiah, Second Temple Period," *Encyclopaedia Judaica* (17 vols.; Jerusalem: Keter; New York: Macmillan, 1971), 11. 1408-10.

Fritsch, C. T., "The So-called 'Priestly Messiah' of the Essenes," *JEOL* 6 (1959-66) 242-48.

García Martínez, F., "Los manuscritos del Mar Muerto y el mesianismo cristiano," *Los manuscritos del Mar Muerto: Balance de hallazgos y de cuarenta años de estudio* (ed. A. Piñero and D. Fernández-Galiano; Córdoba: Almendro, 1994) 189-206.

———, "Los Mesías de Qumrán: Problemas de un traductor," *Sefarad* 53 (1993) 345-60.

———, "Messianische Erwartungen in den Qumranschriften," *JBT* 8 (1993) 171-208.

———, "Nuevos textos mesiánicos de Qumrán y el Mesías del Nuevo Testamento," *Communio* 26 (1993) 3-31.

———, "Two Messianic Figure in the Qumran Texts," *Current Research* (see above), 14-40.

Giblet, J., "Prophétisme et attente d'un messie prophète dans l'ancien Judaïsme," *L'Attente du Messie* (RechBib 1; ed. B. Rigaux; Bruges: Desclée de Brouwer, 1958) 85-130.

Ginsberg, H. L., "Messiah," *Encyclopaedia Judaica* (see above), 11. 1407.

Gnilka, J., "Bräutigam spätjüdisches Messiasprädikat?" *TTZ* 69 (1960) 298-301.

———, "Die Erwartung des messianischen Hohenpriesters in den Schriften von Qumran und im Neuen Testament," *RevQ* 2 (1959-60) 395-426.

Gordis, R., "The 'Begotten' Messiah in the Qumran Scrolls," *VT* 7 (1957) 191-94.

Greig, J. C. G., "Gospel Messianism and the Qumran Use of Prophecy," *SE I* (= TU 73; Berlin: Akademie-V., 1959) 593-99.

Grelot, P., "Le messie dans les apocryphes de l'Ancien Testament: État de la question," *La venue du Messie: Messianisme et eschatologie* (RechBib 6; ed. E. Massaux; Bruges: Desclée de Brouwer, 1962) 19-50.

Grundmann, W., "Die Frage nach der Gottessohnschaft des Messias im Lichte von Qumran," *Bibel und Qumran: Beiträge zur Erforschung der Beziehungen zwischen Bibel- und Qumranwissenschaft: Hans Bardtke zum 22. 8. 1966* (Berlin: Evangelische Haupt-Bibelgesellschaft, 1968) 86-111.

——— et al., "χρίω, Χριστός . . . ," *TDNT* 9 (1974) 493-580, esp. 509-20.

Héring, J., "Encore le messianisme dans les écrits de Qoumran," *RHPR* 41 (1961) 160-62.

Hess, R. S., "Messiahs Here and There: A Response to Craig A. Evans," *Israel's Messiah* (see above), 103-8.

Higgins, A. J. B., "Jewish Messianic Belief in Justin Martyr's *Dialogue with Trypho*," *NovT* 9 (1967) 298-305.

———, "Priest and Messiah," *VT* 3 (1953) 321-36.

———, "The Priestly Messiah," *NTS* 13 (1966-67) 211-39.

Horbury, W., *Messianism among Jews and Christians: Twelve Biblical and Historical Studies* (London/New York: Clark, 2003).

Horsley, R. A. and J. S. Hanson, *Bandits, Prophets and Messiahs: Popular Movements in the time of Jesus* (Minneapolis, MN: Winston Press, 1985; repr. San Francisco, CA: Harper & Row, 1988).

Hurst, L. D., "Did Qumran Expect Two Messiahs?" *BBR* 9 (1999) 157-80.

Jonge, M. de, "Jewish Expectations about the 'Messiah' according to the Fourth Gospel," *NTS* 19 (1972-73) 246-70.

———, "Messiah," *ABD*, 4. 777-88.

———, "Two Messiahs in the Testaments of the Twelve Patriarchs?" *Tradition and Reinterpretation in Jewish and Early Christian Literature: Essays in Honour of Jürgen C. H. Lebram* (ed. J. W. van Henten et al.; Leiden: Brill, 1986) 150-62.

———, "The Use of the Word 'Anointed' in the Time of Jesus," *NovT* 8 (1966) 132-48.

Knibb, M. A., "Messianism in the Pseudepigrapha in the Light of the Scrolls," *DSD* 2 (1995) 165-84.

———, "The Teacher of Righteousness — a Messianic Title?" *A Tribute to Geza Vermes: Essays on Jewish and Christian Literature and History* (JSOTSup

100; ed. P. R. Davies and R. T. White; Sheffield, UK: Sheffield Academic, 1990) 51-65.

Kuhn, K. G., "Die beiden Messias Aarons und Israels," *NTS* 1 (1954-55) 168-79; adapted translation in Stendahl, *The Scrolls and the New Testament* (see section X, 12), 54-64.

———, "Die beiden Messias in den Qumrantexten und die Messiasvorstellung in der rabbinischen Literatur," *ZAW* 70 (1958) 200-208.

Laperrousaz, E.-M., *L'Attente du Messie en Palestine à la veille et au début de l'ère chrétienne* (Collection Empreinte; Paris: Picard, 1982).

LaSor, W. S., "'The Messiahs of Aaron and Israel,'" *VT* 6 (1956) 425-29.

———, "The Messianic Idea in Qumran," *Studies and Essays in Honor of Abraham A. Neuman* (ed. M. Ben-Horin et al.; Leiden: Brill, 1962) 343-64.

Laurin, R. B., "The Problem of Two Messiahs in the Qumran Scrolls," *RevQ* 4 (1963-64) 39-52.

Levey, S. H., *The Messiah: An Aramaic Interpretation: The Messianic Interpretation of the Targum* (MHUC 2; Cincinnati, OH: Hebrew Union College, 1974).

Lichtenberger, H., "Messianische Erwartungen und messianische Gestalten in der Zeit der Zweiten Tempels," *Messiasvorstellungen bei Juden und Christen* (ed. E. Stegemann; Stuttgart: Kohlhammer, 1993) 9-20.

———, "Qumran — Messianism," *Emanuel: Studies in Hebrew Bible, Septuagint, and Dead Sea Scrolls in Honor of Emanuel Tov* (VTSup 94/1-2; ed. S. M. Paul et al.; Leiden: Brill, 2003) 323-33.

Liver, J., "The Doctrine of the Two Messiahs in the Sectarian Literature in the Time of the Second Commonwealth," *HTR* 52 (1959) 149-85.

Loader, B., "The New Dead Sea Scrolls: New Light on Messianism and the History of the Community," *Colloquium* 25 (1993) 67-85.

Lohse, E., "Der König aus Davids Geschlecht: Bemerkungen zur messianischen Erwartung der Synagoge," *Abraham unser Vater: Juden und Christen im Gespräch über die Bibel: Festschrift für Otto Michel . . .* (AGJU 5; ed. O. Betz et al.; Leiden: Brill, 1963) 337-45.

Martone, C., "Un testo qumranico che narra la morte del Messia? A proposito del recente dibattito su 4Q285," *RivB* 42 (1994) 329-36.

Oegema, G. S., "Tradition-Historical Studies on 4Q252," *Qumran-Messianism* (see above), 154-74.

Pearson, B. W. R., "Dry Bones in the Judean Desert: The Messiah of Ephraim, Ezekiel 37, and the Post-Revolutionary Followers of Bar Kokhba," *JSJ* 29 (1998) 192-201.

Priest, J. F., "Mebaqqer, Paqid, and the Messiah," *JBL* 81 (1962) 55-61.

———, "The Messiah and the Meal in 1QSa," *JBL* 82 (1963) 95-100.

Prigent, P., "Quelques testimonia messianiques: Leur histoire littéraire de Qoumran aux Pères de l'Église," *TZ* 15 (1959) 419-30.

Puech, E., "Une apocalypse messianique (4Q521)," *RevQ* 15 (1991-92) 475-522.

———, "Messianic Apocalypse," *EDSS,* 543-44.

———, "Messianism, Resurrection, and Eschatology at Qumran and in the New Testament," *The Community of the Renewed Covenant* (see above), 235-56.

———, "Préséance sacerdotale et Messie-Roi dans la Règle de la Congrégation (*1QSa* ii 11-22)," *RevQ* 16 (1993-95) 351-65.

———, "Some Remarks on 4Q246 and 4Q521 and Qumran Messianism," *The Provo International Conference* (see above), 545-65.

Rainbow, P., "Melchizedek as a Messiah at Qumran," *BBR* 7 (1997) 179-94.

Rivkin, F., "The Meaning of Messiah in Jewish Thought," *USQR* 26 (1971) 383-406.

Sabugal, S., "1 Q Regla de la comunidad ix, 11: Dos ungidos, un Mesias," *RevQ* 8 (1972-75) 417-23.

Sacchi, P., "Esquisse du Développement du Messianisme Juif à la lumière du Texte Qumranien 11 Q Melch," *ZAW* 100 (1988) Supplement, 202-14.

Schiffman, L. H., "The Concept of the Messiah in Second Temple and Rabbinic Literature," *RevExp* 84 (1987) 235-46.

———, "Messianic Figures and Ideas in the Qumran Scrolls," *The Messiah: Developments* (see above), 116-29.

Schreiber, S., "König JHWH und königlicher Gesalbter: Das Repräsentanzverhältnis in 4Q174," *SNTSU* 26 (2001) 205-19.

Schubert, K., "Der alttestamentliche Hintergrund der Vorstellung von den beiden Messiassen im Schrifttum von Chirbet Qumran," *Judaica* 12 (1956) 24-28.

———, "Die Messiaslehre in den Testamenten der 12 Patriarchen im Lichte der Texte von Chirbet Qumran," *Akten des 24. internationalen Orientalisten-Kongresses München 28. August bis 4. September 1957* (Wiesbaden: F. Steiner, 1959) 197-98.

———, "Die Messiaslehre in den Texten von Chirbet Qumran," *BZ* 1 (1957) 177-97.

———, "Zwei Messiasse aus dem Regelbuch von Chirbet Qumran," *Judaica* 11 (1955) 216-35.

Segert, S., "Der Messias nach neueren Auffassungen," *Communio viatorum* 2 (1959) 343-53.

Sen, F., "Los Mesías de Qumrán: Textos mesiánicos," *Cultura Bíblica* 29 (1972) 158-67.

Sigal, P., "Further Reflections on the 'Begotten' Messiah," *HAR* 7 (1983) 221-33.

Silberman, L. H., "The Two 'Messiahs' of the Manual of Discipline," *VT* 5 (1955) 77-82.

Smith, M., "'God's Begetting the Messiah' in 1QSa," *NTS* 5 (1958-59) 218-24.

———, "What Is Implied by the Variety of Messianic Figures?" *JBL* 78 (1959) 66-72.

Smyth, K., "The Dead Sea Scrolls and the Messiah," *Studies* 45 (1956) 1-14.

Starcky, J., "Les quatre étapes du messianisme à Qumran," *RB* 70 (1963) 481-505.

Stefaniak, L., "Messianische oder eschatologische Erwartungen in der Qumransekte?" *Neutestamentliche Aufsätze: Festschrift J. Schmid* (Regensburg: Pustet, 1962) 294-302.

Stuckenbruck, L. T., "'Messias' Texte in den Schriften von Qumran," *Mogilany 1993: Papers on the Dead Sea Scrolls Offered in Memory of Hans Burgmann* (Qumranica mogilanensia 13; ed. Z. J. Kapera; Cracow: Enigma, 1996) 129-39.

Tabor, J. D., "A Pierced or Piercing Messiah? The Verdict Is Still Out," *BARev* 18/6 (1992) 58-59.

Talmon, S., "Typen der Messiaserwartung um die Zeitenwende," *Probleme biblischer Theologie, Gerhard von Rad . . .* (ed. H. W. Wolff; Munich: Kaiser, 1971) 571-88.

VanderKam, J. C., "Messianism in the Scrolls," *The Community of the Renewed Covenant* (see above), 211-34.

Vermes, G., "The Oxford Forum for Qumran Research: Seminar on the Rule of War from Cave 4 (4Q285)," *JJS* 43 (1992) 85-90.

Villalón, J. R., "Sources vétéro-testamentaires de la doctrine des deux Messies," *RevQ* 8 (1972-75) 53-63.

Weymann, E., *Zepter und Stern: Die Erwartung von zwei Messiasgestalten in den Schriftrollen von Qumran* (Stuttgart: Urachhaus, 1993).

Winter, P., "The Holy Messiah," *ZNW* 50 (1959) 275.

Wise, M. O. and J. D. Tabor, "The Messiah at Qumran," *BARev* 18/6 (1992) 60-63, 65.

Woude, A. S. van der, *Die messianischen Vorstellungen der Gemeinde von Qumran* (Studia semitica neerlandica 3; Assen: Van Gorcum, 1957).

———, "Le Maître de Justice et les deux messies de la communauté de Qumran," *La secte de Qumrân et les origines chrétiennes* (RechBib 4; Bruges: Desclée de Brouwer, 1959) 121-34.

Wurz, H., "Die Messiashoffnung in der Zeit zwischen Altem und Neuem Testament," *BL* 53 (1980) 140-46.

Xeravits, G., "Précisions sur le texte original et le concept messianique de *CD* 7:13–8:1 et 19:5-14," *RevQ* 19 (1999-2000) 47-59.

Zimmermann, J., *Messianische Texte aus Qumran* (WUNT 2/104; Tübingen: Mohr Siebeck, 1998).

———, "Observations on 4Q246 — The 'Son of God,'" *Qumran-Messianism* (see above), 175-90.

7. The Qumran Calendar

The Qumran Calendar

Instead of the luni-solar calendar of 354 days, apparently used officially in the Jerusalem Temple, the Essenes of Qumran employed an older solar calendar of 364 days (see 11QPs[a] DavComp 27:6, "songs to sing . . . for all the days of the year, 364"); cf. *Jub.* 6:38. For the importance of the calendar, see 1QS 1:14-15; 10:3-8; 1QH[a] 9(old 1):15-20; CD 6:18-19; 3:13-15; 16:1-5; 1QpHab 11:4-8 [the last-mentioned text indicates a different calendar being used by the Qumran community from that used by the Wicked Priest of Jerusalem who persecuted it]. See especially the various calendrical texts in 4Q317-4Q330, 4Q335-4Q337, 4Q394, 6Q17. Cf. S. Talmon, "Calendars and Mishmarot," *EDSS,* 108-16.

In such a calendar the year is divided into four groups of 91 days or three months, each of which has 30, 30, and 31 days. The week has seven days, with the Sabbath as the middle day. Hence a feast day will fall on the same day of the week every year. The problem is: How did the Essenes make up for the extra year and a quarter? Did they have a method of intercalation?

Day of the Week	I	IV	VII	X		II	V	VIII	XI			III	VI	IX	XII
4 (Wed.)	1	8	15	22	29		6	13	20	27		4	11	18	25
5 (Thur.)	2	9	16	23	30		7	14	21	28		5	12	19	26
6 (Fri.)	3	10	17	24		1	8	15	22	29		6	13	20	27
7 (Sabb.)	4	11	18	25		2	9	16	23	30		7	14	21	28
1 (Sun.)	5	12	19	26		3	10	17	24		1	8	15	22	29
2 (Mon.)	6	13	20	27		4	11	18	25		2	9	16	23	30
3 (Tues.)	7	14	21	28		5	12	19	26		3	10	17	24	31
	(30 days)					(30 days)					(31 days)				

(Column group header: *Months*)

Basic Discussions

Barthélemy, D., "Notes en marge de publications récentes sur les manuscrits de Qumrân," *RB* 59 (1952) 187-218, esp. 200-202.

Baumgarten, J. M., "The Calendar," *Studies in Qumran Law* (Leiden: Brill, 1977) 101-44.

Jaubert, A., "Le calendrier des Jubilés et de la secte de Qumrân: Ses origines bibliques," *VT* 3 (1953) 250-64.

Milik, J. T., "Le travail d'édition des manuscrits du Désert de Juda," *Volume du Congrès, Strasbourg, 1956* (VTSup 4; Leiden: Brill, 1957) 17-26, esp. 24-25.

Talmon, S., "The Calendar of the Covenanters of the Judean Desert," *The World of Qumran from Within: Collected Studies* (Jerusalem: Magnes Press, Hebrew University; Leiden: Brill, 1989) 147-85.

———, "The Calendar Reckoning of the Sect from the Judaean Desert," *Aspects of the Dead Sea Scrolls* (Scripta hierosolymitana 4; Jerusalem: Magnes, 1958) 162-99.

Further Discussions

Baumgarten, J. M., "The Beginning of the Day in the Calendar of Jubilees," *JBL* 77 (1958) 355-60.

———, "The Calendars of the Book of Jubilees and the Temple Scroll," *VT* 37 (1987) 71-78.

———, "The Counting of the Sabbath in Ancient Sources," *VT* 16 (1966) 277-86.

———, "4 Q 503 (Daily Prayers) and the Lunar Calendar," *RevQ* 12 (1985-87) 399-407.

———, "4Q Halakah[a] 5, the Law of *Ḥadash,* and the Pentecontad Calendar," *JJS* 27 (1976) 36-46; repr. in *Studies in Qumran Law* (SJLA 24; Leiden: Brill, 1977) 131-42.

———, "Some Problems of the Jubilees Calendar in Current Research," *VT* 32 (1982) 485-89.

Beckwith, R. T., "The Earliest Enoch Literature and Its Calendar: Marks of Their Origin, Date and Motivation," *RevQ* 10 (1979-81) 365-403.

———, "The Modern Attempt to Reconcile the Qumran Calendar with the True Solar Year," *RevQ* 7 (1969-71) 379-96.

———, "The Qumran Calendar and the Sacrifices of the Essenes," *RevQ* 7 (1969-71) 587-91.

———, "St. Luke, the Date of Christmas and the Priestly Courses at Qumran," *RevQ* 9 (1977-78) 73-94.

———, "The Significance of the Calendar for Interpreting Essene Chronology and Eschatology," *RevQ* 10 (1979-81) 167-202.

Burgmann, H., "Die Interkalation in den sieben Jahrwochen des Sonnenkalenders," *RevQ* 10 (1979-81) 67-81.

———, "Ein Schaltmonat nach 24,5 Jahren im chasidischen Sonnenkalender?" *RevQ* 8 (1972-75) 65-73.

Callaway, P. R., "The 364-Day Calendar Traditions at Qumran," *Mogilany 1989:*

Papers on the Dead Sea Scrolls Offered in Memory of Jean Carmignac: Part 1 . . . (ed. Z. J. Kapera; Cracow: Enigma, 1993) 19-28.

Carmignac, J., "Les apparitions de Jésus ressuscité et le calendrier biblico-qumranien," *RevQ* 7 (1969-71) 483-504.

Chyutin, M., "The Redaction of the Qumranic and the Traditional Book of Psalms as a Calendar," *RevQ* 16 (1993-95) 367-95.

Cryer, F. H., "The 360-Day Calendar Year and Early Judaic Sectarianism," *SJOT* 1 (1987) 116-22.

Davies, P. R., "Calendrical Change and Qumran Origins: An Assessment of VanderKam's Theory," *CBQ* 45 (1983) 80-89.

Ettisch, E. E., "Die Gemeinderegel und der Qumrankalender," *RevQ* 3 (1961-62) 125-33.

Jaubert, A., "Le calendrier des Jubilés et les jours liturgiques de la semaine," *VT* 7 (1957) 35-61.

———, "Fiches de calendrier," *Qumrân: Sa piété, sa théologie et son milieu* (BETL 46; ed. M. Delcor; Paris/Gembloux: Duculot; Louvain: Leuven University Press, 1978) 305-11.

Kimbrough, S. T., "The Concept of Sabbath at Qumran," *RevQ* 5 (1964-66) 483-502.

Kutsch, E., "Der Kalender des Jubiläenbuches und das Alte and das Neue Testament," *VT* 11 (1961) 39-47.

Leach, E. R., "A Possible Method of Intercalation for the Calendar of the Book of Jubilees," *VT* 7 (1957) 392-97.

Maier, J., "Shîrê ʿÔlat hash-Shabbat: Some Observations on Their Calendaric Implication and on Their Style," *The Madrid Qumran Congress: Proceedings of the International Congress on the Dead Sea Scrolls, Madrid 18-21 March, 1991* (STDJ 11/1-2; ed. J. Trebolle-Barrera and L. Vegas Montaner; Leiden: Brill; Madrid: Editorial Complutense, 1992) 543-60.

Martone, C., "Un Calendario proveniente da Qumran recentemente pubblicato," *Henoch* 16 (1994) 49-76.

Meysing, J., "L'Énigme de la chronologie biblique et qumrânienne dans une nouvelle lumière," *RevQ* 6 (1967-69) 229-51.

Morgenstern, J., "The Calendar of the Book of Jubilees: Its Origin and Its Character," *VT* 5 (1955) 34-76.

Obermann, J., "Calendaric Elements in the Dead Sea Scrolls," *JBL* 75 (1956) 285-97.

Pelletier, A., "La nomenclature du calendrier juif à l'époque hellénistique," *RB* 82 (1975) 218-33 (+ pl. XVII).

Rook, J. T., "A Twenty-Eight-Day Month Tradition in the Book of Jubilees," *VT* 31 (1981) 83-87.

Strobel, A., "Zur Funktionsfähigkeit des essenischen Kalenders," *RevQ* 3 (1961-62) 395-412.

———, "Zur kalendarisch-chronologischen Einordnung der Qumran-Essener," *TLZ* 86 (1961) 179-84.

———, "Der 22. Tag des XI. Monats im essenischen Jahr," *RevQ* 3 (1961-62) 539-43.

VanderKam, J. C., "The Origin, Character, and Early History of the 364-Day Calendar: A Reassessment of Jaubert's Hypotheses," *CBQ* 41 (1979) 390-411.

———, "A Twenty-Eight Day Month Tradition in the Book of Jubilees?" *VT* 32 (1982) 504-6.

Wacholder, B. Z., "The Calendar of Sabbatical Cycles during the Second Temple and the Early Rabbinic Period," *HUCA* 44 (1973) 153-96.

8. Qumran Wisdom Literature

The most important lengthy sapiential text is called today 4QInstruction (olim 4QSapiential Work A), or 1Q26; 4Q415-4Q418, 4Q423 (in DJD 34). It is not, however, the kind of text that one can outline; hence its absence in section IX above. It has generated considerable discussion and secondary literature, of which the following items are the most important, even though 4QInstruction is not the only instance of Wisdom Literature in the Qumran texts.

Aitken, J. K., "Apocalyptic, Revelation and Early Jewish Wisdom Literature," *New Heaven and New Earth: Prophecy and the Millennium: Essays in Honour of Anthony Gelston* (VTSup 77; ed. P. J. Harland and C. T. R. Hayward; Leiden: Brill, 1999) 181-93.

Baumgarten, J. M., "Some Astrological and Qumranic Terms in 4QInstruction," *Tarbiz* 72 (2003) 321-28 (Hebrew).

Brooke, G. J., "Biblical Interpretation in the Wisdom Texts from Qumran," *Wisdom Texts from Qumran* (see Hempel below), 201-20.

Burns, J. E., "Practical Wisdom in 4QInstruction," *DSD* 11 (2004) 12-42.

Caquot, A., "Les textes de sagesse de Qoumran (Aperçu préliminaire)," *RHPR* 76 (1996) 1-34.

Collins, J. J., "In the Likeness of the Holy Ones: The Creation of Humankind in a Wisdom Text from Qumran," *The Provo International Conference on the Dead Sea Scrolls: Technological Innovations, New Texts, and Reformulated Issues* (STDJ 30; ed. D. W. Parry and E. Ulrich; Leiden: Brill, 1999) 609-18.

———, "The Mysteries of God: Creation and Eschatology in 4QInstruction and the Wisdom of Solomon," *Wisdom and Apocalypticism* (see García Martínez below), 287-305.

——— et al. (eds.), *Sapiential Perspectives: Wisdom Literature in Light of the Dead Sea Scrolls: Proceedings of the Sixth International Symposium of the Orion Center . . .* (STDJ 51; Leiden: Brill, 2004).

Coulot, C., "L'Image de Dieu dans les écrits de sagesse," *Wisdom and Apocalypticism* (see García Martínez below), 171-81.

Dochhorn, J., "'Sie wird dir nicht ihre Kraft geben' — Adam, Kain und der Ackerbau in 4Q423 2,3 und Apc Mos 24," *Wisdom Texts from Qumran* (see Hempel below), 351-64.

Elgvin, T., "Early Essene Eschatology: Judgment and Salvation according to *Sapiential Work A*," *Current Research and Technological Developments on the Dead Sea Scrolls: Conference on the Texts from the Judean Desert, Jerusalem, 30 April 1995* (STDJ 20; ed. D. W. Parry and S. D. Ricks; Leiden: Brill, 1996) 126-65.

———, "Priestly Sages? The Milieus of Origin of *4QMysteries* and *4QInstruction*," *Sapiential Perspectives* (see above), 67-87.

———, "The Reconstruction of Sapiential Work A," *RevQ* 16 (1993-95) 559-80.

———, "'To Master His Own Vessel': 1 Thess 4.4 in Light of New Qumran Evidence," *NTS* 43 (1997) 604-19.

———, *Wisdom and Apocalyptic in 4QInstruction* (STDJ 38; Leiden: Brill, 2001).

———, "Wisdom and Apocalypticism in the Early Second Century BCE — The Evidence of 4QInstruction," *The Dead Sea Scrolls Fifty Years after Their Discovery: Proceedings of the Jerusalem Congress, July 20-25, 1997* (ed. L. H. Schiffman et al.; Jerusalem: Israel Exploration Society and the Shrine of the Book, Israel Museum, 2000) 226-47.

———, "Wisdom in the *Yaḥad: 4 Ways of Righteousness*," *RevQ* 17 (1996-97) 205-32.

Frey, J., "Flesh and Spirit in the Palestinian Jewish Sapiential Tradition and in the Qumran Texts: An Inquiry into the Background of Pauline Usage," *Wisdom Texts from Qumran* (see Hempel below), 367-404.

———, "The Notion of 'Flesh' in 4QInstruction and the Background of Pauline Usage," *Sapiential, Liturgical and Poetical Texts from Qumran: Proceedings of the Third Meeting of the International Organization for Qumran Studies, Oslo 1998* (STDJ 35; ed. D. K. Falk et al.; Leiden: Brill, 2000) 197-226.

García Martínez, F., "Marginalia on 4QInstruction," *DSD* 13 (2006) 24-37.

——— (ed.), *Wisdom and Apocalypticism in the Dead Sea Scrolls and in the Biblical Tradition* (BETL 168; Louvain: Peeters/Leuven University Press, 2003).

Goff, M. J., "The Mystery of Creation in 4QInstruction," *DSD* 10 (2003) 163-86.

———, "Reading Wisdom at Qumran: 4QInstruction and the Hodayot," *DSD* 11 (2004) 263-88.

———, *The Worldly and Heavenly Wisdom of 4QInstruction* (STDJ 50; Leiden: Brill, 2003).

Harrington, D. J., "The *rāz nihyeh* in a Qumran Wisdom Text *(1Q26, 4Q415-418, 423),*" *RevQ* 17 (1996-97) 549-53.

———, "Two Early Jewish Approaches to Wisdom: Sirach and Qumran Sapiential Work A," *JSP* 16 (1997) 25-38; revised in *Wisdom Texts from Qumran* (see Hempel below), 263-75.

———, *Wisdom Texts from Qumran* (London/New York: Routledge, 1996).

Hempel, C., *The Wisdom Texts from Qumran and the Development of Sapiential Thought* (BETL 159; Louvain: Peeters/Leuven University Press, 2002).

——— and A. Lange, "Literature on the Wisdom Texts from Qumran," ibid., 445-86.

Jefferies, D. F., *Wisdom at Qumran: A Form-Critical Analysis of the Admonitions in 4QInstruction* (Gorgias Dissertations, Near Eastern Studies 3; Piscataway, NJ: Gorgias Press, 2002).

Kister, M., "A Qumranic Parallel to 1 Thess 4:4? Reading and Interpretation of 4Q416 2 ii 21," *DSD* 10 (2003) 365-70.

———, "Wisdom Literature and Its Relation to Other Genres: From Ben Sira to *Mysteries,*" *Sapiential Perspectives* (see above), 13-47.

Knibb, M. A., "The Book of Enoch in the Light of the Qumran Wisdom Literature," *Wisdom and Apocalypticism* (see above), 193-210.

Lange, A., "The Determination of Fate by the Oracle of the Lot in the Dead Sea Scrolls, the Hebrew Bible and Ancient Mesopotamian Literature," *Sapiential, Liturgical and Poetic Texts from Qumran* (see above), 39-48.

Morgenstern, M., "The Meaning of בית מולדים in Qumran Wisdom Texts," *JJS* 51 (2000) 141-44.

Murphy, C. M., *Wealth in the Dead Sea Scrolls and in the Qumran Community* (STDJ 40; Leiden: Brill, 2002) 163-209.

Niehr, H., "Die Weisheit des Achikar und der *musar lammebin* im Vergleich," *Wisdom Texts from Qumran* (see Hempel above), 173-86.

Perdue, L. G., "Wisdom and Apocalyptic: The Case of Qoheleth," *Wisdom and Apocalypticism* (see above), 231-58.

Puech, E., "Apports des textes apocalyptiques et sapientiels de Qumrân à l'eschatologie du judaïsme ancien," *Wisdom and Apocalypticism* (see above), 133-70.

———, "La croyance à la résurrection des justes dans un texte qumranien de sagesse: 4Q418 69 ii," *Sefer Moshe: The Moshe Weinfeld Jubilee Volume:*

Studies in the Bible and the Ancient Near East, Qumran, and Post-Biblical Judaism (ed. C. Cohen et al.; Winona Lake, IN: Eisenbrauns, 2004) 427-44.

———, *La croyance des Esséniens en la vie future: Immortalité, résurrection, vie éternelle?: Histoire d'une croyance dans le judaïsme ancien* (EBib 21; 2 vols.; Paris: Gabalda, 1993).

——— and A. Steudel, "Un nouveau fragment du manuscrit *4QInstruction (XQ7 = 4Q417* ou *418)*," *RevQ* 19 (1999-2000) 623-27.

Reymond, E. D., "The Poetry of 4Q416 2 iii 15-19," *DSD* 13 (2006) 177-93.

Rofé, A., "Revealed Wisdom: From the Bible to Qumran," *Sapiential Perspectives* (see above), 1-11.

Rudman, D., "4QInstruction & Ecclesiastes: A Comparative Study," *QC* 9 (2000) 153-63.

Schiffman, L. H., "Halakhic Elements in the Sapiential Texts from Qumran," *Sapiential Perspectives* (see above), 89-100.

Schoors, A., "The Language of the Qumran Sapiential Works," *Wisdom Texts from Qumran* (see Hempel above), 61-95.

Scott, J. M., "Korah and Qumran," *The Bible at Qumran: Text, Shape, and Interpretation* (SDSSRL; ed. P. W. Flint; Grand Rapids, MI: Eerdmans, 2001) 182-202.

Smith, J. E., "Another Look at 4Q416 2 ii.21, a Critical Parallel to First Thessalonians 4:4," *CBQ* 63 (2001) 499-504.

Strugnell, J., "More on Wives and Marriage in the Dead Sea Scrolls: (*4Q416* 2 ii 21 [Cf. *1 Thess* 4:4] and *4QMMT* §B)," *RevQ* 17 (1996-97) 537-47.

———, "The Sapiential Work 4Q415ff. and Pre-Qumranic Works from Qumran: Lexical Considerations," *Provo International Conference* (see above), 595-608.

Stuckenbruck, L. T., "4QInstruction and the Possible Influence of Early Enochic Traditions: An Evaluation," *Wisdom Texts from Qumran* (see Hempel above), 245-61.

Tigchelaar, E. J. C., "The Addressees of 4QInstruction," *Sapiential, Liturgical and Poetical Texts from Qumran* (see above), 62-75.

———, "הבא ביחד in *4QInstruction* (*4Q418* 64 + 199 +66 par *4Q417* 1 i 17-19) and the Height of the Columns of *4Q418*," *RevQ* 18 (1997-98) 589-93.

———, *To Increase Learning for the Understanding Ones: Reading and Reconstructing the Fragmentary Early Jewish Sapiential Text 4QInstruction* (STDJ 44; Leiden: Brill, 2001).

———, "Towards a Reconstruction of the Beginning of 4QInstruction (4Q416 Fragment 1 and Parallels)," *Wisdom Texts from Qumran* (see Hempel above), 99-126.

Werman, C., "What is the *Book of Hagu?*" *Sapiential Perspectives* (see above), 125-40.

Wold, B. G., "Reconsidering an Aspect of the Title *Kyrios* in Light of Sapiential Fragment 4Q416 2 iii," *ZNW* 95 (2004) 149-60.

Wolters, A., "*Anthrōpoi eudokias* (Luke 2:14) and *'nšy rṣwn (4Q416),*" *JBL* 113 (1994) 291-92.

Wright III, B. G., "The Categories of Rich and Poor in the Qumran Sapiential Literature," *Sapiential Perspectives* (see above), 101-23.

9. Qumran Halakhah or Legal Issues

Baumgarten, J. M., "The Cave 4 Versions of the Qumran Penal Code," *JJS* 43 (1992) 268-76.

———, "The Disqualifications of Priests in 4Q Fragments of the 'Damscus Document,' a Specimen of the Recovery of pre-Rabbinic Halakha," *The Madrid Qumran Congress: Proceedings of the International Congress on the Dead Sea Scrolls, Madrid 18-21 March, 1991* (STDJ 11/1-2; ed. J. Trebolle Barrera and L. Vegas Montaner; Leiden: Brill; Madrid: Editorial Complutense, 1992), 2. 503-13.

———, "The Duodecimal Courts of Qumran, Revelation, and the Sanhedrin," *JBL* 95 (1976) 59-78; repr. in *Studies* (see below), 145-71.

———, "The Essene Avoidance of Oil and the Laws of Purity," *RevQ* 6 (1967-69) 183-92; repr. in *Studies* (see below), 88-97.

———, "The 4Q Zadokite Fragments on Skin Disease," *JJS* 41 (1990) 153-65.

———, "The Laws about Fluxes in 4QTohora[a] (4Q274)," *Time to Prepare the Way in the Wilderness: Papers on the Qumran Scrolls by Fellows of the Institute for Advanced Studies of the Hebrew University, Jerusalem, 1989-1900* (STDJ 16; ed. D. Dimant and L. H. Schiffman; Leiden: Brill, 1995) 1-8.

———, "Liquids and Susceptibility to Defilement in New 4Q Texts," *JQR* 85 (1994-95) 91-101; also in *Proceedings of the Eleventh World Congress of Jewish Studies, Jerusalem, June 22-29, 1993* (Jerusalem: World Union of Jewish Studies, 1994) A:193-97.

———, "The Pharisaic-Sadducean Controversies about Purity and the Qumran Texts," *JJS* 31 (1980) 157-70.

———, "Purification after Childbirth and the Sacred Garden in 4Q265 and Jubilees," *New Qumran Texts and Studies: Proceedings of the First Meeting of the International Organization for Qumran Studies* (STDJ 15; ed. G. J. Brooke and F. García Martínez; Leiden: Brill, 1994) 3-10 (+ pl. 1).

———, "The Qumran-Essene Restraints on Marriage," *Archaeology and History in the Dead Sea Scrolls: The New York University Conference in Memory of Yigael Yadin* (JSPSup 8; ed. L. H. Schiffman; Sheffield, UK: Sheffield Academic, 1990) 13-24.

———, "A Qumran Text with Agrarian Halakhah," *JQR* 86 (1995-96) 1-8.

———, "Recent Qumran Discoveries and Halakhah in the Hellenistic-Roman Period," *Jewish Civilization in the Hellenistic-Roman Period* (ed. S. Talmon; Philadelphia, PA: Trinity Press International, 1991) 147-58.

———, "Sadducean Elements in Qumran Law," *The Community of the Renewed Covenant: The Notre Dame Symposium on the Dead Sea Scrolls* (Christianity and Judaism in Antiquity 10; ed. E. Ulrich and J. C. VanderKam; Notre Dame, IN: University of Notre Dame, 1994) 27-36.

———, "Some Remarks on the Qumran Law and the Identification of the Community," *QC* 1 (1990-91) 115-17.

———, *Studies in Qumran Law* (SJLA 24; Leiden: Brill, 1977).

———, "The Unwritten Law in the Pre-Rabbinic Period," *JSJ* 3 (1972) 7-29; repr. in *Studies* (see above), 13-35.

———, "Yom Kippur in the Qumran Scrolls and Second Temple Sources," *DSD* 6 (1999) 184-91.

Bernstein, M. et al. (eds.), *Legal Texts and Legal Issues: Proceedings of the Second Meeting of the International Organization for Qumran Studies, Cambridge 1995: Published in Honour of Joseph M. Baumgarten* (STDJ 23; Leiden: Brill, 1997).

Davies, P. R., "Halakhah at Qumran," *A Tribute to Geza Vermes: Essays on Jewish and Christian Literature and History* (JSOTSup 100; ed. P. R. Davies and R. T. White; Sheffield, UK: SJOT, 1990) 37-50.

Fitzmyer, J. A., "The Essene Community: Essene or Sadducean?" *HeyJ* 36 (1995) 467-76.

Kister, M., "Some Aspects of Qumranic Halakhah," *The Madrid Qumran Congress* (see above), 571-88.

Müller, K.-H., "Geschichte, Heilsgeschichte und Gesetz," *Literatur und Religion des Frühjudentums: Eine Einführung* (ed. J. Maier and J. Schreiner; Würzburg: Echter; Gütersloh: Mohn, 1973) 73-105.

Nodet, É., "La loi à Qumrân et Schiffman," *RB* 102 (1995) 38-71.

Ploeg, J. van der, "Une *halakha* inédite de Qumrân," *Qumrân: Sa piété, sa théologie et son milieu* (BETL 46; ed. M. Delcor; Gembloux: Duculot; Louvain: Leuven University Press, 1978) 107-13.

Rubenstein, J. L., "Nominalism and Realism in Qumranic and Rabbinic Law: A Reassessment," *DSD* 6 (1999) 157-83.

Schiffman, L. H., *The Eschatological Community of the Dead Sea Scrolls: A Study of the Rule of the Congregation* (SBLMS 38; Atlanta, GA: Scholars, 1989).

———, "Halakhah and Sectarianism in the Dead Sea Scrolls," *The Dead Sea Scrolls in Their Historical Context* (ed. T. H. Lim et al; Edinburgh: Clark, 2000) 123-42.
———, *The Halakhah at Qumran* (SJLA 16; Leiden: Brill, 1975).
———, "Jewish Sectarianism in Second Temple Times," *Great Schisms in Jewish History* (ed. R. Jospe and S. M. Wagner; New York: Ktav, 1981) 1-46.
———, הלכה, הליכה ומשיחיות בכת מדבר יהודאה *(Law, Custom and Messianism in the Dead Sea Sect)* (Jerusalem: Merkaz Zalman Shazar, 1993).
———, "Pharisaic and Sadducean Halakhah in Light of the Dead Sea Scrolls: The Case of Ṭevul Yom," *DSD* 1 (1994) 285-99.
———, *Reclaiming the Dead Sea Scrolls: The History of Judaism, the Background of Christianity, the Lost Library of Qumran* (ABRL; New York: Doubleday, 1995) 245-312.
———, *Sectarian Law in the Dead Sea Scrolls: Courts, Testimony and the Penal Code* (BJS 33; Chico, CA: Scholars, 1983).
Schnabel, E. J., "Law and Wisdom in the Dead Sea Scrolls," *Law and Wisdom from Ben Sira to Paul* (Tübingen: Mohr [Siebeck], 1985) 166-226.
Vermes, G., "Sectarian Matrimonial Halakhah in the Damascus Rule," *Post-Biblical Jewish Studies* (Leiden: Brill, 1975) 50-56 (= *JJS* 25 [1974] 197-202).

10. History of the Qumran Community

Adam, A., *Antike Berichte über die Essener* (KlT 182; Berlin/New York: de Gruyter, 1972).
Allegro, J., *The Dead Sea Scrolls: A Reappraisal* (Pelican Books A376; Baltimore: Penguin, 1964) 103-9.
Amusin, J. D., "The Reflection of Historical Events of the First Century BC in Qumran Commentaries (4Q161; 4Q169; 4Q166)," *HUCA* 48 (1977) 123-52.
Beall, T. S., *Josephus' Description of the Essenes Illustrated by the Dead Sea Scrolls* (SNTSMS 58; Cambridge, UK: Cambridge University Press, 1988).
Beckwith, R. T., "The Pre-History and Relationships of the Pharisees, Sadducees and Essenes: A Tentative Reconstruction," *RevQ* 11 (1982-84) 3-46.
Bergmeier, R., *Die Essener-Berichte des Flavius Josephus: Quellenstudien zu den Essenertexten im Werk des jüdischen Historiographen* (Kampen: Kok Pharos Publishing House, 1993).
Bowman, J., "Contact between Samaritan Sects and Qumran?" *VT* 7 (1957) 184-89.
Burgmann, H., *Die Geschichte der Essener von Qumran und "Damaskus"* (Qumranica mogilanensia 5; Cracow: Privately published, 1990).

———, *Vorgeschichte und Frühgeschichte der essenischen Gemeinden von Qumran und Damaskus* (Arbeiten zum Neuen Testament und Judentum 7; Frankfurt am M./Bern/New York: P. Lang, 1987).

Callaway, P. R., *The History of the Qumran Community: An Investigation* (JSPSup 3; Sheffield, UK: JSOT, 1988).

Campbell, J. G., "Essene-Qumran Origins in the Exile: A Scriptural Basis?" *JJS* 46 (1995) 143-56.

Caquot, A., "Questions qoumrâniennes et esséniennes," *Annuaire du Collège de France* 85 (1984-85) 629-32.

Carmignac, J., "Les Esséniens et les sacrifices," *Monde de la Bible* 4 (1978) 34-35.

Carnevale, L., "Le fonti storiche in 'Khirbet Qumrân,'" *Euntes docete* 35 (1982) 233-48.

Charlesworth, J. H., "The Origin and Subsequent History of the Authors of the Dead Sea Scrolls: Four Transitional Phases among the Qumran Essenes," *RevQ* 10 (1979-81) 213-33.

Collins, J. J., "Essenes," *ABD*, 2. 619-26.

Cross, F. M., *ALQ*, 54-120.

———, The Early History of the Qumran Community," *NDBA*, 3-79.

Davies, P. R., *Behind the Essenes: History and Ideology in the Dead Sea Scrolls* (BJS 94; Atlanta, GA: Scholars, 1987).

———, "Was There Really a Qumran Community?," *Currents in Research: Biblical Studies* 3 (1995) 9-35.

Dionisio, F., "A Qumran con gli Esseni," *BeO* 30 (1988) 3-34, 85-100.

Fitzmyer, J. A., "The Essene Community: Essene or Sadducean?" *HeyJ* 36 (1995) 467-76.

Fritsch, C. T., "Herod the Great and the Qumran Community," *JBL* 74 (1955) 175-81.

García Martínez, F., "Essénisme qumranien: Origines, caractéristiques, héritage," *Atti del congresso tenuto a S. Miniato dal 12 al 15 novembre 1984: Associazione italiana per lo studio del giudaismo, Testi e studi* (Rome: Carucci, 1987) 37-57.

———, "Origenes apocalípticos del movimiento esenio y origenes de la secta qumránica," *Communio* 18 (1985) 353-68.

———, "Priestly Functions in a Community without Temple," *Gemeinde ohne Tempel/Community without Temple: Zur Substituierung und Transformation des Jerusalemer Tempels und seines Kults im Alten Testament, antiken Judentum und frühen Christentum* (WUNT 118; ed. B. Ego et al.; Tübingen: Mohr Siebeck, 1999) 303-19.

Ginzberg, L., *Eine unbekannte jüdische Sekte: Erster Teil* (Hildesheim: Olms, 1972 [reprint of 1922 ed.]); *An Unknown Jewish Sect* (New York: Jewish Theological Seminary of America, 1976).

Goranson, S., "'Essenes': Etymology from עשה," *RevQ* 11 (1982-84) 483-98.

Hayward, C. T. R., "Behind the Dead Sea Scrolls: The Sons of Zadok, the Priests and Their Priestly Ideology," *Toronto Journal of Theology* 13 (1997) 7-21.

Hengel, M., "Die Essener von Qumran," *Schriftauslegung im antiken Judentum und im Urchristentum* (ed. M. Hengel and H. Löhr; Tübingen: Mohr [Siebeck], 1994) 51-60.

Iwry, S., "'Was There a Migration to Damascus?' The Problem of שבי ישראל," *W. F. Albright Volume* (ErIsr 9; Jerusalem: Israel Exploration Society, 1969) 80-88.

Jastram, N., "Hierarchy at Qumran," *Legal Texts and Legal Issues: Proceedings of the Second Meeting of the International Organization for Qumran Studies, Cambridge 1995: Published in Honour of Joseph M. Baumgarten* (STDJ 23; ed. M. Bernstein et al.; Leiden: Brill, 1997) 349-76.

Jeremias, G., *Der Lehrer der Gerechtigkeit* (SUNT; Göttingen: Vandenhoeck & Ruprecht, 1963).

Jones, A. H., *Essenes: The Elect of Israel and the Priests of Artemis* (Lanham, MD: University Press of America, 1985).

Kister, M., "לתולדות כת האיסיים: עיונים בחזון החיות ספר היובלימו ברית דמשק (On the History of the Essene Sect: Studies in the Animal Apocalypse, the Book of Jubilees, and the Damascus Document)," *Tarbiz* 56 (1986-87) 1-18.

Laperrousaz, E.-M., *Les Esséniens selon leur témoignage direct* (Religion et culture; Paris: Desclée, 1982).

Liver, J., "The 'Sons of Zadok the Priests' in the Dead Sea Sect," *RevQ* 6 (1967-68) 3-30.

Mealand, D. L., "Community of Goods at Qumran," *TZ* 31 (1975) 129-39.

Metso, S., "Qumran Community Structure and Terminology as Theological Statement," *RevQ* 20 (2001-2) 429-44.

Milik, J. T., *Ten Years of Discovery in the Wilderness of Judaea* (SBT 26; Naperville, IL: Allenson, 1959) 44-98.

Murphy-O'Connor, J., "Demetrius I and the Teacher of Righteousness (*I Macc.*, x, 25-45)," *RB* 83 (1976) 400-420.

———, "The Essenes and Their History," *RB* 81 (1974) 215-44.

———, "The Essenes in Palestine," *BA* 40 (1977) 100-124.

Newsom, C. A., *The Self as Symbolic Space: Constructing Identity and Community at Qumran* (STDJ 52; Leiden: Brill, 2004).

Rabinowitz, I., "Sequence and Dates of the Extra-Biblical Dead Sea Scroll Texts and 'Damascus' Fragments," *VT* 3 (1953) 175-85.

Regev, E., "The *Yaḥad* and the *Damascus Covenant:* Structure, Organization and Relationship," *RevQ* 21 (2003-4) 233-62.

Rowley, H. H., "The History of the Qumran Sect," *BJRL* 49 (1966-67) 203-32.

Schiffman, L. H. (ed.), *Archaeology and History in the Dead Sea Scrolls: The New York University Conference in Memory of Yigael Yadin* (JSPSup 8; Sheffield, UK: JSOT, 1990).

———, "Community without Temple: The Qumran Community's Withdrawal from the Jerusalem Temple," *Gemeinde ohne Tempel* (see above), 267-84.

Sivertsev, A., "Sects and Households: Social Structure of the Proto-Sectarian Movement of Nehemiah 10 and the Dead Sea Sect," *CBQ* 67 (2005) 59-78.

Smith, M., "The Description of the Essenes in Josephus and the Philosophoumena," *HUCA* 29 (1958) 273-313.

Stegemann, H., *Die Entstehung der Qumrangemeinde* (Dissertation, Bonn: Rheinische Friedrich-Wilhelms Universität, 1965; privately published, 1971).

———, "The Qumran Essenes — Local Members of the Main Jewish Union in the Late Second Temple Times," *The Madrid Qumran Congress: Proceedings of the International Congress on the Dead Sea Scrolls Madrid 18-21 March, 1991* (STDJ 11/1-2; ed. J. Trebolle Barrera and L. Vegas Montaner; Leiden: Brill; Madrid: Editorial Complutense, 1992) 83-166.

Talmon, S., "A Further Link between the Judean Covenanters and the Essenes?" *The World of Qumran from Within: Collected Studies* (ed. S. Talmon; Jerusalem: Magnes Press; Leiden: Brill, 1990) 61-67.

Thiering, B. F., *Redating the Teacher of Righteousness* (Australian and New Zealand Studies in Theology and Religion 1; Sydney: Theological Explorations, 1979); see the reviews by J. Murphy-O'Connor, *RB* 87 (1980) 425-30; M. P. Horgan, *CBQ* 43 (1981) 143-45; B. Z. Wacholder, *JBL* 101 (1982) 147-48.

VanderKam, J. C., "The Judean Desert and the Community of the Dead Sea Scrolls," *Antikes Judentum und frühes Christentum: Festschrift für Hartmut Stegemann . . .* (BZNW 97; ed. B. Kollmann et al.; Berlin: de Gruyter, 1999) 159-71.

———, "The Qumran Residents: Essenes not Sadducees!" *QC* 1 (1990-91) 105-8.

Vermes, G., "The Essenes and History," *JJS* 32 (1981) 18-31.

———, "The Leadership of the Qumran Community: Sons of Zadok — Priests — Congregation," *Geschichte — Tradition — Reflexion: Festschrift für Martin Hengel . . .* (3 vols.; ed. H. Cancik et al.; Tübingen: Mohr [Siebeck], 1996), 1. 375-84.

——— and M. D. Goodman (eds.), *The Essenes According to the Classical Sources* (Oxford Centre Textbooks 1; Sheffield, UK: JSOT, 1989).

Wagner, S., *Die Essener in der wissenschaftlichen Diskussion vom Ausgang des 18. bis zum Beginn des 20. Jahrhunderts* (BZAW 79; Berlin: Töpelmann, 1960).

Woude, A. S. van der, "Wicked Priest or Wicked Priests? Reflections on the Identification of the Wicked Priest in the Habakkuk Commentary," *JJS* 33 (1982) 349-59.

11. The New Testament in Qumran Cave 7?

This question was raised by the writings of José O'Callaghan about the Greek fragments of Qumran Cave 7 ("¿Papiros neotestamentarios en la cueva 7 de Qumrān?" *Bib* 53 [1972] 91-100). He identified 7Q4 as 1 Tim 3:16; 4:1, 3; 7Q5 as Mark 6:52-53; 7Q6 1 as Mark 4:28; 7Q6 2 as Acts 28:38; 7Q7 as Mark 12:17; 7Q8 as Jas 1:23-24; 7Q9 as Rom 5:11-12; 7Q10 as 2 Pet 1:15; and 7Q15 as Mark 6:48. Most scholars have been skeptical about the claims that O'Callaghan had been making. He had not proved his case before his death. His claims generated a considerable amount of secondary literature. Anyone who is interested in it can find a list of most of the earlier reactions in the revised edition of my book, *The Dead Sea Scrolls: Major Publications and Tools for Study* (1990), 169-72. The entries that follow are intended only to list the material that O'Callaghan published and selected items of secondary literature addressing the most recent reactions and counter-claims since that date.

Writings of José O'Callaghan (listed by the date of publication)

(English translation of O'Callaghan's first article: W. L. Holladay: "New Testament Papyri in Qumran Cave 7?" Supplement to *JBL* 91/2 [1972] 1-14).

"Tres probables papiros neotestamentarios en la cueva 7 de Qumran," *SP* 11 (1972) 83-89.

"¿1 Tim 3,16; 4,1.3 en 7Q4?" *Bib* 53 (1972) 362-67.

"Die griechischen Papyri aus der Höhle 7 von Qumran," *BL* 45 (1972) 121-22.

"¿Un fragmento del Evangelio de San Marcos en el papiro 5 de la cueva 7 de Qumrān?" *Arbor* 81/316 (1972) 429-31.

"Notas sobre 7Q tomadas en el 'Rockefeller Museum' de Jerusalén," *Bib* 53 (1972) 517-33.

"Sobre los papiros griegos de la cueva 7 de Qumrān," *Boletín de la asociación española de orientalistas* 8 (1972) 205-6.

"Les papyrus de la grotte 7 de Qumrân," *NRT* 95 (1973) 188-95.

"El ordenador, 7Q5 y Homero," *SP* 12 (1973) 73-79.

"La identificación de papiros literarios (bíblicos)," *SP* 12 (1973) 91-100.

"El cambio *d* > *t* en los papiros bíblicos," *Bib* 54 (1973) 415-16.

Los papiros griegos de la cueva 7 de Qumrán (BAC 353; Madrid: Editorial Católica, 1974).

"El ordenador, 7Q5 y los autores griegos (Apolonio de Rodas, Aristóteles, Lisias)," *SP* 13 (1974) 21-29.

"Sobre la identificación de 7Q4," *SP* 13 (1974) 45-55.

"Nota sobre 704 y 7Q5," *SP* 13 (1974) 61-63.

"¿El texto de 7Q5 es Tuc. I 41,2?" *SP* 13 (1974) 125 (+ pl.) [Tuc. = Thucydides].

"Paleografía herculanense en algunos papiros griegos de Qumrān," *Homenaje a Juan Prado: Miscelanea de estudios bíblicos y hebráicos* (ed. L. Alvarez Verdes et al.; Madrid: C.S.I.C., Institulo "B. Arias Montano," 1975) 529-32.

"The Identifications of 7Q," *Aegyptus* 56 (1976) 287-94.

"7Q5: Nuevas consideraciones," *SP* 16 (1977) 41-47.

"Verso le origini del Nuovo Testamento," *Civiltà cattolica* 139 (1988) 269-72.

"Sobre el papiro de Marcos en Qumran," *FilNeot* 5 (1992) 191-97.

"L'ipotetico papiro di Marco a Qumran," *Civiltà cattolica* 143 (1992) 464-73.

"El papir de Marc a Qumran: incògnites i consequències," *Teologia Actual* 2 (1993) 52-54.

Los primeros testimonios del Nuevo Testamento: Papirología neotestamentaria (Córdoba: El Almendro, 1995).

Recent Secondary Literature

Backhaus, K., "Qumran und die Urchristen: Zu einem neueren Diskussionsbeitrag," *TGl* 83 (1993) 364-68.

Boismard, M.-E., "À propos de 7Q5 et Mc 6,52-53," *RB* 102 (1995) 585-88.

Enste, S., *Kein Markustext in Qumran: Eine Untersuchung der These: Qumran-Fragment 7Q5 = Mk 6,52-53* (NTOA 45; Freiburg Schweiz: Universitäts-V.; Göttingen: Vandenhoeck & Ruprecht, 2000).

———, "Qumran-Fragment 7Q5 ist nicht Markus 6,52-53," *ZPE* 126 (1999) 189-93.

Flint, P. W., "That's No Gospel. It's Enoch!" *Bible Review* 19/2 (2003) 37-40, 52-53.

Grelot, P., "Note sur les propositions du Pr Carsten Peter Thiede," *RB* 102 (1995) 589-91.

Hunger, H., "7Q5: Markus 6,52-53 — oder ? Die Meinung des Papyrologen," *Christen und Christliches in Qumran?* (Eichstätter Studien 32; ed. B. Mayer; Regensburg: Pustet, 1992) 33-56.

Jaroš, K., "Die Qumranfragments der Höhle 7 (7Q) im Computertest," *Aegyptus* 80 (2000) 147-68. (7Q5 = Mark 6:52-53; 7Q1 = Exod 28:4-7; 7Q2 = EpJer 43-44; 7Q4 = perhaps 1 Tim 3:15; 4:1, 3; 7Q8 = perhaps Jas 1:23-24.)

Kraus, T. J., "*7Q5: Status Quaestionis* und grundlegende Anmerkungen zur

Relativierung der Diskussion um das Papyrusfragment," *RevQ* 19 (1999-2000) 239-58.

Massana, R. P., "Acerca de una reciente publicación de José O'Callaghan sobre los papiros de la cueva 7 de Qumrán (*Los primeros testimonios del Nuevo Testamento: Papirología neotestamentaria,* El Almendo, Cordoba, 1995)," *FilNeot* 9 (1996) 51-59.

Muro, E. A., "The Greek Fragments of Enoch from Qumran Cave 7 (*7Q4, 7Q8, & 7Q12 = 7QEn gr = Enoch* 103:3-4, 7-8)," *RevQ* 18 (1997-98) 307-12.

Nickelsburg, G. W. E., "The Greek Fragments of *1 Enoch* from Qumran Cave 7: An Unproven Identification," *RevQ* 21 (2003-4) 631-34.

Peláez del Rosal, J., "El debate sobre los papiros neotestamentarios de Qumrán," *EstBíb* 57 (1999) 517-38.

Pickering, S. R., "Palaeographical Details of the Qumran Fragment 7Q5," *Christen und Christliches* (see above), 28-31.

Puech, E., "Des fragments grecs de la grotte 7 et le Nouveau Testament? 7Q4 et 7Q5, et le Papyrus Magdalen grec 17 = P^{64}," *RB* 102 (1995) 570-84.

———, "Notes sur les fragments grecs du manuscrit 7Q4 = 1 Hénoch 103 et 105," *RB* 103 (1996) 592-600.

———, "Sept fragments grecs de la *Lettre d'Hénoch* (*1 Hén* 100, 103 et 105) dans la grotte 7 de Qumrân (= *7QHén gr*)," *RevQ* 18 (1997-98) 313-23.

Rohrhirsch, F., *Markus in Qumran? Eine Auseinandersetzung mit den Argumenten für und gegen das Fragment 7Q5 mit Hilfe des methodischen Fallibilismus-prinzips* (Wuppertal: Brockhaus, 1990).

———, "Zur Relevanz wissenschaftstheoretischer Implikationen in der Diskussion um das Qumranfragment 7Q5 und zu einem neuen Identi-fizierugsvorschlag von 7Q5 mit Zacharias 7,4-5," *TGl* 85 (1995) 80-95.

Ruckstuhl, E., "Zur Frage einer Essenergemeinde in Jerusalem und zum Fundort von 7Q5," *Christen und Christliches* (see above), 131-37.

Scibona, R., "Un frammento di Marco a Qumran? Ipotesi sulla comunità cristiana di Gerico," *Asprenas* 44 (1997) 385-400.

———, "7Q5 e il 'calcolo delle probabilità' nella sua identificazione," *BeO* 42 (2001) 133-81.

———, "7Q5 — O'Callaghan: Formule simboliche, numerali, e analogie," *BeO* 46 (2004) 163-86.

Slaby, W. A., "Computer-unterstützte Fragment-Identifizierung," *Christen und Christliches* (see above), 83-88.

Spottorno, M. V., "Can Methodological Limits Be Set in the Debate on the Identi-fication of 7Q5?" *DSD* 6 (1999) 66-80.

———, "Una nueva posible identificación de 7Q5," *Sefarad* 52 (1992) 541-43.

Thiede, C. P., "Bericht über die kriminaltechnische Untersuchung des Fragments 7Q5 in Jerusalem," *Christen und Christliches* (see above), 239-45.
———, "Greek Qumran Fragment 7Q5: Possibilities and Impossibilities," *Bib* 75 (1994) 394-98.
———, *The Earliest Gospel Manuscript? The Qumran Papyrus 7Q5 and Its Significance for New Testament Studies* (Carlisle, UK: Paternoster, 1992).
———, "7Q5 — Facts or Fiction?" *WTJ* 57 (1995) 471-74.
———, "Das unbeachtete Qumran-Fragment 7Q19 und die Herkunft der Höhle 7," *Aegyptus* 74 (1994) 123-28.
Vernet, J. M., "Si riafferma il papiro 7Q5 come Mc 6,52-53?" *RivB* 46 (1998) 43-60.
Wallace, D. B., "7Q5: The Earliest NT Papyrus?" *WTJ* 56 (1994) 173-80.

12. The Qumran Scrolls and the New Testament

Much has been written about the bearing of the Qumran texts on the New Testament writings. For the many articles on various aspects of the relationship between these two bodies of literature, consult the topical bibliographies of W. S. LaSor and B. Jongeling, and the yearly bibliography of P. Nober, R. North, and R. Althann (noted in section III above); as well as *NTA* (ed. D. J. Harrington; Cambridge, MA: Weston Jesuit School of Theology [3 times a year]). Listed below are only the more important books on the general topic and on two specific areas of it (in the latter cases, some of the more important articles are included).

Badia, L. F., *The Qumran Baptism and John the Baptist's Baptism* (Lanham, MD: University Press of America, 1980).
Black, M., *The Dead Sea Scrolls and Christian Doctrine* (Ethel M. Wood Lecture; London: Athlone, 1966).
———, *The Scrolls and Christian Origins: Studies in the Jewish Background of the New Testament* (New York: Scribner's Sons, 1961; repr. as BJS 48; Atlanta, GA: Scholars, 1983).
——— (ed.), *The Scrolls and Christianity* (SPCK Theological Collections 11; London: SPCK, 1969).
Braun, H., *Spatjüdisch-häretischer und frühchristlicher Radikalismus: Jesus von Nazareth und die essenische Qumransekte* (BHT 24; 2 vols.; Tübingen: Mohr [Siebeck], 1957; 2d ed., 1969).
———, *Qumran und das Neue Testament* (2 vols.; Tübingen: Mohr [Siebeck], 1966). Vol. 1 is a reprint of articles that appeared in *TRu* 28-30 (1962-64); it is an analytical survey of QL in the preceding ten years; vol. 2 is a synthetic

approach to many topics of the New Testament. This is a fundamental, indispensable work for the period surveyed.

Brooke, G. J., *The Dead Sea Scrolls and the New Testament* (Minneapolis, MN: Fortress, 2005).

Carmignac, J., *Christ and the Teacher of Righteousness: The Evidence of the Dead Sea Scrolls* (Baltimore: Helicon, 1962).

Casciaro Ramírez, J. M., *Qumran y el Nuevo Testamento: Aspectos eclesiológicos y soteriológicos* (Pamplona: Ediciones Universidad de Navarra, 1982).

Charlesworth, J. H. and W. P. Weaver, *The Dead Sea Scrolls and Christian Faith: In Celebration of the Jubilee Year of the Discovery of Qumran Cave 1* (Harrisburg, PA: Trinity Press International, 1998).

Charlesworth, J. H. (ed.), *Jesus and the Dead Sea Scrolls* (ABRL; New York: Doubleday, 1992).

Daniélou, J., *The Dead Sea Scrolls and Primitive Christianity* (2d ed.; Baltimore: Helicon, 1963); revised French edition, *Les manuscrits de la Mer Morte et les origines du christianisme* (Paris: Editions de l'Orante, 1974).

Davila, J. R. (ed.), *The Dead Sea Scrolls as Background to Postbiblical Judaism and Early Christianity: Papers from an International Conference at St. Andrews in 2001* (STDJ 46; Leiden, Brill, 2003).

De Waard, J., *A Comparative Study of the Old Testament Text in the Dead Sea Scrolls and in the New Testament* (STDJ 4; Leiden: Brill, 1966).

Fujita, N. S., *A Crack in the Jar: What Ancient Jewish Documents Tell Us about the New Testament* (New York: Paulist, 1986).

Galbiati, E., "Qumrân e il Nuovo Testamento," *Scritti Minori* (2 vols.; Brescia: Paideia, 1979), 1. 379-408.

Gärtner, B., *The Temple and the Community in Qumran and the New Testament* (SNTSMS 1; Cambridge, UK: Cambridge University Press, 1965).

Graystone, G., *The Dead Sea Scrolls and the Originality of Christ* (New York: Sheed and Ward, 1956).

Heline, C., *The Scrolls and the New Testament* (New York: Crossroad, 1992).

Jeremias, J., *Die theologische Bedeutung der Funde am Toten Meer* (2d ed.; Göttingen: Vandenhoeck & Ruprecht, 1962).

LaSor, W. S., *The Dead Sea Scrolls and the New Testament* (Grand Rapids, MI: Eerdmans, 1972).

McNamara, M., *Palestinian Judaism and the New Testament* (Dublin: Veritas Publications, 1983).

Mowry, L., *The Dead Sea Scrolls and the Early Church* (Chicago: University of Chicago Press, 1962).

Piñero, A., "Los manuscritos del Mar Muerto y el Nuevo Testamento," *Paganos, judíos y cristianos en los textos de Qumrán* (ed. J. Trebolle Barrera; Madrid: Trotta, 1999) 287-317.

Ploeg, J. van der (ed.), *La secte de Qumrân et les origines du Christianisme* (RechBib 4; Bruges: Desclée de Brouwer, 1959).

Praag, H. van (ed.), *Studies on the Jewish Background of the New Testament* (Assen: Van Gorcum, 1969).

Rowley, H. H., *The Dead Sea Scrolls and the New Testament* (London: SPCK, 1957).

———, *The Qumran Sect and Christian Origins* (Manchester, UK: John Rylands Library, 1961; originally an article in *BJRL* 44 [1961] 119-56).

Schelkle, K. H., *Die Gemeinde von Qumran und die Kirche des Neuen Testaments* (Die Welt der Bibel; 2d ed.; Düsseldorf: Patmos, 1965).

Stauffer, B., *Jesus und die Wüstengemeinde am Toten Meer* (Calwer Hefte 9; 2d ed.; Stuttgart: Calwer V., 1960).

Stegemann, H., *The Library of Qumran: On the Essenes, Qumran, John the Baptist, and Jesus* (Grand Rapids, MI: Eerdmans; Leiden: Brill, 1998).

Stendahl, K. (ed.), *The Scrolls and the New Testament* (New York: Harper, 1957; repr. with a new introduction by J. H. Charlesworth, New York: Crossroad, 1992).

Thiering, B. E., *The Gospels and Qumran: A New Hypothesis* (Australian and New Zealand Studies in Theology and Religion; Sydney: Theological Explorations, 1981); see reviews by J. C. VanderKam, *CBQ* 45 (1983) 512-14; C. Y. Lambert, *REJ* 145 (1986) 431-32.

———, *Jesus & the Riddle of the Dead Sea Scrolls: Unlocking the Secrets of His Life Story* (San Francisco, CA: HarperSanFrancisco, 1992); see reviews by R. A. Burridge, *Sewanee Theological Review* 36 (1993) 435-39; G. F. Snyder, *Chicago Theological Seminary Register* 83 (1993) 14-15.

———, *The Qumran Origins of the Christian Church* (Australian and New Zealand Studies in Theology and Religion; Sydney: Theological Explorations, 1983); see reviews by A. Caquot, *RHR* 202 (1985) 309; B. A. Mastin, *RevQ* 12 (1985-87) 125-28.

Qumran Literature and Pauline Writings

In addition to the literature surveyed in H. Braun, *Qumran und das Neue Testament* (see above), 1. 169-240; 2. 165-80, and that collected in K. Stendahl (ed.), *The Scrolls and the New Testament,* 65-113, 157-82, one should note in particular the following title, which contains a good collection of articles on this topic: J. Murphy-O'Connor (ed.), *Paul and Qumran: Studies in New Tes-*

tament Exegesis (Chicago: Priory; London: G. Chapman, 1968; repr. with a new Foreword by J. H. Charlesworth, New York: Crossroad, 1990).

Barré, M. L., "Qumran and the 'Weakness' of Paul," *CBQ* 42 (1980) 216-27.

Braun, H., "Römer 7,7-25 und das Selbstverständnis des Qumran-Frommen," *ZTK* 56 (1959) 1-18.

Brown, R. E., *The Semitic Background of the Term "Mystery" in the New Testament* (Facet Books, Biblical Series 21; Philadelphia, PA: Fortress, 1968).

Cadbury, H. J., "A Qumran Parallel to Paul," *HTR* 51 (1958) 1-2.

Casciaro Ramírez, J. M., "Los 'himnos' de Qumran y el 'misterio' paulino," *Scripta theologica* 8 (1976) 9-56.

Derrett, J. D. M., "New Creation: Qumran, Paul, the Church, and Jesus," *RevQ* 13 (1988) 597-608.

Fitzmyer, J. A., "A Feature of Qumrân Angelology and the Angels of I Cor. xi. 10," *NTS* 4 (1957-58) 48-58; repr. in *ESBNT* or *SBNT*, 187-204.

———, "Paul and the Dead Sea Scrolls," *The Dead Sea Scrolls after Fifty Years: A Comprehensive Assessment* (2 vols.; ed. P. W. Flint and J. C. VanderKam; Leiden: Brill, 1998-99), 2. 599-621.

———, "Qumrân and the Interpolated Paragraph in 2 Cor 6,14–7,1," *CBQ* 23 (1961) 271-80; revised, *ESBNT* or *SBNT*, 205-17; translated into German: *Qumran* (WF 410; ed. K. E. Grözinger et al.; Darmstadt: Wissenschaftliche Buchgesellschaft, 1981) 385-98.

Flusser, D., "The Dead Sea Sect and Pre-Pauline Christianity," *Aspects of the Dead Sea Scrolls* (Scripta hierosolymitana 4; ed. C. Rabin and Y. Yadin; Jerusalem: Magness Press, The Hebrew University, 1958) 215-66.

Grundmann, W., "Der Lehrer der Gerechtigkeit von Qumran und die Frage nach der Glaubensgerechtigkeit in der Theologie des Apostels Paulus," *RevQ* 2 (1959-60) 237-59.

Kertelge, K., *"Rechtfertigung" bei Paulus: Studien zur Struktur und zum Bedeutungsgehalt des paulinischen Rechtfertigungsbegriffs* (NTAbh ns 3; 2d ed.; Münster: Aschendorff, 1967).

Kuhn, H.-W., "The Impact of the Qumran Scrolls on the Understanding of Paul," *The Dead Sea Scrolls: Forty Years of Research* (STDJ 10; ed. D. Dimant and U. Rappaport; Leiden: Brill, 1992) 327-39.

Kuhn, K. G., "Der Epheserbrief im Lichte der Qumrantexte," *NTS* 7 (1960-61) 334-46.

Lang, F., "Gesetz und Bund bei Paulus," *Rechtfertigung: Festschrift für Ernst Käsemann . . .* (ed. J. Friedrich et al.; Tübingen: Mohr [Siebeck]; Göttingen: Vandenhoeck & Ruprecht, 1976) 305-20, esp. 311-12.

Lestaspis, S. de, "Les Pastorales à la lumière des manuscrits de la Mer Morte," *L'Énigme des Pastorales de Saint Paul* (Paris: Gabalda, 1976) 395-98.

Lim, T. H., *Holy Scripture in the Qumran Commentaries and Pauline Letters* (Oxford: Clarendon, 1997).

———, "Paul, Letters of," *EDSS*, 638-41.

Murphy-O'Connor, J., "Saint Paul et Qumrân," *Monde de la Bible* 4 (1978) 60-61.

Osborne, R. E., "Did Paul Go to Qumran?" *CJT* 10 (1964) 15-24.

Penna, A., "L'elezione nella lettera ai Romani e nei testi di Qumran," *Divinitas* 2 (1958) 597-614.

———, "Testi d'Isaia in S. Paolo," *RivB* 5 (1957) 25-30, 163-79.

Rad, G. von, "Die Vorgeschichte der Gattung vom 1. Kor. 13,4-7," *Festschrift Albrecht Alt* . . . (BHT 16; Tübingen: Mohr [Siebeck], 1953) 153-68.

Röhser, G., *Prädestination und Verstockung: Untersuchungen zur frühjudischen, paulinischen und johanneischen Theologie* (Tübingen: Francke, 1994).

Sabugal, S., *Análisis exegético sobre la conversión de San Pablo: El problema teológico et histórico* (Barcelona: Editorial Herder, 1976) 200-220.

———, "La conversión de S. Pablo en Damasco: ¿ciudad de Siria o región de Qumrán?" *Augustinianum* 15 (1975) 213-24.

Sanders, J. A., "Dissenting Deities and Philippians 2:1-11," *JBL* 88 (1969) 279-90.

———, "Habakkuk in Qumran, Paul, and the Old Testament," *JR* 39 (1959) 232-44.

Schneider, C., "Die Idee der Neuschöpfung beim Apostel Paulus und ihr religionsgeschichtlicher Hintergrund," *TTZ* 68 (1959) 257-70.

Schulz, S., "Zur Rechtfertigung aus Gnaden in Qumran und bei Paulus: Zugleich ein Beitrag zur Form und Überlieferungsgeschichte der Qumrantexte," *ZTK* 56 (1959) 155-85.

Schweizer, E., "Rom. 1,3f. und der Gegensatz von Fleisch und Geist vor und bei Paulus," *EvT* 12 (1952-53) 563-71.

———, "Zur Interpretation des Römerbriefes," *EvT* 22 (1962) 105-7.

Stanley, C. D., *Paul and the Language of Scripture: Citation Technique in the Pauline Epistles and Contemporary Literature* (SNTSMS 74; Cambridge, UK: Cambridge University Press, 1992) 292-303.

Stendahl, K., "Hate, Non-Retaliation, and Love (1QS x, 17-20 and Rom. 12:19-21)," *HTR* 55 (1962) 343-55.

Stuhlmacher, P., *Gerechtigkeit Gottes bei Paulus* (FRLANT 87; Göttingen: Vandenhoeck & Ruprecht, 1965).

Thierry, J. J., "Der Dorn im Fleische (2 Kor. xii 7-9)," *NovT* 5 (1962) 301-10.

Wibbing, S., *Die Tugend- und Lasterkataloge im Neuen Testament und ihre Traditionsgeschichte unter besonderer Berücksichtigung der Qumrantexte* (BZNW 25; Berlin: Töpelmann, 1959).

Wood, J. E., "Pauline Studies and the Dead Sea Scrolls," *ExpTim* 78 (1966-67) 308-10.

Yamauchi, E., "Qumran and Colossae," *BSac* 121 (1964) 141-52.

Zedda, S., "II carattere gnostico e giudaico dell'errore colossese nella luce dei manoscritti del Mar Morto," *RivB* 5 (1957) 31-56.

Qumran Literature and Johannine Writings

Again in addition to the literature surveyed in H. Braun, *Qumran und das Neue Testament* (see above), 1. 96-138, 290-326; 2. 118-44 and that collected in K. Stendahl (ed.), *The Scrolls and the New Testament*, 183-207, one should note in particular the following title, which contains a good collection of articles on this topic: J. H. Charlesworth (ed.), *John and Qumran* (London: Chapman, 1972; repr. New York: Crossroad, 1990).

Bauckham, R., "The Qumran Community and the Gospel of John," *The Dead Sea Scrolls Fifty Years after Their Discovery: Proceedings of the Jerusalem Congress, July 20-25, 1997* (ed. L. H. Schiffman et al.; Jerusalem: Israel Exploration Society and Shrine of the Book, Israel Museum, 2000) 105-15.

Baumbach, G., *Qumran und das Johannes-Evangelium* (Aufsatze und Vorträge zur Theologie und Religionswissenschaft 6; Berlin: Evangelische Verlagsanstalt, 1957).

Bergmeier, R., "Glaube als Werk? Die 'Werke Gottes' in Damaskusschrift ii, 14-15 und Johannes 6, 28-29," *RevQ* 6 (1967-69) 253-60.

Böcher, O., *Der johanneische Dualismus im Zusammenhang des nachbiblischen Judentums* (Gütersloh: Mohn, 1965).

Boismard, M.-E., "Qumrán y los escritos de s. Juan," *Cultura bíblica* 12 (1955) 250-64.

Braun, F.-M., "L'Arrière-fond judaïque du quatrième évangile et la communauté de l'alliance," *RB* 62 (1955) 5-44.

Brown, R. E., "John and Qumran," *The Gospel According to John* (AB 29; Garden City, NY: Doubleday, 1966) lxii-lxvi.

———, "John, Gospel and Letters of," *EDSS*, 414-17.

———, "The Qumran Scrolls and John: A Comparison in Thought and Expression," *Companion to John: Readings in Johannine Theology* (ed. M. Taylor; New York: Alba, 1977) 69-90.

———. "The Qumran Scrolls and the Johannine Gospel and Epistles," *CBQ* 17 (1955) 403-19, 559-74; revised and reprinted in *New Testament Essays* (3d ed.; New York: Paulist, 1982) 102-31.

———, "Die Schriftrollen von Qumran und das Johannesevangelium und die Johannesbriefe," *Johannes und sein Evangelium* (WF 82; ed. K. H. Rengstorf; Darmstadt: Wissenschaftliche Buchgesellschaft, 1973) 486-528.

Charlesworth, J. H., "Reinterpreting John: How the Dead Sea Scrolls Have Revolutionized Our Understanding of John," *Bible Review* 9/1 (1993) 18-25, 53.

Cullmann, O., "L'Opposition contre le Temple de Jérusalem, motif commun de la théologie johannique et du monde ambiant," *NTS* 5 (1958-59) 157-73.

———, "Secte de Qumran, Hellénistes des Actes et quatrième évangile," *Les manuscrits de la Mer Morte: Colloque de Strasbourg 25-27 mai 1955* (Paris: Presses Universitaires de France, 1957) 61-74, 135-36.

Fitzmyer, J. A., "Qumran Literature and the Johannine Writings," *Life in Abundance: Studies of John's Gospel in Tribute to Raymond E. Brown* (ed. J. R. Donahue; Collegeville, MN: Liturgical Press, 2005) 117-33.

Frey, J., "Licht aus den Höhlen? Der 'johanneische Dualismus' und die Texte von Qumran," *Kontexte des Johannesevangeliums* (WUNT 175; ed. J. Frey and U. Schnelle; Tübingen: Mohr Siebeck, 2004) 117-203.

Grelot, P., "Jean 8, 56 et Jubilés 16, 16-29," *RevQ* 13 (1988) 621-28.

Kuhn, K. G., "Johannesevangelium und Qumrantexte," *Neotestamentica et patristica: Eine Festgabe, Herrn Professor Dr. Oscar Cullmann . . . überreicht* (Leiden: Brill, 1962) 111-22.

Lákatos, F., "El cuarto evangelio y los descubrimientos de Qumrán," *Revista de teología* 21 (1956) 67-77.

Leaney, A. R. C., "John and Qumran," *SE VI* (TU 112; Berlin: Akademie-V., 1973) 296-310.

Mowry, L, "The Dead Sea Scrolls and the Gospel of John," *BA* 17 (1954) 78-97.

Painter, J., "John and Qumran," *The Quest for the Messiah* (Edinburgh: Clark, 29-39.

Röhser, G., *Prädestination* . . . (see above, under Pauline Writings).

Roloff, J., "Der johanneische 'Lieblingsjünger' und der Lehrer der Gerechtigkeit," *NTS* 15 (1968-69) 129-51.

Shafaat, A., "Geber of the Qumran Scrolls and the Spirit-Paraclete of the Gospel of John," *NTS* 27 (1980-81) 263-69 (R. E. Brown: "debatable interpretation of two difficult passages").

Teeple, H. M., "Qumran and the Origin of the Fourth Gospel," *NovT* 4 (1960) 6-25.

Witmer, S. E., "Approaches to Scripture in the Fourth Gospel and the Qumran *Pesharim*," *NovT* 48 (2006) 313-28.

XI

The Copper Plaque Mentioning Buried Treasure (3Q15)

This copper plaque, which is also called "Copper Scroll" or "Copper Rolls" (because it was found rolled in two parts, resembling scrolls), is really not a scroll at all. It was found in Qumran Cave 3 in 1952. The archaeological institutions, which were involved that year in exploring the cliffs along the northwest shore of the Dead Sea, discovered it in Cave 3 and entrusted the publication of it to J. T. Milik. Attempts to unroll the brittle oxidized copper were unsuccessful. Then attempts were made to restore it to a supple copper form, and they were on the verge of success, when it was decided to saw it open in strips at Manchester in England. J. M. Allegro was there at the time it was opened in this way. He published the first reading of the text with a translation (see below). Milik's publication of the text in DJD 3 is, however, the official publication and is regarded as the *editio princeps*, despite Allegro's prior efforts to make the text known quickly to the public.

Although it was found in Qumran Cave 3, it may have had nothing to do with the other Qumran texts or the Qumran community. It resembles the rest of the Qumran writings neither in its content, its palaeography, nor in the language in which the text was written, for the latter is an early form of what is called usually Mishnaic Hebrew.

3Q15 3QTreasure

Milik, J. T., "Le rouleau de cuivre provenant de la grotte 3 (3Q15)," *Les 'Petites Grottes' de Qumrân: Exploration de la falaise, Les grottes 2Q, 3Q, 5Q, 6Q, 7Q à 10Q; Le rouleau de cuivre* (DJD 3; 2 parts: Textes; Planches; ed. M. Baillet et al.; Oxford: Clarendon, 1962) 199-302.

Cross, F. M., "Excursus on the Palaeographical Dating of the Copper Document," DJD 3. 217-21.

Earlier Publications (prior to 1962)

Kuhn, K. G., "Les rouleaux de cuivre de Qumrân," *RB* 61 (1954) 193-205.

———, "Die Kupferrollen von Qumran und ihr Inhalt," *TLZ* 79 (1954) 303-4.

Baker, H. W., "Notes on the Opening of the 'Bronze' Scrolls from Qumran," *BJRL* 39 (1956) 45-56 (a revised form of these notes is found in DJD 3. 203-10).

Kuhn, K. G., "Bericht über neue Qumranfunde und über die Offnung der Kupferrolle," *TLZ* 81 (1956) 541-46.

Milik, J. T., "The Copper Document from Cave III, Qumran," *BA* 19 (1956) 532.

Dupont-Sommer, A., "Les rouleaux de cuivre trouvés à Qoumrân," *RHR* 151 (1957) 22-35.

Mowinckel, S., "The Copper Scroll — An Apocryphon," *JBL* 76 (1957) 261-65.

Milik, J. T., "Le rouleau de cuivre de Qumran (3Q15): Traduction et commentaire topographique," *RB* 66 (1959) 321-57.

———, "Notes d'épigraphie et de topographie palestiniennes," *RB* 66 (1959) 550-75, esp. 567-75; 67 (1960) 354-67.

———, "The Copper Document from Cave III of Qumran: Translation and Commentary," *ADAJ* 4-5 (1960) 137-55.

Allegro, J. M., *The Treasure of the Copper Scroll* (Garden City, NY: Doubleday, 1960). (See reviews by de Vaux, *RB* 68 [1961] 146-47; Fitzmyer, *TS* 22 [1961] 292-96.)

Rengstorf, K. H., *Ḫirbet Qumrân und die Bibliothek vom Toten Meer* (Stuttgart: Kohlhammer, 1960) 26-28.

Jeremias, J., "The Copper Scroll from Qumran," *ExpTim* 71 (1959-60) 227-28.

———, "Remarques sur le rouleau de cuivre de Qumran," *RB* 67 (1960) 220-22.

Milik, J. T., "Observations," *RB* 67 (1960) 222-23 (on preceding article of Jeremias).

Silberman, L. H., "A Note on the Copper Scroll," *VT* 10 (1960) 77-79.

Laperrousaz, E.-M., "Remarques sur l'origine des rouleaux de cuivre découverts dans la grotte 3 de Qumrân," *RHR* 159 (1961) 157-72.

Nötscher, F., "Die Kupferrolle von Qumran (3 Q 15)," *BZ* 5 (1961) 292-97.

Later Secondary Publications

Contenson, H. de and E.-M. Laperrousaz, "La grotte 3 de Qoumrân et le 'Rouleau de Cuivre,'" *Qoumrân et les manuscrits de la Mer Morte: Un cinquantenaire* (ed. E.-M. Laperrousaz; Paris: Cerf, 1997) 205-13.

Golb, N., "The Problem of Origin and Identification of the Dead Sea Scrolls," *Proceedings of the American Philosophical Society* 124 (1980) 1-24, esp. 5-8.

Goranson, S., "Sectarianism, Geography, and the Copper Scroll," *JJS* 43 (1992) 282-87.

Jeremias, J., *Abba: Studien zur neutestamentlichen Theologie und Zeitgeschichte* (Göttingen: Vandenhoeck & Ruprecht, 1966) 361-64.

———, *The Rediscovery of Bethesda: John 5:2* (NT Archaeology Monograph 1; Louisville, KY: Southern Baptist Theological Seminary, 1966).

Jiménez Bedman, F., "El misterio del *Rollo de Cobre* de Qumrán (3Q15)," *Paganos, judíos y cristianos en los textos de Qumrán* (ed. J. Trebolle Barrera: Madrid: Trotta, 1999) 229-41.

Laperrousaz, E.-M., "Méthodologie et datation des manuscrits de la Mer Morte: *Le rouleau de cuivre* 3Q15," *New Qumran Texts and Studies: Proceedings of the First Meeting of the International Organization for Qumran Studies, Paris 1992* (ed. G. J. Brooke; Leiden: Brill, 1994) 233-39.

Lefkovits, J. K., *The Copper Scroll, 3Q15: A Reevaluation: A New Reading, Translation, and Commentary* (STDJ 25; Leiden: Brill, 2000).

Lehmann, M. R., "Identification of the Copper Scroll Based on Its Technical Terms," *RevQ* 5 (1964-66) 97-105.

———, "Where the Temple Tax Was Buried," *BARev* 19/6 (1993) 38-43.

Luria, B. Z., **מגילת הנחשת ממדבר יהודה** (Publications of the Israel Bible Research Society 14; Jerusalem: Kirjath-Sepher, 1963). (Based on Allegro's reading of 3Q15).

McCarter, Jr., P. K., "The Copper Scroll Treasure as an Accumulation of Religious Offerings," *Methods of Investigation of the Dead Sea Scrolls and the Khirbet Qumran Site: Present Realities and Future Prospects* (Annals of the New York Academy of Sciences 722; ed. M. O. Wise et al.; New York: New York Academy of Sciences, 1994) 133-48.

———, "The Mystery of the Copper Scroll," *Understanding the Dead Sea Scrolls* (ed. H. Shanks; New York: Random House, 1992) 227-41.

Morawiecki, L., "The Copper Scroll Treasure: A Fantasy or Stock Inventory?" *QC* 4 (1994) 169-74.

Muchowski, P., "Bibliography of the Copper Scroll (3Q15)," *FO* 26 (1989) 65-70.

———, "Language of the Copper Scroll in the Light of the Phrases Denoting the Directions of the World," *Methods of Investigation* (see above), 319-27.

Pixner, B., "Copper Scroll (3Q15)," *ABD*, 1. 1133-34.

———, "Unravelling the Copper Scroll Code: A Study on the Topography of 3 Q 15," *RevQ* 11 (1982-84) 323-65.

Puech, E., "Quelques résultats d'un nouvel examen du *Rouleau de Cuivre (3Q15)*," *RevQ* 18 (1997-98) 163-90.

———, "Some Results of the Restoration of the Copper Scroll by *EDF Mécénat*," *The Dead Sea Scrolls Fifty Years after Their Discovery: Proceedings of the Je-*

rusalem Congress, July 20-25, 1997 (ed. L. H. Schiffman et al.; Jerusalem: Israel Exploration Society and the Shrine of the Book, Israel Museum, 2000) 889-94.

——— and N. Lacoudre, "The Mysteries of the 'Copper Scroll,'" *NEA* 63 (2000) 152-53.

Thorion, Y., "Beiträge zur Erforschung der Sprache der Kupfer-Rolle," *RevQ* 12 (1985-87) 163-76.

Wise, M. O., "The Copper Scroll," *Parabola* 19/4 (1994) 44-52.

———, "The Dead Sea Scrolls: Part 2. Nonbiblical Manuscripts," *BA* 49 (1986) 228-43.

Wolters, A., "Apocalyptic and the Copper Scroll," *JNES* 49 (1990) 145-54.

———, "The Copper Scroll," *Dead Sea Scrolls after Fifty Years: A Comprehensive Assessment* (2 vols.; ed. P. W. Flint and J. C. VanderKam; Leiden: Brill, 1998-99), 1. 302-23.

———, "The Copper Scroll," *EDSS*, 143-48; repr. with plates and translation as *The Copper Scroll: Overview, Text and Translation* (Sheffield, UK: Sheffield Academic, 1996).

———, "The *Copper Scroll* and the Vocabulary of Mishnaic Hebrew," *RevQ* 14 (1989-90) 483-95.

———, "The Fifth Cache of the Copper Scroll: 'The Plastered Cistern of Manos,'" *RevQ* 13 (1988) 167-76.

———, "History and the Copper Scroll," *Methods of Investigation* (see above), 285-98.

———, "The Last Treasure of the Copper Scroll," *JBL* 107 (1988) 419-29.

———, "Literary Analysis and the Copper Scroll," *Intertestamental Essays in Honour of Jósef Tadeusz Milik, Vol. I* (Qumranica mogilanensia 6; ed. Z. J. Kapera; Cracow: Enigma, 1992) 239-52.

———, "Notes on the Copper Scroll (3Q15)," *RevQ* 12 (1985-87) 589-96.

Zissu, B., "The Identification of the Copper Scroll's *Kaḥelet* at ʿEin Samiya," *PEQ* 133 (2001) 145-58.

XII

Alphabetical List of Sigla and Their Corresponding Numbers

Listed here are only the sites that are most commonly referred to (Qumran, Naḥal Ḥever, Naḥal Ṣe'elim, and the Papyrus Yadin Collection)

1. Qumran

N.B. Some Qumran texts are not numbered; so there will be missing numbers below.

Sigla	**Corresponding Numbers**
1QapGen ar	1Q20
1QApocryphal Prophecy	1Q25
1QDan[a]	1Q71
1QDan[b]	1Q72
1QDeut[a]	1Q4
1QDeut[b]	1Q5
1QDM	1Q22
1QEnGiants[a] ar	1Q23
1QEnGiants[b] ar	1Q24
1QExod	1Q2
1QEzek	1Q9
1QGen	1Q1
1QH[a]	
1QH[b]	1Q35
1QHymComp	1Q37-40
1QHymns	1Q36
1QInstruction	1Q26
1QIsa[a]	
1QIsa[b]	*DSSHU* + 1Q8
1QJub[a]	1Q17
1QJub[b]	1Q18
1QJudg	1Q6
1QLevi ar	1Q21
1QLitA	1Q30
1QLitB	1Q31
1QLitPr[a]	1Q34
1QLitPr[b]	1Q34bis
1QLiturgy of the Three Tongues of Fire	1Q29
1QM	1Q33
1QMyst	1Q27
1QNJ ar	1Q32
1QNoah	1Q19
1QNoah[bis]	1Q19bis
1QpaleoLev	1Q3
1QpapUncA	1Q70
1QpapUncB	1Q70bis
1QpHab	
1QPhyl	1Q13
1QpMic	1Q14

1QpPs	1Q16
1QPs^{a}	1Q10
1QPs^{b}	1Q11
1QPs^{c}	1Q12
1QpZeph	1Q15
1QS	
1QSa	1Q28a
1QSb	1Q28b
1QSam	1Q7
1QStitle	1Q28
1QUncA	1Q41-62
1QUncB ar	1Q63-67
1QUncC	1Q68-69
2QapocrDavid	2Q22
2QapocrMoses	2Q21
2QapocrProph	2Q23
2QDeut^{a}	2Q10
2QDeut^{b}	2Q11
2QDeut^{c}	2Q12
2QEnGiants	2Q26
2QExod^{a}	2Q2
2QExod^{b}	2Q3
2QExod^{c}	2Q4
2QGen	2Q1
2QJer	2Q13
2QJob	2Q15
2QJub^{a}	2Q19
2QJub^{b}	2Q20
2QJuridical text	2Q25
2QNJ ar	2Q24
2QNum^{a}	2Q6
2QNum^{b}	2Q7
2QNum^{c}	2Q8
2QNum$^{d?}$	2Q9
2QpaleoLev	2Q5
2QPs	2Q14
2QRuth^{a}	2Q16
2QRuth^{b}	2Q17
2QSir	2Q18
2QUnc	2Q27-33
3QCopScr	3Q15
3QEzek	3Q1
3QHymn	3Q6
3QJub	3Q5
3QLam	3Q3
3QpIsa	3Q4
3QPs	3Q2
3QSectarian text?	3Q9
3QTJudah	3Q7
3QUnc	3Q10-11
3QUncA ar	3Q12
3QUncB ar	3Q13
3QUncC	3Q14
3QUnid	3Q8
4QAccB	4Q354
4QAccC	4Q355
4QAccD	4Q356
4QAccE	4Q357
4QAccCerealA	4Q351
4QAcc gr	4Q350
4QAdmonFlood	4Q370
4QAgesCreat^{a}	4Q180
4QAgesCreat^{b}	4Q181
4QApocMess	4Q521
4QApocWeeks	4Q247
4QapocrDan ar	4Q246
4QapocrElisha	4Q481a
4QapocrJerA	4Q383
4QapocrJerB	4Q384
4QapocrJerC^{a}	4Q385a
4QapocrJerC^{b}	4Q387
4QapocrJerC^{c}	4Q388a
4QapocrJerC^{d}	4Q389
4QapocrJerC^{e}	4Q390
4QapocrJerC^{f}	4Q387a
4QapocrJosh^{a}	4Q378
4QapocrJosh^{b}	4Q379
4QapocrLam^{a}	4Q179
4QapocrLam^{b}	4Q501
4QapocrLevi^{a} ar	4Q540
4QapocrLevi^{b} ar	4Q541
4QapocrMoses^{a}	4Q375
4QapocrMoses^{b}	4Q376
4QapocrMoses^{c}	4Q408
4QapocrPentA	4Q368
4QapocrPentB	4Q377
4QapocrPsPr	4Q448
4QAstrCrypt	4Q317
4QBarNaf^{a}	4Q434
4QBarNaf^{b}	4Q435
4QBarNaf^{c}	4Q436
4QBarNaf^{d}	4Q437
4QBarNaf^{e}	4Q438
4QBeat	4Q525

4QBer^{a}	4Q286
4QBer^{b}	4Q287
4QBer^{c}	4Q288
4QBer^{d}	4Q289
4QBer^{e}	4Q290
4QBirthNoah^{a} ar	4Q534
4QBirthNoah^{b} ar	4Q535
4QBirthNoah^{c} ar	4Q536
4QCalDocC	4Q326
4QCalDocD	4Q394 1-2
4QCalDocDM	4Q325
4QCalDocE	4Q337
4QCalDocMA	4Q320
4QCalDocMB	4Q321
4QCalDocMC	4Q321a
4QCant^{a}	4Q106
4QCant^{b}	4Q107
4QCant^{c}	4Q108
4QCatena^{a}	4Q177
4QCatena^{b}	4Q182
4QCatSpir^{a}	4Q230
4QCatSpir^{b}	4Q231
4QChr	4Q118
4QcitJub	4Q228
4QComCer	4Q275
4QComConf	4Q393
4QCommGenA	4Q252
4QCommGenB	4Q253
4QCommGenC	4Q254
4QCommGenD	4Q254a
4QCommMal	4Q253a
4QCongLord	4Q466
4QCourt	4Q440b
4QCreation	4Q457a
4QcryptACalDocB	4Q313c
4QcryptACalDocFG	4Q324g-h
4QcryptALitCal^{a-c}	4Q324d-f
4QcryptAMišmarotJ	4Q324i
4QcryptAMMT^{g}	4Q313
4QcryptAUnidP-Q	4Q313a-b
4QcryptBUnidB	4Q363
4QcryptCUnid	4Q363a
4QcryptMisc	4Q363b
4QCurses	4Q280
4QD^{a}	4Q266
4QD^{b}	4Q267
4QD^{c}	4Q268

4QD^{d}	4Q269
4QD^{e}	4Q270
4QD^{f}	4Q271
4QD^{g}	4Q272
4QD^{h}	4Q273
4QDan^{a}	4Q112
4QDan^{b}	4Q113
4QDan^{c}	4Q114
4QDan^{d}	4Q115
4QDan^{e}	4Q116
4QDanSuz ar	4Q551
4QDebtAck ar	4Q344
4QDeedA	4Q345
4QDeedB	4Q348
4QDeedSale ar	4Q346
4QDeluge	4Q577
4QDescDavid	4Q479
4QDeut^{a}	4Q28
4QDeut^{b}	4Q29
4QDeut^{c}	4Q30
4QDeut^{d}	4Q31
4QDeut^{e}	4Q32
4QDeut^{f}	4Q33
4QDeut^{g}	4Q34
4QDeut^{h}	4Q35
4QDeut^{i}	4Q36
4QDeut^{j}	4Q37
4QDeut^{k1}	4Q38
4QDeut^{k2}	4Q38a
4QDeut^{k3}	4Q38b
4QDeut^{l}	4Q39
4QDeut^{m}	4Q40
4QDeut^{n}	4Q41
4QDeut^{o}	4Q42
4QDeut^{p}	4Q43
4QDeut^{q}	4Q44
4QDibHam^{a}	4Q504
4QDibHam^{b}	4Q505
4QDibHam^{c}	4Q506
4QDibMask	4Q298
4QDidWC	4Q455
4QDivProv	4Q413
4QEn^{a} ar	4Q201
4QEn^{b} ar	4Q202
4QEn^{c} ar	4Q204
4QEn^{d} ar	4Q205
4QEn^{e} ar	4Q206

4QEn^{f} ar	4Q207
4QEn^{g} ar	4Q212
4QEnastr^{a} ar	4Q208
4QEnastr^{b} ar	4Q209
4QEnastr^{c} ar	4Q210
4QEnastr^{d} ar	4Q211
4QEnGiants^{a} ar	4Q203
4QEnGiants^{b} ar	4Q530
4QEnGiants^{c} ar	4Q531
4QEnGiants^{d} ar	4Q532
4QEnGiants^{e} ar	4Q533
4QEschHymn	4Q457b
4QEschWA	4Q468g
4QEschWB	4Q472
4QExerCalA	4Q234
4QExerCalB	4Q360
4QExerCalC	4Q341
4QExod^{b}	4Q13
4QExod^{c}	4Q14
4QExod^{d}	4Q15
4QExod^{e}	4Q16
4QExod^{g}	4Q18
4QExod^{h}	4Q19
4QExod^{j}	4Q20
4QExod^{k}	4Q21
4QExodConq	4Q374
4QExod-Lev^{f}	4Q17
4QExorcism ar	4Q560
4QExpoPatr	4Q464
4QEzek^{a}	4Q73
4QEzek^{b}	4Q74
4QEzek^{c}	4Q75
4QEzra	4Q117
4QFalProph ar	4Q339
4QFlor	4Q174
4QFourKgdms^{a} ar	4Q552
4QFourKgdms^{b} ar	4Q553
4QFourLots	4Q279
4QFrgQoh	4Q468l
4QFrgRedInk	4Q481d
4QGen^{b}	4Q2
4QGen^{c}	4Q3
4QGen^{d}	4Q4
4QGen^{e}	4Q5
4QGen^{f}	4Q6
4QGen^{g}	4Q7
4QGen^{h}	4Q8
4QGen^{j}	4Q9
4QGen^{k}	4Q10
4QGen^{n}	4Q576
4QGen-Exod^{a}	4Q1
4QGenealogy	4Q338
4QH^{a}	4Q427
4QH^{b}	4Q428
4QH^{c}	4Q429
4QH^{d}	4Q430
4QH^{e}	4Q431
4QHalleluyah	4Q456
4QHarvest	4Q284a
4QHistTextA	4Q248
4QHistTextB	4Q578
4QHistTextD	4Q332
4QHistTextE	4Q333
4QHistTextF	4Q468e
4QHistTextG	4Q468f
4QHistTextH	4Q322a
4QH-likeA	4Q433
4QH-likeC	4Q440
4QH-likeD	4Q440a
4QHlkA	4Q251
4QHlkB	4Q264a
4QHlkC	4Q472a
4QHoroscope	4Q186
4QHymB	4Q468k
4QHymSapB	4Q528
4QHymW	4Q579
4QIncant	4Q444
4QIndThanksB	4Q442
4QInstrCompA	4Q419
4QInstrCompB	4Q424
4QInstruction^{a}	4Q415
4QInstruction^{b}	4Q416
4QInstruction^{c}	4Q417
4QInstruction^{d}	4Q418
4QInstruction^{e}	4Q418a
4QInstruction^{f}	4Q418c
4QInstruction^{g}	4Q423
4QIsa^{a}	4Q55
4QIsa^{b}	4Q56
4QIsa^{c}	4Q57
4QIsa^{d}	4Q58
4QIsa^{e}	4Q59
4QIsa^{f}	4Q60
4QIsa^{g}	4Q61

4QIsa^{h}	4Q62
4QIsa^{i}	4Q62a
4QIsa^{j}	4Q63
4QIsa^{k}	4Q64
4QIsa^{l}	4Q65
4QIsa^{m}	4Q66
4QIsa^{n}	4Q67
4QIsa^{o}	4Q68
4QIsa^{q}	4Q69a
4QIsa^{r}	4Q69b
4QJer^{a}	4Q70
4QJer^{b}	4Q71
4QJer^{c}	4Q72
4QJer^{d}	4Q72a
4QJer^{e}	4Q72b
4QJN?	4Q232
4QJob^{a}	4Q99
4QJob^{b}	4Q100
4QJonathan	4Q523
4QJosh^{a}	4Q47
4QJosh^{b}	4Q48
4QJub^{a}	4Q216
4QJub^{c}	4Q218
4QJub^{d}	4Q219
4QJub^{e}	4Q220
4QJub^{f}	4Q221
4QJub^{g}	4Q222
4QJudg^{a}	4Q49
4QJudg^{b}	4Q50
4QKgs	4Q54
4QLam	4Q111
4QLamentA	4Q445
4QLamentB	4Q453
4QLamLeader	4Q439
4QLetter ar	4Q342
4QLetter nab	4Q343
4QLev^{b}	4Q24
4QLev^{c}	4Q25
4QLev^{d}	4Q26
4QLev^{e}	4Q26a
4QLev^{g}	4Q26b
4QLevi^{a} ar	4Q213
4QLevi^{b} ar	4Q213a
4QLevi^{c} ar	4Q213b
4QLevi^{d} ar	4Q214
4QLevi^{e} ar	4Q214a
4QLevi^{f} ar	4Q214b
4QLev-Num^{a}	4Q23
4QLightJacob	4Q467
4QLitWA	4Q409
4QLitWB	4Q476
4QLitWD	4Q527
4QLXXDeut gr	4Q122
4QLXXLev^{a} gr	4Q119
4QLXXNum gr	4Q121
4QM^{a}	4Q491
4QM^{b}	4Q492
4QM^{c}	4Q493
4QM^{d}	4Q494
4QM^{e}	4Q495
4QMedCreatA	4Q303
4QMedCreatB	4Q304
4QMedCreatC	4Q305
4Qmez^{a}	4Q149
4Qmez^{b}	4Q150
4Qmez^{c}	4Q151
4Qmez^{d}	4Q152
4Qmez^{e}	4Q153
4Qmez^{f}	4Q154
4Qmez^{g}	4Q155
4QmidrEschat^{e}?	4Q183
4QMiscRules	4Q265
4QMišmarotA	4Q322
4QMišmarotB	4Q323
4QMišmarotC	4Q324
4QMišmarotD	4Q324a
4QMišmarotE	4Q324c
4QMišmarotF	4Q328
4QMišmarotG	4Q329
4QMišmarotH	4Q329a
4QMišmarotI	4Q330
4QMixedKinds	4Q481
4QM-likeB	4Q471
4QMMT^{a}	4Q394
4QMMT^{b}	4Q395
4QMMT^{c}	4Q396
4QMMT^{d}	4Q397
4QMMT^{e}	4Q398
4QMMT^{f}	4Q399
4QMyst^{a}	4Q299
4QMyst^{b}	4Q300
4QMyst^{c}?	4Q301
4QNarrA	4Q458
4QNarrB	4Q461

4QNarrC	4Q462
4QNarrD	4Q463
4QNarrE	4Q464a
4QNarrF	4Q480
4QNarrG	4Q481b
4QNarrH	4Q481e
4QNarrI	4Q469
4QNarrLeb	4Q459
4QNarrWPr	4Q460
4QNetinim	4Q340
4QNJ^{a} ar	4Q554
4QNJ^{b} ar	4Q554a
4QNJ^{c} ar	4Q555
4QJN?	4Q232
4QNoncanPsA	4Q380
4QNoncanPsB	4Q381
4QNPC^{a}	4Q371
4QNPC^{b}	4Q372
4QNPC^{c}	4Q373
4QNum^{b}	4Q27
4QOrd^{a}	4Q159
4QOrd^{b}	4Q513
4QOrd^{c}	4Q514
4QOrdo	4Q334
4QOtot	4Q319
4QpaleoDeut^{r}	4Q45
4QpaleoDeut^{s}	4Q46
4QpaleoExod^{m}	4Q22
4QpaleoGen-Exod^{l}	4Q11
4QpaleoGen^{m}	4Q12
4QpaleoJob^{c}	4Q101
4QpaleoParaJosh	4Q123
4QpaleoUnid 1	4Q124
4QpaleoUnid 2	4Q125
4QpapAccA	4Q352a
4QpapAccF	4Q358
4QpapAccCerealB	4Q352
4QpapAccCerLiq	4Q353
4QpapAdmonPar	4Q302
4QpapApoc ar	4Q489
4QpapApocr ar	4Q488
4QpapapJerB	4Q384
4QpapBened	4Q500
4QpapBibChron ar	4Q559
4QpapCalDocA	4Q324b
4QpapcryptA^{a-j}, etc.	4Q249-250j
4QpapDeedC	4Q359
4QpapFest	4Q478
4QpapFrgs ar	4Q490
4QpapGen^{o}	4Q483
4QpapH^{f}	4Q432
4QpapHistTextC	4Q331
4QpapH-likeB	4Q433a
4QpapHymPr	4Q499
4QpapHymSap	4Q498
4QpapJub^{b}	4Q217
4QpapJub^{h}	4Q223-224
4QpapJub^{i}	4Q482
4QpapM^{f}	4Q496
4QpapM-likeA	4Q497
4QpapparaKgs	4Q382
4QpapPrFetes	4Q509
4QpapProph	4Q485
4QpapPrQuot	4Q503
4QpappsEzek^{e}	4Q391
4QpapRitMar	4Q502
4QpapRitPur	4Q512
4QpapS^{a}	4Q255
4QpapS^{c}	4Q257
4QpapSamson	4Q465
4QpapSap^{a}	4Q486
4QpapSap^{b}	4Q487
4QpapTJud	4Q484
4QpapTob^{a} ar	4Q196
4QpapUnc^{c}	4Q515
4QpapUnc^{d}	4Q517
4QpapUnc^{e}	4Q518
4QpapUnc^{f}	4Q519
4QpapUncFrgs	4Q51a
4QpapUnc^{g}	4Q520
4QpapUnid^{a}	4Q516
4QpapUnidB ar	4Q360a
4QpapUnid gr	4Q361
4QpapVision^{b}	4Q558
4QparaGenExod	4Q422
4QpCant?	4Q240
4QPeopErr	4Q306
4QPersPr	4Q443
4QpHos^{a}	4Q166
4QpHos^{b}	4Q167
4Qphyl^{a}	4Q128
4Qphyl^{b}	4Q129
4Qphyl^{c}	4Q130
4Qphyl^{d}	4Q131

4Qphyl^{e}	4Q132
4Qphyl^{f}	4Q133
4Qphyl^{g}	4Q134
4Qphyl^{h}	4Q135
4Qphyl^{i}	4Q136
4Qphyl^{j}	4Q137
4Qphyl^{k}	4Q138
4Qphyl^{l}	4Q139
4Qphyl^{m}	4Q140
4Qphyl^{n}	4Q141
4Qphyl^{o}	4Q142
4Qphyl^{p}	4Q143
4Qphyl^{q}	4Q144
4Qphyl^{r}	4Q145
4Qphyl^{s}	4Q146
4Qphyl^{t}	4Q147
4Qphyl^{u}	4Q148
4QPhysHor ar	4Q561
4QpIsa^{a}	4Q161
4QpIsa^{b}	4Q162
4QpIsa^{c}	4Q163
4QpIsa^{d}	4Q164
4QpIsa^{e}	4Q165
4QPlaces	4Q233
4QpMic(?)	4Q168
4QpNah	4Q169
4QPoetTextA	4Q446
4QPoetTextB	4Q447
4QPolText	4Q471a
4QpPs^{a}	4Q171
4QpPs^{b}	4Q173
4QPrA	4Q449
4QPrB	4Q450
4QPrC	4Q451
4QPrD	4Q452
4QPrE	4Q454
4QprEnosh	4Q369
4QPrFêtes^{a}	4Q507
4QPrFêtes^{b}	4Q508
4QPrFêtes^{c}	4Q509
4QPrGodIsr	4Q471c
4QPrMercy	4Q481c
4QprNab ar	4Q242
4QprophJosh^{c}	4Q522
4QProtoEsth^{a} ar	4Q550
4QProtoEsth^{b} ar	4Q550a
4QProtoEsth^{c} ar	4Q550b
4QProtoEsth^{d} ar	4Q550c
4QProtoEsth^{e} ar	4Q550d
4QProtoEsth^{f} ar	4Q550e
4QProv ar	4Q569
4QProv^{a}	4Q102
4QProv^{b}	4Q103
4QPs^{a}	4Q83
4QPs^{b}	4Q84
4QPs^{c}	4Q85
4QPs^{d}	4Q86
4QpsDan^{a} ar	4Q243
4QpsDan^{b} ar	4Q244
4QpsDan^{c} ar	4Q245
4QPs^{e}	4Q87
4QpsEzek^{a}	4Q385
4QpsEzek^{b}	4Q386
4QpsEzek^{c}	4Q385b
4QpsEzek^{d}	4Q388
4QpsEzek$^{?}$	4Q385c
4QPs^{f}	4Q88
4QPs^{g}	4Q89
4QPs^{h}	4Q90
4QPs^{j}	4Q91
4QpsJub^{a}	4Q225
4QpsJub^{b}	4Q226
4QpsJub^{c}	4Q227
4QPs^{k}	4Q92
4QPs^{l}	4Q93
4QPs^{m}	4Q94
4QPs^{n}	4Q95
4QPs^{o}	4Q96
4QPs^{p}	4Q97
4QPs^{q}	4Q98
4QPs^{r}	4Q98a
4QPs^{s}	4Q98b
4QPs^{t}	4Q98c
4QPs^{u}	4Q98d
4QPs^{v}	4Q98e
4QPs^{w}	4Q98f
4QPs^{x}	4Q98g
4QpTrueIsr	4Q239
4QpUnid	4Q172
4QPurLit	4Q284
4QpZeph	4Q170
4QQoh^{a}	4Q109
4QQoh^{b}	4Q110
4QQuoPs107	4Q418b

4QRachJos	4Q474
4QRebukes	4Q477
4QRenewEarth	4Q475
4QRitPurA	4Q414
4QRP^{a}	4Q158
4QRP^{b}	4Q364
4QRP^{c}	4Q365
4QRP^{d}	4Q366
4QRP^{e}	4Q367
4QRuth^{a}	4Q104
4QRuth^{b}	4Q105
4QS^{b}	4Q256
4QS^{d}	4Q258
4QS^{e}	4Q259
4QS^{f}	4Q260
4QS^{g}	4Q261
4QS^{h}	4Q262
4QS^{i}	4Q263
4QS^{j}	4Q264
4QSam^{a}	4Q51
4QSam^{b}	4Q52
4QSam^{c}	4Q53
4QSapDidC	4Q294
4QSapDidWB	4Q425
4QSapHymn	4Q411
4QSapHymWA	4Q426
4QSapiential Work	4Q185
4QSectText	4Q468i
4QSefM	4Q285
4QSelfGH^{a}	4Q471b
4QSelfGH^{b}	4Q491c
4QShir^{a}	4Q510
4QShir^{b}	4Q511
4QShirShabb^{a}	4Q400
4QShirShabb^{b}	4Q401
4QShirShabb^{c}	4Q402
4QShirShabb^{d}	4Q403
4QShirShabb^{e}	4Q404
4QShirShabb^{f}	4Q405
4QShirShabb^{g}	4Q406
4QShirShabb^{h}	4Q407
4QSon of God	4Q246
4QTanh	4Q176
4QTemple^{a}	4Q365a
4QTemple^{b}	4Q524
4QTestament^{a}	4Q526
4QTestament^{b} ar	4Q581
4QTestim	4Q175
4QtgJob	4Q157
4QtgLev	4Q156
4QTimeRight	4Q215a
4QTJacob ar	4Q537
4QTJoseph ar	4Q539
4QTJudah ar	4Q538
4QTNaph	4Q215
4QTob^{b} ar	4Q197
4QTob^{c} ar	4Q198
4QTob^{d} ar	4Q199
4QTob^{e}	4Q200
4QTohorotA	4Q274
4QTohorotB^{a}	4Q276
4QTohorotB^{b}	4Q277
4QTohorotC	4Q278
4QTQahat ar	4Q542
4QTwoWays	4Q473
4QUnc^{a}	4Q464b
4QUnc^{b}	4Q468j
4QUnid^{a}	4Q178
4QUnidAa-f	4Q281a-f
4QUnidA ar	4Q562
4QUnidBa-t	4Q282a-t
4QUnidB ar	4Q563
4QUnidCa-d	4Q468a-d
4QUnidC ar	4Q564
4QUnidCcc-dd	4Q468cc-dd
4QUnidD	4Q468m-bb
4QUnidD ar	4Q565
4QUnidE ar	4Q566
4QUnidF ar	4Q567
4QUnidFrgA	4Q346a
4QUnidFrgC	4Q360b
4QUnidG ar	4Q568
4QUnid gr	4Q126
4QUnidH ar	4Q570
4QUnidI ar	4Q571
4QUnidJ ar	4Q572
4QUnidK ar	4Q573
4QUnidL ar	4Q574
4QUnidM ar	4Q575
4QUnidN ar	4Q580
4QUnidO ar	4Q582
4QUnidText	4Q332a
4QVisAmram^{a} ar	4Q543
4QVisAmram^{b} ar	4Q544

4QVisAmram[c] ar	4Q545
4QVisAmram[d] ar	4Q546
4QVisAmram[e] ar	4Q547
4QVisAmram[f] ar	4Q548
4QVisAmram[g] ar	4Q549
4QVisInterp	4Q410
4QVision[a] ar	4Q556
4QVision[c] ar	4Q557
4QVisSam	4Q160
4QWaysRight[a]	4Q420
4QWaysRight[b]	4Q421
4QWCPrA	4Q291
4QWCPrB	4Q292
4QWCPrC	4Q293
4QWiles	4Q184
4QWordJudg	4Q238
4QWordsMich ar	4Q529
4QWorksGod	4Q392
4QXII[a]	4Q76
4QXII[b]	4Q77
4QXII[c]	4Q78
4QXII[d]	4Q79
4QXII[e]	4Q80
4QXII[f]	4Q81
4QXII[g]	4Q82
4QZedekiah	4Q470
4QZodBront ar	4Q318
4Q?	4Q229
pap4QIsa[p]	4Q69
pap4QLXXLev[b] gr	4Q120
pap4QParaExod gr	4Q127
5QAmos	5Q4
5QapocrMal	5Q10
5QCurses	5Q14
5QD	5Q12
5QDeut	5Q1
5QIsa	5Q3
5QKgs	5Q2
5QLam[a]	5Q6
5QLam[b]	5Q7
5QNJ ar	5Q15
5Qphyl	5Q8
5QPs	5Q5
5QRègle	5Q13
5QS	5Q11
5QToponyms	5Q9
5QUnc	5Q25
5QUnid	5Q16-24
6QAllegory	6Q11
6QApoc ar	6Q14
6QapProph	6Q12
6QCalDoc	6Q17
6QCant	6Q6
6QD	6Q15
6QDeut(?)	6Q20
6QfrgProph	6Q21
6QGen(?) ar	6Q19
6QpaleoGen	6Q1
6QpaleoLev	6Q2
6QpapProv	6Q30
6QPriestProph	6Q13
6QUnidB	6Q24-31
pap6QapocrSam/Kgs	6Q9
pap6QBen	6Q16
pap6QDan	6Q7
pap6QDeut	6Q3
pap6QEnGiants ar	6Q8
pap6QHymn	6Q18
pap6QKgs	6Q4
pap6QProph	6Q10
pap6QPs	6Q5
pap6QUnidA	6Q22
pap6QUnidA ar	6Q23
pap7QLXXEpJer gr	7Q2
pap7QLXXExod gr	7Q1
pap7QUnid[a] gr	7Q3-5
pap7QUnid[b] gr	7Q6-18
pap7QUnid[c] gr	7Q19
8QGen	8Q1
8QHymn	8Q5
8Qmez	8Q4
8Qphyl	8Q3
8QPs	8Q2
11QapocrPs	11Q11
11QcryptAUnid	11Q23
11QDeut	11Q3
11QEzekiel	11Q4
11QHymns[a]	11Q15
11QHymns[b]	11Q16
11QJub	11Q12
11QLev[b]	11Q2
11QMelch	11Q13
11QNJ ar	11Q18
11QpaleoLev[a]	11Q1

11QpaleoUnid	11Q22
11QpapUnidD	11Q28
11QPs^{a}	11Q5
11QPs^{b}	11Q6
11QPs^{c}	11Q7
11QPs^{d}	11Q8
11QPs^{e}	11Q9
11QSefM	11Q14
11QShirShabb	11Q17
11QS-like	11Q29
11QTemple^{a}	11Q19
11QTemple^{b}	11Q20
11QTemple^{c}	11Q21
11QtgJob	11Q10
11QUnc	11Q30
11QUnid ar	11Q24
11QUnidA	11Q25
11QUnidB	11Q26
11QUnidC	11Q27
11QUnidWads	11Q31
KhQOstr 1	KhQ1
KhQOstr 2	KhQ2
KhQOstr 3	KhQ3
XQOffering ar	XQ6
XQpapEn	XQ8
XQphyl 1-4	XQ1-4
XQTextA	XQ5a
XQTextB	XQ5b
XQUnid	XQ7

2. Naḥal Ḥever

Sigla	Corresponding Numbers
5/6ḤevBarKLettA	5/6Ḥev49
5/6ḤevBarKLettB ar	5/6Ḥev50
5/6ḤevBarKLettC	5/6Ḥev51
5/6ḤevBarKLettD gr	5/6Ḥev52
5/6ḤevBarKLettE ar	5/6Ḥev53
5/6ḤevBarKLettF ar	5/6Ḥev54
5/6ḤevBarKLettG ar	5/6Ḥev55
5/6ḤevBarKLettH ar	5/6Ḥev56
5/6ḤevBarKLettI ar	5/6Ḥev57
5/6ḤevBarKLettJ ar	5/6Ḥev58
5/6ḤevBarKLettK gr	5/6Ḥev59
5/6ḤevBarKLettL-M	5/6Ḥev60-61
5/6ḤevBarKLettN ar	5/6Ḥev63
5/6ḤevContA gr	5/6Ḥev31
5/6ḤevContB gr	5/6Ḥev32
5/6ḤevContC gr	5/6Ḥev32a
5/6ḤevDateCrop gr	5/6Ḥev21
5/6ḤevDateCropSale gr	5/6Ḥev22
5/6ḤevDebenture nab	5/6Ḥev1
5/6ḤevDeedGiftA ar	5/6Ḥev7
5/6ḤevDeedGiftB gr	5/6Ḥev19
5/6ḤevDepositA gr	5/6Ḥev5
5/6ḤevDepositB	5/6Ḥev17
5/6ḤevDepositionA gr	5/6Ḥev15
5/6ḤevDepositionB gr	5/6Ḥev24
5/6ḤevExtract gr	5/6Ḥev12
5/6ḤevGuarantee nab	5/6Ḥev4
5/6ḤevHypothec-Loan gr	5/6Ḥev11
5/6ḤevJudicRule gr	5/6Ḥev28-30
5/6ḤevLand-Registration gr	5/6Ḥev16
5/6ḤevLease ar	5/6Ḥev42
5/6ḤevLegalPap	5/6Ḥev44-46
5/6ḤevMarrContA ar	5/6Ḥev10
5/6ḤevMarrContB gr	5/6Ḥev18
5/6ḤevMarrContC gr	5/6Ḥev37
5/6ḤevNum^{a}	5/6Ḥev1a
5/6ḤevPetitionA gr	5/6Ḥev13
5/6ḤevPetitionB gr	5/6Ḥev33
5/6ḤevPetitionC gr	5/6Ḥev34
5/6ḤevPs	5/6Ḥev1b
5/6ḤevPurchaseCont ar	5/6Ḥev8
5/6ḤevReceiptA gr	5/6Ḥev27
5/6ḤevReceiptB ar	5/6Ḥev43
5/6ḤevRedemption nab	5/6Ḥev36
5/6ḤevRights gr	5/6Ḥev20
5/6ḤevSaleContA nab	5/6Ḥev2-3
5/6ḤevSaleContB ar	5/6Ḥev47
5/6ḤevSummonsA gr	5/6Ḥev14
5/6ḤevSummonsB gr	5/6Ḥev23
5/6ḤevSummonsC gr	5/6Ḥev25
5/6ḤevSummonsD gr	5/6Ḥev26
5/6ḤevSummonsE gr	5/6Ḥev35
5/6ḤevTenancy nab	5/6Ḥev6
5/6ḤevUncFrg nab	5/6Ḥev39
5/6ḤevUncText nab	5/6Ḥev38

5/6ḤevWaiver nab	5/6Ḥev9
5/6Ḥev?	5/6Ḥev48
5/6Ḥev? ar	5/6Ḥev62
5/6Ḥev? gr	5/6Ḥev64
8ḤevostrA	8Ḥev5
8ḤevostrB	8Ḥev6
8Ḥevostrfrgs	8Ḥev7
8ḤevpapFrgs	8Ḥev3
8ḤevpapUnid gr	8Ḥev4
8ḤevPrayer	8Ḥev2
8ḤevXII gr	8Ḥev1
XḤev/SeBarKLett	XḤev/Se30
XḤev/SeCancMarr gr	XḤev/Se69
XḤev/SeConclusion gr	XḤev/Se61
XḤev/SeDeclaration gr	XḤev/Se62
XḤev/SeDepositBarley ar	XḤev/Se26
XḤev/SeDeut	XḤev/Se3
XḤev/SeEndDoc gr	XḤev/Se73
XḤev/SeEschHymn	XḤev/Se6
XḤev/SeFrgDeed ar	XḤev/Se14
XḤev/SeGiftDeed gr	XḤev/Se64
XḤev/SeGuardian gr	XḤev/Se68
XḤev/SeLoan gr	XḤev/Se66
XḤev/SeMarrCont ar	XḤev/Se11
XḤev/SeMarrCont gr	XḤev/Se65
XḤev/SeNum[a]	XḤev/Se1
XḤev/SeNum[b]	XḤev/Se2
XḤev/SepapDeedA ar	XḤev/Se24
XḤev/SepapDeedB ar	XḤev/Se24a
XḤev/SepapDeedC ar	XḤev/Se25
XḤev/SepapDeedD ar	XḤev/Se27
XḤev/SepapDeedE ar	XḤev/Se31
XḤev/SepapDeedF ar	XḤev/Se32
XḤev/SepapDeedG ar	XḤev/Se34
XḤev/SepapDeedH ar	XḤev/Se37
XḤev/Sephyl	XḤev/Se5
XḤev/SePromNoteA	XḤev/Se49
XḤev/SePromNoteB ar	XḤev/Se52
XḤev/SePs	XḤev/Se4
XḤev/SeReceiptA ar	XḤev/Se10
XḤev/SeReceiptB ar	XḤev/Se12
XḤev/SeRenunciation gr	XḤev/Se63
XḤev/SeSaleDeedA ar	XḤev/Se7
XḤev/SeSaleDeedB ar	XḤev/Se8
XḤev/SeSaleDeedC ar	XḤev/Se8a
XḤev/SeSaleDeedD ar	XḤev/Se9
XḤev/SeSaleDeedE ar	XḤev/Se21
XḤev/SeSaleDeedF ar	XḤev/Se22
XḤev/SeSaleDeedG ar	XḤev/Se23
XḤev/SeSaleDeedH ar	XḤev/Se50
XḤev/SeSaleDeedI ar	XḤev/Se51
XḤev/SeTaxReceipt gr	XḤev/Se60
XḤev/SeTimber gr	XḤev/Se67
XḤev/SeUncFrgA ar	XḤev/Se9a
XḤev/SeUncFrgB	XḤev/Se15
XḤev/SeUncFrgC-D	XḤev/Se16-17
XḤev/SeUncFrgE	XḤev/Se18
XḤev/SeUncFrgF	XḤev/Se19
XḤev/SeUncFrgG ar	XḤev/Se28
XḤev/SeUncFrgH	XḤev/Se29
XḤev/SeUncFrgI ar	XḤev/Se33
XḤev/SeUncFrgJ ar	XḤev/Se35
XḤev/SeUncFrgK ar	XḤev/Se36
XḤev/SeUncFrgL-BB	XḤev/Se38-47h
XḤev/SeUnid	XḤev/Se?1-57
XḤev/SeUnidFrgA gr	XḤev/Se70
XḤev/SeUnidFrgB gr	XḤev/Se71
XḤev/SeUnidFrgC gr	XḤev/Se72
XḤev/SeUnidFrgs gr	XḤev/Se74-169
XḤev/SeWaiver ar	XḤev/Se13

3. Naḥal Ṣe'elim (Wadi Seiyal)

34SeAcc gr	34Se5
34SeCensus gr	34Se4
34SeNum	34Se2
34SepapDeed ar	34Se3
34Sephyl	34Se1

4. The Papyrus Yadin Collection

For some reason, Israeli scholars have added to the conventional sigla another mode of reference, using "P.Yadin" and a number. Sixty-four texts bear this designation, and since it is often used alone, this list is intended to line up the texts with their corresponding conventional sigla. A more complete listing, giving each its Museum number, genre of text, and language, can be found in Y. Yadin et al. (eds.), *The Documents from the Bar Kokhba Period in the Cave of Letters: Hebrew, Aramaic and Nabatean-Aramaic Papyri* (JDS 3; Jerusalem: Israel Exploration Society; Institute of Archaeology, Hebrew University; Shrine of the Book, Israel Museum, 2002) xvi-xvii.

P.Yadin 1	5/6Ḥev1
P.Yadin 1a	5/6Ḥev1a
P.Yadin 1b	5/6Ḥev1b (see p. 121 above)
P.Yadin 2	5/6Ḥev2
P.Yadin 3	5/6Ḥev3
P.Yadin 4	5/6Ḥev4
P.Yadin 5	5/6Ḥev5
P.Yadin 6	5/6Ḥev6
P.Yadin 7	5/6Ḥev7
P.Yadin 8	5/6Ḥev8
P.Yadin 9	5/6Ḥev9
P.Yadin 10	5/6Ḥev10
P.Yadin 11	5/6Ḥev11
P.Yadin 12	5/6Ḥev12
P.Yadin 13	5/6Ḥev13
P.Yadin 14	5/6Ḥev14
P.Yadin 15	5/6Ḥev15
P.Yadin 16	5/6Ḥev16
P.Yadin 17	5/6Ḥev17
P.Yadin 18	5/6Ḥev18
P.Yadin 19	5/6Ḥev19
P.Yadin 20	5/6Ḥev20
P.Yadin 21	5/6Ḥev21
P.Yadin 22	5/6Ḥev22
P.Yadin 23	5/6Ḥev23
P.Yadin 24	5/6Ḥev24
P.Yadin 25	5/6Ḥev25
P.Yadin 26	5/6Ḥev26
P.Yadin 27	5/6Ḥev27
P.Yadin 28	5/6Ḥev28
P.Yadin 29	5/6Ḥev29
P.Yadin 30	5/6Ḥev30
P.Yadin 31	5/6Ḥev31
P.Yadin 32	5/6Ḥev32
P.Yadin 32a	5/6Ḥev32a
P.Yadin 33	5/6Ḥev33
P.Yadin 34	5/6Ḥev34
P.Yadin 35	5/6Ḥev35
P.Yadin 36	5/6Ḥev36 (see p. 125 above)
P.Yadin 37	5/6Ḥev37
P.Yadin 38	5/6Ḥev38
P.Yadin 39	5/6Ḥev39
P.Yadin 40	5/6Ḥev40
P.Yadin 41	5/6Ḥev41
P.Yadin 42	5/6Ḥev42
P.Yadin 43	5/6Ḥev43
P.Yadin 44	5/6Ḥev44
P.Yadin 45	5/6Ḥev45
P.Yadin 46	5/6Ḥev46
P.Yadin 47	5/6Ḥev47
P.Yadin 48	5/6Ḥev48
P.Yadin 49	5/6Ḥev49
P.Yadin 50	5/6Ḥev50
P.Yadin 51	5/6Ḥev51
P.Yadin 52	5/6Ḥev52
P.Yadin 53	5/6Ḥev53
P.Yadin 54	5/6Ḥev54
P.Yadin 55	5/6Ḥev55
P.Yadin 56	5/6Ḥev56
P.Yadin 57	5/6Ḥev57
P.Yadin 58	5/6Ḥev58
P.Yadin 59	5/6Ḥev59
P.Yadin 60	5/6Ḥev60
P.Yadin 61	5/6Ḥev61
P.Yadin 62	5/6Ḥev62
P.Yadin 63	5/6Ḥev63
P.Yadin 64	5/6Ḥev64

XIII

Electronic Resources for the Study of the Dead Sea Scrolls

(N.B. I have been aided greatly by the series editor, P. W. Flint, and his assistants in the composition of this section.)

In the last fifteen years, there has been a tremendous advance in computer research on the Dead Sea Scrolls, and electronic resources abound. These resources are of different sorts:

A. On p. 12 above, mention has already been made of the three volumes of *The Dead Sea Scrolls Reference Library,* which has been made available by Oxford University Press and Brill Academic Publishers, working together with the Foundation for Ancient Research and Mormon Studies and other scholars (1997, 1999, 2006). Volume 1 contains 3,500 excellent black-and-white images of scrolls and fragments, which can be handled in various ways for simultaneous consultation or comparison of multiple images. Information is given for each scroll or fragment (PAM, IAA, or SHR plate numbers, DJD references, place of publication, secondary literature). Volume 2 contains about 800 digitized images of nonbiblical texts, which were selected from the collection housed at the Ancient Biblical Manuscript Center, Claremont, CA. It includes Hebrew and Aramaic transcriptions from *The Dead Sea Scrolls Database* (ed. E. Tov) and the English translation of them from F. García Martínez and W. G. E. Watson, *The Dead Sea Scrolls Translated* (Grand Rapids, MI: Eerdmans; Leiden: Brill, 1996); also Hebrew and Aramaic word-lists. It contains biblical versions as well: the unvocalized Hebrew Bible text; Septuagint; Latin Vulgate and King James version of the Old Testament. These nonbiblical texts are classified by language and cave, with the DJD numbers and PAM plate numbers; a search feature enables the user to look for words, even letters, and to construct a concordance. Volume 3 of 2006 is a revision of the earlier volumes, containing a valuable introduction, texts and images, English translations (of M. Wise, M. Abegg, Jr., and E. Cook, *The Dead Sea Scrolls: A New Translation* [San Francisco, CA: HarperSanFrancisco, 1996, 2005]), and Hebrew Scriptures.

B. *Accordance for Mac* (http://www.accordancebible.com). This is an important software program for the Bible, with original-language texts and powerful search features. It has valuable modules for the study of the Dead Sea Scrolls, with grammatically tagged texts (information for the gender, number, aspect, stem, and lexical form of each word). Three modules are available: (1) *Qumran Sectarian Manuscripts in Hebrew/Aramaic* (version 2.6), by M. G. Abegg, Jr.; (2) *Qumran Sectarian Manuscripts in English* (based on Wise-Abegg-Cook translation mentioned above); (3) *An Index of Qumran Manuscripts* (version 4.0), by S. W. Marler and C. Toews. This index lists the Qumran texts by cave, describes the content of each writing along with its approximate date and language, and supplies palaeographic and bibliographic information. All three modules have been designed to work together, but each can be used separately. The texts can be copied into word processors and used in various ways.

C. *BibleWorks for PC* (http://www.bibleworks.com). This is the premier original-language Bible software program for PC, which has an integrated collection of tools for the study of both ancient and modern Bibles, along with lexicons, dictionaries, and grammars. For QL, *BibleWorks 7* has two modules: (1) *Qumran Sectarian Manuscripts in Hebrew/Aramaic;* (2) *Qumran Sectarian Manuscripts in English.*

D. *Logos Bible Software for PC* (http://www.logos.com). *Logos 3* is a virtual library, having the following modules: (1) *Qumran Sectarian Manuscripts;* (2) *Qumran Sectarian Manuscripts in English;* (3) *Studies in the Dead Sea Scrolls* (e.g., on CD, 11QTemple, 1QM and related texts); (4) *DSSSE* (by F. García Martínez and E. J. C. Tigchelaar); (5) *The Dead Sea Scrolls Today* (by J. C. VanderKam).

In addition to the four resources just mentioned, there are numerous further sources of information on the Internet (World Wide Web), but they are not always easy to use, because of changes of Internet addresses. Moreover, what information comes from such sources always has to be checked in other forms. Many of these sources can be accessed through *Google* (http://www.google.com). Among them the more important are the following:

E. *The Orion Center for the Study of the Dead Sea Scrolls and Associated Literature* (http://orion.mscc.huji.ac.il). The Orion Center was established in 1995 as part of the Institute for Jewish Studies at the Hebrew University of Jerusalem, which sought to encourage research on these ancient documents, especially with a view to situating the information gained from them in the context of Jewish history and religion. From this source, one can learn much about the Old Testament, Jewish literature of the Second Temple period, New Testament, early Christianity, and rabbinic Judaism. Specifically, it has a comprehensive bibliography (the source of those that appear now regularly in the recent issues of *RevQ*), a beginner's guide to the Scrolls, a cave tour, an index of official editions, and relevant news articles.

F. *Foundation for Ancient Research and Mormon Studies [FARMS]* (http://farms.byu.edu/dss/index.html?selection=&cat=dss_site). This important source has been used in the production of the *Electronic Reference Library* mentioned above under A. It provides basic information about contents of the texts, authors and their publications, etc.

G. *Sundry Other Internet Sources:*

(1) *Bible Places* (http://www.bibleplaces.com/qumran.htm) and (http://www.bibleplaces.com/qumrancaves.htm)
(2) *Biblical Archaeology Society* (http://www.bib-arch.org)
(3) *Center for the Study of Early Christianity* (http://www.uhl.ac/dss.html)
(4) *Israel Antiquities Authority* (http://www.antiquities.org.il/home_eng.asp)
(5) *Israel Museum* (http://www.english.imjet.org.il/HTMLs/Home.aspx)
(6) *Library of Congress* (http://www.loc.gov/exhibits/scrolls)
(7) *Oriental Institute Museum, University of Chicago* (http://oi.uchicago.edu/research/projects.scr/)
(8) *Schøyen Collection* (http://www.schoyencollection.com/dsscrolls.htm)
(9) *Taylor-Schechter Genizah Research Unit, Cambridge University Library* (http://www.lib.cam.ac.uk/Taylor-Schechter)
(10) *University of Southern California, West Semitic Research Project* (http://www.usc.edu/dept/LAS/wsrp)

Index of Modern Authors